PIERO DI COSIMO

PIERO DI COSIMO
Fiction, Invention and *Fantasìa*

SHARON FERMOR

REAKTION BOOKS

Published by Reaktion Books Ltd
1–5 Midford Place, Tottenham Court Road
London W1P 9HH, UK

First published 1993

Distributed in USA and Canada by the
University of Washington Press, PO Box 50096,
Seattle, Washington 98145–5096, USA

Designed by Ron Costley
Photoset by Rowland Phototypesetting Ltd,
Bury St Edmunds, Suffolk
Printed and bound in Great Britain by
Balding and Mansell plc
Wisbech, Cambs

British Library Cataloguing in Publication Data

Fermor, Sharon
Piero di Cosimo: Fiction, Invention and
Fantasìa
I. Title
709.45

ISBN 0–948462–36–1

Contents

Acknowledgements

Of the many people who have assisted in different ways in the preparation of this book, I owe particular thanks to Alison Cole Shadwick, William Griswold, Ann Guité, Maurice Howard, Nigel Llewellyn, David Membrey, Patricia Rubin and Richard Townsend. A Small Personal Research Grant from the British Academy enabled me to study Piero di Cosimo's works in collections in Canada and the USA, and a Grant in Aid of Research from the British School at Rome gave me the opportunity to study those works in Italian collections at length. I have also received financial assistance from the University of Sussex, and from Mr Glen Erikson. Aidan Weston-Lewis at the Witt Library has assisted greatly in providing illustrations. I am also very much indebted to Elspeth Crichton Stuart and Thomas Puttfarken for their moral and intellectual support. This book is dedicated to them.

Introduction

Ever since the appearance of Giorgio Vasari's *Lives of the Artists* in 1550, with a revised edition following in 1568, the persona of Piero di Cosimo has remained an object of fascination for historians and non-historians alike. Vasari's brief biography of Piero, written almost thirty years after the artist's death, is one of the liveliest and most original of those in part Three of the *Lives*, in which Vasari chronicles the achievements of the artists of the Modern Age, from Leonardo da Vinci up to his own day. Vasari describes Piero as a solitary, abstracted, often misanthropic man, wholly engrossed in his study of the subtleties of nature, and living a life 'more animal than human'. Taking little heed of his material well-being, he ate only when hungry, and refused to allow his rooms to be cleaned, or his garden cultivated, insisting on letting everything grow wild.[1] Vasari also relates that Piero was intensely secretive about his work, and although witty and engaging in his conversation, drove people from him by his strangeness. Enraged by the noises of human existence around him, he was beset by irrational fears and had a terror of storms, although he delighted in the sight of torrential rain. At the end of his life he became ever more solitary and eccentric, cursing the doctors who tried to torture him with their cures and the priest who sought to reconcile his soul to God. Refusing all help, he died miserably and alone, found by one of his few remaining friends at the bottom of a flight of stairs.

Vasari's compelling account of Piero has been accepted without question by most writers on the artist. It has also been subject to considerable elaboration, in ways that would have seemed quite foreign to Vasari himself. At the end of the eighteenth century, for example, the German literary critic Wilhelm Wackenroder transformed Vasari's mild eccentric into a man whose imagination was always in turmoil:

> Nature had filled his soul with a continuously seething fantasy and had covered his mind with heavy and dark storm clouds, so that his spirit was constantly in restless toil and moved about amidst extravagant pictures, without ever being reflected in simple and serene beauty. Everything about him was extraordinary and unusual; the writers of the past do not know how to heap up enough powerful words to give us a conception of the intemperance and the atrocity in his entire being.[2]

In the nineteenth century, the novelist George Eliot made Piero a central figure in her historical novel *Romola*, set in fifteenth-century Florence, basing her work on Vasari's account, while embroidering its more colourful details to set the artist in a studio teeming with toads, lizards and other beasts and insects.[3] Inevitably, Vasari's Piero exercised a particular appeal for the Surrealists. In an article entitled 'Piero di Cosimo, Peintre Bizarre', published in the Surrealist journal *Minotaure* in 1938, Georges Pudelko, who planned to write a book on the artist, envisaged Piero as a tortured personality, a man not master of himself. He also transformed Piero into a social and political rebel, a revolutionary whose search for a primitive life signalled a profound disillusionment with the mores of his age. In addition, Pudelko drew a comparison between Piero and another revolutionary of the period, Girolamo Savonarola, seeing the two as united by 'a profound hatred of a liberal and decaying society . . . and a passionate longing for a new simple and natural man'.[4]

These accretions to Vasari's account have persisted. In Eugenio Battisti's *L'Anti-rinascimento* of 1962, Piero's works are seen to reflect the conflicts engendered by the teachings of Savonarola, while his apparent reaction against the classicism of Florentine culture is said by the author to show all the hallmarks of a profound religious crisis. Although for Battisti the expression of these anxieties was not peculiar to Piero, but characteristic of a whole group of seemingly anti-Renaissance, anti-classical artists working in the late fifteenth and early sixteenth centuries, the author is quick to stress Piero's personal religious doubts, citing Vasari's report that 'day after day he turned away the priest who was awaiting his last confession'.[5] In their important book, *Born Under Saturn*, published in 1963, which in many ways is an exemplary study of the tradition of artists' biographies, Rudolf and Margot Wittkower assert that 'We cannot doubt that artists like Piero di Cosimo and Pontormo were deeply disturbed men and probably clinical cases', while in Mina Bacci's monograph of 1966, the most recent and most authoritative on Piero, the artist still appears as 'one of that group of eccentrics who, at the turn of the fifteenth century, anticipated the ferments and anxieties which were to be taken up, after the second decade of the Cinquecento, by the greatest exponents of Mannerism'.[6]

In taking Vasari's biography as a literal account of the artist's life and work, writers have, however, overlooked the fact that, like all the biographies in the *Lives*, it was part of a larger critical and historical project. Vasari's self-acknowledged task in the *Lives* was to chart the development of Italian art from the time of Cimabue in the late thirteenth century up to his own day; more precisely, it was to demonstrate the stages and the means by which Florentine art had developed to its perceived peak of perfection in the art of Vasari's contemporary Michelangelo. This not only entailed the description and characterization of the styles successive artists had evolved, and the means by which they had achieved technical perfection in their art; it also involved consideration of the way in which they lived their lives and managed their affairs. Vasari's aim in this was not just to record the history of Florentine art for posterity, but to demonstrate to contemporary and future artists how to achieve greatness in their works, and fame and fortune through the conduct of their lives. Within that framework, the individual biographies in the *Lives* perform an overtly didactic function. For Vasari, working within a tradition of biographical writing inherited from Antiquity, the purpose of recounting men's lives was to provide examples of virtue and virtuous conduct, or to demonstrate the consequences of unwise action. Factual accuracy was therefore less important than overall credibility; above all, in the construction of each Life, Vasari sought a structural and thematic coherence, and a vividness of detail that would make the whole persuasive, and maximise the impact of the moral or didactic point.

That is not to say that Vasari's account of Piero is wholly invented, for his description is certainly based on fact. At the same time, there is little doubt that he exaggerated and embellished aspects of Piero's character in line with his overall purpose. There are also conventional threads within the Life, motifs that appear in numerous of the other biographies, and which are best understood not as literal accounts of the artist or his behaviour, but as rhetorical devices serving a particular end, in this case that of showing how the talented and virtuous artist should conduct his life. Vasari's biography should thus be seen as part of a concern with the status of the artist that forms one of the most important themes in the *Lives* as a whole. As a practising architect and painter Vasari was deeply concerned with the social and intellectual standing of artists, and was instrumental in the foundation, in January 1563, of the Florentine Accademia del Disegno, one of whose aims was to raise their professional status.[7] Like Alberti in the previous century he cherished an ideal of the artist as a man of education and refinement, whose learning and manners would allow him to mix on equal terms with his patrons.[8] He was thus profoundly critical of artists whose lifestyles appeared to him uncivilized or plebeian, and deeply suspicious of displays of eccentricity. While for the nineteenth century eccentric behaviour was almost a *sine qua non* of artistic genius, both a mark and a guarantee of great talent – a legacy that persists today – sixteenth-century writers on art, and especially Vasari, were more ambivalent about those who lived unorthodox lives.

If the literal interpretation and subsequent elaboration of Vasari's account have clouded our view of Piero's historical persona and its significance, they have also had profound consequences for the interpretation of his works. At once compelled by the vivid personality, and constrained by a lack of documentary evidence for Piero's life and work, scholars have leant heavily on Vasari as a starting-point for the discussion of the paintings. Almost invariably, therefore, these have been interpreted as the products of an eccentric or disordered personality, and of an artist out of tune with his times, although the implications of this have not always been perceived in the same way. Piero's imagined persona has been adduced as an explanation for his apparent stylistic diversity – his seeming failure to develop a distinctive pictorial mode – just as it has been used to explain, and also to argue for, apparent iconographic obscurities in his works. For other writers, and especially Pudelko, Piero's 'bizarre' character is registered primarily in the unusual anthropomorphic forms of his landscape backgrounds, to which Pudelko gave a Freudian interpretation. More recently, scholars have perceived in Piero's mythological paintings an ironic, anti-intellectual, anti-humanist vein, symptomatic of his assumed distaste for the society of Medicean Florence, while his paintings of Early Man, such as the *Hunt* panels (illus. 22 and 23), have appeared as natural reflections of a character described by Vasari as 'bestial' and 'untamed'.[9]

Such elisions between Piero's alleged character and the analysis of his work would, however, have bemused Vasari, and are generally remote from his own critical method. That is not to say that Vasari did not posit a connection between Piero's character as he described it, and the nature of his work. On the contrary, as with all the artists in the *Lives*, Vasari saw the man and the work as largely of a piece, and the notion that that artist's behaviour has consequences for his work plays an essential part in the didactic function of the individual Lives. But the nature of that relationship was by no means as direct or as simple as scholars have assumed; Vasari never suggests, for example, that Piero's paintings are obscure in their meaning, or that his approach to his subject-matter was unorthodox; and it is by no means clear that he had seen the paintings of Early Man, which are now seen as the artist's most characteristic works. Most important, in describing Piero's work as 'bizarre', a word that has been fatally misinterpreted in discussions of the artist, Vasari was alluding less to a perceived oddness in the artist's works, or to an unacceptable eccentricity, than to an acceptable, even desirable degree of inventiveness and imagination – an element of *fantasìa*, as he termed it – which he perceived as an essential achievement of the artists of the Modern Age. If Vasari had reservations about Piero's works, these are a matter less of what Piero actually did than of what, in Vasari's eyes, he ultimately failed to do.

My aim in this book is thus to reconsider aspects of Piero's life and work within their contemporary context by re-evaluating Vasari's account and, by setting the Life within its own historical framework, to reconsider its implications for our understanding of Piero's art. Vasari was undoubtedly the most important and influential writer on art of the sixteenth century, and the *Lives* constitute the most illuminating guide to the perception of art in the years after Piero's death. Furthermore, since Vasari's account has coloured all subsequent writings on Piero, and successive misreadings of the Life have been the source of so many misconceptions, any new discussion of the artist must inevitably start from this point. This is particularly important in view of the fact that, as yet, there exists no comprehensive study of Vasari's biographical technique to which readers may refer in order to see the Life of Piero in a more historical light.[10] In taking Vasari as the point of departure, my intention is not, however, to rely on his words alone. In attempting to set Piero in context, and re-examine the significance of his works, it will be necessary to consider what Vasari does not say, as well as that which he does. It will also be important to consider the extent to which the *Lives* may be taken as representative of Renaissance art criticism more generally, and the possible divergences between Vasari's views and those of the people who commissioned Piero's works.

Although his critical stance on Piero has generally been misconstrued, Vasari was an astute and sensitive observer of the artist's works – although his knowledge of his *oeuvre* was only partial – and his discussion of the paintings provides important insights into the way in which they were seen by a sixteenth-century audience. At the same time, there are ways in which we can now see Piero and his work that Vasari could not, and aspects he chose to leave aside – such as Piero's skill in pictorial composition, and his role as a producer of objects for private religious devotion – to which he alludes only in passing. Just as his construction of and attitude to Piero's life depend on his aims for the artist's status, so his assessment of Piero's work is conditioned by his views on the nature of good art. There are also aspects of Piero's art that Vasari lacked the vocabulary to describe, particularly his use of landscape, which he mentions only briefly. Generally speaking, landscape is not an aspect of painting that Vasari discusses at length in the *Lives*, partly because it was not yet recognized as an independent genre. Thus, while Vasari's comments on Piero's wild or untamed lifestyle can be seen as one way of commenting on his mode of depicting nature, he lacked the kind of critical vocabulary necessary for a detailed discussion of what seems to us to be one of the most distinctive aspects of Piero's work, and which forms the basis of chapter Four of this book, 'Piero and the Depiction of Landscape'.

It will be clear from this that my intention has not been to produce a straightforward monograph, and that my coverage of Piero's work is selective. Although reference is made to most of his securely attributed works, these are not all discussed in the same degree of detail, while his drawings are not dealt with under a separate heading, but where they are felt to be illuminating. Nor do I discuss in detail questions of chronology or attribution, or the complex range of stylistic influences that appears in Piero's work. Since the publication in 1966 of Mina Bacci's authoritative monograph, and of her *L'Opera Completa di Piero di Cosimo* of 1976, these matters have been largely resolved, although on some of these the reader will find opinions and amendments of my own.[11] My main aim has been to locate Piero's life and work within their cultural and artistic contexts, and to redress the view of him as an isolated eccentric by looking at key works from each aspect of his *oeuvre*. The point is not to deny the originality of Piero's works: it is rather to consider the nature of that originality in a more precise and systematic way, particularly in relation to contemporary art theory and practice.

My starting-point, therefore, and the subject of chapter One, is a discussion of Vasari's account, set against the documentary evidence for Piero's life and work and considered in the light of other, complementary, biographies in the *Lives*, such as the Life of Leonardo. Of particular importance here is the analysis of the terms in which Vasari describes Piero's life and work, such as 'imagination' (*fantasia*), 'wildness' (*selvatichezza*) and 'brutishness' (*bestialità*), the historical meaning of which requires close examination, as does the conventional aspect of the biography itself. In the absence of a separate study of Vasari's biographical technique, or an extended discussion of his critical language, these issues will need to be examined at some length, although, it is hoped, without losing sight of the figure of Piero himself.[12]

Piero's major secular works are the subject of chapter Two, in which I look in detail at Vasari's concepts of imagination, 'invention' and the 'bizarre' in their application to individual works. I also consider the iconography of these works, their relation to the physical and intellectual settings for which they were designed, and the approach to composition which, it is suggested, make these some of Piero's most distinctive and original works. This inevitably entails some consideration of a number of broader issues of importance for the period as a whole, such as the tastes and identity of Piero's patrons, the requirements and expectations they had of works intended for domestic decoration, and the degree of control Piero and other painters could expect to exercise in the choice of subject-matter for such works. Previous discussions of these works have often left such questions aside, for in approaching Piero's works first and foremost as expressions of his assumed eccentricity, or by invoking his personality as the primary explanation of his works, scholars have tended to lose sight of the social and intellectual contexts of his paintings, and of the physical settings and constraints within which, like all Renaissance artists, he had to work. Likewise, in construing his mythologies as ironic or anti-humanist, scholars have tended to assume in the minds of artists and patrons a normative attitude to Classical myth, and to its representation, the existence of which may also be open to question.

In chapter Three I turn to Piero's religious works, an aspect of his *oeuvre* to which Vasari paid relatively little attention, although works of this kind, and especially those intended for private devotion, formed the largest part of his output. It is here that we see the more conventional aspect of Piero's production, although in his numerous variations on the theme of the Virgin and Child he showed himself to be a sensitive and original interpreter of standard iconographic themes, one of the features that led to the many contemporary copies that were made of his devotional works. It is also here that we see most clearly his response to the major artistic figures of his day and their influence on his style, as well as his manner of using preparatory drawings.

Piero's use of landscape is the subject of my final chapter. In some ways this is the most tentative and speculative part of my discussion, for the use of landscape in Renaissance art has yet to be seriously studied. Piero's works also occupy an awkward place in the history of landscape painting, between a time when landscape featured primarily as background setting, or as a demonstration of artistic skill, and a period when, with the works of artists such as Giorgione, it began to emerge as an independent genre. Consideration will be given to the narrative and symbolic functions of Piero's landscape backgrounds, their possible sources and the terms Vasari and earlier writers on art used to describe the depiction of landscape.

While this book is intended primarily to be about Piero and his works, in attempting to retrieve the historical view of the artist it will inevitably raise questions of more general significance for our understanding of Renaissance art and theory even if, within its particular scope, it cannot answer them in full. Writings on Piero have often seemed to bring together many of the most crucial questions about the interpretation of Renaissance art, just as paintings like his so-called *Simonetta Vespucci* (illus. 34), discussed in chapter Two, have become a meeting-point for some of our most cherished misconceptions about the period as a whole. A book of this nature will necessarily be wide-ranging in its implications, and it is hoped, therefore, that it will not only be of interest to those concerned with Piero, but to all those with an interest in the period as a whole, particularly in art criticism and theory, and the fiction, invention and *fantasia* that are Vasari's as well as Piero's own.

CHAPTER ONE

Vasari's Life of Piero di Cosimo

The Documented Life of Piero di Cosimo

While Vasari's biography of Piero is one of the most colourful and evocative in the *Lives*, the known facts of the artist's life are few. He was born in 1461 or 1462, almost certainly in Florence, his date of birth being indicated by property tax or *catasto* declarations made by his father Lorenzo di Piero d'Antonio in 1469 and 1480, in which Piero is described as eight and eighteen years old respectively.[1] Although Vasari describes Lorenzo as a goldsmith, he seems rather to have been a toolmaker, an artisan of modest means who, in his first *catasto* declaration of 1457, stated that he and his brother rented a workshop, and had no property other than the tools of their trade. In 1461, however, Lorenzo bought a house in the Via della Scala in Florence, and by 1469 he had also acquired a workshop in the Por San Piero quarter of the city. In that year, he was living in the house in Via della Scala with his wife Alessandra, the eight-year-old Piero and three younger children, Giovanni, Girolamo and Vanna.

By 1480 Piero had left the family home, and according to the *catasto* declarations of that year was working without pay in the studio of the painter Cosimo Rosselli (1439–1507), from whom he took the *di Cosimo* of his name. The date of his entry into Cosimo's studio, and the precise nature of his position in it are unknown. In the first edition (1550) of the *Lives*, Vasari states that Piero joined Cosimo at the age of twelve, the usual age for apprentices to enter the workshop of the master;[2] in the second edition, however, he states only that Piero entered as a boy.[3] The fact that Piero was still working for Cosimo without pay at the age of eighteen might suggest that he entered later in his adolescence, and was still an apprentice, rather than an assistant, at this date. In his Life of Cosimo Rosselli, however, and in the Life of Piero, Vasari also records that, just over a year later, Piero was working as an assistant to Cosimo in the Sistine Chapel in Rome, where he painted the landscape in Cosimo's fresco of the *Sermon on the Mount and the Healing of the Leper* (illus. 1), and portraits of Virginio Orsini and Roberto Sanseverino in Cosimo's *Crossing of the Red Sea*.[4] Piero is said by Vasari to have painted a number of panel portraits of Roman notables during the same period, including Valentino, son of Pope Alexander VI, which suggests that he had already begun to establish a name as an independent master. None the less, if Vasari's testimony is to be believed, Piero retained close links with Cosimo's workshop until the latter's death in 1507, after which he became increasingly withdrawn, shutting himself away to devote his time to the finer problems of his art.

Subsequent to this period of work in the Sistine Chapel no documentation exists for Piero's life or artistic undertakings until 1489 when, on 13 October, the woodcarver Chimenti del Tasso received six gold florins for making the frame of an altarpiece destined for the Capponi Chapel in S. Spirito in Florence. This can almost certainly be identified with Piero's *Visitation* (illus. 87), now in Washington, and since the likelihood is that the frame was made first, the document establishes a *terminus post quem* for the execution of the altarpiece, which can probably be dated to *c.*1490.[5]

By 1498 Piero was living in the family house in Via della Scala, and made his own tax declaration as the head of the household, in which he also claimed to own a house and land in nearby Carmignano. Between 1503 and 1505, and by then over forty years of age, he joined the Confraternity of St Luke, an informal religious brotherhood for painters, and on 8 May 1504 he became inscribed in the painters' official guild, that of the Doctors and Apothecaries. On 25 January that year he served on the committee of thirty artists and other citizens convened by the Florentine Signoria to decide on a site for Michelangelo's marble statue *David*, together with Leonardo da Vinci, Botticelli, Perugino, Filippino Lippi, Granacci, Lorenzo di Credi, Andrea Sansovino, Cosimo Rosselli and Giuliano da Sangallo.[6] The individuals included in the committee provide a fair indication of the richness and diversity of artistic talent in Florence at the time, and the complexity of the cultural situation that existed when Piero was at the height of his career.

On 10 March 1506 Piero was paid fifteen gold florins by the convent of the Suore Muntalve at S. Cresci in Valcava for a painting of the Virgin. The painting was being sent to Naples, presumably to a sister convent, but it cannot be securely identified with any extant work.[7] On 12 February 1507 he received the first of several payments from his patron Filippo Strozzi the younger in recompense for his part in designing a procession for the Glovemakers' Guild.[8] Vasari himself records that, as a young man, Piero was much sought after as a designer of processions, and claims that he was the first to arrange them in the form of triumphal entries. He describes one such, a Triumph of Death, in great detail, noting that it was still talked about in his own day for its inventiveness and originality, and that it had been said at the time to symbolize the return in 1512 of the Medici from exile.[9] The payment from Filippo Strozzi, and a further payment made to Piero on 8 December 1515 for his contribution to the triumphal entry of Leo X into Florence, would seem to confirm Vasari's report, even though on this occasion the amount paid to Piero was small in relation to what most of the other artists involved received.[10]

A further documented date relating to work by Piero is 11 September 1510, when he received six gold florins for unspecified work in Filippo Strozzi's antechamber. At the same time, the sculptor and woodcarver Baccio d'Agnolo was paid for work on some wooden chests, described as *cassoni con spalliere*, and it may be that Piero was involved in painting them.[11] Piero's panel of the *Liberation of Andromeda* (illus. 43) was in all likelihood also painted for Filippo Strozzi the younger, intended to decorate the *spalliera*, or wainscoting, of a room. Vasari identifies Filippo Strozzi the elder as the patron of this work, but since he died in 1491 – which, on stylistic grounds, it is generally agreed is too early a date for the painting – it seems likely that Vasari confused the two men, and that the patron was again the younger Filippo.[12]

The year of Piero's death is undocumented. Vasari puts it at 1521, and states that the artist was buried in S. Pier Maggiore in Florence. While this date cannot be verified, and Vasari certainly exaggerated Piero's age at his death, describing him as around eighty years old, none of Piero's works shows an awareness of artistic developments post-1520, and it seems unlikely that he was active for very long after this date. In the family's tax returns of 1534 Piero's name is not mentioned, the declaration being made by his brothers Bastiano and Raffaello, both of whom were shoemakers.[13]

Little is known of Piero beyond these documented facts; thus it is difficult to say whether his life and career were in any sense unusual in relation to those of other painters of his time. The late date of his entry into both the Confraternity of St Luke and the painters' official guild may mean that he had relatively little interest in the public life of artists, and this is supported by Vasari's image of him as a solitary man, keeping himself apart from the artistic community as a whole. It is possible, however, that Vasari exaggerated this aspect of Piero's personality to suit his own purposes, and it is worth noting that both Perugino and Botticelli entered the painters' guild well into their careers, a fact that may be attributed to certain fluctuations in the strictness with which regulations were enforced.[14] If Piero did avoid contact with his fellow artists, this does not appear to have affected his reputation as a painter or his ability to attract prestigious patrons, despite Vasari's claim that his bizarre behaviour prevented the proper recognition of his talent. His inclusion in the committee of 1504 may itself bear witness to the esteem in which he was held, and in his Life of Piero's pupil, Andrea del Sarto, Vasari states that at the beginning of the sixteenth century Piero was considered to be one of the finest masters in Florence.[15] He certainly received commissions from some of the city's most prominent and discerning patrons, among them the Strozzi, the Capponi and the del Pugliese, while his works were later acquired by the Medici, as well as by Vasari himself.[16] His popularity as an artist is also attested by the numerous copies of his works produced in the first decades of the sixteenth century.[17]

Piero does not appear to have had a large workshop, or to have employed many assistants: Vasari names both Andrea del Sarto and Pontormo as his pupils, while drawings by Ridolfo Ghirlandaio after Piero's compositions suggest that he too may have been a pupil or assistant at some stage.[18] His work undoubtedly had an influence on a number of his contemporaries, particularly Fra Bartolommeo and Albertinelli, but he does not appear to have been a particularly active teacher, or to have had many collaborators. This may have been because his temperament made it uncongenial to him, as Vasari suggests, although here again his comments should be treated with caution. More important, perhaps, is that Piero did not undertake the type of large-scale fresco commission that necessitated using large numbers of assistants of different grades from time to time. After his period with Cosimo Rosselli in the Sistine Chapel, Piero appears to have abandoned fresco, although a set of drawings showing scenes from the life of Joachim could possibly have been executed in preparation for a fresco cycle, perhaps the decoration of a private chapel.[19]

The bulk of Piero's commissions consisted of religious works for private devotion and secular scenes for domestic settings, although he also painted a number of important altarpieces, and, as we have seen, Vasari suggests that he was frequently involved in designing triumphal entries. His account of Piero's time in Rome suggests that he was also in demand as a portraitist, although no trace of the Roman portraits remained by the time Vasari wrote, with the exception of the drawing for that of Duke Valentino, son of Pope Alexander VI, which Vasari records as being in the possession of Cosimo Bartoli, provost of the Baptistery in Florence. However, Piero's extant portrait of his friend the architect Giuliano da Sangallo (illus. 2), and his posthumous portrait of Sangallo's father, the musician Francesco Giamberti (illus. 3), as well as the portrait-like heads of some of his religious figures are evidence of his skill in this respect, and it likely that a number of other portraits existed at one time.[20]

Vasari's Life of Piero di Cosimo

Despite this paucity of facts, not all of which were known to him, Vasari's biography of Piero is one of the most vivid in the *Lives*. He relates that Piero showed a lively and original mind as a child; recognizing this, and noting his natural inclination for the art of design, his father placed him in Cosimo's studio, where his singular imagination (*fantasia*) and tendency to self-absorption (*astrattezza*) marked him out from his fellow apprentices. On occasions when discussions arose in the workshop, Piero would become so engrossed in his own thoughts that the others would have to repeat everything for him at the end. Solitary by nature, he was only content when he was free to wander off alone, absorbed in his thoughts and giving his imagination free rein. Piero's taste for solitude is said to have intensified after Cosimo's death, when he shut himself away and refused to allow anyone to see him at work. He ate only when he was hungry, and later in life reduced himself to living off hard-boiled eggs, which he cooked fifty at a time when boiling the size for his paintings, in order to save fuel. He would not allow his rooms to be cleaned or his garden hoed. He refused to prune his plants or trim the fruit trees, and let the vines run wild and the shoots spread over the ground, for he loved to see everything grow wild and uncultivated (*selvatico*) around him. Vasari describes Piero's way of life as more animal (*bestiale*) than human, noting that Piero took such pleasure in it that anything else struck the artist as a form of slavery.

Piero is portrayed by Vasari as an artist wholly absorbed in his work, especially in his study of the subtleties of the natural world; he is said to have been particularly enthralled by the freaks or accidents of nature, and often sought out strange plants or other objects that nature had produced by chance or from some unfathomable whim. Transported by his enthusiasm for these objects he would describe them at such length that it became tedious even to those who were interested in such things. Vasari also records Piero's fascination with the shapes that appeared on walls against which sick people had spat, or those in the clouds, which he would stop to contemplate, and

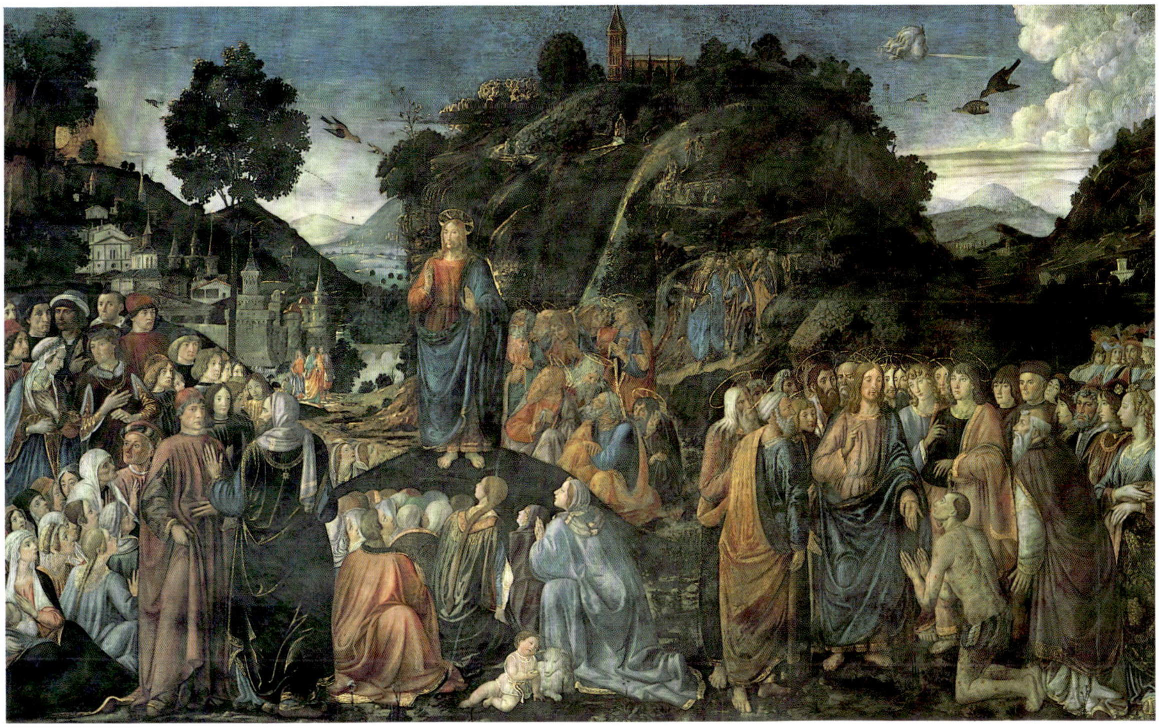

1 Cosimo Rosselli and Piero di Cosimo, *The Sermon on the Mount and the Healing of the Leper*, 1481–2, fresco. Sistine Chapel, Rome.

2 *Giuliano da Sangallo*, *c.*1500–4, oil on panel. Rijksmuseum, Amsterdam.

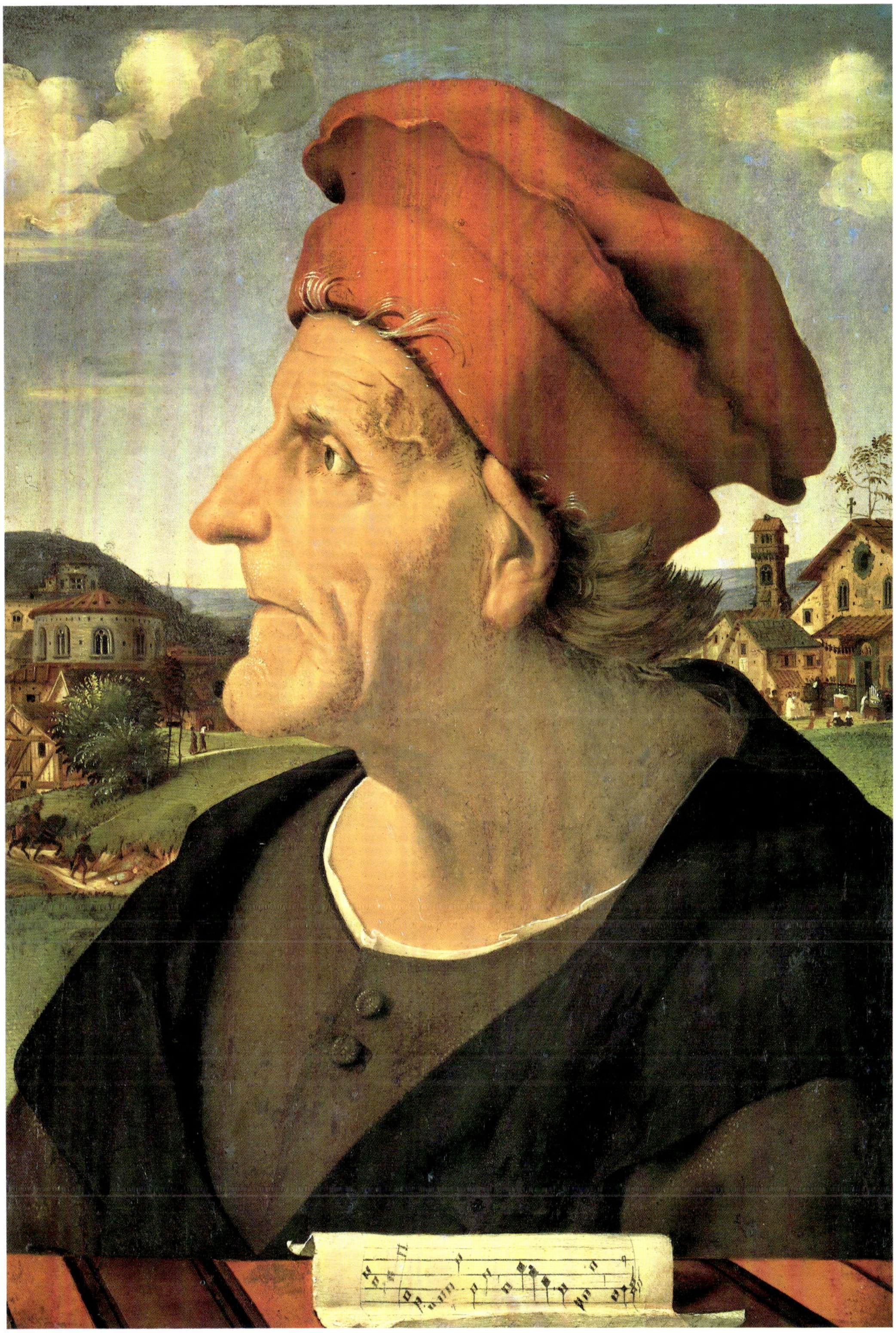

3 *Francesco Giamberti*, *c.*1500–4, oil on panel. Rijksmuseum, Amsterdam.

from which he would then extract the forms of battles, fantastic cities or vast landscapes. Despite his solitary nature Piero is said to have been amusing and original in conversation, and could double up his listeners with laughter. But as he grew older and his eccentricities increased he became prey to odd fears and fancies, and so strange and eccentric (*fantastico*) in his manner that no-one could endure him, nor did he want anyone with him, but sent his apprentices and assistants away. At the end of his life, ill and enfeebled by age, and visited only by the occasional friend, he was urged to make his peace with God; but refusing to believe he was going to die, he kept everyone hanging on from one day to the next. In his last hours he inveighed from time to time against the torments inflicted on the dying: the doctors who starved him or refused to let him sleep, for example, requests to make a will, or being forced to watch relatives weep. Death, he claimed, was thus a welcome release, and fortunate was the man who died quickly. He was eventually found dead one morning at the bottom of a staircase, and was buried in S. Pier Maggiore.

Vasari's image of Piero must certainly be based on fact: at the time he was collecting material for the first edition of the *Lives* Piero had only been dead twenty years, and Vasari would have been able to draw on the reminiscences of those who knew him personally, such as his (Vasari's) own master, Andrea del Sarto, as well as Pontormo and Andrea di Cosimo Feltrini and Piero's friends Giuliano and Francesco da Sangallo.[21] Furthermore, while some of the characteristics Vasari ascribes to Piero, namely his love of solitude, abstractedness and lack of care for his material existence, reappear in other biographies in the *Lives*, and to some extent have the character of *topoi*, others, such as his fears and dislikes, eating habits, attitude to death and love of untamed nature, are peculiar to Piero. Lacking an obvious precedent in the Classical accounts of artists on which Vasari sometimes drew for such details, they also appear too original and distinctive to be wholly invented.[22] At the same time, and especially in his description of the artist as untamed (*selvatico*) and brutish, Vasari probably exaggerated aspects of Piero's character in order to underline the theme of the biography as a whole, and to clarify its moral and instructive point.

The Didactic Function of the Life: Vasari and the Solitary Artist

The didactic function of Piero's Life, and its exemplary role in the *Lives*, were made explicit by Vasari in the second edition:

> if Piero had not been so abstracted, and had thought more carefully about his way of life, he would have made known his great talent in such a way that he would have been truly adored; whereas instead, on account of his bestial life, he was rather thought to be mad, even if in the end he brought harm to no-one but himself, and profit to the art of painting with his works. All great talents and every excellent artist should therefore take instruction from this example, and always consider the consequences of their actions.[23]

This admonitory note is even clearer in the first edition, where, in place of the laudatory passage that opens the revised Life, Vasari begins with an invective against

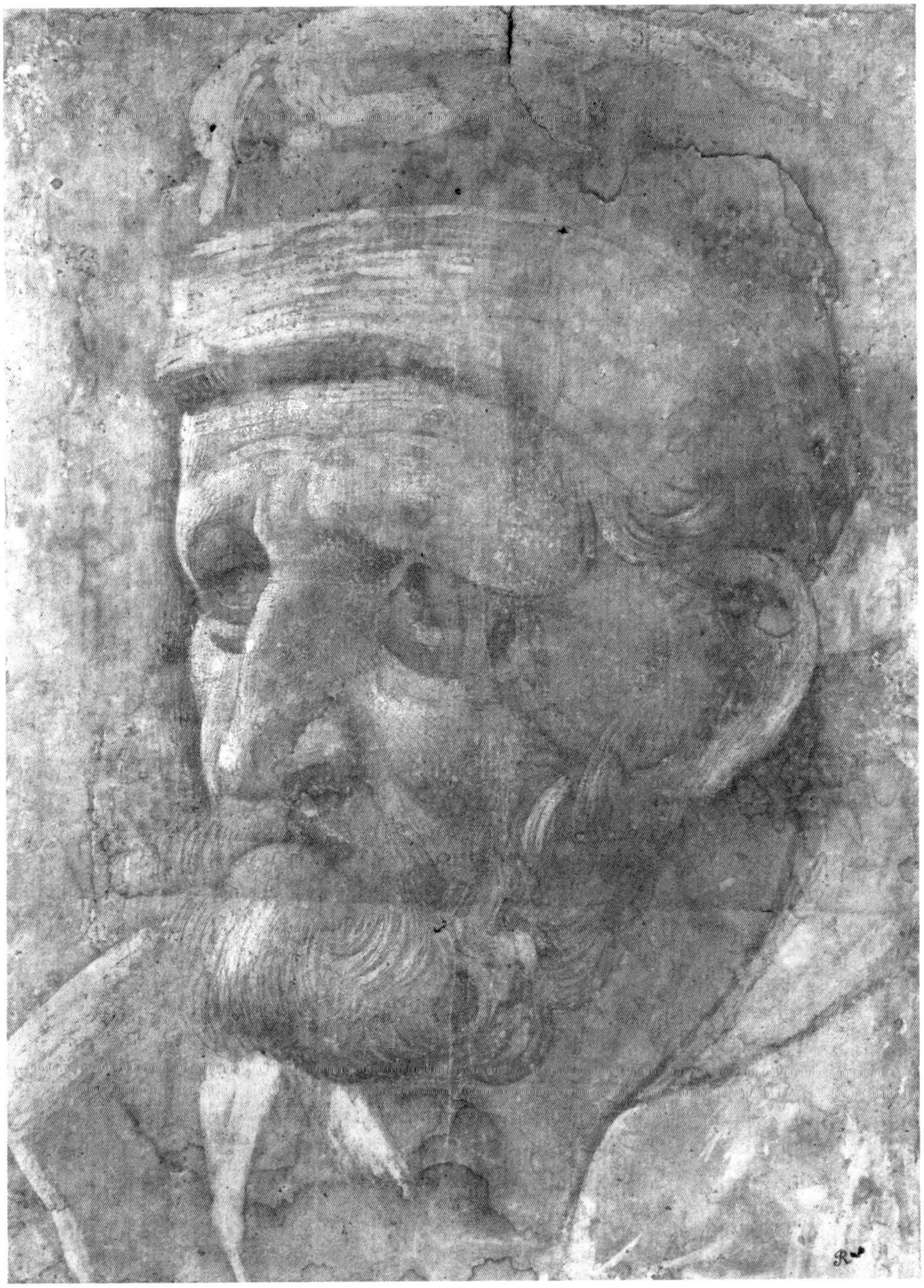

4 *Head of a Bearded Old Man Wearing a Cap* (verso of illus. 35), pen, ink and wash. Musée du Louvre, Paris.

those 'singular and malformed intellects' who seek only solitude, and live meanly and in poverty, passing off their disreputable lives under a veil of philosophical speculation.[24] Such men, like Piero, having lived in isolation and eschewed friendship, end their lives lonely and abandoned, while their art appears to the world to have been pursued out of knavery and perverseness rather than true virtue.

The primary theme of the Life, therefore, and the focus of Vasari's criticism, is Piero's solitary and uncivilized behaviour. Throughout the *Lives* Vasari expresses reservations about artists who withdraw from society, or display a lack of sociability. In the Life of Pontormo, who showed a similar antipathy to human company, Vasari implies that solitude need not necessarily be a vice, and acknowledges that artists should have the freedom to live as they choose; he also admits that solitude can assist artists in their work, a notion he may have derived from Leonardo's *Notebooks*, where Leonardo urges a certain isolation on the painter as the best way in which to perfect his art.[25] According to Vasari,

> although Pontormo's behaviour, and his singular and solitary life were little praised, it is not that such habits cannot be excused should one feel so inclined . . . As for solitude, I have always heard it said that it is most conducive to study: but even if this were not the case, one should not perhaps condemn those who, without giving offence to God or to their neighbours, choose to live in their own way.[26]

There is no doubt, however, that on a personal level Vasari disapproved of artists who led solitary lives, and in his biography of Pontormo he is careful to stress that the artist's behaviour was little commended by his contemporaries. It is also significant that in the above passage the benefits of solitude are reported rather than personally endorsed, and that in his Life of Leonardo, a deliberate counterpart to that of Piero, Vasari is at pains to stress Leonardo's own sociability, and the way in which, unlike Piero, he drew people to him by his manners, generosity and charm. Only in the Life of Michelangelo, in fact, does Vasari condone unsocial behaviour as a necessary concomitant of the artist's exceptional talent.

Michelangelo's solitary nature and avoidance of human company were reported by a number of sixteenth-century writers, including Ascanio Condivi and Francisco de Hollanda.[27] Like Vasari, de Hollanda felt obliged to defend Michelangelo's personal reputation, making the point that solitude is an essential corollary of great art. In his *Dialogues on Painting*, published in 1548, de Hollanda argues that genius has no time for social niceties, but requires total self-absorption, so that the artist can maintain the purity of his thoughts:

> There are many who maintain a thousand lies, and one is to say that eminent painters are strange, harsh and unbearable in their manner, although they are really human and humane . . . And these fools . . . consider them fantastic and capricious (*fantasticos e fantesiosos*) and are loath to tolerate such characteristics in a painter . . . But idle unskilled persons are wrong to demand great ceremony from a busy, skilful man . . . For excellent painters are not unsociable from pride, but either because they find few minds capable of the art of painting or in order not to corrupt themselves with the vain conversation of idle persons and degrade their thoughts from the continuous and lofty imaginings in which they are always rapt.[28]

It was particularly important for Vasari to vindicate Michelangelo, for whom he had a deep personal admiration and whose work represents the pinnacle of perfection in the *Lives*. In order to uphold his praise of Michelangelo, and the critical structure of the *Lives* as a whole, Vasari had to find a means of justifying the artist's unsocial conduct:

> No one should think it strange that Michelangelo loved solitude, as one who was deeply in love with his art, which claims a man with all his thoughts for itself alone. And so it is necessary for anyone who wants to devote himself to the study of art to avoid the company of others, for he who spends time on such study will never be truly alone, or without his own thoughts. And those who attribute this desire in him to a fantastic and strange nature (*a fantasticheria et a stranezza*) are wrong, because whoever wants to do good work must leave behind all cares and burdens, since his talent requires concentration, solitude and time to reflect, with nothing to distract the mind.[29]

The idea that artists were inclined to seek solitude, and could even require it in order to perfect their art, had been voiced before the fifteenth century, and by the time of Vasari's writing it was something of a commonplace, as de Hollanda implies.[30] Yet such behaviour was by no means universally approved, and the desire for solitude was not necessarily seen as a mark of great talent. Both de Hollanda and Vasari are clearly defensive in their discussions of Michelangelo's conduct; most important, Vasari makes clear that in this respect Michelangelo is exceptional, and not to be taken as a model for imitation by other artists. His lack of sociability, frugality in material matters and ascetic lifestyle – traits Vasari censures in Piero – are made part of the Christ-like persona with which he endows the hero of the *Lives*. The Messianic note that runs throughout Michelangelo's Life, from the moment he was sent into the world by God 'in order to redeem artists from ignorance and error', is calculated by Vasari precisely to emphasize the artist's uniqueness, the fact that in his case alone can a hermitic life be condoned.[31]

As one of the models against which Piero is judged, the Life of Michelangelo is important, for one of the functions of Piero's Life is to illustrate the consequences of unorthodox behaviour for an artist whose work is less than divinely inspired. His account of Michelangelo, and that by de Hollanda, are also important for their vocabulary. Both writers are at pains to stress that although Michelangelo was solitary he was not 'bizarre', 'fantastic' or 'strange', the last two being terms that Vasari frequently uses of Piero. Vasari's insistence on this point underlines the fact that, in discussions of artists' behaviour, solitude is frequently associated with these less desirable characteristics; it also emphasizes the fine line that existed between a tolerable desire for solitude and an unacceptable eccentricity. Vasari's reservations about artists who seek solitude spring partly from the fact that he saw this as a sign of an obsessive personality, and artists of this kind, including Piero, are frequently described as abstracted (*astratto*) or as *fantastico*, that is, prone to follow the dictates of their own *fantasìa*. Consequently, it is often seen as characteristic of artists who have an unbalanced attitude to their work, and who pursue one aspect of their art at the expense of others, and to the detriment of their natural talent. The *locus classicus* for this idea in the *Lives* is the biography of Uccello in part Two, although Vasari makes the same point about Pontormo, and elsewhere in the *Lives* cites Pontormo and Uccello together as artists who betrayed their natural gifts.[32] Obsessed by the problems of perspective to the point of neglecting other essential aspects of painting, Uccello developed a manner that was dry and harsh. Not only did he thus do violence to his natural talent, which, like Piero's, is described as whimsical (*capriccioso*) and charming, producing works that invited ridicule rather than praise, he also became strange, solitary and melancholic, ending his life poverty-stricken and in obscurity.

In Piero's case, his love of solitude and tendency to abstractedness are linked by Vasari to his pursuit of the subtleties of nature and his obsessive interest in her more recondite forms. While his studies of bizarre flora and fauna, like Uccello's perspective studies, are not in themselves to be condemned, Vasari sees this preoccupation as a diversion from the human form, which he presents in the *Lives* as the artist's ultimate goal and the most important object of artistic representation. Although Vasari does not state this explicitly, among the biographies in part Three of the *Lives* Piero's is rare in the extent to which, in describing the artist's works, Vasari fails to mention the human figure. Furthermore, in the one case – the *Liberation of Andromeda* (illus. 43) – where Vasari praises Piero for his figures, and for his rendering of human emotions, mention of this aspect of the work comes after that of the sea-monster:

> Piero never painted a more pleasing work than this, or one which was more finely finished, seeing that one could not possibly see a more bizarre (*bizzarro*) or capricious (*capriccioso*) sea monster than that which Piero imagined, or a bolder attitude in a figure of Perseus . . . and one can also see the bound Andromeda, who has the most beautiful face, torn between hope and fear . . . and a crowd of people in front of her with different strange costumes, singing and dancing . . .[33]

This implied lack of interest in the human form, regrettable in the case of Uccello, would have appeared particularly lamentable to Vasari in an artist of the Modern Age. Here again, the point can be clarified in relation to the Life of Michelangelo, for if Michelangelo shared Piero's abstractedness and tendency to singlemindedness, the object of his obsession was precisely that which Vasari saw as the central subject of artistic imitation. Following his description of Michelangelo's *Last Judgement* fresco, Vasari observed that

> this extraordinary man chose always to refuse to paint anything save the human body in its most beautifully proportioned and perfect forms and in the greatest variety of attitudes, and thereby to express the wide range of the soul's emotions and joys . . . Thus he has demonstrated how painting can achieve facility in its chief province: namely, the reproduction of the human form. And concentrating on this subject he left to one side the charm of colouring and the caprices (*capricci*) and novel fantasies (*nuove fantasie*) of certain minute and delicate refinements that many other artists, and not without reason, have not entirely neglected.[34]

While Michelangelo's obsession produced endless variations on the human form, Piero's generated instead those 'caprices and novel fantasies' that should be the ornament rather than the substance of art.

On the one hand, then, a taste for solitude was associated with a certain obsessiveness, and seen as both a cause and a symptom of a misplaced concentration in the artist's approach to his work, while also engendering eccentric behaviour. On the other, a degree of sociability and a refined manner were essential parts of Vasari's notion of the ideal artist. This is made clear in the opening passage to his Life of Raphael, who constitutes the model in the *Lives* of how artists should behave: just as artists should look to Michelangelo in perfecting their art, so Raphael demonstrates the way they should fashion their lives. Vasari describe Raphael in terms that directly counterpoint those he uses of Piero; conversely, the eccentricity, the lack of refinement and the element of the *fantastico* that characterize Piero here constitute everything the artist should avoid:

> Nature sent Raphael into the world after it had been vanquished by the art of Michelangelo and was ready, through Raphael, to be vanquished by character as well. Indeed, until Raphael most artists had in their temperament a touch of uncouthness and even madness that made them abstracted (*astratti*) and eccentric (*fantastichi*); the dark shadows of vice were often more evident in their lives than the shining light of the virtues that can make men immortal. So nature had every reason to display in Raphael, in contrast, the finest qualities of mind accompanied by such grace, industry, looks, modesty, and excellence of character as would offset every defect, no matter how serious, and any vice, no matter how ugly.[35]

Throughout the *Lives* manners are seen as the means by which the artist may assert or improve his social status, and claim his right to be considered more than a mere craftsman. Manners are also a sign of virtue, and of the moral and ethical composure that is a mark of breeding and education. Conversely, uncouth behaviour and any form of eccentricity – any deviation indeed from the measured rationality exemplified in Raphael – suggests a lowly status for both the painter and his art. While Vasari states that Raphael's fine temperament and noble manner were gifts of God, he also stresses that these virtues were enhanced by a judicious upbringing: Raphael, the son of a painter, was nursed at home rather than 'in the houses of peasants or common people with their less gentle, indeed their rough manners and behaviour'.[36] Gentlemen, he implies, can be made as well as born, a notion that has crucial implications for the standing of the artist and his potential for social advancement. Vasari also emphasizes the fact that Raphael was treated as an equal by his patrons, enjoying the friendship of those at the papal court as well as that of his fellow artists.

The acquisition of manners is not only desirable in itself, however, and as a means to social respectability. It also has a practical end, for in terms of securing commissions, protection from poverty and the acquisition of fame and reputation (the latter a central theme in the *Lives*), the artist's behaviour is seen as equal in importance to the quality of his works. While Piero's behaviour is unacceptable in itself, and exemplifies the eccentric stereotype of the artist that Vasari aims to dispel, it is also seen to deny him fame and fortune. Piero's isolation, and his idiosyncratic lifestyle, are said by Vasari to have deprived him of the fame his talent deserved, for his contemporaries, deterred by his odd manner, remained largely unaware of, or unable to appreciate, his talent. Thus, not only was he not revered as an artist, he was actually considered to be mad. The artist who seeks fame and prosperity should cultivate his lifestyle as carefully as his talent.

Piero and Leonardo: the Eccentric and the Refined Artist

Vasari underlines the didactic significance of Piero's Life, if only implicitly, by comparison with that of Leonardo, which opens part Three of the *Lives*, and by the contrasts he draws between their respective fortunes.[37] While Raphael can be said to provide the model of behaviour for the *Lives* as a whole, it is Leonardo who reveals most clearly the point of Piero's example, partly because of their proximity in the overall sequence of the *Lives*. It is no coincidence that Piero is included in a group of four painters that opens with Leonardo (Giorgione and Correggio are the other two), for not only does Vasari suggest stylistic affinities between them, but the significance of their lives is mutually reinforcing. Unlike Piero, both Leonardo and Giorgione are praised for their refined manners, sociable natures and musical accomplishments, gifts that, as much as their works, made them revered and sought after by patrons.

The relationship between Leonardo and Piero is, however, particularly telling; the two have many traits in common and their Lives are couched in the same descriptive language. Both artists are described as being of great natural talent, or *elevato ingegno*, and in his accounts of their works Vasari stresses the same quality of imagination, or *fantasìa*, as well as their inventiveness, and the elements in their art of the whimsical (*capriccioso*) and bizarre. Both display a certain secretiveness about their work and Leonardo, like Piero, pursues his interests obsessively, to the point of a certain abstractedness. Most important, both are seen as artists who fail sufficiently to discipline their natural talent, a trait that in the case of Leonardo led him to finish few works – one aspect of his career of which Vasari could not entirely approve. Leonardo also shares Piero's fascination with the natural world in both its perfect and imperfect forms, and with the fine details of flora and fauna. Fascinated by the oddities of nature, he is said to have taken a particular delight in the bizarre physiognomies he encountered in the street, his drawings of which are well known. Vasari also relates how Leonardo liked to invent fantastic and grotesque forms, such as the head of Medusa he painted on a peasant's buckler, which Leonardo made up of the lizards, crickets, snakes, butterflies, locusts and bats that he brought into his workshop. Vasari describes the result as

> a fearsome and horrible monster, which emitted poisonous breath and turned the air to fire; and he depicted the creature emerging from the dark cleft of a rock, belching forth venom from its throat, fire from its eyes and smoke from its nostrils in so strange a fashion that the effect was altogether monstrous and horrible.[38]

Leonardo is also said to have made an oil painting of the head of Medusa, with a coiffure of snakes, described by Vasari as 'the strangest and most extravagant (*stravagante*) invention that one could possibly imagine.[39] Vasari's accounts of these paintings resonate strongly with his descriptions of Piero's own works, such as his painting of a sea monster that 'by virtue of its deformity is so extravagant, fantastic and bizarre, that it seems impossible that nature herself could produce such strangeness and such deformity in her works'.[40] Vasari also describes a dragon painted by Piero in a predella panel depicting St Margaret, claiming that

> he made the animal so ugly and deformed, showing venom in its eyes, and in the fire of its breath, and revealing the face of death in its truly fearsome appearance, that I do not think one could see a better example of such a thing.[41]

The similarity in the language Vasari uses of these works is not simply a reflection of the fact that, within the *Lives*, objects of this genre are frequently described in such terms; it also serves to underline the similarities between the artists' interests and talents, and in some respect of their achievements.

At the same time, however, Vasari is at pains to stress the universality of Leonardo's talent, and his mastery of every aspect of nature, especially the human figure. Within this context, a fascination with the more exotic and recondite forms of nature becomes a permissible facet of the pursuit of mimesis, one aspect of an interest in the workings of the natural world that Leonardo also harnessed for more serious purposes. That which, in Piero, appears as an unworthy preoccupation with the abnormal, which diverts him from the proper subject-matter of art is, in Leonardo, at worst a harmless caprice. And, while their artistic interests, and the nature of their talents, are similar, as a person Leonardo is the very opposite of Piero and the antithesis of all that is coarse and eccentric, being beautiful to look at, graceful in his manner and virtuous in his every action. While Piero is said to have repelled even his friends by his strangeness, Leonardo is presented as a model of courtly behaviour, one who drew people to him by his charm and accomplishment, delightful conversation, musical gifts and personal generosity. Patronized and feted by kings and popes, and living like a prince despite his humble birth, Leonardo's death was as noble and ceremonious as Piero's was solitary and mean. Exemplary in his piety to the last, Leonardo was visited in his final days by Francis I, and died in the arms of his royal patron, following which he was universally mourned. 'His name', Vasari writes, 'became so famous that not only was he esteemed during his lifetime but his reputation endured and became even greater after his death'.[42] The key themes of Leonardo's life are nobility and fame, and Vasari makes clear the relationship between them: it is the combination of attributes in Leonardo, not his talent alone, that attracted fame and fortune.

In this first cluster of biographies in part Three of the *Lives*, Piero thus functions as the antithesis of Leonardo as the model painter, with his life and inglorious death serving as examples of what happens when a talented artist fails to nurture his reputation, or to match the nobility of his gifts to an equally noble lifestyle. While endowed with similar interests and talents, Piero, if not wholly Leonardo's equal, pursues a completely different path. The implication is that, with a judicious control of his natural talent and the proper attention to good manners, Piero could have gained prosperity and renown and a similarly ceremonious end.

Vasari's attitude to Piero's life is therefore inextricable from his views on the artist and his status, and his lively account of Piero's eccentricities serves always to reinforce the moral point. His description of him as 'brutish' (*bestiale*) and 'untamed' (*selvatico*) should also be seen in this context: while these terms serve as a means of describing his work and the way in which he deploys his talent, they also allude to the solitary habits and roughness of manner that constitute the Life's main theme.

While a degree of sociability is essential for the artist's ability to win patrons, it is also an intrinsic part of the level of refinement that Vasari wishes him to display. More specifically, the desire for company and the ability to enjoy the society of others are attributes of the civilized man. They are also one aspect of that which distinguishes men from beasts, an idea that had been formulated quite clearly by Cicero, whose views on the nature and evolution of man were highly influential in the Renaissance, and which Vasari certainly knew. For Cicero, man is inherently sociable in a way that animals are not, and not simply as a means of survival.[43] Cicero also stresses that man, unlike animals, is able to assess the consequences of his actions, to view the course of his life as a whole and to use his reason when evaluating the best course of action.[44] Vasari's description of Piero as 'brutish' should perhaps be read against this background, and it is significant that in the opening to the Life he stresses Piero's failure to foresee or to calculate the consequences of his unsocial behaviour. The term must also allude to the uncouth nature of the artist's existence – his domestic uncleanliness and frugal diet. Living without care for one's appearance, and eating only in order to survive, his is a life governed by instinct rather than by reason, one devoid of the delight in gracious living that is a mark of man's greater civilization – his superiority over the animal world. While in the Life of the artist Sodoma, whose conduct also earned Vasari's disapproval, *bestialità* refers to sexual vice, incontinence and impiety, in the case of Piero, who Vasari insists was pious despite his bestial life, it alludes rather to his solitary nature, and to a life dictated by brute instinct.[45]

The term *selvatico* – uncultivated or wild – while most important, perhaps, as a means of describing Piero's art and the undisciplined nature of his talent, is also related to his desire to be alone, and in contemporary religious and philosophical literature it was sometimes used as a synonym for solitariness or for the desire to live apart from civilization.[46] Vasari means it to refer also to Piero's undisciplined habits, and to the lack of care he bestowed on his well-being and appearance: the man is as untamed as the garden he left to grow wild 'like his own nature'.

It is in the use of these terms and in the picture he paints of Piero's primitive habits, that we can discern most clearly the element of invention, or at least of exaggeration, in Vasari's Life. While there is no reason to doubt that Piero led a solitary and frugal existence, the very coherence of this aspect of Vasari's account, and the metaphorical and didactic function of his terms, suggest that such details are embellishments designed to serve a wider purpose. At once a means of describing Piero's works, and in part inferred or abstracted from them, they make the account more vivid, and underline more clearly the consequences of such a life. In his description of Piero as bestial or savage, Vasari presents him less as an individual than as an exemplar of an uncivilized man, a definition of the solitary in all its aspects, just as Raphael serves to demonstrate what it means to be fully human. In this respect at least, the individual is subordinate to the type.

Piero and the Notion of *Fantasìa*

We have seen that, in the *Lives*, artists who seek solitude are often also described as *fantastico*, and that for Vasari, as for other sixteenth-century writers, such as de Hollanda, the two characteristics are frequently related. We have also seen that both writers were anxious to make clear that although Michelangelo was a solitary he was not 'fantastic' in his behaviour. The term *fantastico* does, however, play a critical role in Vasari's characterization of Piero and his work. It is also inextricable from his discussion of Piero's *fantasìa*, which constitutes one of the most important and revealing aspects of the Life as a whole.

It is important to establish at the outset that the term *fantasìa* as used in the fifteenth and sixteenth centuries has relatively little to do with the notion of fantasy as presently conceived, especially in so far as it relates to the expression of subconscious desires, or the workings of the unconscious mind. In terms of the theory of faculty psychology that underpinned most Renaissance discussions of the term, including Vasari's, *fantasìa* was a faculty of the mind, positioned between the senses and the intellect.[47] *Fantasìa* was the mind's image-forming capacity, its ability to construct mental images or impressions on the basis of things actually seen, although it could also be responsible for dreams and illusions. For Aristotle, whose definitions of the faculties formed the basis of most later thought on the matter, and which were largely sustained in the Renaissance, *fantasìa* was an indispensable part of all rational thought, for thought cannot take place without images.[48] It was the function of *fantasìa* to produce clear mental images of the objects in the world as the basis for contemplation, providing the subject-matter of intellectual activity. It was also allied to memory, for on the basis of stored sense-impressions *fantasìa* could construct images of objects not immediately present before the eyes, enabling contemplation of the things of the world in their absence. Most important for our purposes, writers after Aristotle, beginning with St Augustine, also attributed to *fantasìa* the power to produce compound images, and to construct objects that do not exist in reality by combining parts from things actually seen. Avicenna used the example of a flying man or an emerald mountain to illustrate this second function of *fantasìa*, which he named *imaginativa*.[49]

It should be clear from this that *fantasìa*, as defined by faculty psychology, was not a counterpart of rational thought, but operated in conjunction with reason and the intellect, furnishing them with the basic material of contemplation. It could also be controlled by reason and the will, a notion that had particular importance for Stoic and Christian writers, who emphasized that *fantasìa* should be properly directed. For while it was an essential instrument of rational activity, *fantasìa* was also related to both intention and desire, and could be used to construct foolish and vain images, or which incited vicious rather than virtuous thoughts. Writers such as St Augustine therefore stressed that *fantasìa* must not be allowed to run free or weave vain fancies, but should be harnessed to rational ends and used to furnish images that would aid virtuous contemplation.[50]

It is also important to note that *fantasìa* was seen to have as its objects the things of the real world; the images it constructed come not from the intellect itself, or solely from within the mind, but from things experienced and seen. While it could construct from these objects that do not actually exist, *fantasìa* always remained rooted in the sensory experience of reality. This proximity to and dependence on the sense of sight was also thought to give a particular vividness and intensity to the images *fantasìa* produced, a notion of some importance for discussions of its role in the visual arts. As the basic image-forming capacity of the mind, *fantasìa* was part of the psychological make-up of all men, and was not peculiar to artists. At the same time, for Classical and Renaissance writers there was an obvious analogy between the operations of *fantasìa* and the activity of the artist in his task of *mimesis* – the faithful and convincing representation of the external world. Almost inevitably, therefore, writers on the arts discussed the role of *fantasìa* in artistic production, just as they sometimes used the example of artistic activity to illustrate its workings.[51] From the late fourteenth century onwards, the term appears with some frequency in discussions of the visual arts, although it is not always used in the same way, and writers by no means established a consistent definition or a coherent view of the role of *fantasìa* in artistic creation. In his *Libro dell'Arte*, for example, written around 1397, Cennino Cennini assigns to *fantasìa* the function of constructing compound images, enabling the artist to reproduce objects that do not actually exist, such as centaurs. It is also an example of a faculty shared by painters and poets, and of the licence accorded to both, an idea Cennini probably derived from the *Ars Poetica* of Horace.[52]

Fantasìa could also be used to describe the theme or idea for a painting, the invention of subject-matter by the artist or his patron. In the instructions given by Isabella d'Este to the artists engaged to paint mythologies for her studiolo in Mantua, her ideas for particular subjects and their arrangement are called both *fantasìe* and inventions (*invenzioni*) – *fantasìa* thus referring both to her discovery of a theme and to its imaginative composition through specific arrangements of figures.[53] Along slightly different lines, the term appears occasionally in artists' contracts towards the end of the fifteenth century, where it seems to be associated primarily with objects of secondary importance, and particularly with the decorative elements of a work. In the contract Pintoricchio signed in 1502 for the painting of the Piccolomini Library in Siena, it is used particularly in relation to grotesque ornaments, such as were often comprised of different natural forms: the artist is asked to paint the ceiling with 'those *fantasìe* . . . that are nowadays called *grottesche*'.[54]

While the uses of the term *fantasìa* were not always consistent in the fifteenth century, it retained a decidedly rational slant. *Fantasìa* remained allied to the rational intellectual process of invention, whether this related to the conception of the *istoria*, or narrative theme, or to the composition of decorative motifs. Within these contexts, *fantasìa* is seen as a means of extending the artist's creative powers, enabling him to produce forms not seen in nature, to devise new subjects, or to create variations on a familiar iconographic theme or motif. For the most part Vasari retains this rational view of *fantasìa* and its link with the intellectual process of invention, and his conception of the term remains broadly within the tradition of faculty psychology. Like many of his contemporaries he has an ambivalent attitude towards *fantasìa*: while recognizing its ability to increase the artist's creative potential, and especially his capacity for invention, he implies that it must be carefully controlled, and exercised within certain limits. Although Vasari does not make the point explicitly, in his discussion of individual works he suggests that *fantasìa* must not be allowed to run too freely, or be allowed to create excessively bizarre objects. The products of *fantasìa*, even if they do not exist in reality, must retain the appearance of verisimilitude, and must not degenerate into the ugly or grotesque. They must also be appropriate to the painting's main theme, and placed in such a way as to maintain an overall decorum. In this respect it is significant that, within the *Lives*, unlike terms such as 'grace' (*grazia*) or 'charm' (*leggiadrìa*), those which Vasari associates with *fantasìa* and its products, such as 'capricious' or 'whimsical' (*capriccioso*) and 'extravagant' (*stravagante*), while often terms of praise, may also be used with negative connotations.[55]

Although artists who display *fantasìa*, and whose works are described in these terms in the *Lives*, are not necessarily unorthodox or eccentric in their behaviour, an excess of *fantasìa* is also seen to make artists abstracted or bizarre. Piero tended to allow his imagination free rein and to indulge his *fantasìa* or, as Vasari put it, to build castles in the air, rendering him strange and self-absorbed. The description of him as *fantastico* refers less, in fact, to distinct quirks of behaviour or particular eccentricities than to his tendency to *fantasticare*, and to an immersion in his own imaginings that renders him abstracted and distant from his fellow men. That is not to say that Vasari disapproved of the products of Piero's imaginings or considered them unacceptably strange, for as we shall see later, in his descriptions of Piero's works *fantasìa* is invariably used as a term of praise. The real point is that the artist spends too much time indulging this aspect of his talent and following its whims, to the ultimate detriment of his art.

The Limits of *Fantasìa*: Imagination and Design

As defined by faculty psychology – as the capacity to conceive vivid mental images – *fantasìa* would of course play a role in the production of all the painter's forms, each of which would be formed initially in his mind. In theory, therefore, it would contribute to the artist's representation of all aspects of the visible world. Vasari, however, assigns it a more limited role, one more in line with its second function, that of producing compound images. In the *Lives* he uses it almost exclusively of subsidiary or decorative subjects, especially those that, like *grotteschi*, are made up of different forms, and which combine the objects of nature in various imaginative ways. Not surprisingly it is also used of unusual or exotic animals and landscapes that, although rooted in the natural world, combine different parts of nature to produce variations not seen in reality. Most important, Vasari does not use *fantasìa* in relation to the human form or the composition of dramatic narrative, and it does not appear at all in the Life of

Raphael, while in that of Michelangelo it is used only in relation to architectural ornament. Following his account of Michelangelo's designs for the New Sacristy in S. Lorenzo in Florence, Vasari adds:

> The licence he allowed himself has served as a great encouragement to others to follow his example; and subsequently we have seen the creation of new kinds of fantastic ornamentation containing more of the grotesque than of rule or reason.[56]

The implication is that *fantasìa* alone is of limited value, its role being to embellish and give variety to forms conceived in other, more elevated ways. We saw earlier how, in discussing Michelangelo's *Last Judgement*, Vasari contrasted the artist's understanding of design and mastery of the human form with the 'caprices and novel fantasies' produced by his contemporaries. Following on from this, Vasari notes that

> some artists, lacking Michelangelo's profound knowledge of design, have tried by using a variety of tints and shades of colour, by including in their work various novel and bizarre inventions . . . to win themselves a place among the most distinguished masters.[57]

While Vasari may not have had a coherent theory of *fantasìa* and its role in the creative process, there are signs none the less that he saw it as subsidiary and inferior to the process of *disegno*, or design, of which the main object, though not the only one, was the ideal human form. This is particularly interesting in relation to previously established notions of the limits of *fantasìa*, limits that were seen to arise from its position between the intellect and the senses. Within the framework of faculty psychology, *fantasìa*, while it worked in conjunction with the intellect, was seen as inferior to it because it was dependent on sensory data for its operations, even if it could combine the objects of sensory experience in various novel ways. This also meant that it was bound to particulars, and lacked the capacity to abstract general forms or ideas from them, a process that was properly the activity of the intellect.

It is precisely the ability to abstract from particular forms that characterizes the process of design as Vasari understands it, the intellectual nature of which is stressed throughout the *Lives*. For Vasari design, unlike *fantasìa*, originates in the intellect, not in the world of the senses. This is made explicit in the second edition of the *Lives*, in which Vasari added an extended definition of design to the Technical Preface on Painting, underlining its intellectual and generalizing qualities:

> Seeing that Design . . . having its origin in the intellect, draws out from many single things a general judgement, it is like a form or idea of all the objects in nature, most marvellous in what it encompasses, for not only in the bodies of men and of animals but also in plants, in buildings, in sculpture and in painting, design is cognisant of the proportion of the whole to the parts and of the parts to each other and to the whole. Seeing too that from this knowledge there arises a certain conception and judgement, so that there is formed in the mind that something which afterwards, when expressed by the hands, is called design, we may conclude that design is not other than a visible expression and declaration of our inner conception and of that which others have imagined and given form to in their idea.[58]

The addition of this passage was almost certainly partly made in response to the writings of Venetian art theorists, particularly Ludovico Dolce, and their claims for the superiority of the Venetian painters' emphasis on colour as a means of representation. In his *Dialogue on Painting* of 1555, for example, which appeared between the two editions of the *Lives*, Dolce stresses both the particularity of colour or colouring (*colorito*) – its ability to capture the specifics of visual experience – and its universal scope. In Dolce's own definition *disegno* is confined to the drawing of outlines, and is of use primarily in the rendering of figures. It is colour that enables the artist to reproduce all the objects of nature, and so to perfect the task of *mimesis*, the imitation of the natural world. This includes the figure, which can only be given a living presence through the rendering of colour and the textural quality of paint itself.[59]

Partly in response to this, and in an attempt to maintain the superiority of Florentine *disegno* over Venetian colouring, in the second edition of the *Lives* Vasari stresses in turn the universality of design. In the first edition, like Dolce, he suggests that design is primarily concerned with the figure, defining it in the third preface as 'the imitation of the most beautiful things in nature, used for the creation of all figures whether in sculpture or painting; and this quality depends on the ability of the artist's hand and mind to reproduce what he sees with his eyes accurately and correctly on to paper or whatever flat surface he may be using'.[60] In the first preface he describes it as

> the animating principle of all creative processes: and surely design existed in absolute perfection before the Creation when Almighty God, having made the vast expanse of the universe and adorned the heavens with His shining lights, directed His creative intellect further, to the clear air and the solid earth. And then, in the act of creating man, He fashioned the first forms of painting and sculpture in the sublime grace of created things.[61]

In the passage added to second edition, however, Vasari stresses the universality of design and its role in the representation of all the things of nature, giving it a scope equivalent to that of Dolce's *colorito*. At the same time he increases the emphasis on the intellectual dimension of design, implicit in the first edition, giving it a measure of superiority over the Venetian *colorito*, which implicitly belongs to the realm of the senses. He also stresses its generalizing activity, its ability to formulate general ideas of the objects of nature, in contrast to the Venetians' colouring, which is more tied to and concerned with the specifics of visual experience.

There is no doubt that this addition, and Vasari's attempt to respond to Dolce's ideas, creates certain tensions within the second edition of the *Lives*. While in the Technical Prefaces Vasari stresses the larger scope of design, in the individual Lives, and in his comments on specific works, his use of *disegno* still relates first and foremost to the figure, and it is clear that this remains for him the highest object of art. What is also clear is the importance he attaches to the intellectual nature of design, reaffirmed in the second edition, and to its generalizing activity, both of which distinguished it from the specificity and sensual nature of the Venetians' use of colour. It is also these qualities that distinguishes design from *fantasìa*. The role of design, and its ultimate aim, is to extract a general idea of the objects of nature, and of the essentials of their forms, from the sensory experience of individual examples. Unlike the *fantasìa* of psychological theory, its function is not the exact reproduction of the world as seen, but the abstraction and representation of its ideal, essential forms based partly on experience and partly on the artist's own inborn vision, which, in the case of Michelangelo, was implanted in his mind by God. As a faculty of the mind, the proximity of *fantasìa* to sight was thought to give the images it produced a certain vividness and grasp of detail, as well as verisimilitude, and it is interesting that these, as we shall see in chapter Two, are among the qualities Vasari commends in the products of Piero's *fantasìa*. He conceives it none the less as both less elevated and more limited in scope than the intellectual, generalizing activity of design, and more akin, perhaps, to the Venetians' *colorito*, although *fantasìa* could act as a complement to design and a means of extending its range.

In the light of these implicit distinctions, it is significant that Vasari rarely praises Piero for his *disegno* and makes little mention of the artist's figures. The implication seems to be that, while the products of Piero's *fantasia* may be commendable *per se*, he indulged this aspect of his talent at the expense of a mastery of design and the painting of the human form. He thus becomes an example of those artists who, lacking Michelangelo's understanding of design, concentrate on producing caprices and *fantasie*, and those new and bizarre inventions that should be the ornament, not the substance, of the painter's art.

Fantasìa and the Image made by Chance

Vasari's discussion of Piero's habit of creating images from spit-stains on walls, or from the shapes of clouds is also best seen within the context of his attitude to *fantasìa*, although he himself does not use the term in relation to this procedure, beyond describing as 'fantastic' (*fantastiche*) the cities Piero invented in this way. The idea that images may appear in irregular shapes, and that artists could use these as an aid to invention, had been discussed in Classical literature, although in differing ways.[62] Even before the phenomenon was related to artistic creation, writers in Antiquity had discussed the appearance of recognizable images in the irregular shapes of clouds and rocks. In Lucretius's *De Rerum Natura*, for example, written in the first century BC and which Piero may have known, the author discusses the way semblances of objects often appear in the sky, and which,

> melting incessantly change their shapes and turn themselves into the outlines of all manner of figures . . . often giants' countenances appear to fly over and to draw their shadows after, sometimes great mountains and rocks . . . [63]

Later writers, such as Philostratus, applied this phenomenon specifically to the activity of the artist. In his *Life of Apollonius of Tyana*, written in the late second or early third century AD, in answer to the question 'What does this art [of painting] do?' posed by Apollonius, Damis explains that the task of the painter is *mimesis*, the imitation of the external world. He reproduces the objects he sees around him, but he can also represent other things, such as the images that appear in the heavens 'whenever the clouds are torn away from one another . . . the centaurs and stag antelopes . . . the wolves and the horses', which he can then rearrange and perfect into regular forms.[64] While this is ostensibly a discussion about painting, and Philostratus does not actually use the term *fantasìa*, it has been suggested that the passage is also intended to serve as an illustration of the workings of the imagination.[65] Certainly, the two can be seen as analogous, the twin functions of *fantasìa*, that of direct representation of the visible – the mirroring of the external world – and that of creative recomposition, being directly comparable to two aspects of the painter's task.

Most important, Philostratus implies that, while the ability to see such images is common to all men, and not peculiar to painters, it can be of particular use to the artist, enabling him to create variations on natural forms by suggesting permutations of real objects he would not ordinarily see. They thus present him with a wider range of forms on which to draw, at the same time releasing him from the limits of direct imitation, for Philostratus also suggests that the semblances of objects that appear in the clouds require imaginative completion or perfection through the artist's intervention. As described by Philostratus, however, this procedure is not contrary to the rational process of *mimesis*, nor does it involve a suspension of the rational faculty. Chance images function primarily as a means of extending the possibilities of *mimesis* by adding variety to the artist's repertory of forms, and the images produced in this way still imitate and resemble the objects of the visible world, or variations of them.

The concept of chance images was a familiar one in the Renaissance through works such as that of Philostratus, and was discussed by a number of writers. In terms of the subject under discussion here, the most important reference to the idea appears in Leonardo's *Notebooks*, which may well have been the source for Vasari's account of Piero's use of spit-stains. Leonardo, however, approaches the subject in terms slightly different from those of Philostratus, for he does not suggest that chance images objectively exist. Rather, it is the artist who creates them, extracting from, or projecting into, amorphous and irregular shapes images not actually present, and he recommends the process to painters as a means of stimulating and enriching their capacity for invention:

> I have in the past seen clouds and wall stains which have inspired me to beautiful inventions of other things. These stains, while wholly in themselves deprived of perfection in any part, did not lack perfection in regard to their movements or other actions . . . I shall not refrain from including among these precepts a new aid to contemplation which, although seemingly trivial and almost ridiculous, is nonetheless of great utility in arousing the mind to various inventions. And this is, if you look at a wall soiled with a variety of stains, or stones with variegated patterns, when you have to invent some location, you will therein be able to see a resemblance to various landscapes, graced with mountains, rivers, rocks, trees, plains, wide valleys and hills in many combinations; or, again, you will be able to see battles and various figures darting about; or strange-looking faces and costumes, and an endless number of objects, which you can distil into complete and finely-rendered forms. And what happens with regard to such walls and variegated stones is just as with the sound of bells, in whose peal you may find any name or word you care to imagine.[66]

The irregular shapes of stains on walls can suggest new forms to the painter's mind, feeding his imagination and increasing his inventive powers. As for Philostratus, however, this procedure is a tool in the task of *mimesis*, a means of enlarging the artist's capacity to depict natural or plausible forms. Leonardo does not recommend it as an alternative to rational invention, or to the scientific study of nature, but as an adjunct to it. It is an aid to the representation of the visible world, and the objects the artist creates in this way must always appear realistic, and grounded in the knowledge of nature itself.

Vasari's use of this idea in relation to Piero is fully in line with Leonardo's discussion, for Vasari does not suggest that such images exist. It is Piero who discovers them, and Vasari indicates this quite precisely by his use of terms, stressing that Piero 'extracted' (*cavava*) battles, landscapes and cities from the irregular shapes he paused to contemplate. Neither Leonardo nor Vasari uses the term *fantasìa* in connection with this procedure. In both cases, however, and especially that of Vasari, the implication seems to be that the ability to see objects or suggestions of objects in this way is a special gift of the painter, rather than being common to all men, and that painters are particularly disposed to 'discover' such forms, especially those with an active *fantasìa*. At the same time, the process of conceiving images in this way has analogies with the activity of *fantasìa* in creating compound images from the parts of different objects; from the suggestion of a natural object, or part of an object in an irregular shape, the artist can imagine new variations on the things of the world as seen. Likewise, the ability to see such semblances and to fashion from vague likenesses images that are both clear and complete, could be seen as a natural extension and combination of the functions of *fantasìa* as conventionally understood. It is certainly significant that Vasari ascribes this procedure to Piero rather than to any other artist, the implication being that his fertile *fantasìa* gives him both the inclination and the capacity to see images in this way, and to fashion new inventions from them.

The important point, however, is not the name that Leonardo or Vasari might assign to this stratagem, but their views of its place in the artistic process. While Leonardo recommends it as an aid to creativity, and a means to variety of invention, Vasari's view was probably more ambivalent. Although he neither praises nor condemns the practice in Piero, it seems likely that he viewed it in the same way as the actions of *fantasìa*, even though he suggests that its scope is broader than that of the latter, and that it gave rise to battles, cities and landscapes, not simply to decorative forms. His account of Piero's use of this procedure also follows directly from description of the artist's enthusiasm for the freaks of nature, perhaps implying that both constitute an element of wasted effort, of interest and attention that could be more usefully directed in other ways. Certainly, the similarity of this process to the actions of *fantasìa*, and its dependence on visual experience, however broadly conceived, would have made it inferior to the intellectual process of design. It is thus significant that, while his source may well have been Leonardo's *Notebooks*, Vasari makes no mention of it in his Life of Leonardo, stressing instead the artist's scientific study of nature and his mastery of design.

We have seen that Piero's lifestyle is censured by Vasari, both because it perpetuates the image of the artist as strange and fantastic and because it has consequences for his art. His behaviour is seen to have damaged his reputation and prevented the proper recognition of his talent. His solitary habits also signal an excessive preoccupation with the secrets of nature, at the same time allowing him to indulge this fascination, to the detriment of his art as a whole. The relationship between Piero's lifestyle and his art is in this respect reciprocal: just as his solitary habits allow him to pursue the mysteries of nature, so this same preoccupation renders him ever more abstracted and self-absorbed, leading him to avoid the company of others.

Vasari also sees Piero's character as having other consequences for his art, although the relationship between the two is largely different from the one that has been projected by subsequent writers. It is particularly important to note that, while stressing the eccentricity in Piero's life, Vasari does not suggest that his work is similarly eccentric, or that it is bizarre in an uncontrolled or unacceptable way, and the terms *bizzarro, capriccioso* and *stravagante* are not used of his works in a pejorative way, as they are in the cases of Pontormo and Tintoretto.[67] The 'bizarre' aspect of Piero's paintings is, for Vasari, the object of unqualified praise, the implication being that the whimsical or fantastic element in his works remains within acceptable bounds and does not stray into the irrational, incomprehensible or grotesque. The consequences of Piero's character are seen more in what he does not do than in the actual products of his brush.

Piero and the Notion of Individual Style

I have suggested that Vasari sees Piero's absorption in nature, and in his own *fantasìa*, as misuses of his talent, and that his description of Piero as *selvatico* is a means of alluding to his failure to impose sufficient control over his natural gifts. His accounts of Piero's untamed nature and his wild garden serve as metaphors for his undisciplined talent, which prevented him from perfecting his art and inhibited the full flowering of his gifts. While this is manifest in the artist's unchecked enthusiasm for the finer points of nature, it also has consequences of another kind, which Vasari signals in more subtle ways. Most important is his implication that Piero failed to develop a distinct personal style – a judgement endorsed by most subsequent writers on the artist and reflected in the complex history of attribution of Piero's works. Although, towards the end of the Life, Vasari writes that 'one recognises in the things that one sees by his hand, a mind and spirit very different and remote from those of others', this is less a question of a specific manner or style than of a particular repertory of objects, and a focus on the subtleties of nature, and Vasari states quite clearly that Piero changed his style from one work to the next. Describing Piero's enthusiasm, at one point in his career, for the manner of Leonardo, Vasari explained that he

> turned his attention to colouring in oils, having seen certain things by Leonardo, in which the colours and tones were subtly blended, and which were finished with that extreme care and diligence which Leonardo used when he wanted to demonstrate his mastery of that art; and so Piero, attracted by this manner of painting, attempted to imitate it, although he himself was very remote from the manner of

Leonardo, and also from other artists' styles; so that one can say truly that he changed his manner almost from one thing to the next, according to what he was doing.[68]

At no point in the Life, in fact, does Vasari describe Piero as having a particular *maniera*. Unusually for an artist included in part Three of the *Lives*, where, for the most part, artists are distinguished from one another by their individual style rather than by the degree of technical achievement or proficiency that divides those in parts One and Two, Piero's work is not described in terms of a specific style. Indeed, Vasari fails quite conspicuously to formulate a vocabulary with which to characterize the visual effect of Piero's art, the common stylistic element that unites his works.

The terms Vasari uses of Piero and his works can be divided into three groups. The first includes 'talent' (*ingegno*), 'imagination' (*fantasìa*), 'invention' (*invenzione*) and 'caprice' or 'whim' (*capriccio*). These refer primarily, although not exclusively, to the artist's natural talent, the inborn qualities of mind that give him the potential to create great works. The second, used primarily of the works themselves, although sometimes of the artist, includes 'bizarre' (*bizzaro*), 'strange' (*strano*), 'extravagant' (*stravagante*) and, in some instances, 'whimsical' (*capriccioso*). As we shall see these do not allude to a style, however, or manner of execution, but to a specific category of object, such as the fantastic sea-monster of the *Liberation of Andromeda*, or the unusual landscape background of the *Incarnation* (illus. 88). The third group includes 'patience', 'diligence', 'unity' (*unione*) and 'harmonious and unified colour' (*colore continovato*), which refer, not to a distinct pictorial manner, but to the technical execution of the works, the care and precision with which Piero applies his paint, or blends his tones and colours.

In contrast, therefore, to the Lives of Piero's contemporaries, especially those in part Three, whose biographies are dense with terms such as 'boldness' (*fierezza*), 'grace' (*grazia*), 'charm' (*leggiadrìa*) or 'sweetness' (*dolcezza*), which describe or characterize individual styles, Piero's Life lacks a vocabulary at this fundamental critical and appreciative level. Furthermore, in his accounts of Piero's works, Vasari tends to focus on individual objects – particularly those noteworthy for their strangeness or their quality of the bizarre – rather than on an overall visual effect, or on the place of a work within the development of the artist's own pictorial mode. So, while Vasari praises Piero's mental or intellectual gifts – his powers of invention and his lively *fantasìa* – and his technical skill, or agility of hand, at the critical level, the level of the final product, there is a striking absence of descriptive and evaluative terms. The implication seems to be that Piero's natural talent, or *ingegno*, was not fully realized; his mental ability and skill of hand did not combine, or come to fruition, in a distinctive pictorial mode. Piero's response to the works of other artists, such as Leonardo, and his own movement between different styles are also seen as arbitrary and haphazard, and not, as in the case of the exemplary Raphael, part of a pattern of continuous and organic development.

Piero's character is, therefore, not manifest in an analogous style, although this is by far the most common model used by Renaissance art critics and theorists in discussing the relationship between the artist and his work. From the fifteenth century onwards, writers on art became increasingly concerned with the question of artistic individuality, and with both describing and accounting for divergent artistic styles.[69] Certainly, for Vasari, one of the main objects of the *Lives* was the description and classification of the different styles and areas of expertise developed by artists from Cimabue onwards.

Vasari does not deal explicitly with the mechanism that causes artists to work in different ways, and the relationship between the man and the work is not always perceived in the same way in the *Lives*. He frequently suggests, however, that the character of the artist both conditions, and is reflected in, the nature of his style, especially in the quality of his figures. Thus, the courtly and gracious Raphael is praised for his graceful style, the refined Parmigianino for the charm and loveliness of his figures and the awesome Michelangelo for his *terribilità*.[70] But Piero's idiosyncratic nature is not registered in a similar way. On the contrary, while Vasari describes Piero as strange, bestial and untamed, these qualities are seen to inhibit, not assist, the development of a distinct pictorial mode or a comparable figural style. Whereas the bestial and licentious Sodoma is said by Vasari to have produced figures that were similarly lascivious and vulgar, and which lacked a proper decorum, the same relationship does not obtain in Piero, whose figures invite little comment in the Life.[71] The consequences of Piero's character are seen rather in his choice of forms – particularly the stranger forms of nature and bizarre types of animal – in his interest in certain, more recondite, natural phenomena, and in his obsessive concentration on naturalistic details, as in, for example, *The Visitation* (illus. 87):

> In the picture Piero represented a book made of parchment, rather old . . . which seems real, and likewise some balls belonging to Saint Nicholas, which appear to shine in a certain way, with the highlights and the dim reflections thrown back from one to the other, and which reveal clearly the singularity of Piero's mind, and the way he sought out the difficulties of his art.[72]

Discussing the *Incarnation* Vasari describes the landscape as 'bizarre', 'on account of certain strange trees and certain rocks', while following his account of the painting of St Margaret's dragon he adds:

> And truly I do not think that anyone painted such things better than Piero, or imagined them so convincingly . . . as is shown by a sea-monster which he painted and gave to the magnificent Giuliano de' Medici, which by virtue of its deformity is so extravagant, fantastic and bizarre, that one cannot possibly imagine nature herself using such deformity and such strangeness . . . this painting is now in the dressing-room of Cosimo de' Medici, as is a book of drawings by Piero of animals of a similar kind, bizarre and very beautiful, and executed with indescribable care.[73]

Vasari's enthusiastic praise for these works, including their fantastic and bizarre elements, makes clear that, like all the biographies in the *Lives*, his account of Piero can and should be read in two ways. I have suggested in this chapter that the Life should be interpreted first and foremost in the context of Vasari's aims for the status of the artist, and in the light of his views on the nature of good art. It must also be seen in relation to the other biographies, for there is no question but that Vasari saw the individual Lives as complementary, and their significance as mutually reinforcing. He makes the didactic function of Piero's Life quite clear and, within the *Lives* as a whole, his account serves as one of the clearest and most complete examples of an eccentric artist, a type that aroused his deep disapproval. While his description of Piero is not necessarily fictional, Vasari's leading purpose was to use him as an exemplar, and elements in both the structure and the details of the Life, as well as the lessons he draws from it, must inevitably have been shaped by that aim. Ultimately, therefore, the issue is not so much whether the account is 'true', a question that would probably have had little significance for the sixteenth-century reader; the real point is to determine what, in constructing the Life, Vasari sought to say.

It will, none the less, be important to us in subsequent chapters to consider those areas in which Vasari may have overstated his case, particularly in relation to his claims concerning Piero's reputation. For while Vasari and other writers in the sixteenth century were at pains to dispel the image of artists as eccentric and uncouth, it is by no means clear that this was of great importance to prospective patrons, or that, as Vasari suggests, ungracious behaviour led to the loss of important commissions. While it may be unwise to argue from an absence of evidence, it does not appear to have been the case that Piero's behaviour lost him commissions, and he certainly did not lack prestigious patrons. Nor is it clear that all Renaissance patrons shared Vasari's view of the primacy of the human figure, especially within the genre of domestic decoration, the type of work in which Piero excelled.

Thus, although the Life of Piero must be seen within the context of the *Lives* as a whole, it must also be seen on its own terms. Like all the artists in the *Lives* Piero is seen as part of the overall development of art, and judged by Vasari in relation to the standard of perfection achieved by Michelangelo. In this context his art is to some extent deficient, and he is compared unfavourably with both Leonardo, the universal painter, and with Michelangelo, who eschewed *capricci* and *fantasìe* in favour of the human form. At the same time, however, Vasari is able to acknowledge that each artist has his merits, and he was quick to appreciate their individual gifts and achievements, even if these did not conform to his personal ideal. Indeed, it is the dialogue between the ideal that he establishes for art and the achievements of individual artists – the reality of their works – that gives the *Lives* its interest, and its critical and descriptive richness.

While in absolute terms, therefore, Vasari sees Piero's work as deficient, he also shows a lively appreciation of his particular gifts, and an acute sense of the originality of his works. This is most evident in his discussions of individual paintings, where his descriptive and narrative technique is designed to match Piero's own, and to evoke quite precisely the experience of viewing the artist's works. It is here that we see the positive connotations of terms such as 'bizarre', 'capricious' and *fantasìa*, which, in describing particular paintings, Vasari almost invariably uses as terms of praise. It is this second aspect of the Life I will consider in chapter Two, in which the use of such terms in the relation to the works themselves will be examined more closely. By so doing we not only gain a clearer insight into the way in which Piero's paintings were viewed by Vasari and his contemporaries, we can also grasp more fully the nature of the dialectic that informs the Life itself.

CHAPTER TWO

Secular Paintings

Of the fifty or so paintings that can be securely attributed to Piero, eighteen are of secular subjects, drawn mainly from Classical history and mythology. Without exception, these secular works were painted for private patrons, to decorate their domestic interiors. Most are on a small scale, and were probably designed to be set at eye level, in or above the wooden wainscoting or *spalliera* that, in the late fifteenth and early sixteenth centuries, typically furnished the lower sections of the walls in the rooms of the grander town-houses, or *palazzi*.[1]

Piero was unusual among Florentine painters of his day in the extent to which he worked for this market while not specializing exclusively in such works. Furthermore, while other major artists who worked on such commissions often provided only the designs, leaving the execution to their workshop, Piero appears to have undertaken most of the works himself.[2] He appears to have placed unusual emphasis on what, for most artists, was a minor aspect of their activity, of less significance than the large-scale narrative compositions that, since the appearance of Alberti's *De Pictura*, had increasingly come to be seen as the highest challenge to the painter.[3]

There can be no doubt that the genre of *spalliera* panels was particularly well-suited to Piero's talents, and allowed him to develop his interests and skills with a freedom rarely possible in religious works or in commissions of a more public nature. During his lifetime private building activity in Florence was intense, with aristocratic and middle-class patrons keen to construct residences that reflected their good taste. The market for works of art to furnish and adorn their interiors was very large, and characterized by an enormous flexibility in terms of subject-matter and style – a phenomenon that painters like Piero encouraged by developing their own specialities and areas of expertise.[4] At the same time, to a greater extent than large-scale fresco cycles or altarpieces, works designed for domestic interiors were expected to be decorative and pleasing to the eye. While they often had a didactic role, a major part of the function of such images was to enliven expanses of wall or wooden panelling through variety of content, colouristic richness and intricacy of design, or to open up the interior of a room with landscape backgrounds or perspective views.

Working within this genre allowed Piero to exploit those aspects of painting at which he excelled – the rendering of landscape, the invention of unusual details and the striking and unusual colouristic harmonies about which Vasari wrote with such praise, as well as his ability to visualize unconventional themes. Conversely, in works such as the *Hunt* panels (illus. 22 and 23), *The Discovery of Honey* (illus. 28), and the *Liberation of Andromeda* (illus. 43), Piero developed both the design and the execution of the *spalliera* panel to a degree of refinement and sophistication unequalled by his

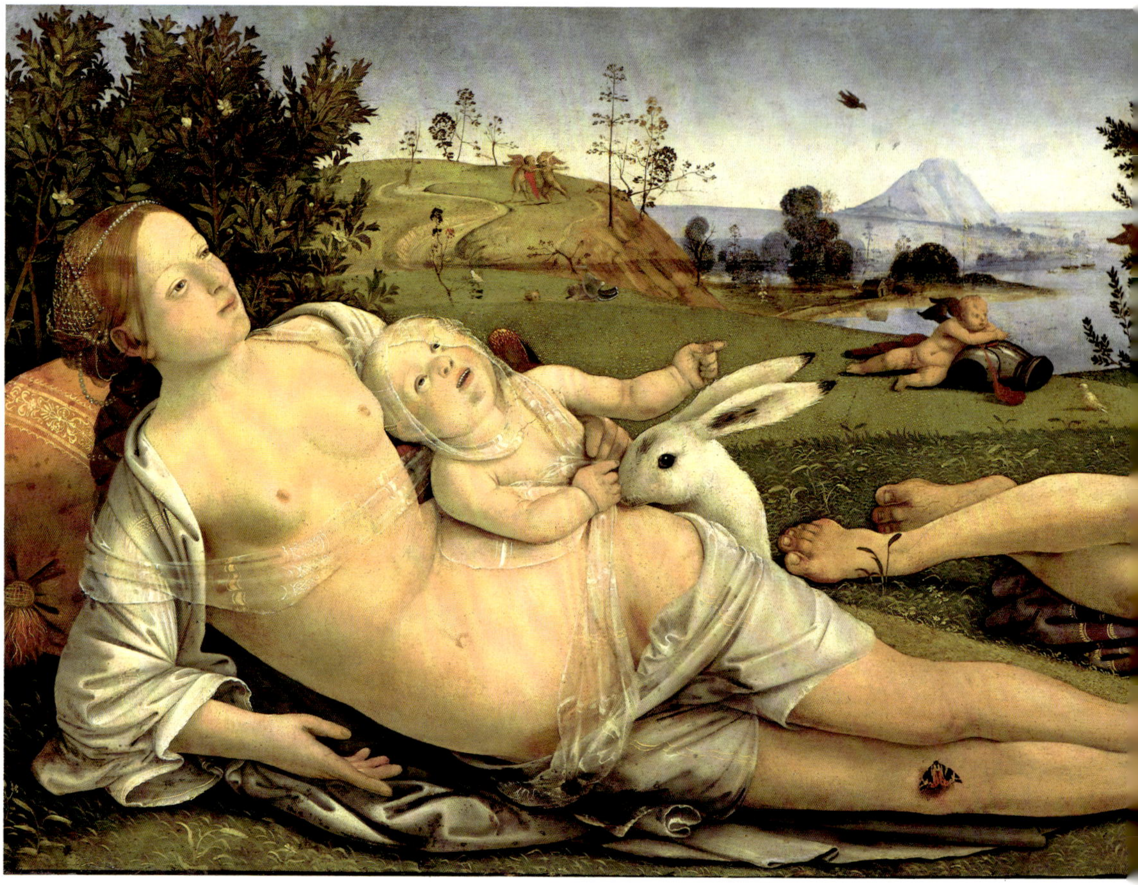

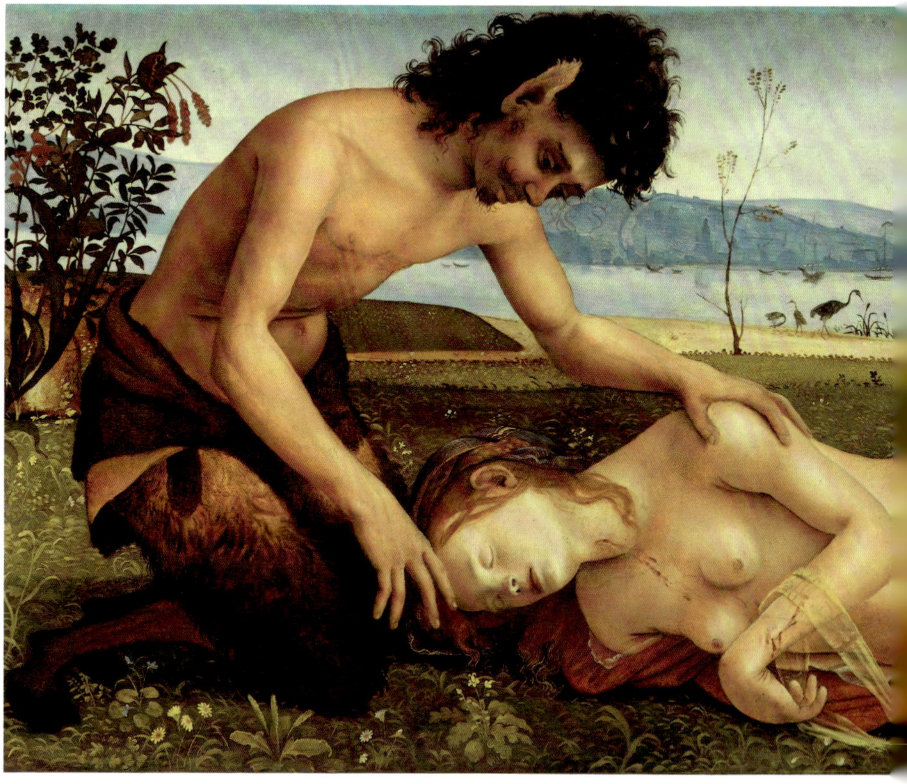

5 *Mars and Venus*, *c*.1500–5, oil on panel. Gemäldegalerie, Berlin.

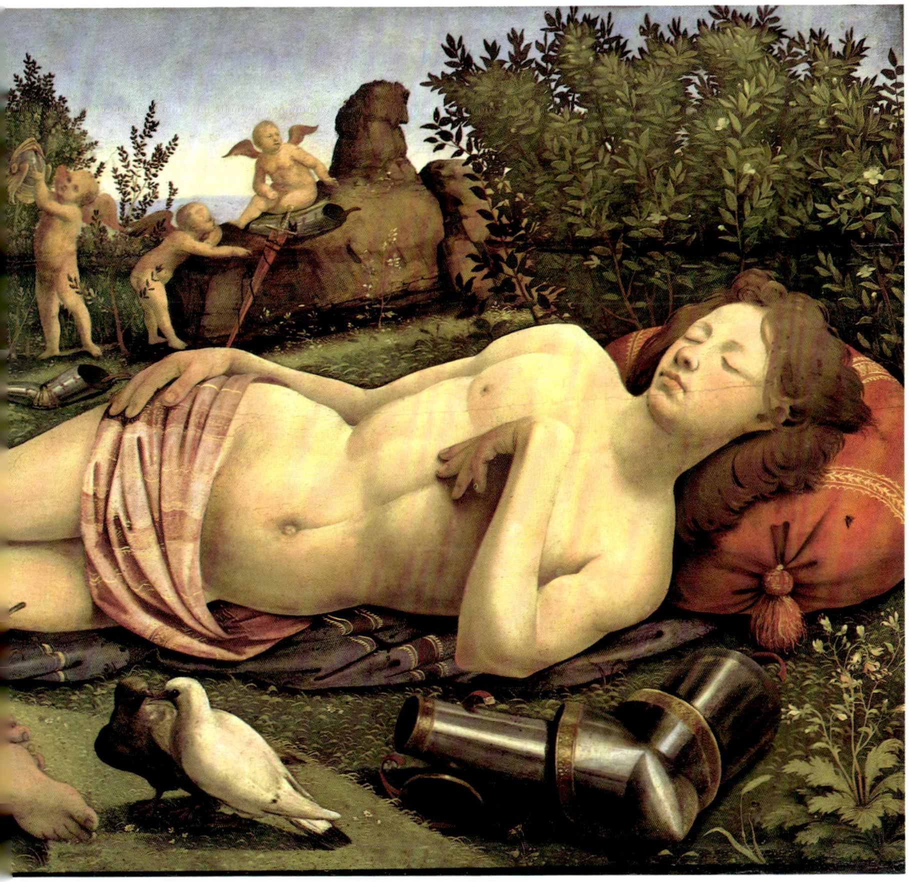

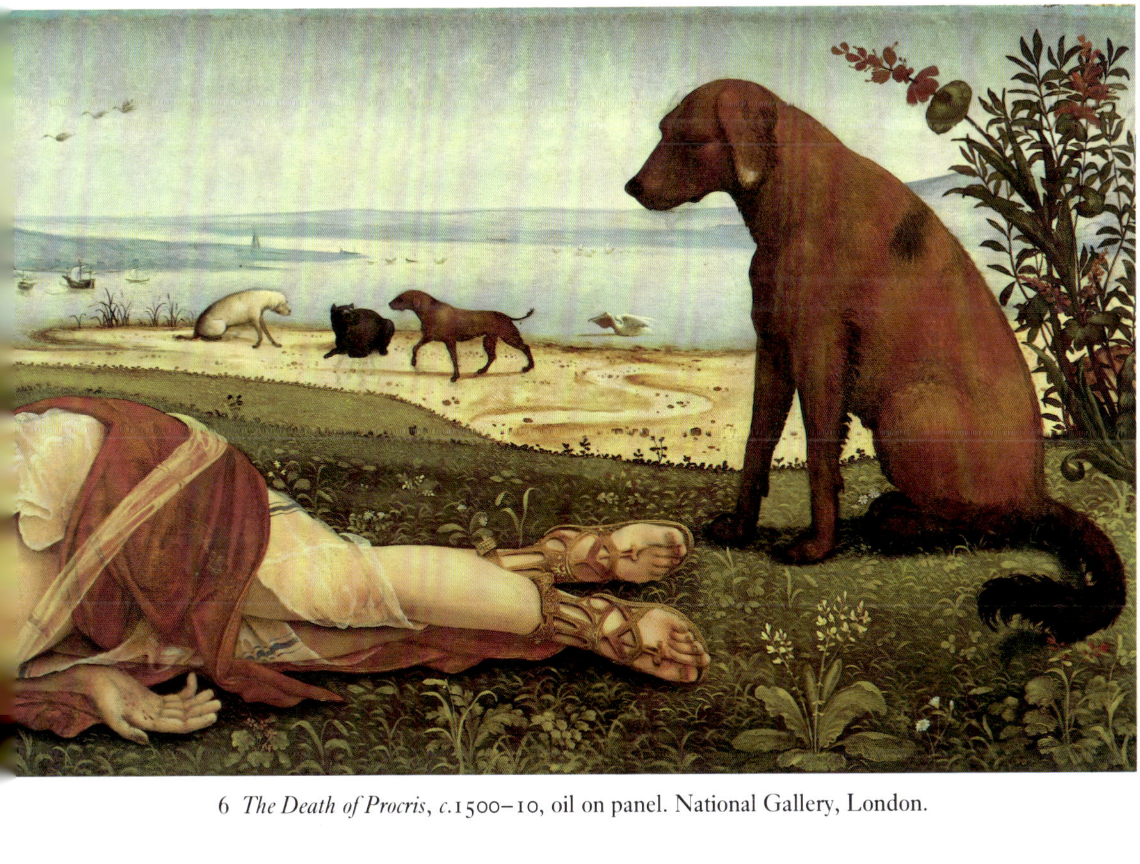

6 *The Death of Procris*, *c.*1500–10, oil on panel. National Gallery, London.

contemporaries, and in ways that displayed a particular sensitivity and responsiveness to the demands and limitations of working on a small scale. Whereas most of his contemporaries transposed to their *spalliera* panels a range of compositional techniques and expressive gestures developed for the purpose of the large-scale dramatic narrative, Piero evolved a range of pictorial techniques more specifically suited to the medium of the small-scale decorative work designed to be viewed at close quarters.[5]

Piero's approach to the design of his *spalliera* panels has had important consequences for the way in which they have been viewed, both by Vasari and by subsequent scholars, and of all his works it is the secular paintings that have proven to be the most controversial. In most cases, the ostensible subject of controversy has been the iconography, which has generally been seen as problematic. Yet a close analysis of the paintings suggests that it is often Piero's approach to composition and gesture, rather than any narrative or iconographic detail, that renders them enigmatic or obscure, and in considering the iconography of the works this must also be taken into account. It is the iconography of the secular works that I will consider first, starting with the single panels, which generally address more conventional themes than those designed as pairs, or as parts of larger cycles. Even here, however, scholars have often found it difficult to determine the significance of Piero's response to his subject-matter, a problem compounded by the lack of information regarding the provenance of the works, or the identity of their patrons.

Mars and Venus

Piero's panel of *Mars and Venus* (illus. 5) is probably the least problematic of his secular works. Nothing is known of its early provenance. It was probably painted between 1500 and 1505, but by the time Vasari published the revised edition of his *Lives* it was in his possession, and he describes it as

> a painting showing a naked Venus with Mars who, similarly stripped naked, sleeps upon a meadow full of flowers, and around them are various cupids who carry Mars' breast-plate, armlets and weapons; and there is also a grove of myrtle, and a Cupid who appears frightened of a rabbit; and also in the picture are doves of Venus and the other appurtenances of love.[6]

Having made love, Mars and Venus recline in a flowering meadow. Mars sleeps under the gaze of his lover, while Cupid nestles under her arm. Cupid's hand is nuzzled by a rabbit, a symbol of fertility and lust, and conventionally associated with venereal love. The billing turtle-doves – birds sacred to Venus – allude to the lovers' embraces, while in the background putti sport with Mars's discarded armour, a motif adapted from a description by the Classical writer Lucian of Aetion's painting of the *Marriage of Alexander and Roxana*, in which putti play with Alexander's weapons.[7] The painting thus records the amorous liaison of the Goddess of Love and the God of War, a story recounted by Homer in the *Odyssey* and by Ovid in the *Metamorphoses*; it does not, however, represent an actual moment described by Classical or contemporary authors, and is unlikely to have derived from a specific text.[8] Nor, in fact, is it intended

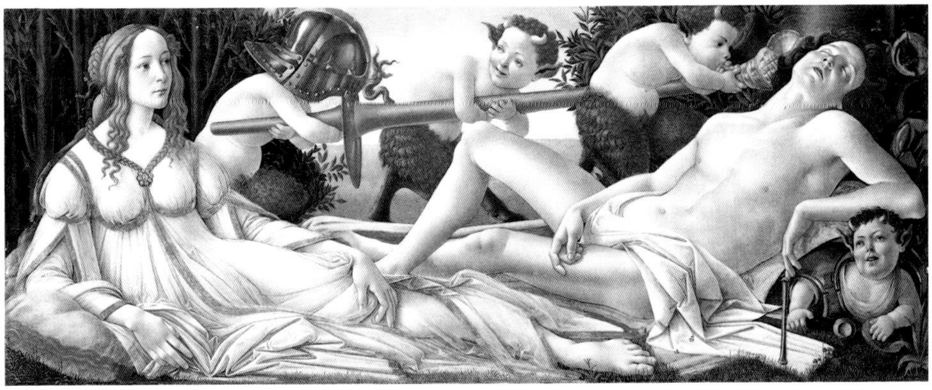

7 Botticelli, *Mars and Venus*, *c.*1483, tempera on panel. National Gallery, London.

as a narrative, but functions, rather, as an allegory of the triumph of love over war, or of the pacifying effects of earthly love.

In view of its subject-matter it seems likely that *Mars and Venus* was commissioned in connection with a marriage, possibly as a *spalliera* panel for a nuptial chamber. During the late fifteenth and early sixteenth centuries it was common practice for wealthy men, on marrying, to refurnish and redecorate their apartments as a gift to their brides and as a sign of their own altered status, and paintings played an important part in this. Indeed, it has recently been observed that, during the period of Piero's career, marriage formed one of the most significant occasions for the acquisition of works of art, and private chambers the most important location for their display.[9] Certainly, while *Mars and Venus* would have been understood as an allegory of love's triumph over war, Piero appears to have been equally concerned to stress the theme of conjugal love, and the reciprocal nature of the couple's affection. Compared, say, to Botticelli's version of the theme (illus. 7), executed around 1483, and which may have influenced Piero, the emphasis is less on the power of Venus over Mars, than on passion given and returned.[10] This is indicated by the turtle-doves, and also, perhaps, by the wrestling putti in the background. Although the significance of these two putti remains unclear, and the nature of their action hard to determine, they may be Eros and Anteros, sons of Venus, whose struggle generally signified reciprocal love, as each sought to prove his devotion the greater.[11]

The theme of mutual love is also suggested in more subtle ways, as in the placement of the figures in almost identical poses, their legs overlapping in a pattern of repeated diagonal lines. Most important, unlike Botticelli's Venus, whose pose suggests composure and control, Piero's appears languorous and abstracted, reclining in dreamy contemplation of her lover. Lost in reverie, she remains oblivious to the antics of Cupid who, entangled in her mantle, attempts to attract her attention to something beyond the grove in which they lie. Like the putti in the background, he appears to point to some danger or intruder unseen by lovers and viewer alike, reinforcing the intimacy of the scene, and the transitoriness of this moment of seclusion.[12] Venus's absorption in her lover, and the stillness of both figures, are further indicated by the butterfly resting on her leg and the fly on Mars's pillow; while these can be seen as humanist conceits, recalling Classical anecdotes concerning the artist's power of illusion, and ability to deceive, they also convey the depth of the couple's repose.[13]

Piero also introduces a subtle eroticism into the image, in the contrast between the semi-nudity of the figures and the opulent richness of their apparel, and between the luxuriance of the cushions and drapery on which they lie, and the seeming naturalness of the landscape. The sensuality of the painting is particularly pronounced in the figure of Venus, more obviously the Venus of earthly love than that of Botticelli, in the grey silk and fine veils in which she is clad, and in her elaborate coiffure of pearls and gold net, the wisp of hair hanging loose over her ear and the delicate flush of her cheeks pointing clearly to the theme of consummated love.

The comparison with Botticelli's *Mars and Venus* is important, not least because it may have provided Piero with a model – he was almost certainly aware of it – and which may have been commissioned by a member of the Vespucci family. Although there is no documentary evidence to support this connection, it has been convincingly suggested that the wasps (*vespae*) buzzing around Mars's ear in Botticelli's work are a punning reference to the Vespucci family name, and to their coat of arms, which included the motif of wasps.[14] Piero's panels of *The Discovery of Honey* and *The Misfortunes of Silenus* were certainly painted for the Vespucci, and although these were executed after his *Mars and Venus*, he may have had previous connections with the family, and been in a position to know Botticelli's work. More important is the fact that Piero's painting has often been compared unfavourably with Botticelli's, in ways that reveal much about the manner in which his mythologies have been perceived. In an essay on Piero's Early Man panels, Erwin Panofsky, for example, described Piero's representation of Mars and Venus as an 'enchantingly primitivistic pastoral' compared to Botticelli's 'solemnly classicizing allegory', while elsewhere he suggested that Piero set out to parody both the myth itself and Botticelli's own painting.[15] Other scholars have corroborated this view of Piero's mythologies as parodic or anti-humanist, or as deliberate counterpoints to Botticelli's 'innocent' renderings of Classical themes.[16]

Yet, while the allegorical implications of the liaison between Venus and Mars may be more overt in Botticelli's work, the notion that his painting is 'solemnly classicizing' is surely open to question. The wasps and the frolicking satyrs who try to awaken Mars – Botticelli's variation on the *amorini* of Aetion's *Marriage of Alexander and Roxana* – lend a note of gentle comedy to the scene, as does Piero's Cupid in his attempt to distract Venus. At the same time, Botticelli's prominent sexual symbols – the conch and lance – would seem to mitigate against an entirely serious reading of his work.[17] Conversely, while the colourful landscape in Piero's painting might justify its description as 'pastoral', it is difficult to see in what sense the artist's interpretation of the theme could be construed as 'primitivistic'.

The assumption that Piero's treatment of the subject is primitive or ironic appears, in part, to stem from a perception of his figures as inelegant or crude, the awkward

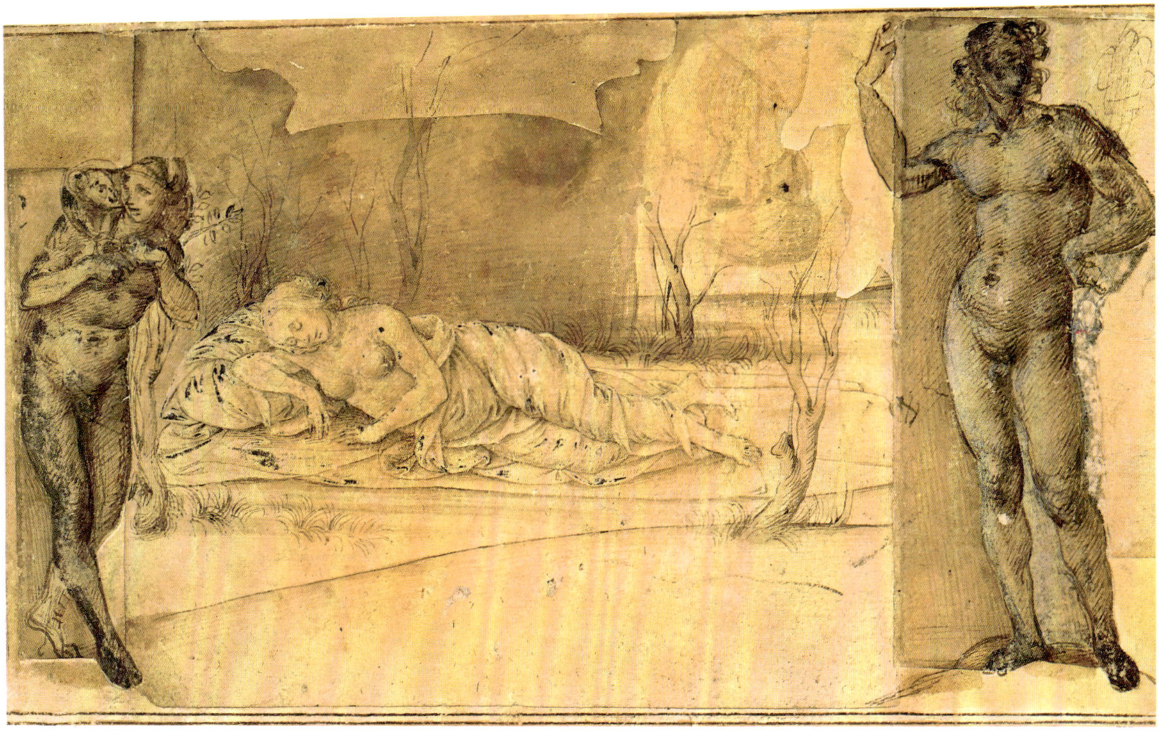

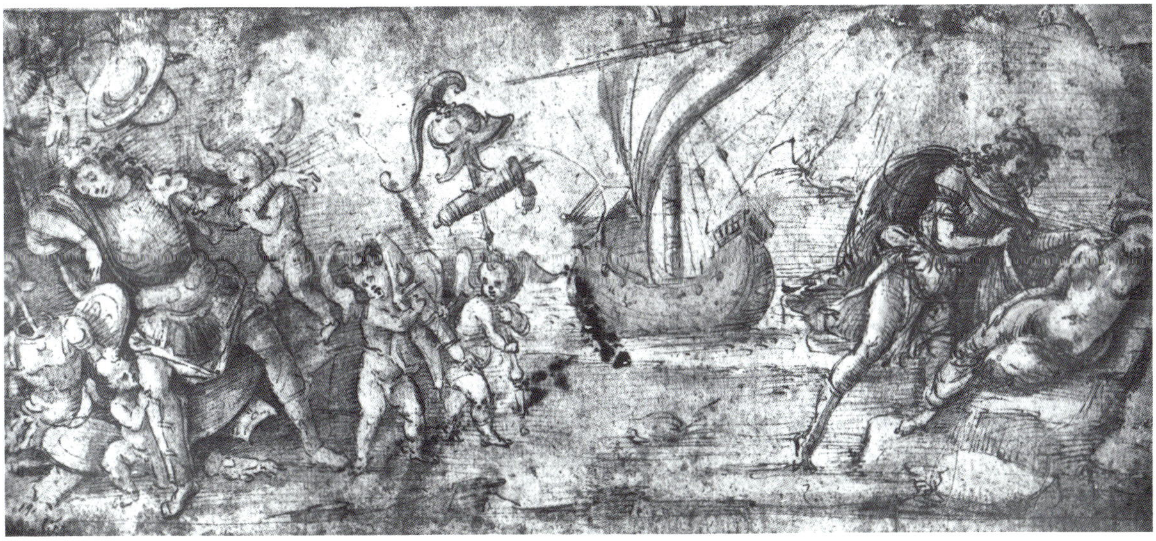

8 *Ariadne Asleep in a Landscape*, pen and ink and wash. British Museum, London.

9 An unidentified mythological subject (possibly 'Mars and Rhea Silvia'), pen, brown ink and wash over chalk. Uffizi, Florence.

anatomy of Venus and the pointing gesture of Cupid being interpreted by some scholars as deliberately vulgar and rustic, and thus as satirical in intent.[18] But although Piero's large-scale figures are sometimes ineptly painted, and their gestures often unconventional, this should not be confused with a fundamental intent of irony on his part. Nor is it clear why he would have taken it on himself to satirize either Botticelli's painting or the myth itself. It is also questionable whether the paintings of Botticelli can necessarily be interpreted as more serious or orthodox than Piero's in their approach to Classical myth. Underlying the interpretation of scholars like Panofsky is not only the assumption that Botticelli's secular works are invariably a matter of high seriousness, but that his attitude to Classical mythology, as well as to Antique forms, can be taken as normative for the period as a whole. Such assumptions are largely a legacy of the nineteenth-century revaluation of Botticelli's work, and there is no reason to suppose that his patrons viewed it in this way, or that contemporary notions of classicism were quite so rigidly defined.[19] Fifteenth-century artists responded to Classical culture in a variety of ways, and there is little evidence to suggest that patrons viewed one as more correct or authentic than another, or that this was an issue of real concern. On the contrary, it seems likely that, until the second decade of the sixteenth century at least, patrons and artists were flexible and pragmatic in their attitude to the Antique, as indicated, not least, by the fact that a number of patrons, including the Vespucci, acquired mythological works by both Piero and Botticelli.[20]

In their depictions of Mars and Venus, neither Piero nor Botticelli seem to have been concerned with the precise or literal recreation of a Classical motif, although both appear to have had ample knowledge of Antique literature and works of art.[21] Both improvise creatively around Classical textual and visual sources, albeit in different ways, and to see one work as more 'classical' than the other, or to construe Piero's as an ironic response to Botticelli's, sets up polarities that may have meant little to people at the time. This reading also obscures the distinctive nature of Piero's approach, and the combination of emotional subtlety and visual richness that characterizes his works. This is not to say that Piero did not develop the theme in ways that best displayed his talent and emphasized his particular gifts. Specialization of this kind was a large and inevitable feature of the market for secular works, and Piero's distinctive skills are clearly apparent in the rich colouristic effects of the figures' accessories and clothing, rendered in striking harmonies of orange, red and grey, in the extensive background, and in the wonderful naturalistic details. Unlike Botticelli, Piero opens up the scene to reveal a landscape of almost encyclopaedic variety and richness, moving from the grove of myrtle and the conventional flowery meadow, or *locus amoenus*, in which the lovers recline – items singled out by Vasari – to a vista of rolling hills and plains, adorned with a wealth of different flora and fauna, rocky outcrops and shimmering sea.[22] In addition to its obvious decorative appeal, the landscape subtly complements the shapes and identity of the figures, as gentle hills and winding paths extend beyond Venus, while Mars reclines before a screen of craggy rocks.

A Nymph and a Faun, or the so-called *Death of Procris*

If the subject-matter of *Mars and Venus* is uncontroversial, Piero's painting of a nymph and faun (illus. 6), probably executed between 1500 and 1510, has proven highly problematic in this respect, and its iconography remains a matter of debate. It has been suggested that the painting depicts the myth of Cephalus and Procris, not as told by Ovid in the *Metamorphoses*, but in a version by the fifteenth-century Ferrarese playwright Niccolò da Correggio.[23] The identification of the work with this particular legend has by no means been universally accepted, however, despite the fact that no more satisfactory interpretation has been advanced.[24]

In the version according to Ovid, Aurora, Goddess of the Dawn, desiring Cephalus and jealous of his fidelity to Procris, leads him to doubt her constancy.[25] In disguise, Cephalus tests Procris's devotion by offering her rich gifts, and succeeds in making her hesitate. When Cephalus reveals his identity Procris flees to join the nymphs of Diana, who, taking Procris under her protection, gives her a javelin, and a hunting-hound named Laelaps. Full of remorse, and desolate without his wife, Cephalus effects a reconciliation with Procris, who hands to him Diana's gifts. One day, while out hunting with the javelin, he stops to rest, calling to the breeze to refresh him. Overhearing his words, and thinking he was calling to a nymph, a passer-by tells Procris that Cephalus is being unfaithful. Her suspicions aroused, Procris spies on Cephalus who, hearing a noise in the bushes, throws the javelin. Mortally wounding Procris in the breast, he thus kills his beloved wife.

There are obvious difficulties in relating Ovid's account to Piero's painting, such as the absence of Cephalus and the javelin, or the location of Procris's wounds, or the presence of the faun and the surrounding landscape, a landscape that does not resemble the woodland setting described by Ovid. Furthermore, while there exists no large-scale representation of the myth prior to Piero's, manuscript illustrations of the story, and later monumental representations of it, almost invariably include Cephalus at the scene of Procris's death, either in the act of throwing the javelin, or reacting in horror to the discovery of his error.[26] The identification of the painting with Correggio's version of the myth appears more convincing, however, although the relationship between the two has yet to be fully explored. As several commentators have observed, the text of the play could account for the presence of the faun (one of the painting's most puzzling features), and the notion that Piero based his work on Correggio's has depended almost exclusively on this detail.[27] Equally important, however, is the fact that the play provides a moral and didactic context for the painting, an issue that has rarely been raised.

Niccolò da Correggio's play was first performed in January 1487 at the court of Ercole d'Este in Ferrara, in honour of the wedding of two young members of the Ferrarese aristocracy, after which it achieved great popularity.[28] In line with the occasion, the playwright altered Ovid's text in a number of significant ways, one of which was to give the story a happy ending. At the end of the play Aurora expresses her remorse for the strife she had caused and Diana restores Procris to life, whereupon the lovers are reconciled. The playwright also introduced other characters, including Procris's nurse (who explains the moral of the tale), and a faun – a substitute for Ovid's nameless passer-by – who, himself in love with Procris, leads her to believe that Cephalus is being unfaithful. Hoping to take Cephalus's place in her affections, the faun tells her he has heard Cephalus calling the name of Aurora, inducing her to seek out and spy upon her husband.

The play could thus explain the presence of Piero's faun, although there is no reference in the text to the creature discovering Procris's body, a role that falls to Cephalus, as in Ovid's account. It seems likely, however, that the real subject of Piero's picture is not the discovery of Procris's death or the actual finding of her body, as has often been assumed, and it is worth noting that the javelin, the actual cause of her death, is omitted. The real subject is that of mourning, and in this respect too the painting appears to follow the play for, unlike Ovid, Correggio includes in his text a protracted scene of the mourning of Procris's lifeless body by nymphs and other woodland creatures after she has been discovered by her grief-stricken husband. Before Diana restores Procris to life, the nymphs lament her fate and prepare to give her a proper burial so that her soul may rest in peace. The assembled Muses sing plaintively over her body, calling on the gods of the woods and mountains and all the things of nature to join in the lament:

> Here lies her lifeless body, its spirit fled
> the soul already gone;
> now she can rest where she will, in quiet tranquillity,
> where tears and lamentations go unheard.
> You, Galatea, light the pyre with that smouldering torch
> and Procris shall be interred,
> then shall the ashes be placed within that urn
> so she may be allowed to cross the Styx.
>
> Weep, mountain glades, rivers and streams,
> Mourn for her, you gods of the woods and hills:
> she who here lies dead, is now in the heavens,
> Nereids, Dryads, and nymphs of the springs
> all weep, and you, sacred semi-gods, of green oak divest your brows!
> Come and lament the death of she who, living,
> enflamed a thousand hearts among you
> with her purity and charm.
> Leave your herds, and shepherds come
> join in the sad and melancholy song
> and make your tears a sacred wine.[29]

Piero's painting captures quite precisely the tenor of this scene of mourning. Procris lies peacefully on the tranquil earth, oblivious to the sorrow of those around her. She is attended by the grieving faun and by the hound Laelaps, the latter a means of identifying the myth and also, perhaps, serving as a symbol of the fidelity of Procris and her absent husband. The background landscape, while remote from the woodland setting of the play, underlines the note of quiet lament, the rolling lines of the river and its banks echoing those of Procris's recumbent form, while the plants framing the composition appear bent in sympathy.

The treatment of the theme is distinctively Piero's, but the extrapolation of this particular moment from the play as the subject for the painting must also relate to the painting's original function. As with *Mars and Venus*, nothing is known of the provenance of the work, or of the patron, but given its subject and the fact that the play was itself written to celebrate a wedding, it is probable that the painting is also connected with a marriage, perhaps intended for the decoration of the marital chamber. More precisely, it seems likely that it belongs with the class of images that functioned as examples of wifely virtue or of the consequences of inappropriate behaviour.[30]

As I have already said, commissioning paintings for a marriage was common practice, whether in the form of panels for chests (*cassoni*) or, increasingly, of panels for *spalliere*. Such works were not purely decorative, for they often had a moral or didactic function. Around the middle of the fifteenth century the imagery employed in such works appears to have undergone a significant change, for reasons not wholly clear, shifting from general images related to love or marriage – often taken from the writings of Boccaccio – to themes that exemplified the kinds of virtue expected of spouses. Themes that illustrated the virtues required in a bride were common, and the period saw a notable increase in representations of virtuous women from Roman history or the Bible.[31] Equally popular were subjects depicting the punishment of women who went astray, a notable example being Botticelli's set of *spalliera* panels illustrating Boccaccio's story of Nastagio degli Onesti (illus. 10 and 11), in which a woman is savaged by hounds for her pride in refusing a suitor, after which she consents to the marriage.[32] Within this context the fate of Procris serves as an example of the consequences of jealousy in a wife, and of the dangers of immoderate love. The image of her prostrate body, mourned by the faun and dog, functions not simply as a reference to the Ovidian myth, or a poetic evocation of Correggio's text, but as a didactic image, an exhortation to proper behaviour that was aimed primarily at the female viewer. Against this background, the absence of Cephalus from the image, and his implicit exoneration from guilt, may also be more easily understood, especially when seen in relation to the play.

The moral implications of the tale as perceived by Correggio are clearly spelt out in the text, and may themselves be symptomatic of a hardening of attitudes towards the role of women in marriage, and the virtues expected of them. Throughout the Middle Ages Ovid's tale was moralized as a lesson in conjugal fidelity and served as a warning against jealousy in spouses. While attitudes to Cephalus and Procris varied, both were generally seen as culpable, although for different reasons and in differing degrees.[33] For Correggio, similarly, the myth served as a warning against jealousy between husband and wife, as Diana remarks at the end of the play. In this case, though, it is

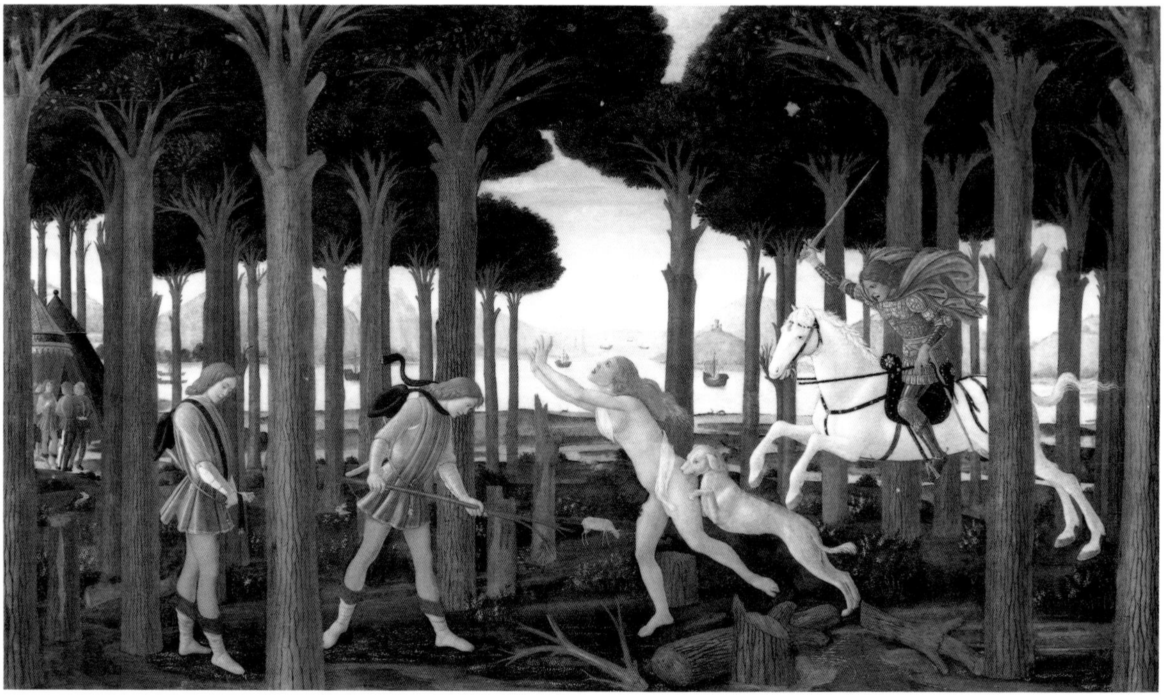

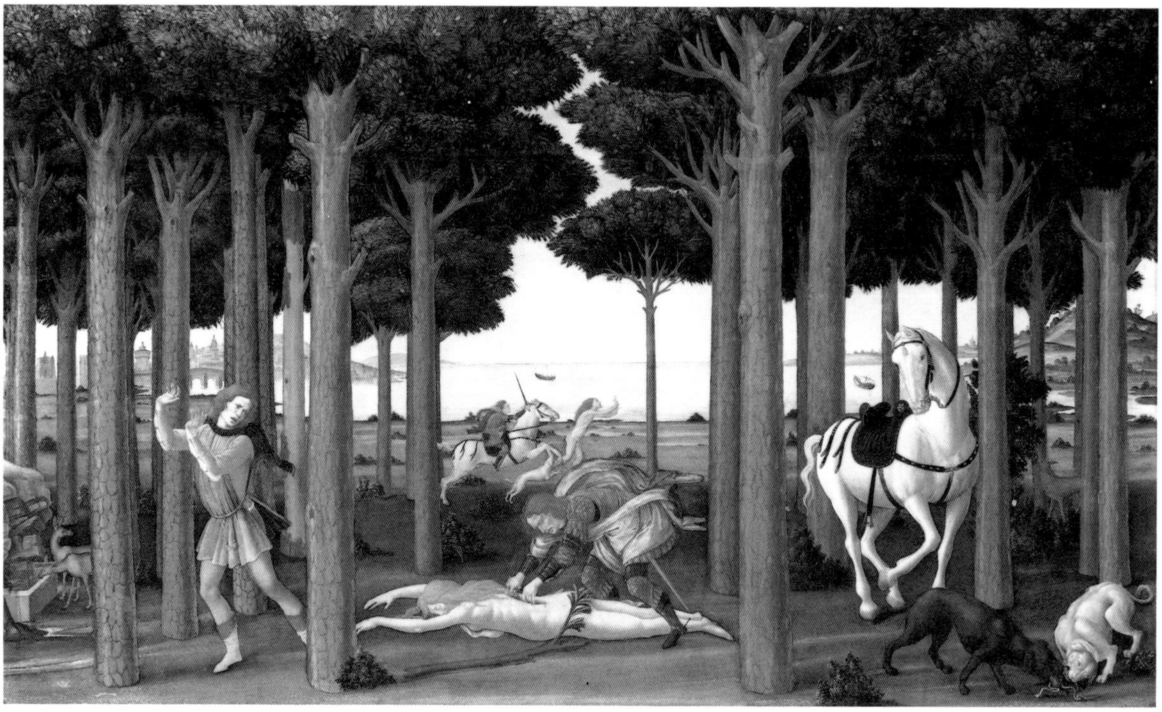

10 Botticelli, *Episodes from the Story of Nastagio degli Onesti* (first panel), *c.*1482–3, tempera on panel. Prado Museum, Madrid.

11 Botticelli, *Episodes from the Story of Nastagio degli Onesti* (second panel), *c.*1482–3, tempera on panel. Prado Museum, Madrid.

Procris who is made to carry the burden of guilt, and who takes responsibility for her own death, which is caused by her jealousy, her unreasonable suspicion of Cephalus's fidelity and her feminine fury. As she dies she thus absolves him of any blame, and begs him not to kill himself as he has sworn to do, but only to remain faithful to her memory:

> Woman's passion caused this death my Cephalus, not you!
> And my too ardent love,
> And so alone I mean to cross this stream.
> If our marriage vows you wish to honour
> I beg you not to forget me for another:
> If you promise me not to take Aurora
> Then you remove this spear from my heart.[34]

Conversely, while at the beginning of the play it is Cephalus who doubts Procris, and who presumes to test her fidelity, he is exonerated from blame on the grounds that he was the victim of a jealous goddess, and of his unwitting insult to Aurora, and not responsible for his actions. The message is further underlined by the interjections of Procris's nurse, who not only vouches for Cephalus's faithfulness, but suggests that it is foolish of wives to expect marital fidelity and that, if necessary, they should turn a blind eye to a husband's indiscretions. Wifely love should be temperate and controlled, and wives should not be led to question a husband's behaviour through jealousy or unseemly or inappropriate passion.

Piero's painting responds quite precisely to the moral tone and lesson of the play, and may well have performed a similar function. Cephalus and the javelin are conspicuous by their absence, while Procris, the instrument of her own death, lies exposed before the viewer, a reminder of the consequences of rash and unseemly action. It may also serve as a warning against calumny, as the faun regards the outcome of his deceit, and of Procris's readiness to believe his false report. At the same time, his penitent gesture, and the plaintive presence of the hound, mitigate the harshness of the theme, as does the tender scene of mourning in the play, and the restoration of Procris to life. For while she is guilty of immoderate behaviour, Procris is also held up as a figure of virtue, whose goodness and purity won the hearts of all who encountered her and for whom death was considered, finally, to be too severe a fate.

Looked at in this way the painting appears less problematic, and it is not difficult to imagine an educated patron suggesting as a theme the mourning of Procris, a prominent feature of Correggio's play, and a performance of which the patron may conceivably have seen. At the same time, if the theme of the painting was chosen by the patron, the particular treatment or formulation of it and the framing of Procris between the dog and the faun were certainly the choice of the artist, and reflect Piero's own interests and skills. As can be seen in various works, the lifelike rendering of creatures such as fauns and centaurs was one of Piero's distinctive gifts. He was also particularly adept at investing them with quasi-human emotions, an aspect of his talent that lends the *Death of Procris* a particular piquancy, since the behaviour of fauns towards nymphs, as represented in both literature and art, was usually characterized by lust rather than by remorse or tender concern.[35] In addition, Piero reveals his affinity with the subtler and more lyrical emotions inherent in this section of the play and his tendency to avoid rhetorical gestures, an aspect of his work that gives the painting both its expressive power and its continued ability to disconcert.

It seems likely, in fact, that the perception of the painting as enigmatic or obscure springs as much from Piero's approach to expressive gesture as from his use of narrative or iconographic detail. In his depiction of the faun he rejected the conventional, more explicit, gestures of grief familiar from the paintings of his contemporaries in favour of a gesture of affectionate sadness, as the creature pulls back Procris's hair from her face, while touching her lightly on the shoulder. The directness and intimacy of the action, at once reticent and deeply emotive, appear in some ways peculiarly modern, while making the didactic significance of the image less than usually overt. Yet this approach to gesture, and a freedom from rhetorical and dramatic convention, are typical of Piero's work, factors that may reflect his lack of experience in large-scale narrative painting. The anecdotal quality of the landscape, which adds to the painting's enigmatic air, is also a recurrent characteristic of his work, and while these features are unusual, they should not lead us to assume that his paintings were equally unconventional in other ways, or to overlook their relationship to the texts on which they are based, or to their didactic and institutional functions.

The Battle of the Lapiths and Centaurs

A similar responsiveness to the tragic possibilities of the text is apparent in Piero's panel of the *Battle of the Lapiths and Centaurs* (illus. 12), painted around 1505–7, although here the results are rather more complex. It is also this eye for pathos, and the subtle humanizing of animal forms that distinguish the painting from contemporary works on similar themes, and from Michelangelo's marble relief of the same subject, executed in 1491–2 (illus. 14).

The story that forms the subject of Piero's panel is recounted in Book XII of the *Metamorphoses*.[36] Ovid relates how the centaurs, invited by the Lapith Pirithous to his wedding feast, become inflamed by wine and lust and violently disrupt the proceedings, led by Eurytus, who abducts Pirithous's bride, Hippodame, dragging her away by the hair. The other centaurs follow suit, seizing whatever maidens they can from among the guests. The description of the ensuing fight constitutes one of the most detailed and vivid in Ovid's text, and Piero followed it closely, reproducing almost exactly its most colourful incidents, and focusing on those that allowed him to depict groups of figures in complex movement. The following parts of Ovid's account are reproduced almost exactly in the painting:

> First Amycus . . . scrupled not to rob the inner sanctuary of its gifts, and first snatched from the shrine a chandelier thick hung with glittering lamps. This, lifted on high . . . he dashed full at the head of Celadon, one of the Lapithae . . . But Pelates of Pella, wrenching off the leg of a table of

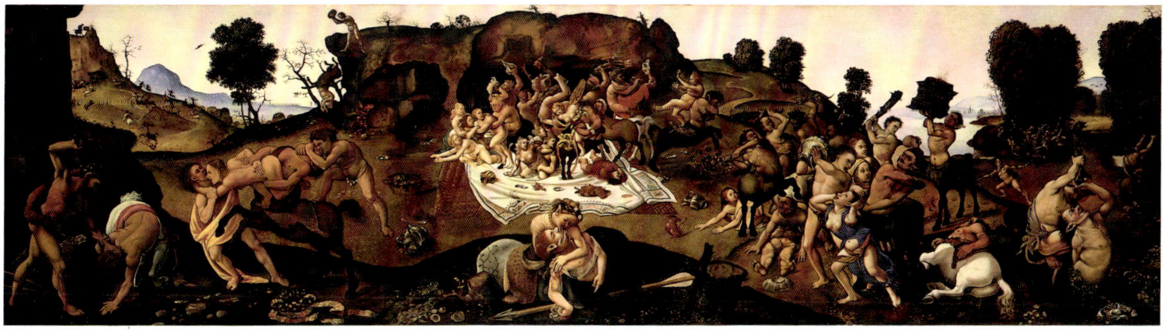

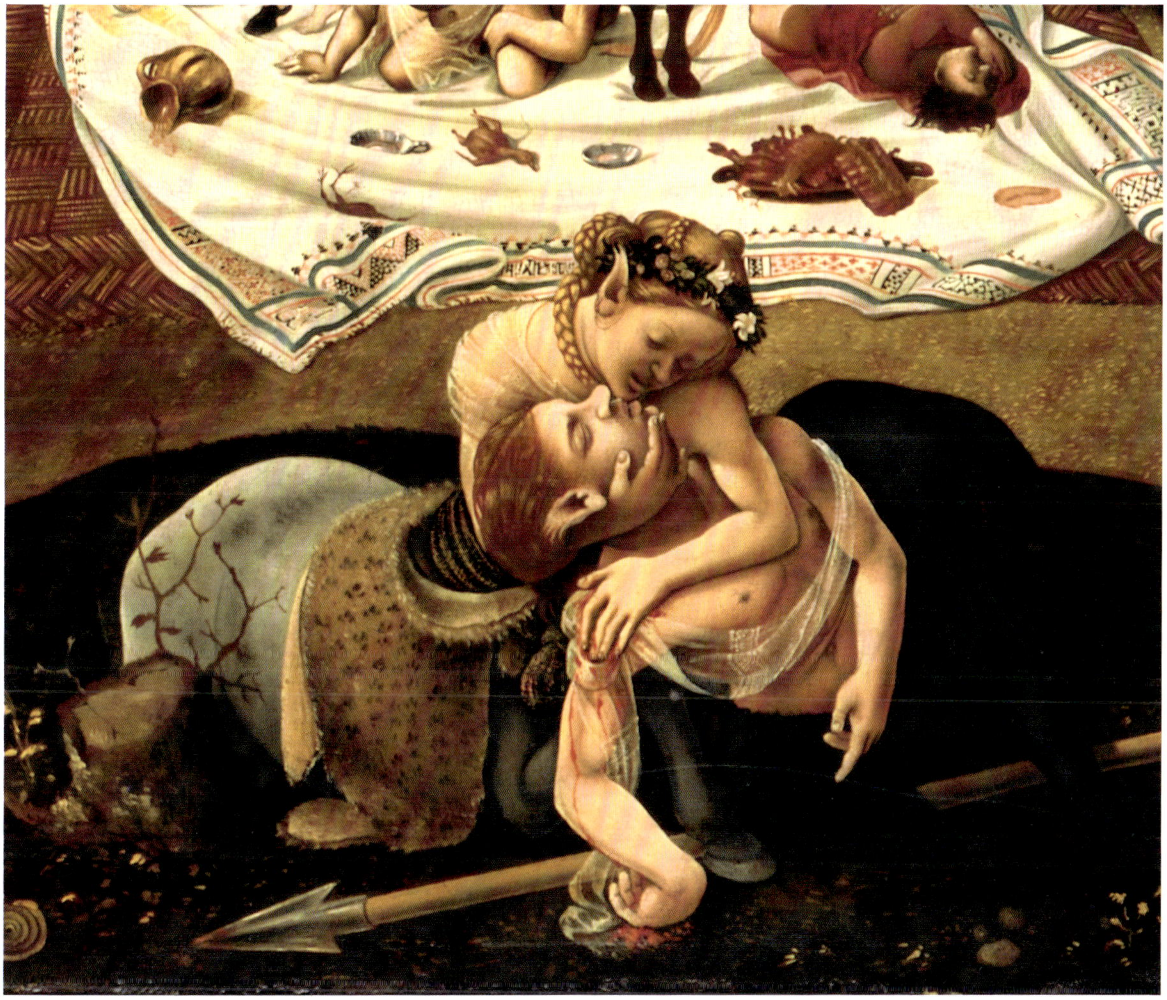

12 *The Battle of the Lapiths and Centaurs*, *c.*1505–7, oil on panel. National Gallery, London.

13 Cyllarus and Hylonome, a detail from *The Battle of the Lapiths and the Centaurs*.

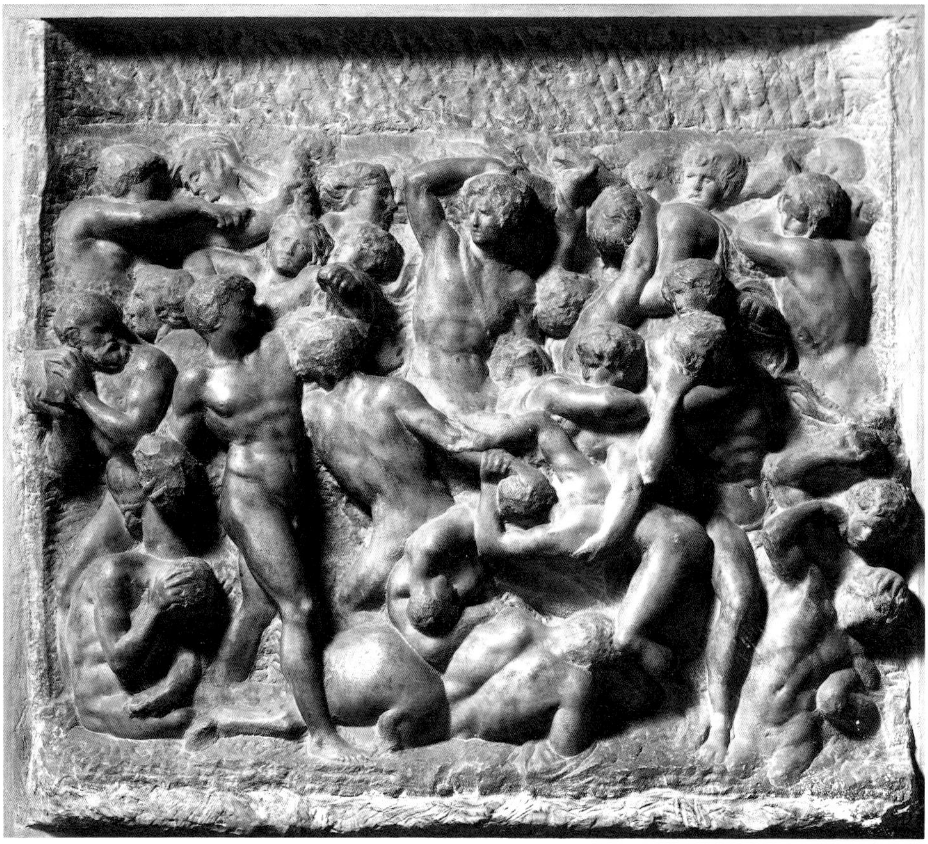

14 Michelangelo, *Battle of the Centaurs*, 1491–2, marble relief. Casa Buonarroti, Florence.

maplewood, hurled Amycus to the ground, his chin driven into his breast . . . Then Gryneus, gazing with wild eyes upon the smoking altar near which he stood, cried out 'Why not use this?' and catching up the huge altar, fire and all, he hurled it amidst a throng of Lapithae . . . Exadius . . . found for weapon the antlers of a stag hung on a tall pine-tree as a votive offering . . . Then Rhoetus caught up a blazing brand of plum-wood from the altar and, whirling it on the right, smashed through Charaxus' temples covered with yellow hair. The hair, caught by the greedy flames, burned fiercely, like a dry field of grain . . . I saw Petraeus striving to tear from the earth an acorn-laden oak. While he held this in both his arms, bending it this way and that, and just as he was wrenching forth the loosened trunk, Pirithous hurled a spear right through his ribs and pinned his writhing body to the hard oak . . . Dictys, while fleeing in desperate haste from Ixion's son who pressed him hard, stumbled on the edge of a steep precipice and, falling headlong, crashed into a huge ash-tree's top with all his weight and impaled his body on the broken spikes . . . Aphareus, at hand to avenge him, heaved to throw a rock torn from the mountain-side; but, even as he heaved, the son of Aegeus caught him with an oaken club and broke the great bones of his elbow-joint. Having no time nor care to inflict further injury on his maimed body, he sprang on tall Bienor's back, who never before had carried any but himself; and, pressing his knees into the centaur's sides and with his left hand clutching his flowing locks, he crushed face and mouth . . . and hard temples with his knotty club.[37]

The struggles between the Lapiths and centaurs thus take up most of the space in the painting. At the same time – and this is the most striking aspect of the work – Piero places equal emphasis on the death of the centaur Cyllarus in the arms of his lover Hylonome, depicted in the centre foreground (illus. 13). Indeed, the focus of the painting might appear to be not the battle itself, or the abduction of Hippodame (shown on the right), but the last embraces of this beautiful centaur pair. Here again, Piero follows Ovid's text almost to the letter:

> [Cyllarus's] beard was just in its first growth, a golden beard, and golden locks fell down upon his shoulders. He had a pleasing sprightliness of face; and his neck, shoulders, breast and hands, and all his human parts you would praise as equal to an artist's perfect work. His equine part, too, was without blemish, no way less perfect than his human part . . . Many females of his own kind sought him, but Hylonome alone had won him, than whom there was no other centaur-maid more comely in all the forest depths. She, by her coaxing ways, by loving and confessing love, alone possessed Cyllarus; and by her toilet, too, so far as such a thing was possible to such a form; for now she smoothed her long locks with a comb, now twined rosemary, now violets or roses in her hair, and sometimes she wore white lilies . . . Nor would she wear on shoulder or left side aught but becoming garments, skins of well-chosen beasts. They both felt equal love . . . Thrown from an unknown hand, a javelin came from the left and pierced you, Cyrallus, below where the chest rises to the neck. The heart . . . grew cold and the whole body also after the weapon had been drawn out. Straightway Hylonome embraced the dying body, fondled the wound with her hand and, placing her lips upon his lips, strove to hold from its passing the dying breath . . . [38]

As in the *Death of Procris*, Piero responds quite precisely to the pathos inherent in the text, depicting the event in the same quiet, intimate manner, accentuating its poignancy, and also the human quality of Hylonome's devotion, arranging the figures in a manner recalling conventional representations of the *Pietà*. The grieving Hylonome cradles the head of her dying lover like the Virgin mourning the dead Christ, an allusion underlined by the use of the familiar religious symbols of the barren and flowering tree stumps (respectively, death and life), which neatly frame the figures. The intimacy of their embrace is further enhanced by their oblivion to the chaos surrounding them as they form the one still point in the mass of fighting forms, and around which these struggles appear to revolve. Thus, while Michelangelo focuses almost exclusively on the struggling male figures (illus. 14), Piero juxtaposes the fight against an intimate scene of leave-taking that strikes a very different note. This duality of focus, and the mixture of pathos and aggression, distinguish the painting clearly from the relief, for in his mass of fighting figures Michelangelo sought a formal and thematic unity that Piero manifestly did not.

The juxtaposition of these two motifs also makes the painting disconcerting, establishing a conflict between parts of the image that is unusual in contemporary narrative works, and which goes against the recommendations for narrative unity put forward in the fifteenth century by writers like Alberti and Leonardo. One of Alberti's main concerns in *De Pictura* was with the narrative coherence of the *istoria*, which, first and foremost, entailed a unity of emotional effect: 'all bodies must move in harmony with each other in accordance with the subject of the action', and, Alberti added, 'if you painted centaurs in an uproar at dinner, it would be absurd among this violent commotion for one of them to be lying there asleep from the effects of wine', a remark that has interesting implications for the construction of Piero's work.[39]

The example chosen by Alberti to illustrate the ideal *istoria* was Giotto's *Navicella* mosaic, of which little of the original survives; in his account of this work he suggests that, while the disciples are shown in different poses, the poses all express variations on the same emotion of fear, evoked by the single action of Peter walking on the water.[40] Narrative unity thus depends on the figures in the painting expressing aspects of the same emotion in response to one main action or event, and the emotional response of the viewer will be controlled accordingly. The implication is that additional incidents that might evoke a different response, even if appropriate to the action, should be placed in the background or to the side, a strategy observed by most of Piero's contemporaries, where the nature of the commission allowed. A similar point was made by Leonardo in his own recommendations for the composition of narrative painting, in which he advised the use of one central, dominant action surrounded by subsidiary, less prominent, *effetti*. Here too, and in his own designs for works such as the *Battle of Anghiari* and the *Adoration of the Magi*, not only is there a main incident around which the others revolve, but the subsidiary incidents Leonardo envisaged are variations on the same theme, and are designed to evoke the same emotions.[41]

In Piero's panel, however, motifs commanding different and conflicting responses are closely juxtaposed, and in compositional terms given almost equal weight. While the death of Cyllarus occupies the centre foreground, thus commanding our immediate attention, it is directly superimposed by a mass of figures in combat amid the remnants of the banquet, while other groups of fighting Lapiths and centaurs take up most of the overall space. The emotional implications of these violent scenes are also evoked with great vividness, so that although all the incidents depicted can be seen as appropriate to the subject, they are placed and depicted in such a way as to form competing foci of attention, rather than being mutually reinforcing in the way that Alberti recommended.

The motivation for Piero's treatment of the theme must remain a subject for speculation. By the time he executed the *Battle of the Lapiths and Centaurs*, scenes of combat had become relatively common as subjects for interior decoration, and also occurred frequently in prints.[42] Most artists exploited the opportunity offered by such themes to depict their mastery of the active male nude, and the potential for such displays of talent must in turn have contributed to the popularity of these subjects among patrons. Piero was certainly aware of this trend, and it is inevitable that he too would have exploited this aspect of his text. His work includes several quotations from, and references to, well-known battle-pieces, including Leonardo's *Battle of Anghiari*, while the densely knit cluster of struggling figures in the centre may reflect the influence of Michelangelo's *Battle of Cascina* cartoon.[43] At the same time, the motif of the death of Cyrallus as described by Ovid would have exerted a strong personal fascination for Piero, and presented an opportunity for the display of his own skills that would hardly have allowed him to make it an incidental motif only. It also seems likely that in terms of composition, as in his use of gesture, Piero was less bound by convention than those of his contemporaries who worked on large-scale didactic narratives, and in some ways his approach to the organization of the theme seems to owe more to the episodic nature of Ovid's text than to Albertian ideas of pictorial organization and dramatic unity. And if the juxtaposition of different motifs creates a sense of unease in the viewer, and fragments our attention in both spatial and dramatic terms, it also gives the painting a complexity and depth of interest that are signally lacking in Michelangelo's relief.

Piero's approach to the subject may also have been dictated by the function of the painting, of which nothing specific is known, and it is possible that the work was meant to be read in an allegorical way. In Classical and Renaissance literature and art, centaurs were often taken or used to represent the bestial part of man's nature, as opposed to the rational or intellectual side, a concept that may form the underlying theme of Botticelli's so-called *Pallas and the Centaur* of *c.*1482–3. While the exact significance of this painting is still disputed, its central motif is the taming and subduing of a centaur by a virtuous female figure, who is possibly the wise and rational Pallas.[44] The battle of the Lapiths and centaurs, and the final victory of the Lapith tribe, could function, in a similar way, as an allegory of the victory of reason over animal instinct, or of civilization over barbarism. Certainly, it has been suggested that Michelangelo may have construed the theme in this way, perhaps under the influence of the poet and humanist Angelo Poliziano who, according to Michelangelo's biographer Condivi, suggested it as a subject for the marble relief.[45]

In Piero's painting, however, it is notable that little distinction is made between the brutality of the two tribes and that two centaurs, Cyllarus and Hylonome, are shown expressing intensely human, almost spiritual, emotions. The emphasis appears to be less on the contrast between the Lapiths and the centaurs, or between reason and bestiality, than on that between lust and conjugal love, both represented chiefly by the centaurs. Piero pointedly contrasts the tenderness and mutual devotion of Cyllarus and Hylonome (Hylonome, in Ovid's account, commits suicide after Cyllarus's death), with the lustful abduction of the Lapith women that was the reason for the battle. Like *Mars and Venus*, this painting can thus be construed as an allegory of the civilizing or pacifying effect of love, and in this respect the image of the grieving Hylonome has analogies with that of the faun mourning Procris, whose natural lustfulness is subdued by her virtue, and by his own devotion. It is not inconceivable, therefore, that the panel had nuptial associations, and although it may seem unduly violent for such a context, scenes of rape and abduction had long featured on the fronts of *cassoni* commissioned in connection with weddings, and they also appeared frequently in *spalliere*.[46]

While the *Battle of the Lapiths and Centaurs* works well as an independent piece, it has been suggested that it originally formed part of a larger cycle, together with two smaller panels, much damaged, showing battling Tritons and Nereids (illus. 15). Mina Bacci has suggested that these two panels were intended as companions to the

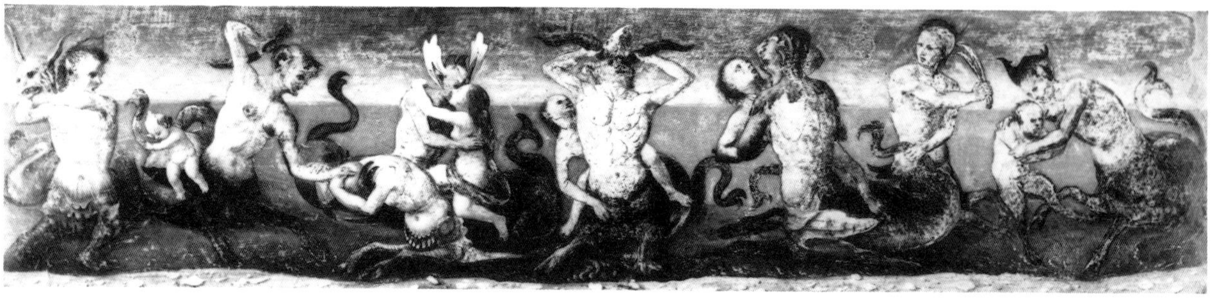

15 *Tritons and Nereids*, *c.*1505–10, oil on panel. S. J. Freedberg Collection, Washington DC.

Battle of the Lapiths and Centaurs, not as part of the narrative, but as subsidiary decorative elements, possibly part of a frieze.[47] Bacci also postulated the existence of a second large panel as a pendant to the *Battle* showing the stories of Theseus, companion to the Lapith king Pirithous, who played a prominent part in the struggle with the centaurs, and who appears in Piero's painting.[48] The two smaller panels would thus form decorative adjuncts to the two narrative images depicting the exploits of the companions according to Ovid's *Metamorphoses*, while their marine setting, and the presence of nereids and tritons, can be explained by the fact that Theseus was the son of Aegeus, the Athenian king of the sea. Such an explanation must remain entirely speculative, however, for there exists no evidence of, or reference to, a lost panel of Theseus by Piero. Furthermore, as Bacci admitted, the smaller panels appear to 'fit' iconographically only very loosely with the *Battle of the Lapiths and Centaurs*, and do not clarify its function or significance in any way. It is also worth noting that these small panels are quite unusual in including satyrs among the tritons and nereids, since satyrs were generally confined to the land.[49] The suggested grouping of these panels with the Ovidian narrative does not serve to clarify or explain this rare combination, and it seems equally likely that the panels were intended as independent works with a purely decorative function, designed to display Piero's inventiveness in the depiction of mythical creatures of all varieties and his skill in rendering shells and other natural forms.[50]

The Liberation of Andromeda

Piero's *Liberation of Andromeda* (illus. 43) is the only single panel in his *oeuvre* for which a reasonably secure provenance can be put forward. The last of Piero's secular works, this painting was probably executed *c.*1515, almost certainly for Filippo Strozzi the younger, for whom Piero also carried out other works, including a commission of an unidentified subject for his *anticamera*. Strozzi had been a supporter of the Medici before their exile, and in 1508 he had married Clarice, daughter of Piero de' Medici. The return of the Medici in 1512 thus relieved the family from the threat and suspicions of the republican regime, and the painting has consequently been construed as an allegory of their reinstatement, the liberation of Andromeda alluding to the freeing of both families from oppression.[51] In support of this, the sprouting tree-stump in the centre foreground has been interpreted as an allusion to the Medici device of the *broncone*, or laurel branch, which featured prominently as a symbol of renewal in the festivals organized to celebrate their return.[52] There is little specific evidence to back up this suggestion, however, and the motif of the flowering tree-stump appears in several of Piero's other works, where it has a conventional role as a symbol of regeneration or renewed life, as in the *Adoration of the Child* in Toledo (illus. 72), while the twin dead and flowering tree-stumps that frame Cyrallus and Hylonome in the *Battle of the Lapiths and Centaurs* refer, as I mentioned earlier, to death and life respectively. Similarly, in the *Liberation of Andromeda*, the dead trunk to the left may allude to the threat to Andromeda's life, and the flowering branch on the right to her rescue and union with Perseus.

This does not mean that paintings for domestic interiors were not sometimes intended to have a moral or allegorical significance. As I have suggested, many of the subjects favoured for such commissions were clearly meant to be understood in this way, and some may have been designed to carry a political significance. For the most part, however, these were only political in the broadest sense of the word, using biblical stories, or scenes from Classical myth or history to illustrate ideas of civic virtue, or provide examples, in a general way, of the virtues expected of good citizens or just rulers.[53] It is less clear that mythological subjects were used to allude to specific political events, especially in works designed for private consumption. While they may have been used in this way in festivals or pageants designed by ruling families for a clear political purpose, or to commemorate specific events, such interpretations have not been applied convincingly to small-scale decorative works, and it remains doubtful whether the majority of patrons would have wished them to function in this way.[54] Given the subject-matter of the *Liberation of Andromeda*, it seems more likely it was commissioned to celebrate a marriage, or that the subject was chosen simply because it was well-suited to Piero's talents.

The myth is taken from Book IV of the *Metamorphoses*, in which Ovid tells how the Ethiopian princess Andromeda is rescued by Perseus from the sea-monster to whom she had been offered as a sacrifice.[55] Having fallen in love with her, Perseus flies down and kills the monster, claiming Andromeda's hand in marriage as a reward. Piero adheres quite closely to Ovid's narrative, and follows it in some details, most notably in the right background, where Perseus sacrifices a cow, a bullock and a bull to Minerva, Mercury and Jupiter as offerings for his success. At the same time, Piero displays his characteristic eye for unusual detail, and a profound originality in the rendering of emotion, exploiting to the full the dramatic and decorative potential of the theme. The sea-monster that occupies the centre of the panel is a masterpiece of imaginative invention, as are the exotic costumes of Andromeda's family and friends, both of which Vasari singles out for praise. The dominance of the sea-monster is not simply a conceit, however, for it is around the monster and its death at the hands of Perseus that the plot revolves, bringing about the dramatic reversal of fortune indicated by the contrasting groups of figures on either side. In this respect, the organization of the panel is more conventional than those of Piero's other works, and he achieves here a narrative cogency and unity of effect less apparent in the *Battle of the Lapiths and Centaurs*, for the phases of the story are placed on either side of the panel, clearly separated by the scene of the monster's death. On the left, in front of the bound Andromeda, her family grieves in a tightly-knit group, while on the right she and Perseus celebrate their union to the accompaniment of musicians. The contrast between sorrow and jubilation is strongly marked in the opposing patterns of movements and gestures, while the theme of each side of the panel is reinforced by smaller incidents in the background – the lovers on the left hiding their eyes from the spectacle of Andromeda's distress, and the sacrificial offerings on the right.

While, compositionally, Piero's treatment of the *istoria* may thus be more in line with conventional theory and practice, he displays his customary originality in the treatment of gesture. On the left, the grieving figures lean over in identical movements of sorrow and despair, forming almost a single body and a single demonstration, and echo one another's movements almost exactly (illus. 44). Rather than displaying different responses to the event, or differing expressions of grief, as recommended, for example, by Alberti, they offer and amplify a single emotional response, and their bending movements are echoed in Andromeda's own, and in the curved forms of the landscape. Similarly, the rejoicing people on the right raise their arms in a pattern of repeated gestures that is reinforced by the gesticulating worshippers in the background. The contrasting patterns of languid curves and vigorous vertical lines express the different emotions, and the dramatic shift in the story, in an almost abstract or diagrammatic way, one remote from both the recommendations of writers on art and the approach to dramatic expression employed by most of Piero's contemporaries.

The Early Man panels

In addition to these single panels, Piero executed a number of pairs or series of works, also for the decoration of *spalliere*, that deal with more unusual subjects, the interpretation of which has proven especially problematic. Particularly important among them are the two panels showing scenes from a primitive hunt (illus. 22 and 23), a third depicting a forest fire (illus. 19), and two canvases with scenes from the life of Vulcan (illus. 20 and 21).[56] As with the single panels, the problem has been less the identification of the actual subject-matter of the works, which are mostly based on identifiable texts, than the question of their precise significance for artist and patron. The fact that the texts on which they draw were unusual as subjects for artistic representation has raised the question of whether the paintings carried a particular moral or allegorical significance for the patron. Since they are all concerned in some measure with the life of early or primitive man, scholars have also speculated extensively about the attitude towards his subject-matter of an artist Vasari described as 'brutish' and 'uncivilized', and it is in the discussion of these works that the influence of Vasari's account has been particularly pervasive and misleading.

The most influential interpretation of these works has been that of Erwin Panofsky, whose views have yet to be seriously challenged.[57] Drawing partly on a passage from Vasari's Life of Piero, Panofsky suggested that the five paintings were intended to form part of a single cycle, commissioned by the wool-merchant Francesco del Pugliese for his town-house. According to Vasari:

> In the house of Francesco del Pugliese [Piero] executed various stories with small figures which are set around a room; nor can one possibly describe the diversity of fantastic things which he was pleased to paint in them, of buildings, animals, garments and various instruments, and other *fantasie* which the myths suggested to his mind. These stories were removed after the death of Francesco and his sons, and I do not know what has become of them. And he also did a painting of Mars and Venus with her Cupids, and Vulcan, executed with great skill and incredible patience.[58]

On the basis of this passage, Panofsky suggested that the two *Hunt* panels and *The Forest Fire* would have constituted the first part of the series, perhaps hung in an anteroom. The two *Vulcan* canvases, together with the *Mars, Venus and Vulcan* mentioned by Vasari, of which no trace survives, would have formed the second, possibly located in a subsequent chamber. Taken together, the works would have formed one comprehensive cycle that, according to Panofsky, would have represented the two earliest phases of human history, as described in Classical writing – the first three depicting the phase before man learned to harness fire, and the second group that when he had been taught its uses by Vulcan.

It is important to note, however, that none of the paintings under discussion can be securely identified with those described by Vasari, and his account of the works made for Francesco del Pugliese does not relate to any of them particularly well. Vasari's description is in fact quite generic, and he appears to be enumerating those objects usually found in or thought appropriate for *spalliera* panels, rather than describing works that he had actually seen or knew well. Furthermore, the subject-matter of the *Hunt* panels and *The Forest Fire* is sufficiently unusual that, had Vasari seen them, it seems likely that he would have remarked on them in a more precise way. Nor does he suggest that the *Mars, Venus and Vulcan* was related to the other works he mentions, even if it can be inferred from his account that it was also painted for Francesco del Pugliese. More important, from an iconographic point of view, Panofsky's grouping together of the works creates more problems than it solves, while also ignoring differences in scale, medium and conception between the five works. As Panofsky pointed out, the two panels in the Metropolitan Museum showing *The Hunt* and the *Return from the Hunt* are based on Book v of Lucretius's *De Rerum Natura*, in which Lucretius describes the emergence of different species at the beginning of the world, and the evolution of man towards civilization. While Lucretius's account of man's progress is not wholly systematic, and the stages by which it occurred are not always clearly distinguished, Piero's paintings can be seen as corresponding in a general way to the first two stages of evolution as described in Lucretius's text.

Lucretius relates how, at the beginning of the world, nature was more fertile and fecund than she has been ever since. Earth first produced grass and 'bright verdure', flowering meadows and trees, and then brought forth animals and man, generated directly from the earth. Such was the fertility of nature at this stage that she produced not only animals and man but also monsters, such as hermaphrodites, which, incapable of reproduction, eventually died out. This left those creatures that were properly equipped for survival, which, in addition to man, included the lion, the wolf, the dog, woolly sheep and horned oxen, most of which appear in *The Hunt*.[59]

According to Lucretius, during the first stage of existence men were indistinguishable in their way of life from beasts. Although they were stronger physically than at later stages of civilization, they did not know how to plough or plant or to prune trees, but lived off acorns and other things the earth provided. They did not know how to use fire, or how to clothe themselves in animal skins, and gave no thought to the common good; each man bore off his own booty, and lived for himself alone. At this stage men also began to chase beasts, and so, according to Lucretius,

> trusting in the wonderful strength of their hands and feet, men chased the woodland beasts with stones and heavy clubs, capturing many, but losing some in their hiding places . . . more than often in those days one of them would be caught and furnish living food to the beasts, mangled by their teeth, and would fill the groves and mountains and forests with his groaning as he saw his living flesh buried in a living tomb.[60]

Yet although human life at this stage was brutish, men did not die in great numbers in battle, but mainly from starvation; nor was the 'wicked art' of navigation invented, which later crushed ships and men among the rocks. In Lucretius's second phase of evolution, there emerged the beginnings of human society. Men equipped themselves with huts, tents of hide, and fire, and men and women began to associate in couples rather than mating indiscriminately. They also began to unite in friendly agreement, and to speak, and although universal concord could not be reached, 'a good and great part kept their covenants inviolate'. The same period saw the beginning of the arts of cooking, weaving and agriculture, and the domestication of animals.[61]

Neither of Piero's paintings corresponds exactly with Lucretius's account. In *The Hunt*, for example, men are already distinguished from beasts, which, unlike them, are seen to attack one another, while man is shown acting and hunting co-operatively, rather than for himself alone. Piero also includes among the men both satyrs and centaurs, whose existence Lucretius denied, and the men are already clothed in rudimentary garments of skins. Yet the motif of the hunt itself corresponds well to Lucretius's account. Men pursue animals using their natural swiftness and the strength of their bare hands, aided by the creatures' flight from the fire raging in the forest. They are armed with primitive clubs made, not of iron, but of branches torn from trees, a point that is emphasized by the broken branch pressed up against the picture plane, and by the discarded club lying alongside the foreshortened corpse. The danger of life at this stage is illustrated by the figure lying dead from wounds in his shoulders and neck, whose face, bared in a grimace, recalls Lucretius's description of the dying men whose groans fill the forest. The rich variety of animals included by

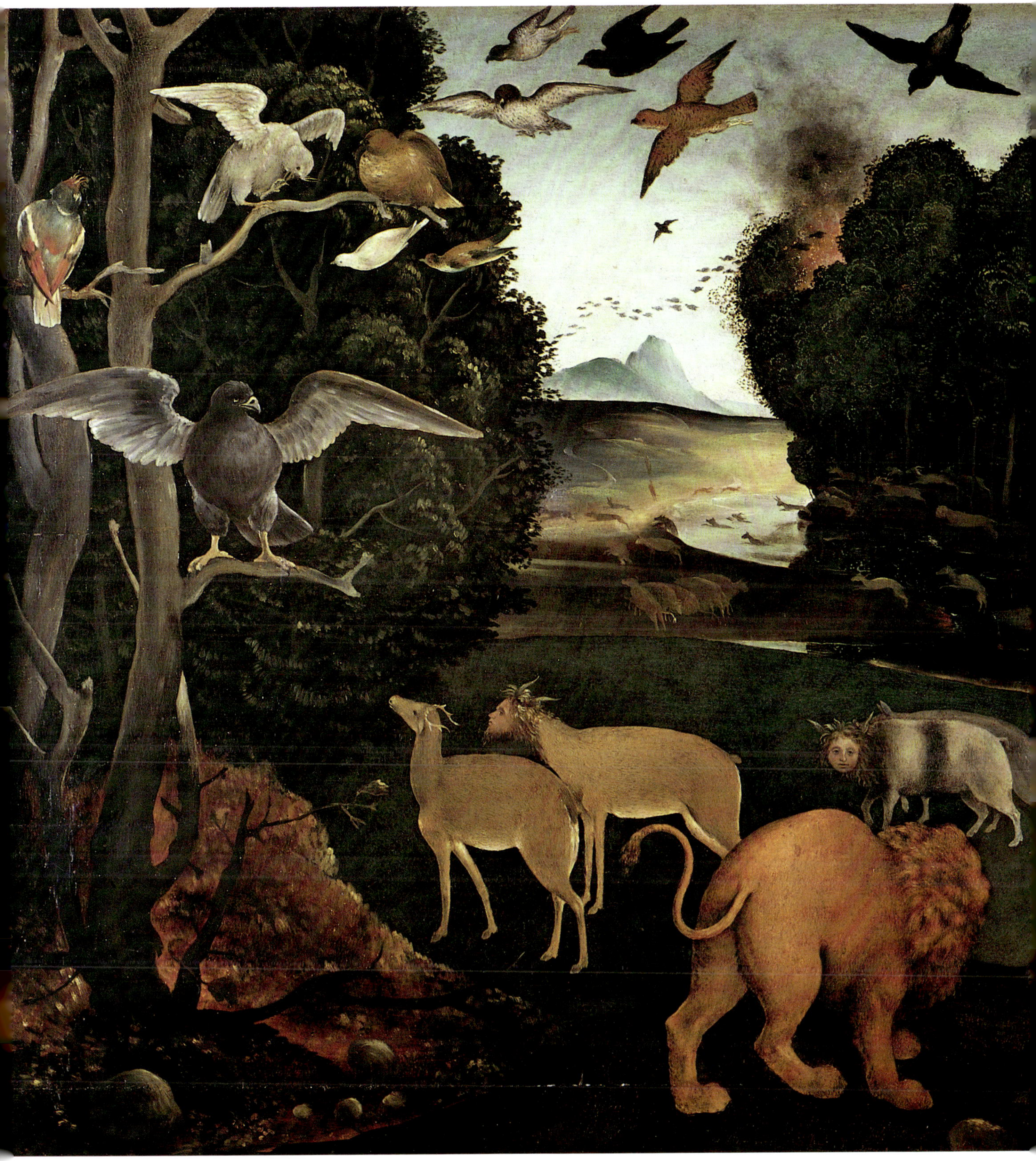

16 Left-hand detail from *The Forest Fire*, illus. 19, *c.*1500–5.

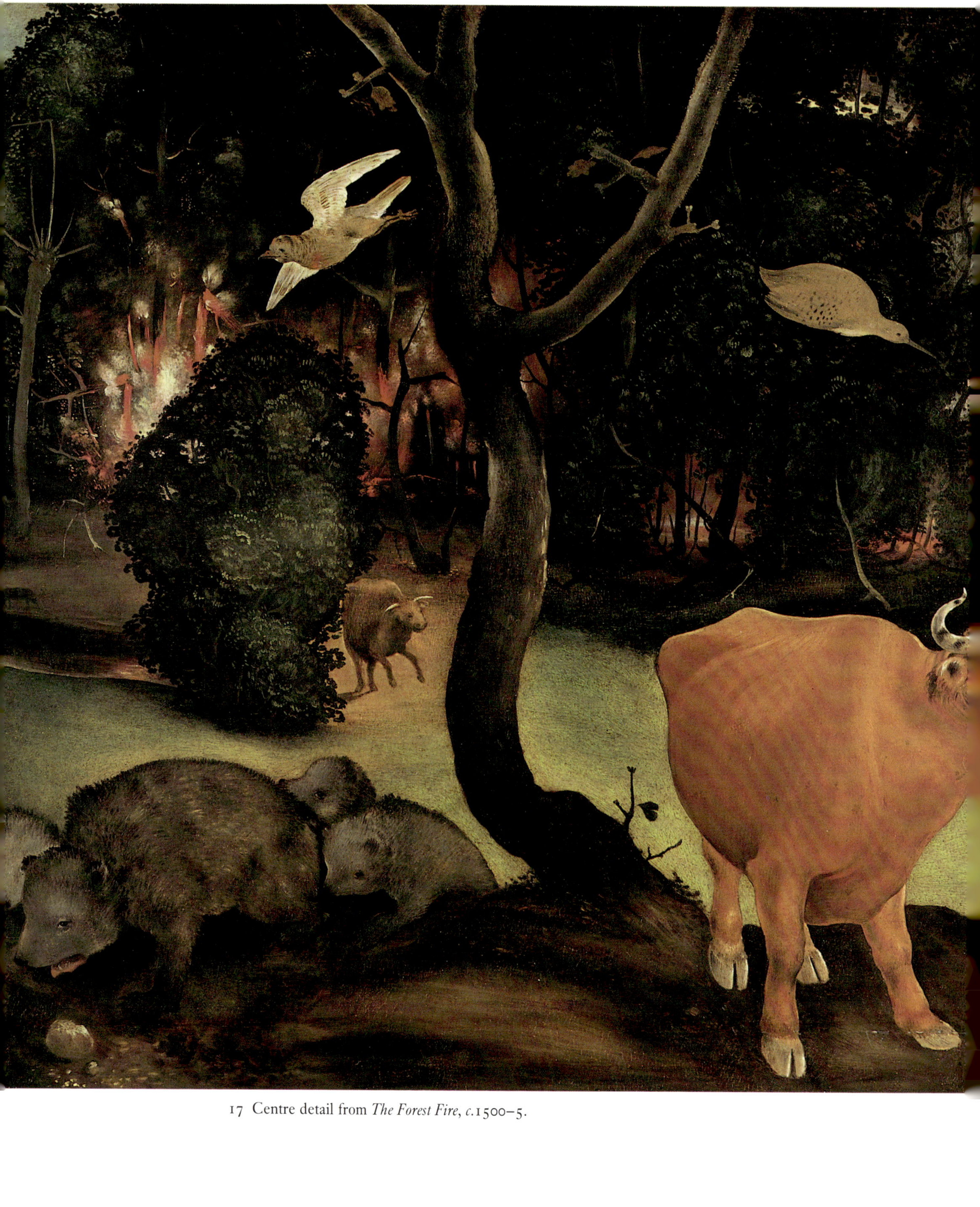

17 Centre detail from *The Forest Fire*, *c.*1500–5.

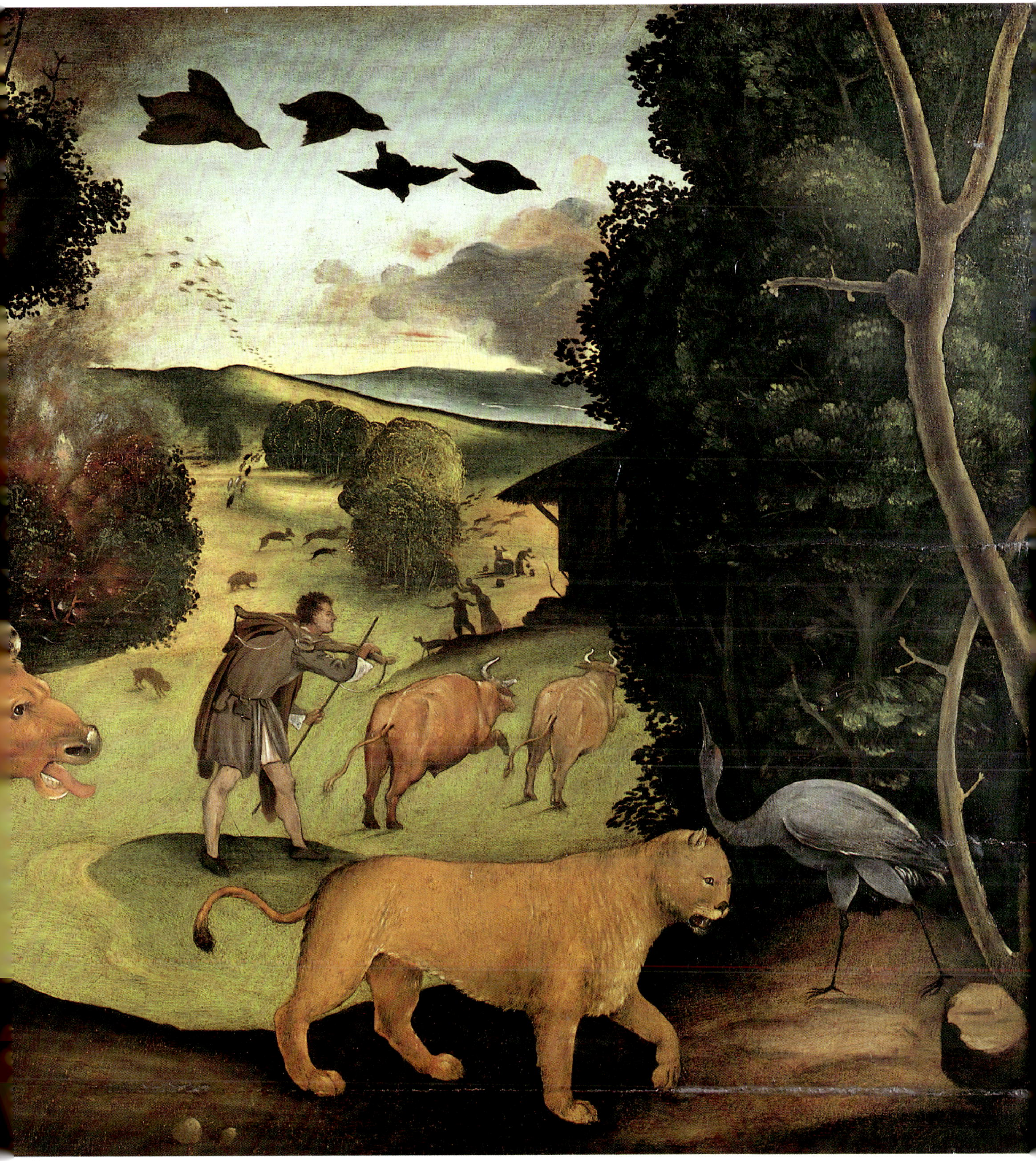

18 Right-hand detail from *The Forest Fire*.

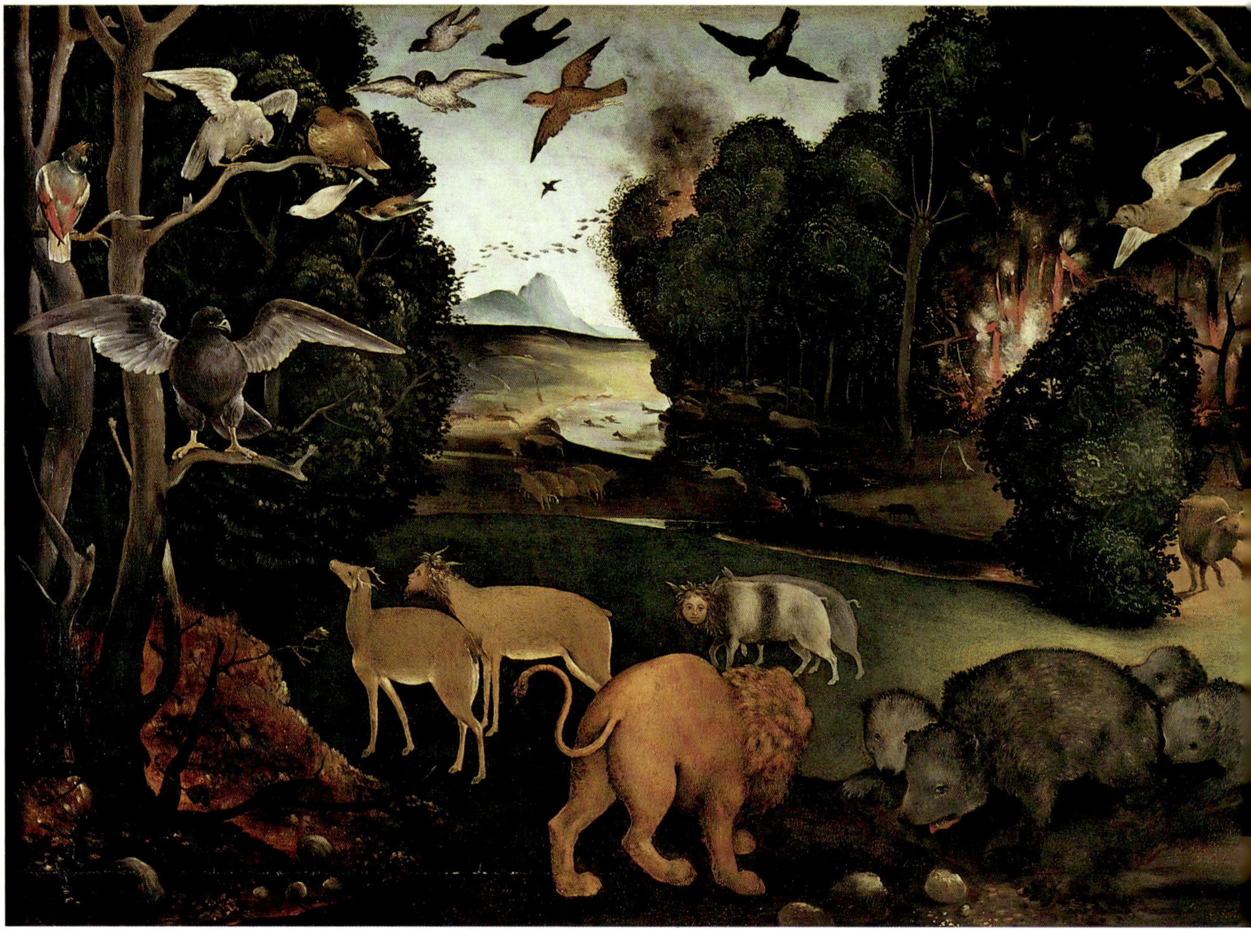

19 *The Forest Fire*, *c.*1500–5, oil on wood. Ashmolean Museum, Oxford.

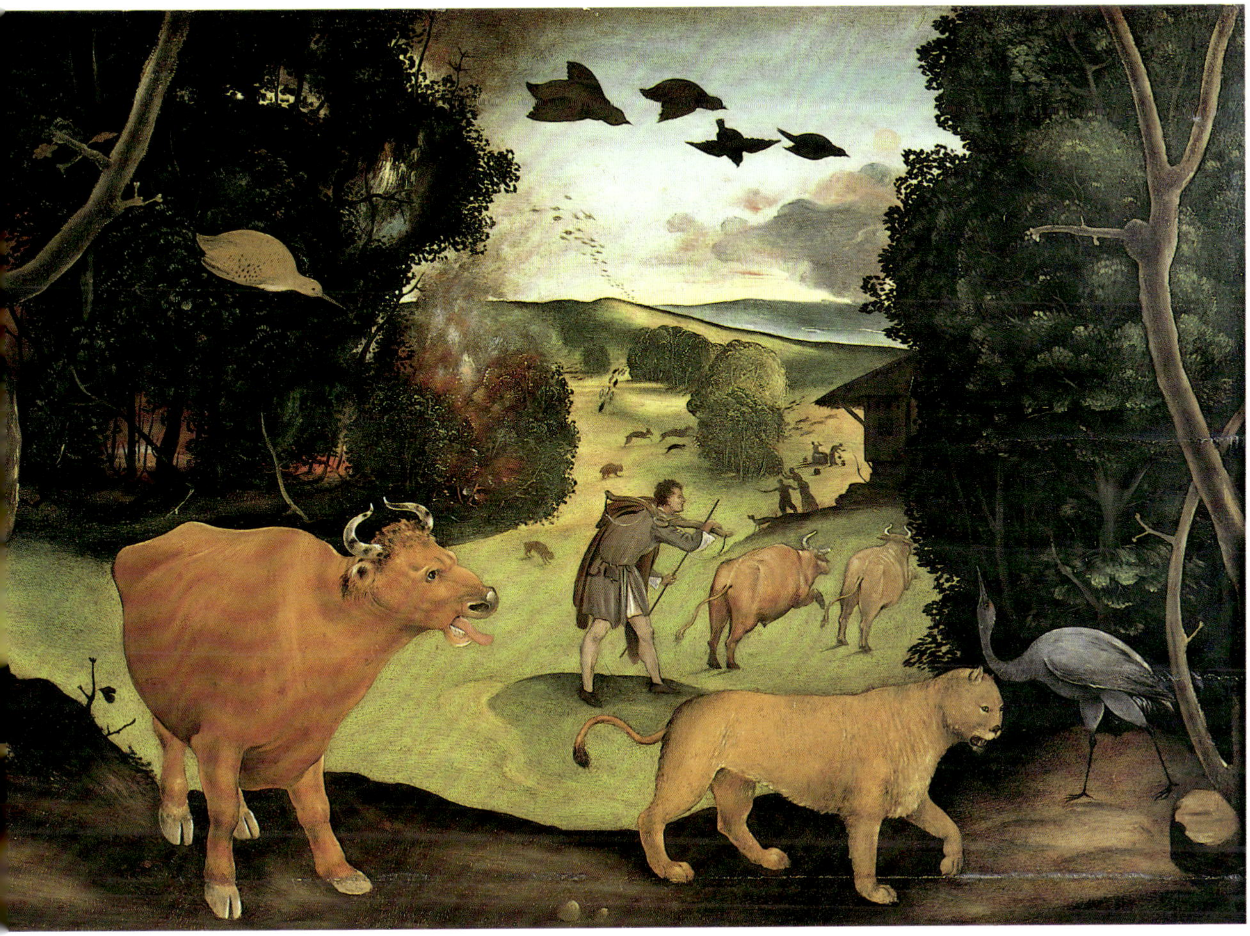

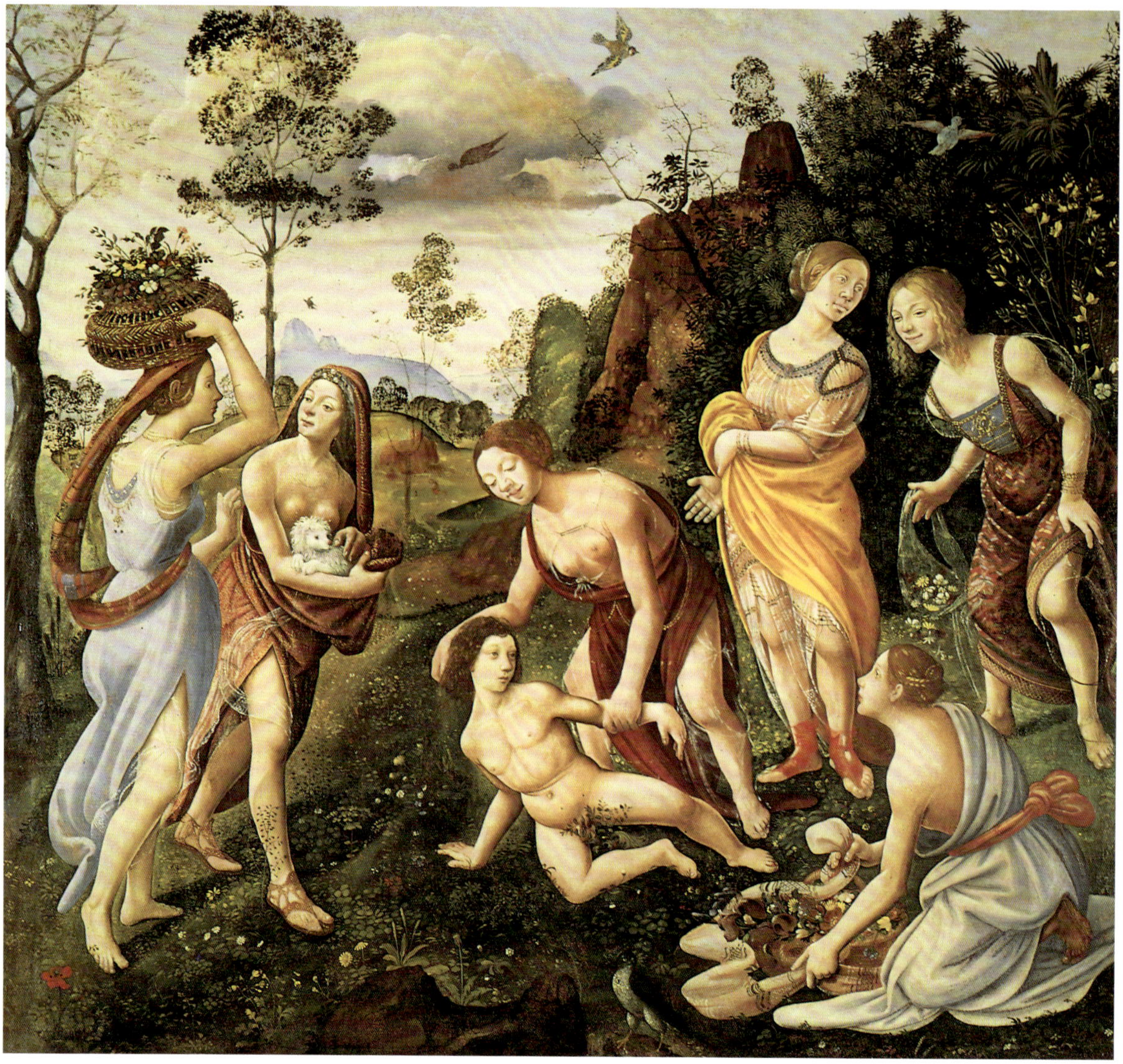

20 *The Finding of Vulcan on Lemnos*, *c.*1495–1505, oil and tempera on canvas. Wadsworth Athenaeum, Hartford, CT.

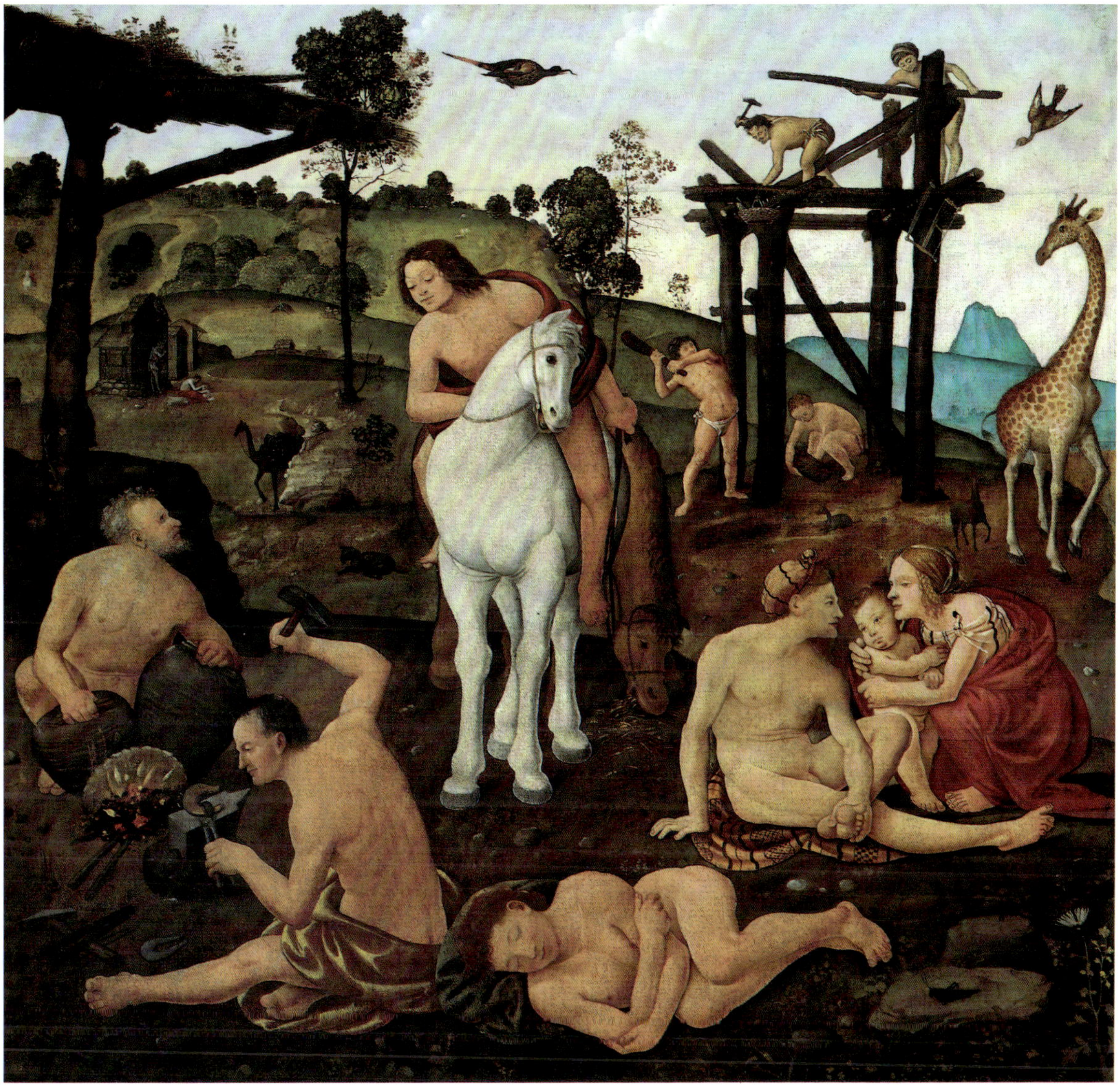

21 *Vulcan and Aeolus*, *c.*1495–1500, oil and tempera on canvas. National Gallery of Canada, Ottawa.

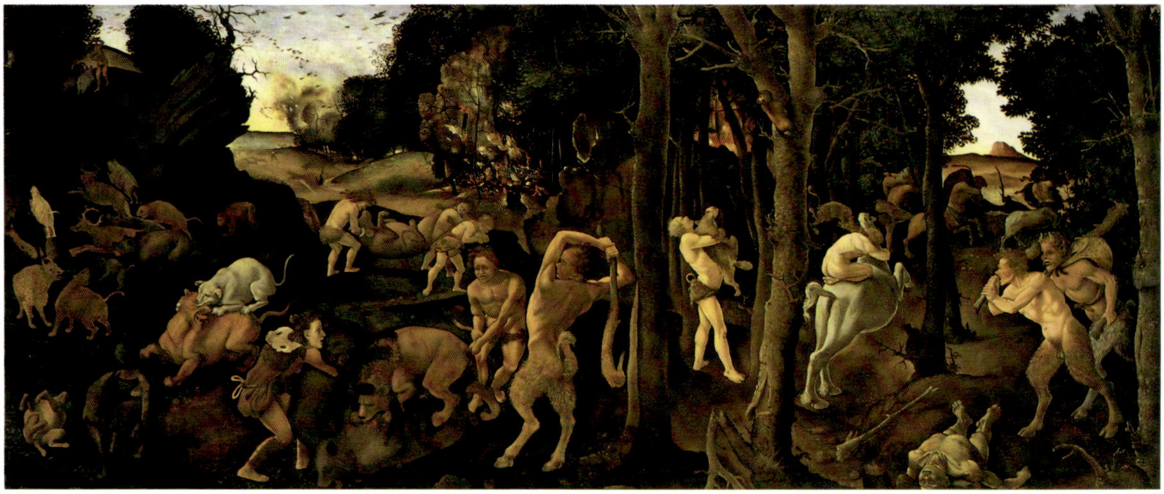

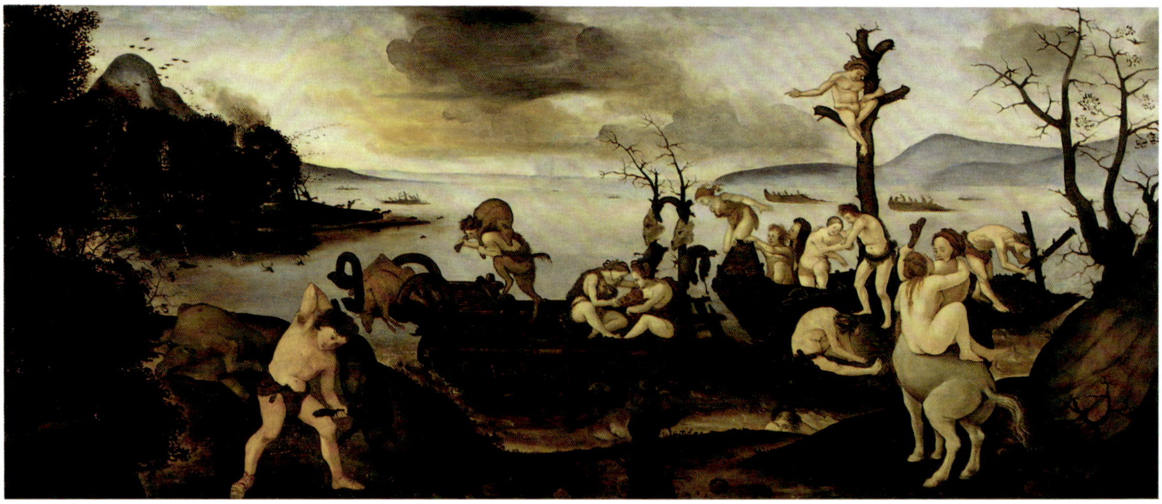

22 *The Hunt*, *c.*1495–1505, tempera and oil on wood. Metropolitan Museum of Art, New York.

23 *Return from the Hunt*, *c.*1495–1505, tempera and oil on wood. Metropolitan Museum of Art, New York.

Piero also recalls Lucretius's notion of the fecundity of nature at the beginning of creation.

The *Return from the Hunt* represents an advance in civilization, primarily in the emergence of basic family units and human bonds, which Lucretius identified as the most important factor in the second phase of evolution. Men and women embrace, and the figures – who still, however, include satyrs and centaurs – display more clearly the signs of co-operation, as they unload their kill from the boat, help each other ashore or keep lookout from the mast, while in the background others paddle towards the forest to take advantage of the conflagration. They wear more sophisticated clothing, and ornaments in their hair, and have discovered the art of building ships, although still without the aid of iron, suggesting that they are as yet unable to harness fire. Thus, although for Lucretius the art of navigation emerged at a later stage, and was a negative development that led to territorial conflicts, in general terms the second panel is in line with his account. The representation of the fire also adheres to Lucretius's account, especially in *The Hunt*, where the flames kindling among the intertwined branches recall Lucretius's description of the origins of fire:

> it was lightning that first brought fire down to the earth for mortals, and from this all blazing flames have been spread abroad. For we can see many things catch fire touched by the flames from on high, when the stroke from heaven has given them its heat. And yet also when a branching tree struck by the winds, swaying and tossed about, leans on the branches of a tree, fire is pressed out by the great force of the friction, and at times the burning glare of flames flashes while branches and twigs are rubbed together.[62]

The alterations that Piero makes to Lucretius's text were almost certainly motivated by aesthetic concerns, and by his desire to bring variety to the panels, both individually and as a pair. The introduction of satyrs and centaurs exploits Piero's *fantasie* – his ability to make the imaginary real – and brings variety and interest to each panel, while the introduction of boats in the second allowed him to create contrasting land- and seascapes, linked by the motif of fire. Furthermore, while the panels differ from Lucretius's text in some details, the development they present is logical and consistent in itself, and conveys clearly the passage of time.

This last point is particularly important as regards the panel of *The Forest Fire*, which most scholars have seen as related to the *Hunt* panels.[63] For Panofsky, the painting represented a still more advanced stage of civilization, and the last phase of the trilogy, in which man has acquired huts, primitive vessels and more advanced clothing, and attempts to put fire to good use by harnessing animals. Other scholars, including those who have disputed Panofsky's linking of the three to the *Vulcan* canvases, have accepted his suggestion that the two *Hunt* panels and *The Forest Fire* were designed to go together.

While *The Forest Fire* may also have been based on Lucretius, its relationship to the text is noticeably looser than that of the *Hunt* panels, and the phases of evolution Lucretius describes are more arbitrarily combined. Like the *Hunt* panels, *The Forest Fire* includes a conflagration, which occupies the centre of the panel, and one of

Piero's two main interests appears to have been the depiction of the fire itself and its reflections in the water below. The other main focus is the group of animals and birds fleeing from the flames, some proto-domestic, some decidedly exotic, and some which belong to the early hybrid and monstrous races that feature in Lucretius's account:

> Many were the monsters . . . that the earth then tried to make, springing up with wondrous appearance and frame: the hermaphrodite, between man and woman yet neither, different from both; some without feet, others again bereft of hands; some found dumb also without a mouth, some blind without face; some bound fast with all their limbs adhering to their bodies . . . [64]

An equally colourful description of such early monstrosities appears in the account of the world before the Age of Love included in the *Fragments* of Empedocles:

> there grew many creatures with double faces and double breasts; offspring of cattle with human faces and conversely human bodies with the heads of oxen sprang up, and mixed kinds partly male and partly female, having ambiguous members . . . [65]

In Piero's picture, however, rather than succeeding or supplanting them, man dwells side by side with these monstrous creatures, and in a relatively advanced stage of civilization. The human inhabitants of the plain, who appear to form an extended family, wear conventional, well-made clothes, live in a relatively sophisticated dwelling of wood and stone and are shown drawing water from their well. They also appear to have manufactured pots, implying that they have discovered the means to harness fire, as is also indicated by the yoke with metal trappings with which the man in the middle-ground attempts to harness the fugitive oxen.

Like the *Return from the Hunt*, these scenes of human life may have been drawn from Lucretius's account of the second stage of existence, which saw the most complex and numerous advances in civilization. In Lucretius's terms, however, by the time man had reached this stage in his development, the monstrous races depicted in the foreground would long since have been extinct. The painting thus dramatically telescopes the phases of primitive life to create an image that, if based on Lucretius's text, extracts and combines its most picturesque incidents in a fairly random way. In this respect *The Forest Fire* differs from the *Hunt* panels, where progress follows a clear and logical pattern along the broad lines of Lucretius's account, and it cannot easily be accommodated within their tight thematic progression. Furthermore, the focus of attention in *The Forest Fire* appears to be less the existence of early man, which, in the *Hunt* panels, is rendered with almost scientific interest and precision, than the combination of a raging fire and an exotic menagerie.

It seems most likely, therefore, that the *Hunt* panels were designed as a pair, for as such they have a visual and thematic coherence and completeness that is wholly disrupted by attempts to link them with *The Forest Fire*, which was probably always intended as a single panel. There is ample precedent for the existence of such single panels within the context of domestic decoration. From the mid-fifteenth century onwards, records survive of single panels of animal hunts, by artists such as Pesellino and Uccello, and at least one painting of a fire, by an unknown artist, is mentioned in

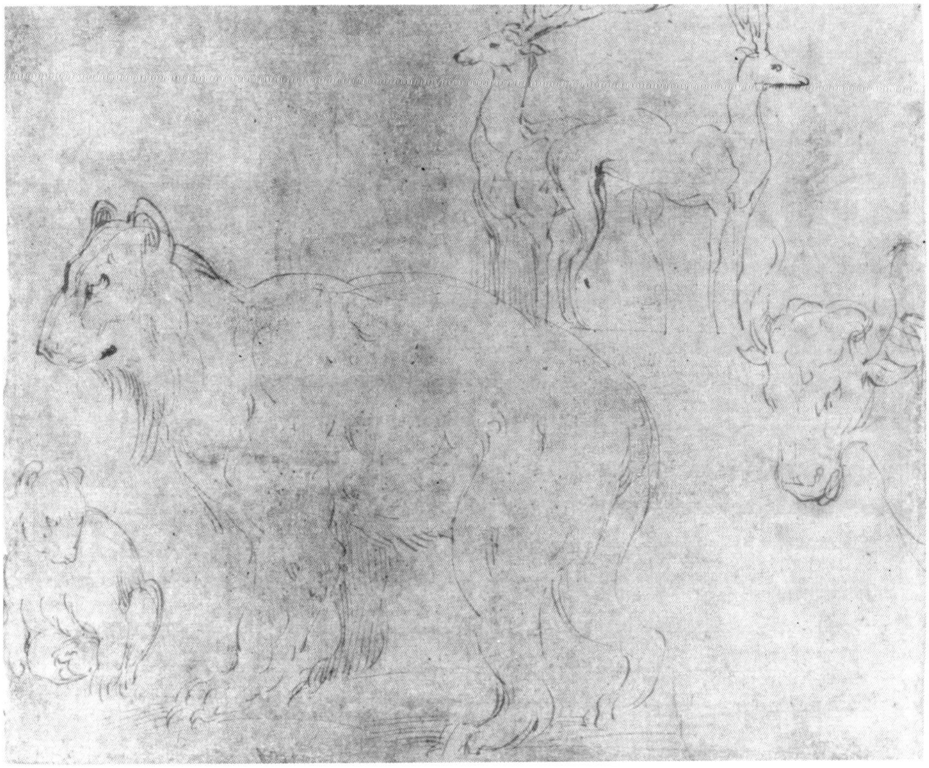

24 *A Bear and Cub; Two Deer; Head of an Ox*, pen and brown ink over metalpoint on rose-salmon prepared paper. Boymans–van Beuningen Museum, Rotterdam.

an inventory of one of the Strozzi collections.[66] The painting of fire could also be seen as a humanist conceit, a demonstration of artistic virtuosity and skill similar to those described by Pliny, who makes admiring mention of paintings of storms and similar phenomena. The subject is certainly one that exploits to the full the range of Piero's talents, in its combination of wild landscape, unusual animals and the variety of colours and reflections engendered by the fire. The value placed on such displays of inventive and painterly skill is eloquently underlined by Vasari's account of a forest fire with animals painted by Francesco Francia, which from the description was strikingly similar to Piero's *The Forest Fire*:

And Francia's fame was increased immeasurably by a pair of harnesses which the Duke of Urbino had him paint, on which he depicted a huge forest of trees set alight by fire, and emerging from it a great number of animals of both land and air, and some figures, a thing truly awesome, terrifying and most beautiful, that was held to be excellent particularly because of the time he spent painting the feathers of the birds, and on the other animals, apart from the variety of the leaves and branches one could see in the different trees. This work was acknowledged by the great gifts that the Duke gave to Francia in recognition of his labours, apart from which the Duke was always in Francia's debt on account of the constant praise the work received.[67]

In Panofsky's view, the cycle initiated by the *Hunt* and *Forest Fire* panels would have been concluded by the two *Vulcan* canvases now in Ottawa and Hartford, and also

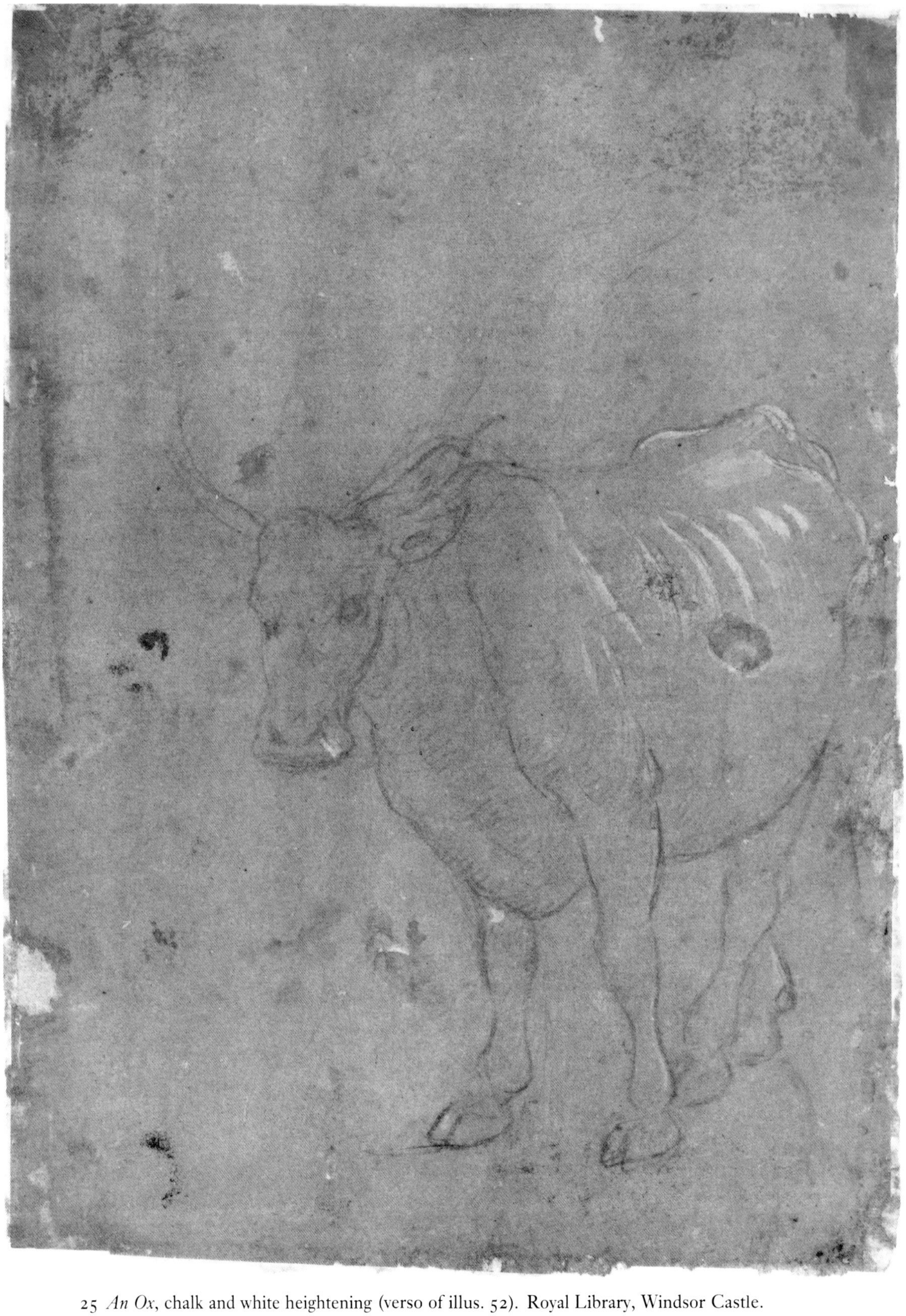

25 *An Ox*, chalk and white heightening (verso of illus. 52). Royal Library, Windsor Castle.

possibly the lost *Mars, Venus and Vulcan* described by Vasari. Panofsky convincingly suggested as a source for the *Vulcan* canvases the account in Virgil's *Aeneid* of the life of the God of Fire. The first – *The Finding of Vulcan on Lemnos* (illus. 20) – would thus show the story told by Virgil of Vulcan's fall to earth, specifically to the island of Lemnos, after he was thrown from Mount Olympus by his parents, Jupiter and Juno, who were disgusted by his deformity. According to Virgil's account, Vulcan was discovered on the island by apes, who took over his education and brought him up.[68]

Piero shows the young god dazed after his fall into the verdant realm of Lemnos. Here he is discovered, not by apes, but by nymphs, an alteration that Piero almost certainly made on artistic grounds, as Panofsky has suggested. The nymphs come upon Vulcan while out gathering flowers, and although Piero's subdued approach to gesture makes their discovery of him undramatic – their surprise is marked only in the upraised hands of the nymph on the right, and the scattering of the flowers – it seems clear that this was intended to be the subject of the work. The second canvas – *Vulcan and Aeolus* (illus. 21) – shows the adult Vulcan, accompanied by Aeolus, God of the Winds, teaching man the uses of fire. In the left foreground Vulcan fashions a horseshoe over a small fire while Aeolus works a primitive bellows; the two are watched by a small family and a man on horseback, while in the background others construct houses with the aid of rudimentary metal tools, the details of which Piero probably derived from Vitruvius's account of the origins of architecture.[69] According to Panofsky's interpretation, the theme that united the five paintings would thus be the importance of fire to the development of civilization, which cannot truly progress until man has learnt its proper uses from the God of Fire himself. It is the theme of the origin and gradual harnessing of fire that is supposed to join the *Vulcan* canvases to the *Hunt* panels and *The Forest Fire*, and make of them a coherent cycle.

But there are significant difficulties with this interpretation, difficulties made particularly acute by Panofsky's inclusion of *The Forest Fire* as part of the first stage of the cycle, for here man appears to have reached a relatively advanced level of civilization without the aid of Vulcan. In *The Forest Fire*, which occurs before the God's arrival, man has evolved houses, clothes and utensils equal in sophistication to those depicted in the canvas of *Vulcan and Aeolus*, although beasts have not yet been harnessed as they have in the latter, which may also represent only the beginnings of technological development. The different phases of man's life are not, however, clearly distinguished from one work to the next, as one might expect in a cycle that had as its theme the progress of civilization. Furthermore, the underlying message of Lucretius's text, which Panofsky acknowledges as the source for the first three works, is that man progresses and discovers the use of technology through his own innate intelligence and by force of necessity, rather than through the intervention of gods.

It is also significant that, in Lucretius's view, neither the technological progress of man, nor his socialization, entirely depended on fire, as might be inferred from the *Vulcan* canvases. Although the use of fire was implicitly essential to the development of technological society, Lucretius does not discuss this *per se*, remarking only in passing that fire enabled men to discover metals. Likewise, in Piero's *Hunt* panels, and in *The Forest Fire*, the progress of man is not shown as linked to fire, which remains an essentially threatening and untamed force, although it might assist him in catching animals for food. Indeed, in both the paintings and Lucretius's text, the motif of fire, and the emergence of civilization, appear almost as separate conceits. It is also worth noting that, despite Panofsky's insistence on the discovery and harnessing of fire as a governing theme, the motif of the working of fire is only one small part of the Ottawa canvas where, as in the *Hunt* panels, Piero appears to be interested in exploring a range of different facets of early life, rather than emphasizing one in particular.

As Panofsky recognized, therefore, if the *Vulcan* canvases are related to the *Hunt* panels, their significance must have been allegorical, for they could not have functioned as part of the historical and chronological progression that Piero charts in the latter. Vulcan would have to be interpreted, not as the inventor of fire, or as the one responsible, in an historical sense, for teaching man its uses, but as a symbol or an allegory of man's innate ability to harness it, and his efforts to keep it alive. The cycle would thus combine Lucretius's evolutionary account of early man with an allegorical use of Virgil's life of Vulcan, and of Virgil's praise of Vulcan as the founder of civilization in bringing fire to mankind, and teaching him its uses. In addition to the fact that this interpretation appears unnecessarily cumbersome and not wholly coherent, such a combination of the narrative and allegorical scenes would certainly have been unusual, particularly within the context of an upper-middle-class home. While cycles comprising a mixture of narrative and allegorical works may sometimes have been used to decorate courtly or princely residences, especially in fresco, such complex and grandiose schemes must surely have been rare as decorations for the houses of bourgeois or mercantile patrons.[70] The combination of small panels and large canvases that Panofsky's interpretation entails is also without obvious precedent, and would have made the cycle unusually difficult to read, especially if, as Panofsky suggested, the parts of the scheme were hung in separate rooms. While our knowledge of the hanging or installation of such works is only fragmentary, what evidence there is suggests that decorative ensembles were generally intended to be visually coherent, and the works complementary in a way that would manifestly not be the case in this instance, where the works are radically different in scale, colouring and support.[71]

It seems more likely that the *Hunt* panels and *The Forest Fire* are the result of distinct commissions, with the *Vulcan* canvases comprising a third. It is also conceivable that the *Vulcan* canvases were intended as part of a larger cycle, whose primary subject was the life of Vulcan rather than the evolution of man, even if Piero treated the second canvas in a manner that allowed him to explore the theme of man's early existence. On the other hand, the two function well as a contrasting pair, linked by the forms of the mountains. And the particular scenes may have been chosen in part because they allowed for a contrast between a verdant and flowery landscape, inhabited by richly adorned nymphs, and a barren, untilled plain, with semi-naked male figures.

Distinguishing between the works, and separating the commissions, does not, of course, answer the question of their significance to the patrons, or to the artist himself, two issues that have preoccupied scholars. Panofsky, for example, was in no doubt that Piero's treatment of the early life of man was a sympathetic and nostalgic one, which reflected his own 'primitive' character and inclinations as described in Vasari's Life. This view has been endorsed since by a number of scholars, while the existence of so many 'primitive' subjects in his *oeuvre* has itself been seen as an indication of Piero's own interests. But even if we accept Vasari's account of Piero's character at face value, it should be stressed that, with the possible exception of *The Forest Fire*, it is unlikely that Piero would have been solely responsible for choosing the subject-matter of the works, or selecting the texts of Lucretius and Virgil on which they are based. In the majority of cases for which documentation exists, the choice of subject-matter for private commissions was made by the patron, although its precise formulation was inevitably the artist's own, and the subjects may have been chosen with an eye to his particular talents.[72] While patrons familiar with Piero's work might conceivably have requested a painting depicting a fire, leaving the details and the setting for the artist to decide, the subjects of the *Hunt* and *Vulcan* panels were almost certainly the result of a specific request, rather than the choice of the painter. Nor is it the case that Piero's view of primitive life is a consistent one, and while an artist's personal attitude to his subject is always difficult to determine, his response to the theme of early existence is not obviously nostalgic or idealizing. If the life depicted in the second canvas, *Vulcan and Aeolus*, appears seductive in its innocence and simplicity, that shown in the *Hunt* panels and *The Forest Fire* is, as Lucretius describes it, hard, brutish and full of danger.

It would also be simplistic to infer from Vasari's view of Piero as a solitary man not given to social niceties that he would have seen such an existence as an ideal or desirable state, or that he would have made no distinction between his sense of his own situation and his depiction of a mythical past. Vasari himself made no connection between Piero's character and the subjects he depicted, or his treatment of the subject-matter. On the contrary, this is an aspect of Piero's work about which he had virtually nothing to say, and it is by no means certain that he knew the *Hunt* panels or *The Forest Fire*, for the only so-called 'primitive' subjects he was undisputably familiar with are *The Discovery of Honey* and *The Misfortunes of Silenus*, both painted for Giovanni Vespucci. To see Piero's treatment of his subjects in terms of his character is to ignore the metaphorical nature of Vasari's account, and the fact that, for Vasari himself, the relationship between the man and his work was of a more complex and subtle kind.

Attempts to assign a political or ideological meaning to the Early Man paintings have been equally unsatisfactory and unconvincing. For Panofsky, the broader political significance of the works was linked in part to the identity of the man whom he assumed was the patron, Francesco del Pugliese, although we have seen that this connection is by no means certain.[73] Pugliese was a rich and successful wool-merchant, and an active participant in the Florentine government, serving as one of the *priori* of Florence in 1490–1 and again in 1497–8.[74] He is known to have had republican and anti-Medicean sympathies, and to have been an active supporter of the radical reformer Girolamo Savonarola, and was exiled from Florence in 1513 for insulting Lorenzo de' Medici, Duke of Urbino. He was also a patron of eclectic and sophisticated tastes who owned an unusual number of devotional paintings, including works by Botticelli, Filippino Lippi and Fra Bartolommeo, and some by Flemish artists.

Taking into account Pugliese's sympathies and interests, Panofsky concluded that Vulcan – 'the only ungentlemanly workman in the Olympian leisure class' – would have been an obvious choice for this 'wealthy, plain-spoken democrat', implying, in addition, that the subject of primitive life would have had a particular resonance for a man out of love with the apparent over-sophistication of the Medicean regime, and whose sympathies lay rather with the policies of Savonarola. Other scholars, however, while accepting Panofsky's grouping of the works, and the link with Francesco del Pugliese, have come to the opposite conclusion, expressing surprise that the same man should have commissioned, for the decoration of his house, an 'anti-humanist cycle of paintings of primitive humanity', considering that their pessimistic and evolutionary view of man's origins sat uneasily with Francesco's profoundly religious bent.[75] This conflict of opinions is important because it highlights the difficulty inherent in assigning to any of these works a clear political or ideological significance, not least because the texts on which they draw had not previously been used as the subject for artistic representation, and there is no established tradition of moral or allegorical interpretation of such subjects to which we may refer. That is not to say that none of the paintings in question had a broader significance for their patrons, or that they could not have been interpreted in allegorical terms. It is unlikely, however, that they were conceived as expressions of nostalgia for a primitive past, or of a dissatisfaction with contemporary society or culture, as scholars have implied, albeit in different ways. Where such sentiments can be discerned in contemporary literature, for example, they are articulated rather within the framework of the myth of the Golden Age, and what has been termed 'soft primitivism', as opposed to the 'hard primitivism' of Lucretius.[76] According to this myth, which originated with Hesiod and was transmitted by Ovid, the earliest age of mankind was the most happy, a time of innocence and abundance, and a state of grace from which man fell through the imperfections of his own nature. Earth gave freely of its gifts, and food dropped into men's laps, for they did not yet eat meat or undertake work, nor was there any sorrow or pain. The subsequent development of civilization and the progress of technology that took place in the successive ages of Silver, Bronze and Iron are here seen as negative processes that led man astray from this simple and innocent age.

This idyllic vision of man's earliest existence is wholly remote from that described by Lucretius and depicted by Piero. For Lucretius, the earliest stages of man's life were brutish rather than idyllic, and although his version of 'hard primitivism' shared with the Hesiodic view the sense that progress towards civilization was essentially a bad thing, he by no means envisaged the age before civilization as one of primordial bliss. If he saw an ideal age in the state of semi civilization that saw the emergence of the first social bonds, this idealization is never strongly marked, and his view of mankind was a profoundly pessimistic one, while his evolutionary account of man's origins was in fundamental contradiction with the Christian notion of Creation. It is thus worth asking why a patron who shared this view of mankind would wish to have it recorded in such vivid pictorial terms.

It is also difficult to see how the works in question could be interpreted allegorically, or how they could function as didactic and moralizing images. Where panels designed for domestic interiors were intended to function in this way, they usually presented images of moral virtue, intended for emulation. Alternatively, where the subject-matter illustrated examples of human vice or failing, they generally did so in an overtly didactic way. In both cases, the moral significance of the theme was usually of a general and fairly obvious kind, while the construction of the image itself invariably made clear that it was intended to be read in this way. None of the five works under discussion fits comfortably into these categories, nor does Piero's presentation of his subject-matter appear to suggest any overriding moral or didactic point. Rather, the images preserve the same air of reportage, and of detached observation that is apparent in Lucretius's text, and which gives them their compelling visual appeal.

It is quite likely that the *Hunt* paintings were designed primarily as vivid illustrations of Lucretius's interesting text, which had only recently been discovered, designed to impress both by the novelty of the subject-matter and by the unconventional nature of the imagery to which they gave rise.[77] In this sense they act as clear demonstrations of the erudition and sophistication of the patron, as well as virtuoso displays of the artist's particular talents. Furthermore, while that does not rule out the possibility that they had or acquired a greater significance for the patron, knowledge of his identity would not inevitably prove enlightening in this respect, for it is not necessarily the case that every painting commissioned during the Renaissance was a reflection of deeply held views on the part of the patron, or an expression of his personal opinions. It is thus eminently conceivable that a man like Francesco del Pugliese could have commissioned such works for the pleasure of owning unusual and sophisticated paintings, irrespective of his religious or political views.

The Vespucci *Bacchanals*

The subject-matter of Piero's most sophisticated pair of mythological panels, *The Discovery of Honey* (illus. 28) and *The Misfortunes of Silenus* (illus. 29), was almost certainly chosen in part because it entailed a reference to the patron's family name, albeit of a light-hearted kind, and these are among the few of the artist's works for which a reasonably secure provenance can be established. Probably painted between 1505 and 1510, they were almost certainly commissioned by Giovanni Vespucci, as stated by Vasari, who appears to have known the panels well:

He painted for Giovanni Vespucci, for his house which stood opposite San Michele in the Via de' Servi . . . some bacchanals which were placed around a room; in which he painted such strange fauns, nymphs and satyrs, and putti and bacchantes, that it is marvellous to behold the diversity of their garments and their implements, and the variety of goatlike forms, rendered with grace and in the most realistic manner. And in one story there is Silenus astride an ass with many young boys around him, some holding him up and some plying him with drink; and one sees in the painting a truly lifelike merriment and glee, rendered with great talent.[78]

Both paintings have as their central motif the discovery of honey in a decaying tree-trunk, indicated by a swarm of bees. As we saw in discussing Botticelli's *Mars and Venus*, wasps featured on the Vespucci crest, while the word *vespa*, the Italian for wasp, could be seen as a punning allusion to their name. While the passage from Ovid's *Fasti* on which the panels are based speaks of *crabrones* (hornets), rather than bees or wasps (*vespae*), Renaissance commentaries on the text referred to both *crabrones* and *vespae*.[79] The precise identity of the insects may also have been less important than the visual pun that gave the subject its personal significance for the patron.

In Book III of the *Fasti*, Ovid describes the discovery of honey by Bacchus and his train when explaining the origins of the sweet cakes or libations traditionally offered to the God. In a subsequent passage he describes how Silenus, greedy for more honey, fell from his ass while trying to reach a honeycomb, and was repeatedly stung by the bees. His companions then soothed the stings by the application of mud:

Libations derive their name from their author, and so do cakes, because part of them is offered on the hallowed hearths. Cakes are made for the god, because he delights in sweet juices, and they say honey was discovered by Bacchus. Attended by the satyrs he was going from sandy Hebrus (my tale includes a pleasant jest) and had come to Rhodope and flowery Pangaeus, when the cymbals in the hands of his companions clashed. Lo, drawn by the tinkle, winged things, as yet unknown assemble, and the bees follow the sounding brass. Liber collected the stragglers and shut them up in a hollow tree; and he was rewarded by the discovery of honey. Once the satyrs and the bald-pated ancient had tasted it, they sought for the yellow combs in every grove. In a hollow elm the old fellow [Silenus] heard the humming of a swarm; he spied the combs and kept his counsel. And sitting lazily on the back of an ass, that bent beneath his weight, he rode the beast up to the elm, where the bark was hollow. Then he stood on the ass, and leaning upon a branching stump he greedily reached at the honey stored in the bole. Thousands of hornets gathered, and thrust their stings into his bald pate, and left their mark on his snub-nosed face. Headlong he fell, and the ass kicked him, while he called to his comrades and implored their help. The satyrs ran to the spot and laughed at their parent's swollen face; he limped on his hurt knee. Bacchus himself laughed and taught him to smear mud on his wounds: Silenus took the hint and smudged his face with mire. The father god enjoys honey, and it is right that we should give to its discoverer clear honey infused in hot cakes. The reason why a woman should knead the cakes is plain enough: Bacchus rouses bands of women by his thyrsus. You ask why it is an old woman who does it. That age is more addicted to wine and loves the bounty of the teeming vine. Why is she wreathed with ivy? Ivy is most dear to Bacchus. Why that is so can also soon be told. They say that when the stepmother was searching for the boy, the nymphs of Nysa screened the cradle in ivy leaves.[80]

Piero's paintings clearly follow the framework of Ovid's text. In *The Discovery of Honey* Bacchus and Ariadne can be seen standing on the right, Ariadne pointing at Bacchus's wreath of ivy, the plant 'most dear' to him. Behind him is Silenus, who arrives with his troupe of satyrs and maenads, while on the left we see the remnants of Bacchus's train. In the centre, two satyrs attempt to trap the bees within a hollow tree, while in the right background others, in a desperate attempt to find more honeycombs, climb trees near the opening to a dark forest. In the second panel, which adheres more closely to Ovid's account, the centre of the painting is occupied by Silenus falling from his ass while searching for more honey. On the right, his laughing companions attempt to raise him from the ground, while on the left they smear mud on his stings.

While the main features of both panels are taken from the *Fasti*, *The Discovery of Honey* departs from Ovid's text, both in certain details and in Piero's interpretation of the theme. Here, for example, the bees are made to swarm by the rattling and banging of kitchen implements, sticks, stones and bones, not by the noise of the maenads' cymbals, a detail that Piero probably derived from Aristotle's *History of Animals*. In it, Aristotle records the opinion that 'Bees seem to take pleasure in listening to a rattling noise; and consequently men say that they can muster them into a hive by rattling with crockery or stones'.[81] In the *Georgics* Virgil also notes that bees follow the tinkling sounds of bronze, as well as of cymbals.[82] More important, the subject of the painting appears not to be the original discovery of honey but, rather, Bacchus and his troupe setting out deliberately to entrap bees, and to gather the honey with a variety of pots, pans and other utensils. The gathering of honey is thus envisaged as one activity in the everyday lives of the God and his entourage, rather than as a specific incident, while the members of the entourage are envisaged, less as mythical personages, than as human beings with ordinary family lives. Similarly, the landscape is not the 'flowery Pangaeus' of Ovid's text, but an unspecific rural setting dotted with religious and domestic buildings. At the same time, as in *The Misfortunes of Silenus*, Piero elaborates on an aspect of the story only hinted at by Ovid, emphasizing the pleasantness and companionship of life in Bacchus's troupe.

In *The Discovery of Honey* Piero thus departs from Ovid's text, and rejects the motif of the Bacchic procession, or *thiasos*, favoured by the majority of artists working on such scenes, especially those in the circle of Botticelli, who also tended to refer quite closely to Classical examples (illus. 26). Bacchic processions were well-known from relief depictions on sarcophagi, and such subjects gave Renaissance artists the opportunity to quote directly from the Antique, while the frenzied maenads and cavorting satyrs that conventionally comprised Bacchus's troupe enabled them to display to the full their ability to show the body in movement, as well as their mastery of *all'antica* drapery.[83] Yet there can be little doubt that such motifs, and the kind of movement typified by the Classical maenad, were ill-suited to Piero's abilities. The element of drama and surprise implicit in Ovid's account of the discovery of honey may also have sat uneasily with the artist's unrhetorical approach to narrative and expressive gesture, and it is also significant that in his depiction of Bacchus's troupe, Piero referred back to an example of narrative painting that he had encountered early in his career – Perugino and Pintoricchio's fresco of the *Events from the Life of Moses*

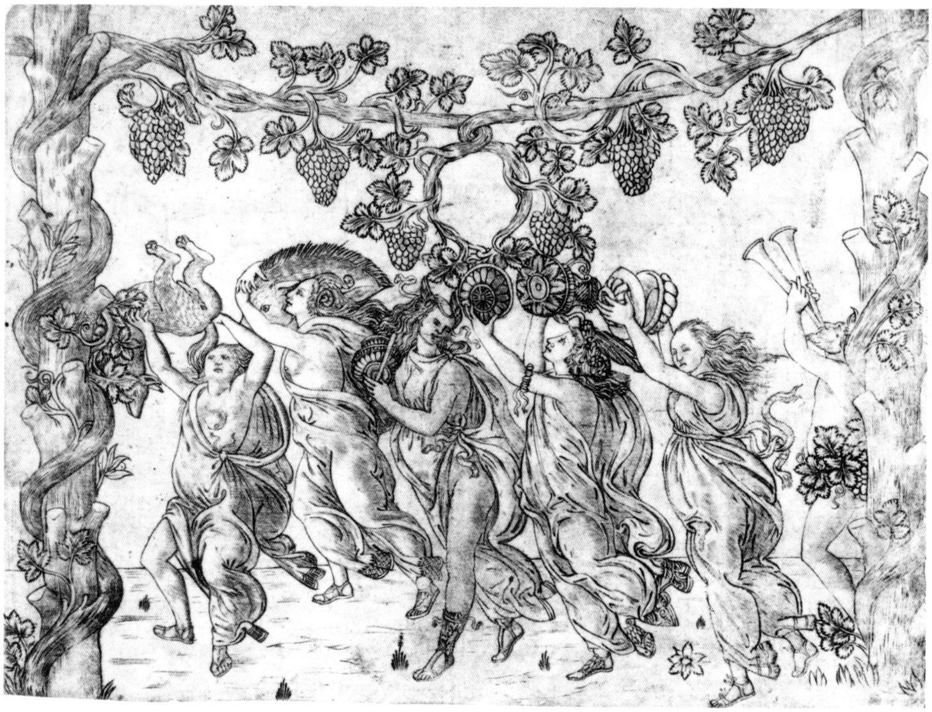

26 Engraving after a drawing by Botticelli, *Bacchic Procession* (detail from the *Triumph of Bacchus and Ariadne*), *c.*1480–90. British Museum, London.

(illus. 27) in the Sistine Chapel – taking as a model the procession of the family of Moses on the left. At the same time, by departing from traditional interpretations of the Bacchic entourage, Piero was able to exercise his characteristic inventiveness in the varied designs of the costumes and implements and in the physiognomy of the satyrs, engendering precisely that sense of wonder and curiosity that Vasari describes.

Almost inevitably, as with *Mars and Venus*, this seemingly 'rustic' interpretation of the subject has prompted the suggestion that the paintings were parodic in tone, and that the artist set out to satirize the myth on which they are based.[84] In this case, however, the suggestion that the artist took a light-hearted view of his subject appears more convincing. At the same time, it is important to realize that the literature of antiquity itself included a strong parodic strain, as illustrated, for example, in the writings of Lucian and Horace, whose satires on the Gods and their amours were well-known. In his account of Bacchus's campaign in India, for example, Lucian includes a lengthy comic description of how Bacchus and his army must have looked to the defending Hindus, and although the joke is ultimately on the latter for underestimating Bacchus, the passage makes clear that Classical writers could themselves conceive of the deities in a humorous vein:

His rank and file are crack-brained crazy women, wreathed with ivy, dressed in fawn-skins, carrying little headless spears which are of ivy too, and light targes that boom if you do but touch them . . . a few clodhoppers are with them, dancing the can-can without any clothes on; they have tails, and have

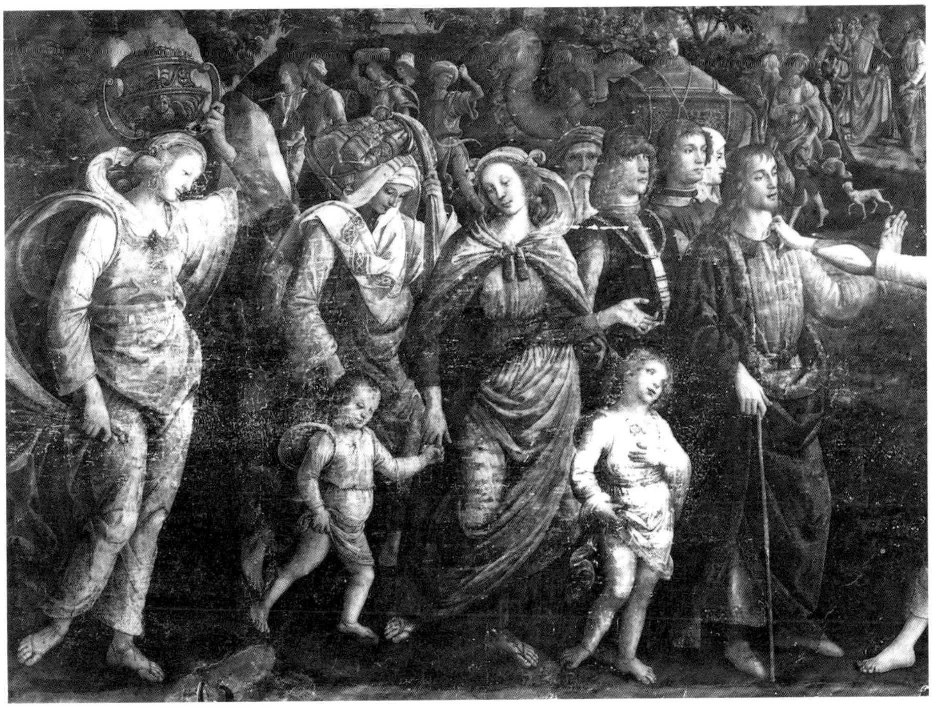

27 Perugino and Pintoricchio, *Moses's Journey into Egypt*, detail from *Events from the Life of Moses*, 1481–2, fresco. Sistine Chapel, Rome.

horns like those which start from the foreheads of new-born kids. As for the general himself . . . he is quite beardless, without even the least bit of down on his cheeks, has horns, wears a garland of grape clusters, ties up his hair with a ribbon . . . [85]

If, then, Piero avoided the more conventional, dionysiac aspect of the theme, and if his depiction of Bacchus and his troupe was parodic or humorous in intent, it could find ample support in Classical texts, and it would be a mistake to construe the paintings as anti-Humanist or as satiric in any more pointed a way. Furthermore, the spirit of fun and laughter that pervades both panels – the 'merriment', or *letizia del vivo*, that Vasari describes – is itself inherent in the passage from the *Fasti* on which Piero drew, Ovid stating that 'my tale includes a merry jest', while the second part of the tale is told at Silenus's expense in a way that is captured quite exactly in Piero's work.

It has also been suggested that the paintings carried an allegorical meaning. Here again, the most significant interpretation has been that of Panofsky, who suggested that the landscape in *The Discovery of Honey* was symbolic or allegorical in intent.[86] As he pointed out, the landscape is clearly divided into two along the lines of a traditional *paysage moralisé*, the dividing point being the tree in which the bees swarm. While the landscape on the left, from which the troupe of Bacchus descends, is sunlit, well-ordered and adorned with well-constructed buildings, that on the right is dark and forbidding, full of blasted trees. In this part of the painting, inhabited by lions and apes, satyrs grope blindly among the trees in their desperate search for more honey:

those who gather the honey inhabit a light and tranquil world, while those who have yet to find it stumble in a twilit and inhospitable realm, in the company of wild beasts.

Panofsky thus concluded that honey was being presented here, not simply as an enjoyable addition to man's diet, but as a civilizing force, like the wine Bacchus also provides, and one of the means by which man's life is lifted above mere survival. Like Vulcan in the canvases discussed earlier, Bacchus himself would not simply be interpreted in literal terms as an historical or mythological figure, but as a benefactor, one of those responsible for the advancement of civilization, who also embodies the gains and principles essential for man's progress. The story would be understood as an allegory of that stage in civilization when men discover the simple pleasures of sweet foods and wine, progressing beyond a life of bestial or unmitigated hardship to a pastoral existence in harmony with nature.[87] Although this aspect of the story of the discovery of honey is not touched on by Ovid, whose primary interest in the *Fasti* is the origins of different religious rituals, it is not inconceivable that the theme would have been seen in this way, although such an interpretation fails to take account of *The Misfortunes of Silenus*, which is more difficult to interpret in allegorical terms. At the same time, it is worth noting that not only is the allegorical significance Panofsky ascribes to the work of a relatively simple kind, but the devices Piero uses are fairly self-evident.

The Stories of Prometheus

The last of Piero's *spalliera* panels to be considered consist of a pair depicting the *Stories of Prometheus* (illus. 32 and 33), probably painted between 1515 and 1520. Both are in poor condition, making the details and the background incidents difficult to decipher, while in some parts the execution appears weak, possibly suggesting the intervention of an assistant. The design, however, is clearly Piero's, and the compositions of the two works match each other closely, almost forming a continuous landscape. Both the figures and the landscape echo one other in a deliberate and methodical way, although the landscape is highly simplified, and the forms of the trees and the curves of the figures' limbs create an insistent pattern across the surface of the work in a manner which recalls *The Discovery of Honey*. The shapes of the clouds are also characteristic of Piero, as are the meticulous and varied still-life of implements in the first panel (illus. 32) and the idiosyncratic costumes of the gods and goddesses in each.

Although the subject is certainly the story of Prometheus, the source for Piero's version remains obscure. Despite suggestions that he derived the main incidents from Boccaccio's *Genealogia Deorum*, the paintings do not follow Boccaccio's text closely, and even the identification of the figures is unclear in some cases.[88] In the panel with which the story begins (illus. 32), Prometheus is seen fashioning the first man from clay in the presence of his brother Epimetheus. Although it has generally been assumed that Prometheus is the figure dressed in red and blue who pulls at the arm of the clay man, this seems more likely to be his brother, while Prometheus, wearing brown, sits back to admire his creation. In this respect Piero may have been following Boccaccio, who relates that Epimetheus also made a man of clay, as a punishment for which Jupiter turned him into an ape. Piero may thus have chosen to show the brothers fashioning the statue together in a compressed version of the text, although the simian creature climbing a tree on the left may be a reference to the state of ignorance that existed prior to the figure of clay receiving the spark of divine wisdom, rather than an allusion to Epimetheus's fate. As regards Prometheus, it is certainly he who, dressed in brown and black, encounters Minerva on the right, and accompanies her to the Heavens to steal fire from the chariot of Phoebus.

In the second panel (illus. 33), Prometheus is seen among the clouds, stealing fire, while on the left he animates his man of clay with the spark he obtains. On the right Mercury punishes Prometheus for the theft by tying him to a tree, where an eagle waits to peck at his liver. The significance of the scene in the centre background is less clear; possibly it alludes to the myth of Pandora, told by Hesiod and Aeschylus, who was sent to earth to become the wife of Epimetheus, and who released innumerable evils on mankind as a further punishment for the theft.[89] If this is the case, the figure left of centre, again dressed in red and blue, is most likely to be Epimetheus, and the standing women in red may be Pandora. Epimetheus, it appears, is being asked to consider the consequences of his actions in accepting Pandora as his wife, which Prometheus had warned him against, as a couple indicate to him a woman reclining in sickness. On the far left of the picture, in the background, a diminutive figure in red appears to wrestle with a snake around his ankle, another possible reference to the evils released from Pandora's urn.

Yet if this is the story of Pandora, Piero is departing from Boccaccio, who does not relate the legend. In Boccaccio's synthetic account, Pandora is the name given to the clay man, Boccaccio having misunderstood its significance in the Greek, while the punishment visited on mankind for the theft of divine wisdom is described simply as 'infirmity, sadness and women'. This is not altogether incompatible with Piero's picture, if the figures in the centre are understood rather as generic illustrations of the evils that befall humanity, including unidentified female figures, some of whom appear to languish in sorrow or sickness, while one is courted by a figure resembling a knight. Whatever the specific source, Prometheus is thus shown as creator of the first man and as the bringer of fire, both roles having been assigned to him by Classical writers, some of whom also ascribed to him the transmission of the arts to man.[90] In Piero's image the two stories are fused in the animation of the man of clay by the stolen fire: the fire that Prometheus gives to mankind is thus to be understood, not simply as the natural element, but as the spark of divine wisdom that distinguishes man from lesser creatures, and which is the source of his knowledge of the arts. The physical torture imposed on Prometheus, and the punishment wrought on mankind by means of Pandora, constitute the revenge of the Gods for his theft.

None the less, the precise significance of the myth for both artist and patron remains problematic. Like many myths of the Creation, or of the origin of mankind, including the myth of the Golden Age, that of Prometheus had always been subject to various interpretations, and even in Antiquity views of its significance invariably differed. Prometheus could be seen as a hero, whose theft of the divine spark released mankind from a state of bestial ignorance, and without whom the arts, sciences and technological improvement would have been impossible. In Aeschylus's *Prometheus Bound*, for example, written *c.* 467 BC, men are described as living life to no purpose prior to the intervention of Prometheus, 'nor had they sunny houses made of bricks, nor woodwork, but buried in the ground they lived like little ants in the recesses of sunless caves'.[91] Alternatively, for Cynic writers such as Diogenes, who saw the primitive state as the most happy, the gift of wisdom could be seen as an evil that disrupted a state of innocence and simplicity, and the inevitable corollary of which was suffering and pain.[92] Piero's paintings do not themselves suggest a particular attitude to or interpretation of the myth, although interpreting them is made more difficult by their poor condition, and if they were intended to offer a moral or didactic point, or to be read allegorically, this is certainly not made overt. In a similar way to the Early Man panels, they appear rather as detached recountings or illustrations of different aspects of and incidents in the Prometheus legend. In the first panel, for example, there are suggestions that life before the gift of fire was bestial and primitive, as implied by the tree-climbing simian and, on the right, the figure blindly crawling from a rock. At the same time, the background is full of brick buildings and dwellings of a sophisticated kind, as if civilization was far advanced. In the second panel, however, the focus appears to be on the punishment of mankind, and the evil consequences of Prometheus's action, both in his own suffering, and in the apparent allusions to the punishment in the centre, which provides a pivotal point for mankind's reversal of fortune. In this respect the paintings may, in fact, follow the view of Boccaccio, for whom the celestial fire, while it dispelled ignorance, could do so only at the expense of happiness and peace of mind.[93]

In the absence of any information about the provenance of the panels, their precise significance will probably remain obscure, especially since there are few previous depictions of the myth with which Piero's can be compared. As Panofsky observed, the two works can be connected in a general or 'abstract' way with the *Hunt* and the *Vulcan* series, in that they deal with the advancement of early man, and particularly with the role of fire.[94] The connection between them is probably no more precise, however, and the appearance of the works in Piero's *oeuvre* probably reflects first and foremost his proven expertise in the rendering of themes of this kind.

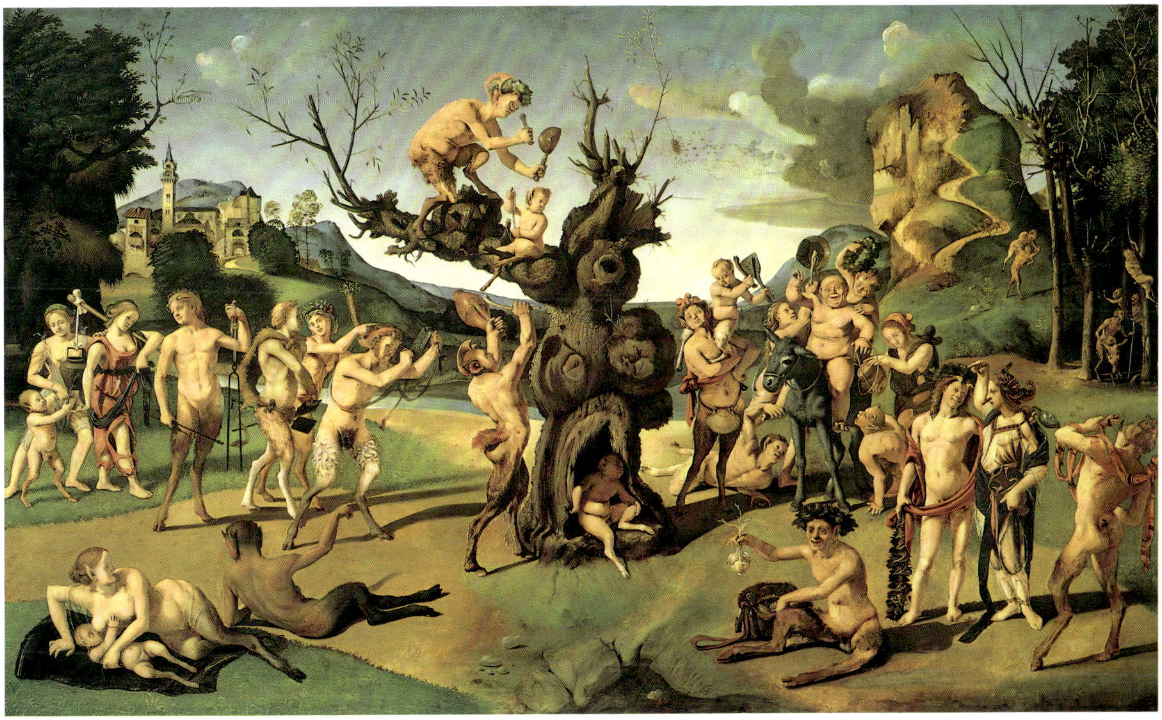

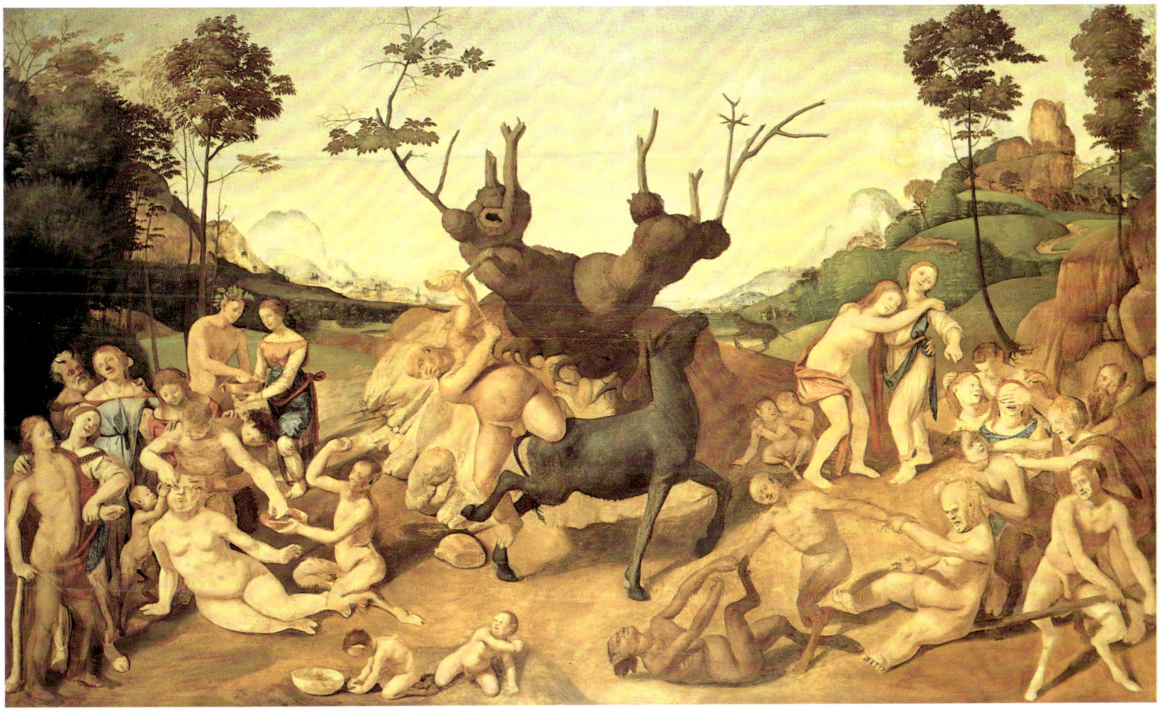

28 *The Discovery of Honey*, *c.*1505–10, oil on panel. Art Museum, Worcester, MA.

29 *The Misfortunes of Silenus*, *c.*1505–10, oil on panel. The Fogg Art Museum, Cambridge, MA.

30 (*Overleaf, left*) Two satyrs in a hollow tree, a detail from *The Discovery of Honey*.

31 (*Overleaf, right*) Satyrs in search of honeycombs, a detail from *The Discovery of Honey*.

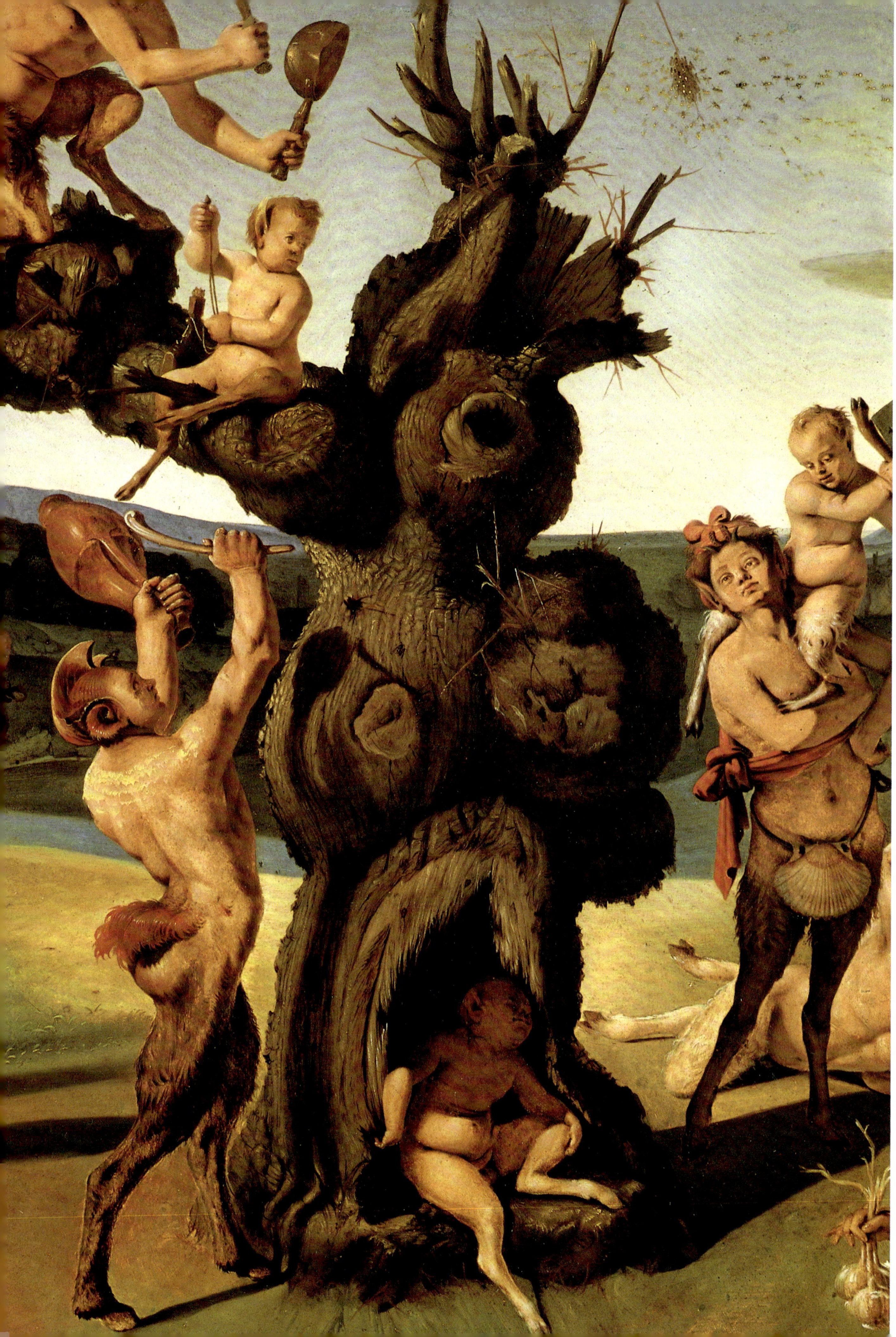

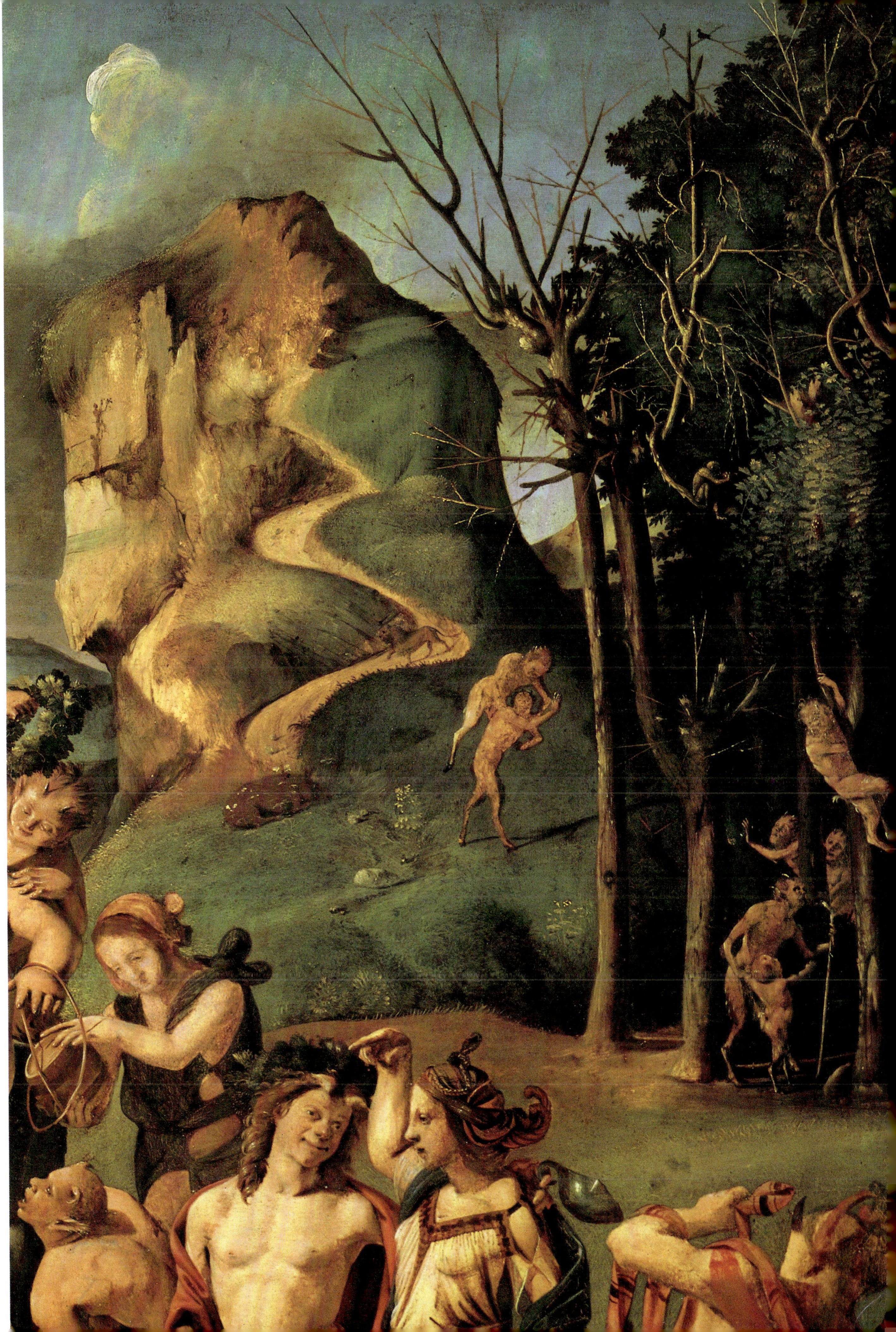

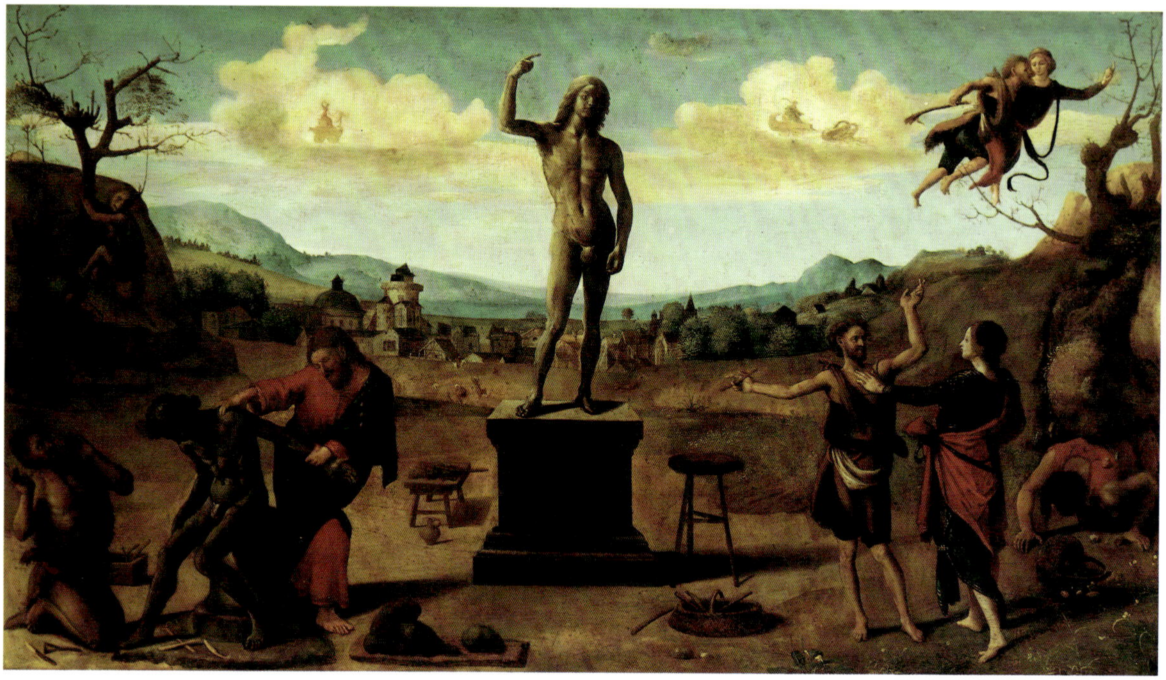

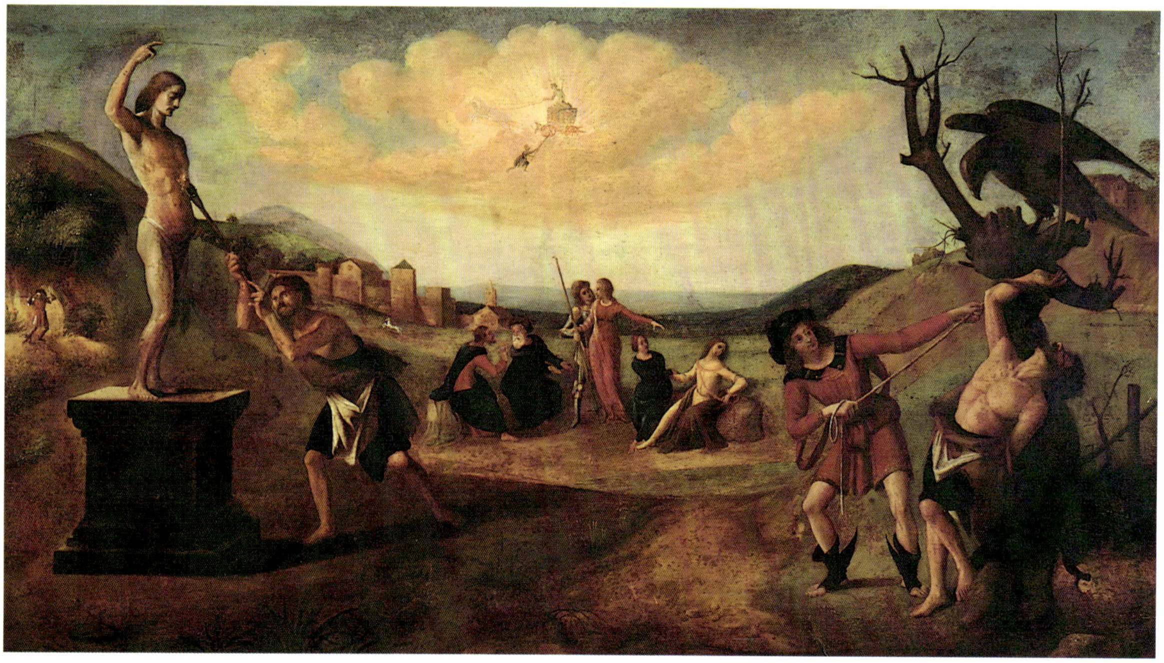

32 'Fashioning the first man', from *Stories of Prometheus*, *c.*1515–20, oil on panel. Alte Pinakothek, Munich.

33 'Stealing fire', from *Stories of Prometheus*, *c.*1515–20, oil on panel. Musée des Beaux-Arts, Strasbourg.

The so-called *Simonetta Vespucci*

In addition to the panels discussed above, which can be identified with some certainty as decorations for *spalliere*, Piero executed a number of secular works that fit less easily into this context. The most important and interesting of these is the so-called *Portrait of Simonetta Vespucci* (illus. 34), executed between 1485 and 1490. Not only has the subject-matter of the painting consistently been a matter of dispute, but the function and original location of the image are also unclear, and to some extent it thus remains problematic.[95] The identification of the woman in the painting with Simonetta Vespucci, the legendary beauty beloved of Giuliano de' Medici (*d.*1476), who was celebrated in Poliziano's *Stanze per la Giostra*, depends almost exclusively on the inscription running along the bottom of the panel. Most scholars have been content to accept the authenticity of the inscription, and have interpreted the other features of the painting accordingly. Thus, the snake winding itself around the sitter's neck has been variously interpreted as a symbol of eternity, of immortality and of the tuberculosis that led to Simonetta's death at the age of 23, while the storm-cloud in the distance has been read as an allusion to her tragic fate, a foreboding of her early death.[96]

The authenticity of the inscription is, however, open to doubt. Recent examinations of the painting suggest that it dates from the late sixteenth century, and while this does not rule out the possibility that the painting is a portrait of Simonetta, it clearly calls into question the truth of this identification, which is also difficult to sustain on other grounds.[97] First, the physiognomy of the woman is relatively generic, and while contemporary writings on Simonetta invariably describe her in terms of ideal beauty of a largely Petrarchan kind, the same facial type appears in a number of Piero's other works of a similar date, such as the '*Innocenti Altarpiece*' (illus. 57) and the *Finding of Vulcan*, and in a drawing by Piero in the Louvre that may be related to the painting (illus. 35).[98] Second, while a snake biting its tail, and thus forming a perfect circle, was an established symbol of eternity, there is no reason to apply this interpretation to the snake in Piero's picture, which appears to be a motif of a rather different order, and arranged largely with an eye to its decorative effect. The symbolic function of the snake depended in large measure on the perfection and completeness of its shape: had Piero intended it to be read in this way he would almost certainly have observed this convention. A circled serpent was also used as a personal emblem by Lorenzo di Pierfrancesco de' Medici, a fact that has been used to support a connection between the picture and the Medici family.[99] Here again, though, while the snake does not bite its tail, it is the rounded form, in which the serpent curves back on itself, that gives the image its significance, so that the same reservations must apply. Similarly, there are no cases in contemporary art where clouds are incontrovertibly used as symbols of death, while the notion that the stormy sky expresses a melancholy mood appropriate to the sitter's fate implies a view of landscape and its function that was largely foreign to fifteenth-century thought.[100]

To interpret the work in this way is also to ignore its evident erotic appeal. Its overt sensuality would have been unthinkable in a work intended as a portrait of a well-bred woman, particularly one who was also renowned for her chastity, even allowing for the fact that, given his age at the time, Piero must have painted it after Simonetta's death.[101] In considering the painting, scholars have consistently overlooked the fact that it openly subverts the conventions of female portraiture, and in its combination of nudity and ornament and the use of a vast open landscape as a background it creates an image that is the very antithesis of all that Simonetta appears to have represented for her contemporaries.[102] The nakedness of the breasts gives the figure an obvious sensuality that is compounded by the elaborate coiffure and the ornate lines of the necklace and the snake. The erotic connotations of elaborate hairstyles are amply demonstrated by contemporary images of women in paintings, prints and ceramics, among them the numerous images of Venus or of the Magdalen, who frequently display complex and ornate coiffures. In Botticelli's *Mars and Venus*, for example, the plaits of the goddess are woven into the fabric of her dress, while in Piero's painting of the same subject, the combination of rich ornament, intricate braids and semi-nudity exerts a similar erotic appeal. In the 'Simonetta', the erotic potential of the motif may have been enhanced by the fact that those who wore their hair bound were generally married women, making the combination of hairstyle and nudity especially piquant, while the addition of rich jewels, which also suggest vanity, further accentuates the sensuality of the image.[103]

It is also significant that, in the fifteenth and sixteenth centuries, where portraits of females include landscapes, these are usually dealt with in very specific ways. For the most part, where the landscape is visible behind the sitter, she herself remains enclosed, often seated on a balcony or at a window, and there are few examples in contemporary Florentine art of female sitters in the midst of open landscapes.[104] While the landscape may serve to create a sense of space behind her immediate domain, the sitter is generally confined within a delimited interior, a pattern that certainly reflects in part the real enclosure of women and the notion that movement outside the home was a threat to their virtue and had to be carefully controlled.[105] The landscapes that appear in such images are also frequently symbolic, almost invariably alluding to the virtues of the sitter, or to her identity and family name. In some cases they resemble the enclosed garden, or *hortus conclusus*, familiar from paintings of the Annunciation, and which alludes to the Virgin's chastity, while the same function may also be fulfilled by individual flowers or trees.[106] Against this background, Piero's image appears particularly provocative, for the sitter is set wholly unconstrained within an extensive landscape, far removed from the enclosed gardens or distant landscapes of conventional female portraiture. Nor does the landscape appear to have any symbolic features, and in its untamed, uncultivated aspect adds to the sense of the sitter as herself free from restraint, and beyond the bounds of decorous female behaviour.

The assumption that the painting was intended as a portrait of Simonetta Vespucci

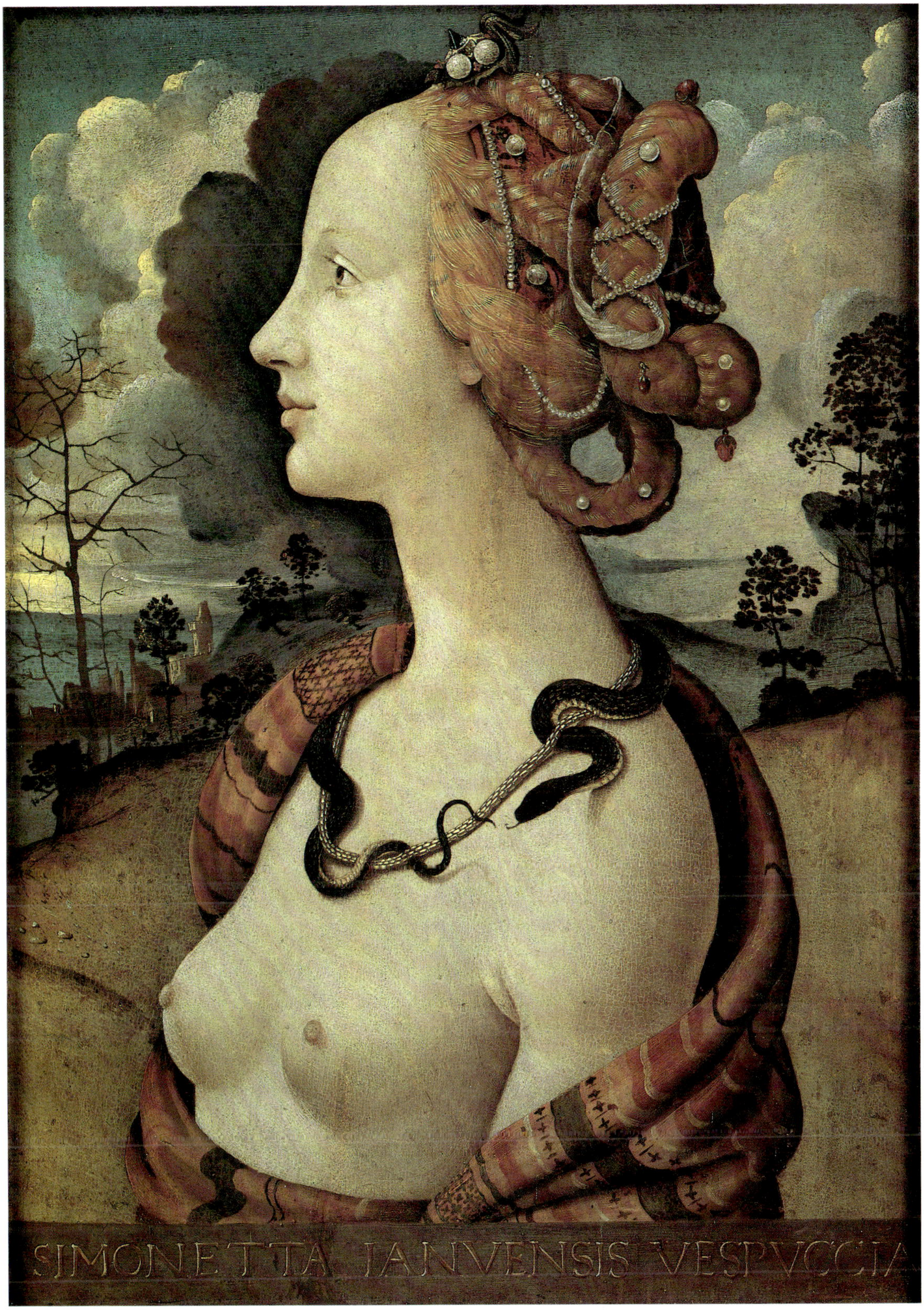

34 *Cleopatra* (the so-called '*Simonetta Vespucci*'), *c.*1485–90, tempera on wood. Musée Condé, Chantilly.

can thus almost certainly be discarded, and it seems more likely that it is the work that Vasari describes in his Life of Piero as 'a very beautiful head of Cleopatra with an asp around her neck', which he saw in the possession of Francesco da Sangallo.[107] Piero's most likely source for an image of Cleopatra was Boccaccio's *On Famous Women*.[108] Like his contemporaries Dante and Petrarch, Boccaccio took a strongly moralizing view of Egypt's queen, presenting her as a prime example of ambition – a woman who came to power by means of vice alone and who was renowned, not for any real achievement, but for her seizure of the throne, her cruelty and greed, and the beauty of her face.[109] Most important, she served as an example of luxury, and of a sensuality that rendered great soldiers powerless – 'splendid in her beauty and capable of ensnaring whoever she desired by the fascination of her sparkling eyes and the seduction of her speech'.[110] Boccaccio also described her as 'the whore of the Kings of the Orient, insatiable in her lust for gold and jewels, [for] not only did she despoil her lovers of such riches, but she also robbed temples and holy places of vases, statues and other treasures'.[111] He also relates the story of her death, which took place in Mark Antony's tomb; opening the veins in her arms and fixing asps to them to hasten the bleeding, she lay down to die beside Mark Antony.

While characteristically inventive in detail, Piero's image is fully in line with Boccaccio's account in concentrating on Cleopatra's sensuality and *luxuria*. The focus is clearly on her seductive appeal, on the beauty of her face and bare torso, and on her love of rich and costly things. Draped in a richly decorated fabric, she wears a gold necklace, while her hair is intertwined with gold and studded with rubies and pearls – the symbol of her love of opulence, but also, perhaps, an allusion to the banquet at which she drank a pearl dissolved in vinegar as proof of her fabulous wealth.[112] The elaborate, Medusa-like hairstyle is an erotic device that is also appropriate to her wealth and royal status, while the snake (which in later representations appears as the cause of her death) serves as an attribute, a means of identification that alludes to her death while allowing Piero to exploit the sensuality of the serpentine form.[113]

The significance of the landscape background and stormy sky are less clear. Although it is fringed by open sea, and includes a crenellated building, the landscape does not obviously allude to Alexandria, nor to any other specific location. The bare terrain and the figure's dominance over it do, however, add to the air of licence and freedom from restraint. It is also impossible to ignore its effectiveness as a foil to Cleopatra herself, accentuating through its plainness and lack of detail the elaborateness of the figure, while the rolling hills echo the roundness of her breasts. The construction of the background may thus have been dictated partly by formal considerations, just as the storm-cloud serves to throw the figure's profile into relief, its convoluted outline repeating those of her face and coiffure. Likewise, the stormy sky constitutes an example of painterly virtuosity, as in Piero's *Madonna and Child* (illus. 37), painted around the same time, and there is no doubt that artists and patrons valued the rendering of atmospheric and meteorological effects as demonstrations of pictorial skill.[114]

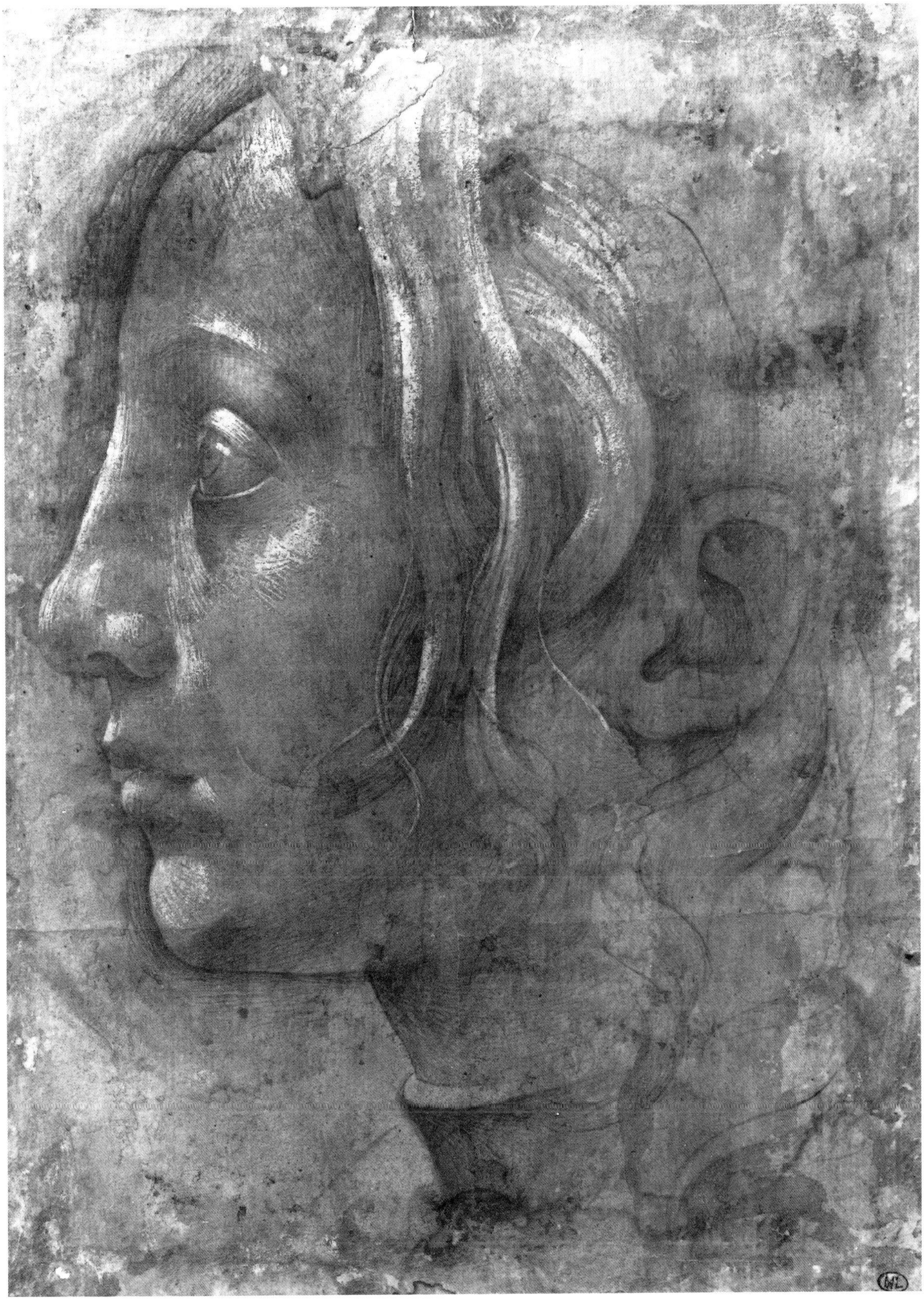

35 *Head of a Youth/Young Woman in Profile to the Left*, pen and ink and wash. Musée du Louvre, Paris.

The question remains as to why the identification of the figure as Cleopatra has proved so difficult for art historians to accept. To some extent this must reflect the fact that fifteenth-century depictions of Cleopatra are relatively rare, and scholars have tended to use sixteenth-century images as the basis for comparison. However, the historical image of Cleopatra underwent a significant transformation during the Renaissance, and while to some extent artists and writers remained ambivalent in their attitudes towards her, in the course of the sixteenth century she came to be seen less as an evil seductress than as a tragic heroine, whose decision to commit suicide rather than face dishonour displayed a certain fortitude and virtue.[115] Accordingly, and perhaps also encouraged by the discovery early in the century of a Roman copy of a Hellenistic statue thought to be that of the dying Cleopatra, artists focused increasingly on her death by the bite of the asp, rather than on her sensuality, although such images, which generally show her full-length and reclining, inevitably retained an element of eroticism.

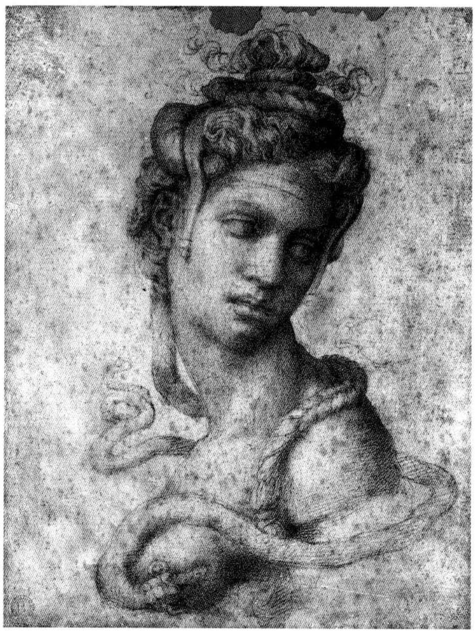

36 Michelangelo, *Cleopatra*, *c.*1534, black chalk. Casa Buonarroti, Florence.

In relation to such images, Piero's half-length figure, wearing her asp as a form of adornment, appears somewhat anachronistic, although it is fully in line with the Late Medieval view of Cleopatra that placed the main emphasis on her dangerous sensuality. In this respect, the most informative comparison is a drawing by Michelangelo that displays the same interest in the erotic potential of the hair and the snake, and in the subtle sensuality of the serpentine form which, as in Piero's painting, pervades every detail of the work (illus. 36).[116] It may also be that we find it hard to associate Piero's snub-nosed sitter with the *femme fatale* either of Classical accounts or

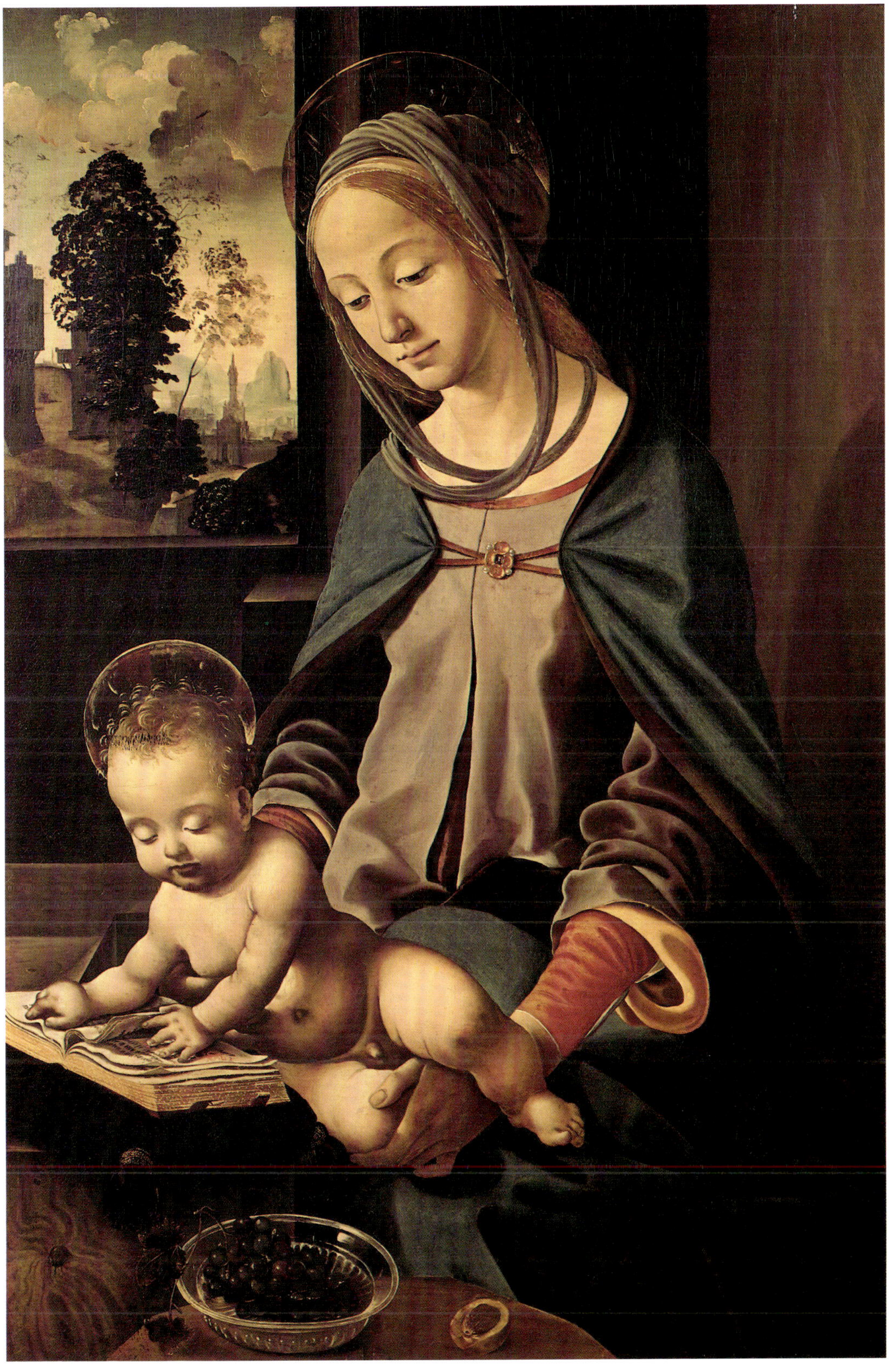

37 *Madonna and Child*, *c.*1485–90, oil on panel. Royal Collection, Stockholm.

of Boccaccio's text, for in terms of facial beauty she is remote both from modern ideas and from the literary and visual images of female beauty that proliferated after the beginning of the sixteenth century. Our knowledge of Renaissance notions of sexuality and sexual attractiveness also remains rudimentary, especially for the Quattrocento, and it is difficult for us to grasp the full significance of devices such as the elaborate coiffure or the averted gaze, which, to the modern eye, appears to repel rather than invite attention. For the contemporary viewer, however, the significance of the profile view was almost certainly different and more complex, and its attraction may have lain in its ability to make the sitter available for contemplation while rendering her unable to engage the viewer's gaze.[117] Similarly, the combination of a seemingly 'natural' landscape with an adorned or decorated figure almost inevitably had resonances that are difficult for us to detect.

That is not to say that such devices were unambiguous, and their precise significance, and the way in which they were perceived, would have depended as much on the viewer as on the artist. They must also have depended on the function and location of the painting, of which nothing specific is known. Its small size might suggest that it was destined for a bedroom or *anticamera* rather than for the larger and more public spaces of a private residence, although its shape makes it less likely to have been designed for a *spalliera*. It may thus have functioned as an image of, and warning against, the vice of *luxuria*, and it is possible that it was intended to have a companion piece illustrating an aspect of female virtue. Contrasting companion prints of Cleopatra and Lucretia were quite common, the latter being an example of chastity and piety, while cycles of famous men and women sometimes juxtaposed Cleopatra with biblical heroines such as Judith.[118] Vasari, though, makes no mention of a companion piece by Piero, and single images of Cleopatra are recorded in contemporary collections.[119] Whether used as a moral warning, or simply as a decorative motif, the figure of Cleopatra had obvious visual appeal, and even where such images were used with a moral intent, they are inevitably erotic in nature. Indeed, it could be said that the very effectiveness of such images as forms of moral instruction depended precisely on their ability to convince and persuade. The devices employed in them might thus serve simultaneously to invite and repel the attention of the viewer, an ambivalence that was recognized by a number of contemporary writers.[120]

Piero's secular works thus include both conventional and less conventional subjects, and if the second group outnumbers the first, this should not be seen as a reflection of his personal preferences or 'bizarre' character, an interpretation that would ascribe to the artist an unprecedented degree of freedom in his choice of themes. Rather, it reflects his ability to visualize unusual subjects in a convincing way, and to formulate interesting compositions for themes that had no tradition of pictorial representation, as well as his ability to produce pleasing and original landscapes. Nor should Piero's treatment of his subjects be seen in terms of a personal sympathy for or identification with the notion of early man, for his depiction of primitive life was by no means always idealistic or nostalgic, and his works are marked less by a consistent personal view than by a scrupulous attention to the texts from which he worked. This is not to deny the originality of Piero's works, but to suggest that their originality resides more in the use of gesture, and in Piero's approach to composition, than in his treatment of his subject-matter, although these are inevitably connected. It is also these aspects of his work, rather than their iconography, that conditioned Vasari's perception of Piero's paintings, as revealed in his choice of descriptive terms.

Composition and the Use of Gesture: Vasari's Response to Piero

I have suggested that Piero's approach to gesture is unusually understated, and that he treats the narratives of his paintings in an unrhetorical way, emphasizing the quieter, more reflective emotions inherent in a text and avoiding the overtly didactic and expressive gestures favoured by most of his contemporaries. This means that the moral or didactic point of his works is rarely made explicit, and their precise significance often appears elusive, a characteristic accentuated by his compositional technique.

Generally speaking, and in line with the theories of Alberti, Florentine painters working at the same time as Piero made the figures the focus and dominant feature of their works, giving them clear priority over their surroundings or background setting.[121] It was the arrangement of the figures themselves, and their relationship to one another, that determined the structure of the painting, as well as its emotional or dramatic tone. While the setting might function as a means of establishing or reinforcing the figures' locations in space, and also their narrative role, it generally played only a subsidiary part. In Piero's works, however, figures and background command equal attention, and neither clearly dominates; thus, not only do his works often lack a clear focus of attention or obvious resting point for the eye, but the gestures of the figures are subsumed within the larger whole. To some extent this is a product of Piero's extensive use of landscape, and his avoidance of the perspectival settings favoured by contemporary artists in the production of *spalliera* panels.[122] Perspective views had always been favoured as subjects for interior decoration.[123] Not only were they valued as examples of artistic virtuosity but, like perspective backgrounds, they acted as a means of opening up the enclosed spaces of the interior, creating the illusion of miniature windows within the panelling of the *spalliera*. At the same time, as in large-scale images, perspective offered artists a means of ordering the space in their works and controlling the placement of their figures. It could also help to establish narrative clarity and create a clear compositional and dramatic focus, as in Botticelli's *Nastagio degli Onesti* panels, where key events in the narrative are placed at the points where the perspective appears to converge (illus. 10 and 11). In this instance, the use of a strictly controlled geometric setting also allowed the artist to stress the actions of the figures, whose pliant gestures stand out against and contrast with the rigid lines of the background.

Landscape backgrounds were less amenable to the application of linear perspec-

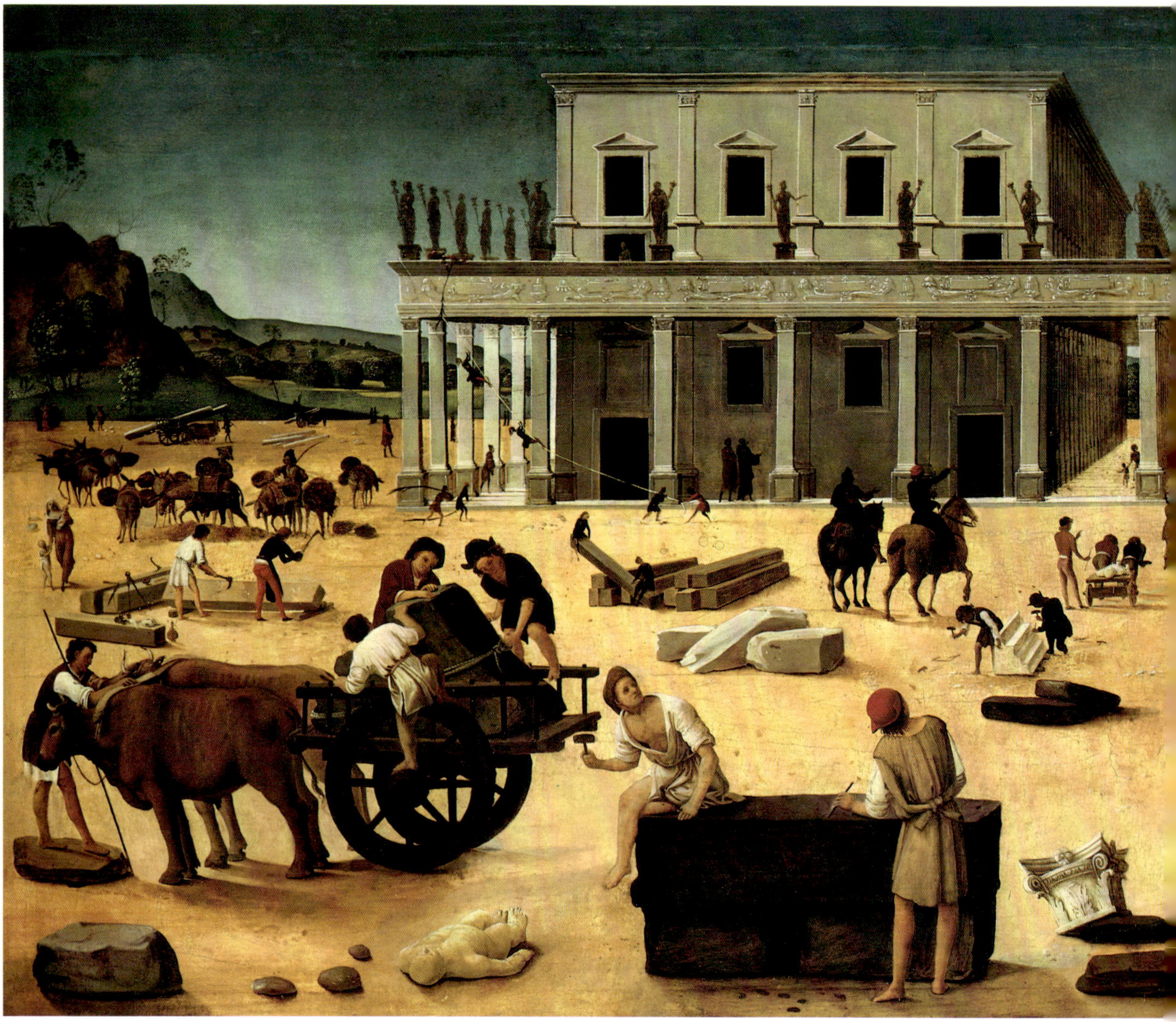

38 *Construction of a Building*, *c.*1515–20, oil on panel. The John and Mable Ringling Museum of Art, Sarasota, FL.

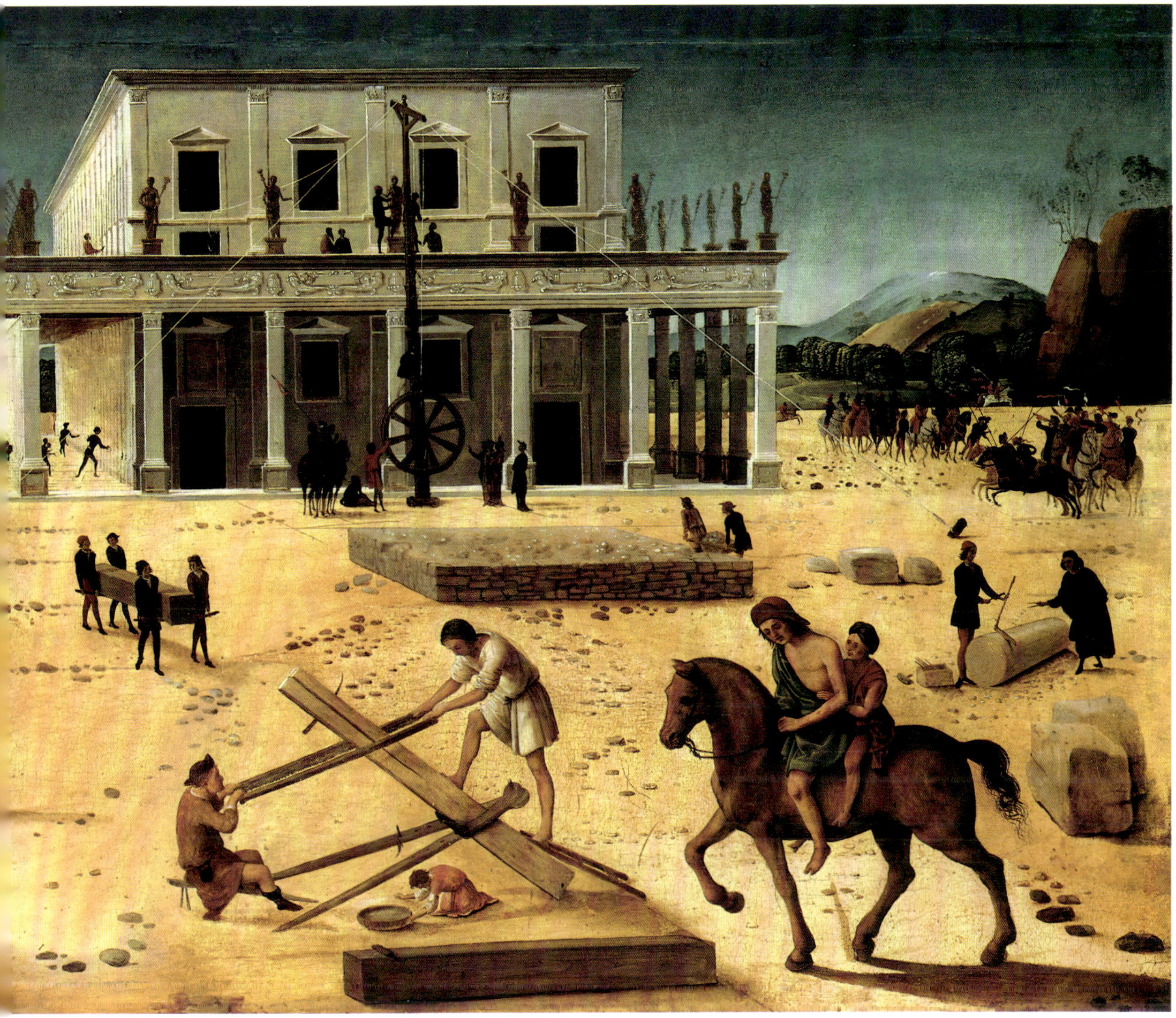

tive, and this is certainly one reason for the relative scarcity of extensive landscape settings in contemporary Florentine art.[124] Not only were the irregular shapes of nature less susceptible to geometrical organization but, if painted in any detail, landscapes could easily compete with or overshadow the figures. Thus, despite the fact that Classical and contemporary writers offered ample justification for the idea that landscape was a legitimate subject for the exercise of the artist's skill, and especially suitable for domestic decoration, landscapes such as Piero's are rare in either large- or small-scale works. Artists who made use of landscape settings often overcame the problems they posed by painting the landscape in broad and generalized terms, or by reducing the forms of nature to artificially regular shapes, imposing on them a strict perspective scheme, as for example Uccello did in his *Hunt in the Forest* (illus. 39), also painted for a *spalliera*, and in his larger *Rout of San Romano* (illus. 40), and Botticelli in the *Nastagio degli Onesti* panels.[125] In each of these works the landscape also retains its status as background, acting as a foil to the animated and brightly coloured figures.

Piero's interest in the reality of landscape and his obsession with the fine details of nature would hardly have allowed him to employ such solutions, and he generally used a different approach, in which the landscape itself establishes the structure of the composition, and the painting is built around shapes apparently inherent in nature. That is not to say that he was unaware of the landscape compositions of other artists, for the *Hunt* panels, *The Forest Fire* and the *Battle of the Lapiths and Centaurs* all show the influence of Uccello's method of imposing on nature the equivalent of a perspectival scheme.[126] In *The Hunt*, for example, the painting is dominated by, and arranged around, the mass of the burning forest. Diagonal clearings running along each side serve to indicate recession into depth, their function emphasized by the foreshortened corpse and discarded club aligned along them in a manner clearly reminiscent of Uccello's *Hunt* and *Rout of San Romano*. Similarly, in the *Return from the Hunt*, Piero uses a conventional device, exploiting the natural shape of a river valley to create the equivalent of a perspective setting, focusing attention on the women embracing in the boat, while depth is suggested by the foreshortened groups of figures to the left and right, placed at an angle to the picture plane.

Yet Piero uses these devices with a subtlety quite foreign to Uccello, and preserves the apparent integrity of the landscape by maintaining a basic asymmetry in the composition. In *The Hunt*, the clearings in the forest do not divide the space into equal parts, while the picture surface is also divided asymmetrically by the two, startlingly real, tree-trunks in the foreground, whose split bark and broken branches project out towards the spectator. Placed to one side of the centre of the panel, and yet commanding attention by their prominence and apparent solidity, these appear less as a means of ordering the composition than as objects around which the viewer must look into the cluttered space of the forest beyond, where separate groups of figures are threaded through the trees in an apparently arbitrary way. Piero thus establishes order in the painting without it appearing deliberately composed, maintaining the seeming

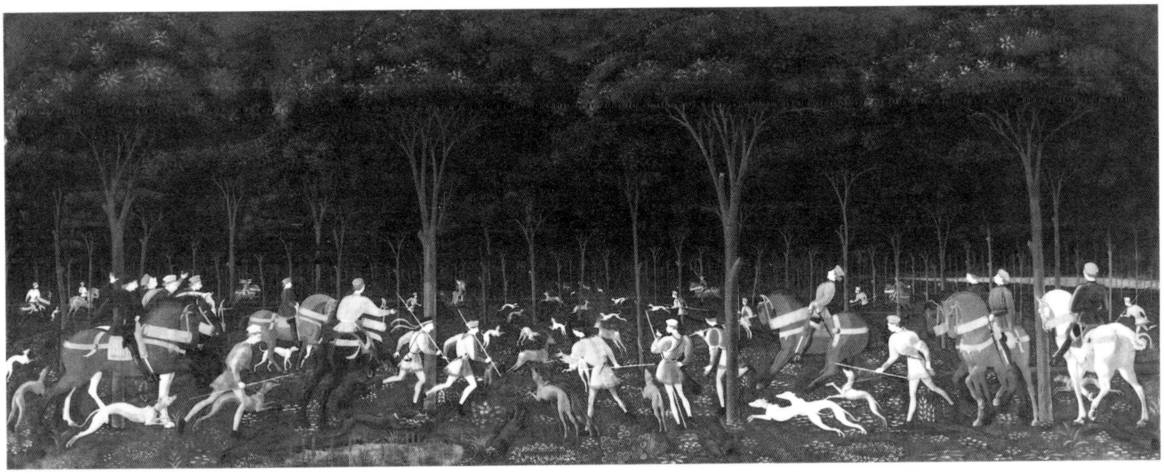

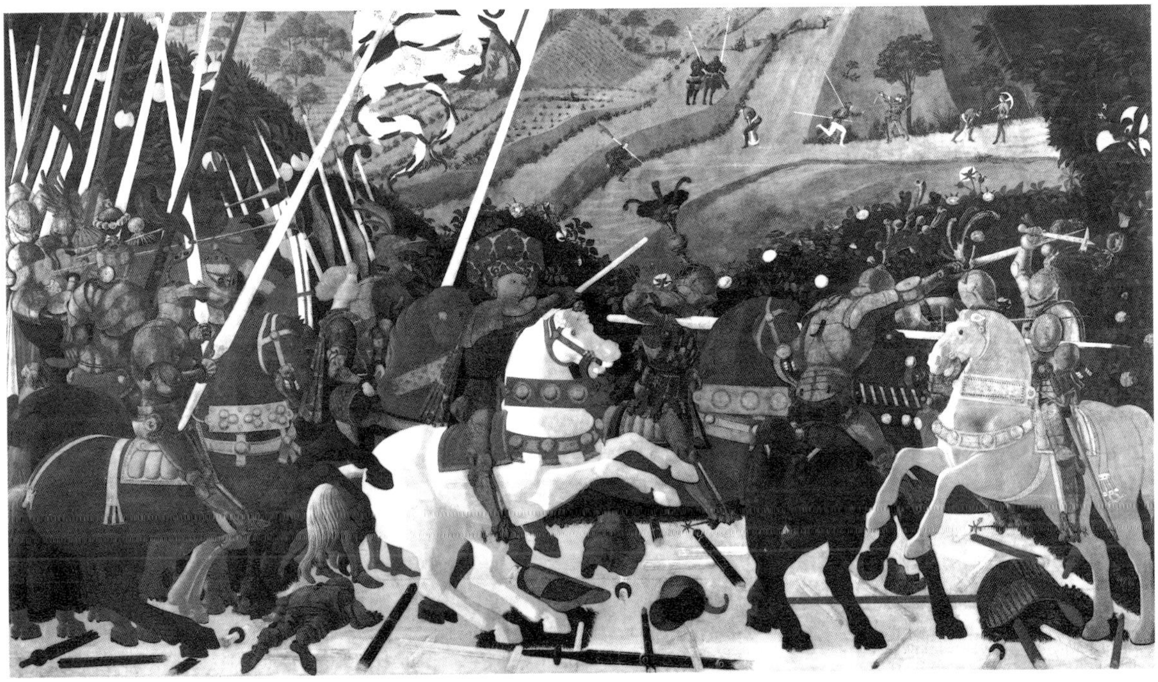

39 Paolo Uccello, *The Hunt in the Forest*, 1460s, tempera with oil glazes on panel. Ashmolean Museum, Oxford.

40 Paolo Uccello, *Rout of San Romano*, early 1450s, panel. National Gallery, London.

naturalness of the landscape while also adding to the painting's air of detached observation or reportage.

In the *Battle of the Lapiths and Centaurs*, it is the rocky mass in the centre that provides the basic compositional structure, enclosing and providing the backdrop for the superimposed motifs of the disrupted banquet, and the dying Cyllarus in the foreground. Marginal vistas to the sea suggest recession and frame the groups of figures. In each case, however, the placement of figures within the whole is underlined by a corresponding landscape motif, such as a tree or an overhanging cliff, or a pair of bushes, so that figures and landscape work together to create an order that is felt, but which is never overt. In Piero's works, it is the landscape itself rather than an imposed geometric framework that appears to determine the structure of the composition. Furthermore, while for Uccello landscape acts primarily as a background and a foil for the actions of the figures, for Piero neither appears to dominate, the two existing in a reciprocal relationship more familiar from the work of Venetian artists such as Giorgione and Titian, or from the landscape compositions of Mantegna. The example of Mantegna is particularly instructive here, for his use of landscape exercised a decisive influence on later artists, and there are clear parallels between a work such as his *Agony in the Garden* (illus. 41) and Piero's *Death of Procris*. The landscape in each of these paintings encloses the figures and serves to underline their positions in space. The shapes of each landscape also echo those of the figures and their gestures, accentuating and clarifying their significance. The relationship between figures and landscape is thus mutually reinforcing in a manner that is both compositionally effective and integral to the narrative and emotional effect. However, while there are clearly parallels between the two artists' works, in paintings such as *The Discovery of Honey* and the *Liberation of Andromeda* Piero develops this approach to landscape to a point of sophistication and abstractness that is quite different from anything by Mantegna, or by contemporary Venetian artists.

In *The Discovery of Honey* (illus. 28), the focus of the painting, in both narrative and compositional terms, is the tree in the centre, in which the bees make their swarm. Silhouetted against the radiant sky, and framed by a river valley whose banks follow exactly the lines of its branches, the tree sets up a vocabulary of shapes that runs insistently through every element of the painting. The lines of its branches, and the knots and whorls of its anthropomorphic trunk, find echoes in every detail of the composition, from the winding path of the mountain on the right and the spiralling clouds above it to the rhythmic flow of the figures' upraised arms and the coils and loops of their garments. The painting is held together by a network of curves and spirals that appears to originate in the forms of the landscape, and which operates on the surface rather than in depth, binding figures and setting together in a complex visual pattern.

In the *Liberation of Andromeda* (illus. 43), Piero develops this device further, so that figures and landscape appear to merge into one. On the left, Andromeda pulls away from a tree that appears to move with her, leaning over to grasp her in a woody

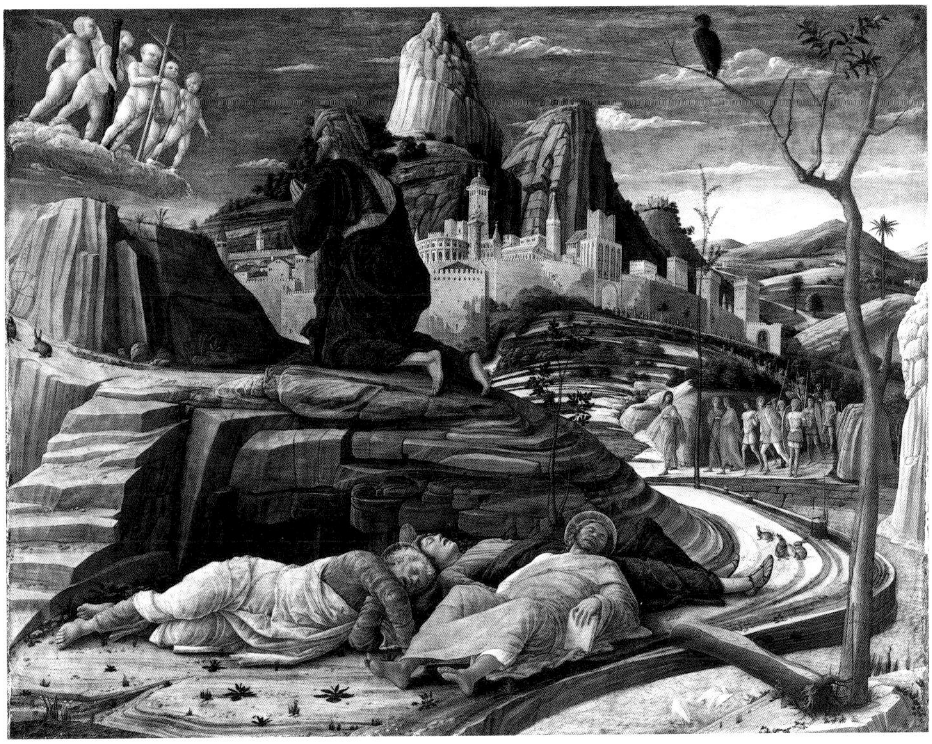

41 Andrea Mantegna, *The Agony in the Garden*, (?)mid-1450s, oil on wood. National Gallery, London.

embrace, while on the other side it turns to the monster a grotesquely human face. The curves they create are insistently repeated in the movements of the sorrowing figures below, and in the menacing shape, half cloud, half mountain, that looms over the scene on the right, while the clothes of the grieving women follow the rippling and swirling waves and the shells on the shore. In the right foreground, figures rejoice with gestures that echo the jaunty spiral of the monster's tail, the serpentine form of Perseus himself and the fluttering scarf, while musicians play instruments which could almost have been fashioned from the twisted branches of the tree-trunk. Figures and landscape are assimilated to each other in such a way that the landscape takes on quasi-human characteristics, while the figures assume the organic qualities of the natural world. In this way not only do the figures not take priority over the landscape, their dramatic gestures blend into and become part of their surroundings, rather than standing out against them, while both are rendered with equal attention to detail.

In terms of composition, Piero's works are thus relatively remote from those of contemporary artists, and also from the theory of composition put forward by Alberti, which influenced Vasari, among others, when writing the *Lives*. Alberti's theory of composition centres almost exclusively on the arrangement of the bodies within the narrative *istoria*, and on their formal and dramatic relationship to one another. Indeed, it is significant in this respect that his use of the term *compositio* is largely confined to the ordering of figures and takes little account of their relationship to their setting.

While he discusses the use of perspective at some length, and the relationship between figures and setting must have been a matter of concern, Alberti does not consider in detail this aspect of the artist's work, and it has less importance within his theory of art than the disposition of figures. Vasari himself does not advance a theory of composition, and it has been suggested that he had little interest in this aspect of a work of art.[127] Yet the influence of Alberti's ideas is clearly apparent in the *Lives* – in the accounts of individual works, which focus first and foremost on the dramatic interaction of figures, and in Vasari's response to the works of Raphael, whom he identifies as the master of dramatic narrative.[128] His interest in Albertian ideas is also apparent in his use of the word 'invention' (*invenzione*), which, like 'design', is one of his most important critical terms. Like most of the terms in the *Lives*, 'invention' has a number of interrelated meanings. Its most significant, however, is that which Vasari gives it in the Technical Prefaces:

> invention . . . groups figures in fours, sixes, tens, and twenties, in such a manner as to represent battles and other great subjects of art. This invention demands an innate propriety springing out of harmony and obedience; thus if a figure move to greet another, the figure saluted, having to respond, should not turn away.[129]

For Vasari, as for Alberti, it is the dramatic arrangement and co-ordination of figures and their movements that constitute the basis of a good composition. It is thus wholly logical that Vasari should praise Raphael as the master of invention, upholding his genius for narrative composition as an achievement almost equal in importance to Michelangelo's skill in design. In the Life of Piero, however, 'invention' is conspicuously not used in this way, nor does Vasari allude to the compositional aspect of the artist's work: 'invention' is used to refer to those aspects or features of Piero's work that are perceived as original motifs and which enlarge the possibilities of art in other, less fundamental ways, such as his designs for triumphs or his paintings of exotic animals, made to impress the observer by their novelty and charm. Accordingly, it is often combined with terms such as 'bizarre' or 'capricious', which also imply originality and whim, and which emphasize the distinctive nature of the artist's imagination rather than his effective deployment of figures.[130]

Neither Piero's figures nor his compositional technique appears deserving of comment in the Life of Piero, and it seems likely that the artist's approach to both aspects of his work conflicted with Vasari's notion of good painting. The frequent lack of dramatic focus in Piero's works, and the relatively unobtrusive nature of his figures almost certainly ran contrary to the emphasis Vasari placed on the *istoria*, and to his belief in the primacy of the human form. Conversely, Vasari was ill-equipped either to appreciate or to describe the zoomorphic nature of Piero's compositions, his use of landscape as an expressive tool, or the subtle combinations of figures and landscape that, to the modern viewer, lend the paintings much of their interest and charm. But concerns such as these were not necessarily shared by Piero's patrons, and while Piero's approach to composition may have fallen short of Vasari's critical ideals, it was ideally suited to the function and physical setting of the *spalliera* panel, and to its relatively small scale. The delicate interweaving of figures and landscape, the constant play of lively, organic forms, collectively give his works an immense visual richness, enhanced by their striking colouristic effects, and the complex play of light and shade unifies the whole. They thus have a strongly decorative quality and an intricate surface pattern that must have been particularly effective as a foil to the *spalliera*, enlivening its expanses of plain wood and contrasting with their own geometric frames. Arranged at eye-level around the room, probably between fluted pilasters, works such as *The Discovery of Honey* and *The Misfortunes of Silenus* broke up the solid surfaces of panelling or wall with their sequence of spirals and curves, while offering the delights of a distant view, and glimpses of a radiant sky.[131]

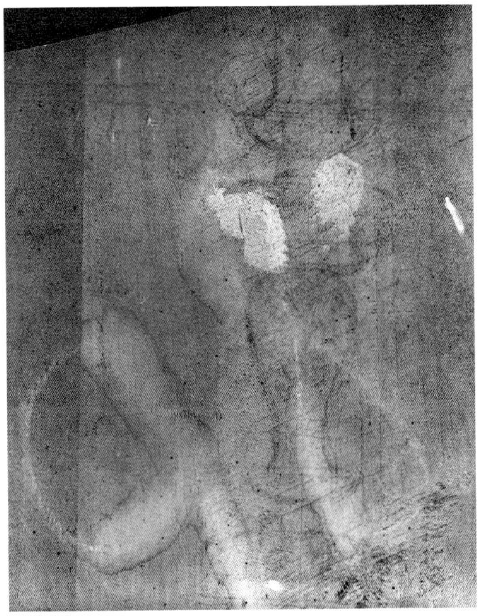

42 Drawing on unprimed wood from reverse of *The Death of Procris* (illus. 6), perhaps for a decorative pilaster of a frame.

The design of Piero's panels is also well-adapted to being seen at close quarters, especially within the relatively small and intimate spaces of the *camera* or *anticamera* where such works were usually to be found.[132] The absence of a single dramatic or compositional focus encourages close and sustained viewing, for rather than being directed to a specific point, the eye scans the picture piece by piece, affording equal attention to each and tracing the details in a less than systematic way. Since Piero painted all his figures and landscapes with the same microscopic attention to detail, each object invites the same minute scrutiny. It is this rendering of detail that is Piero's greatest strength, and which must have constituted a large part of his appeal for contemporary patrons, giving the works both a decorative quality and a high degree of visual interest. It is these qualities, furthermore, that are signalled by Vasari's use of the term *fantasia*, which, together with 'bizarre' and 'capricious', is the most important that Vasari uses in the Life.

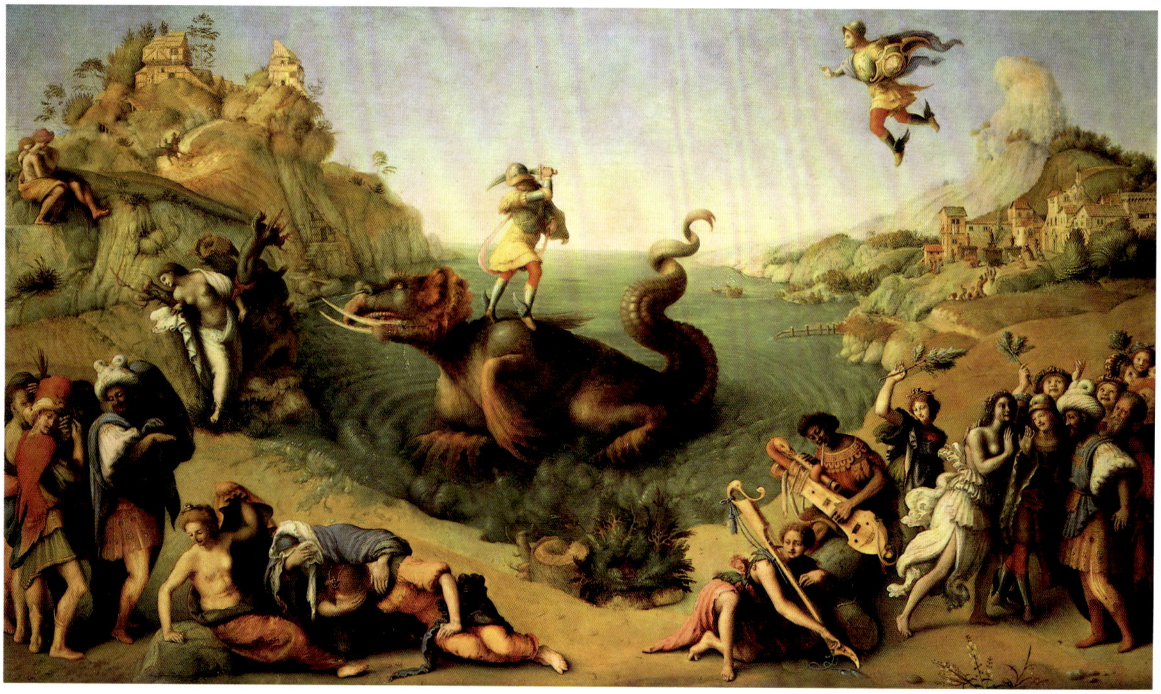

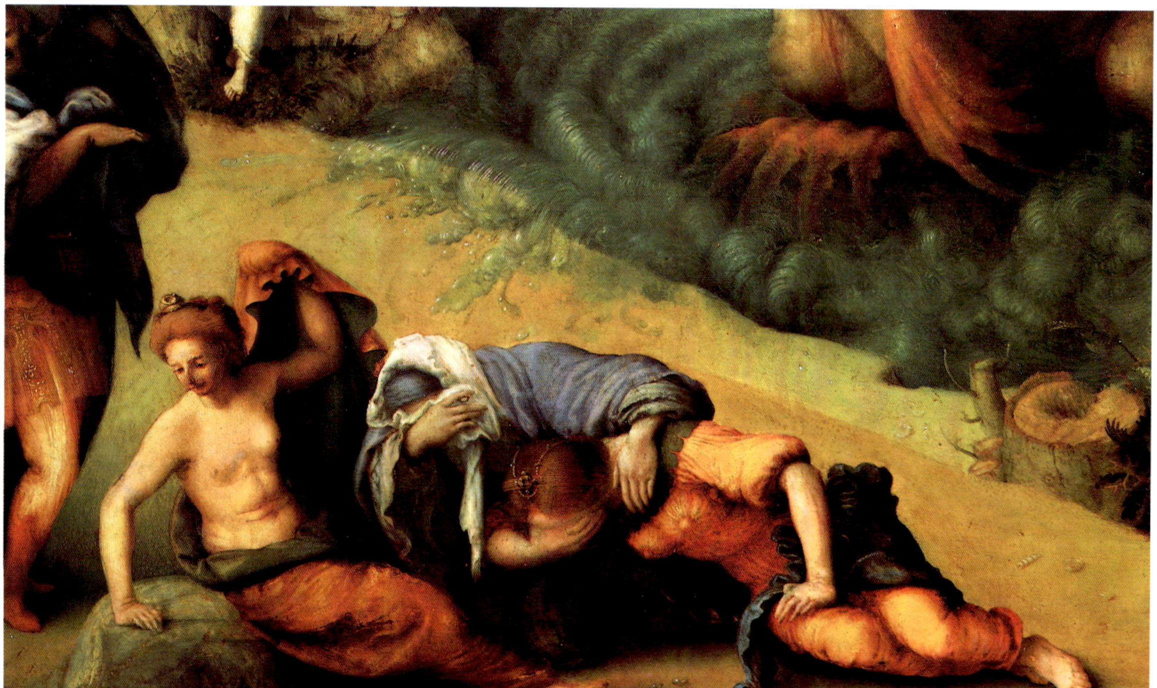

43 *The Liberation of Andromeda*, *c.*1515, oil on panel. Uffizi, Florence.

44 Andromeda's grieving family, a detail from *The Liberation of Andromeda*.

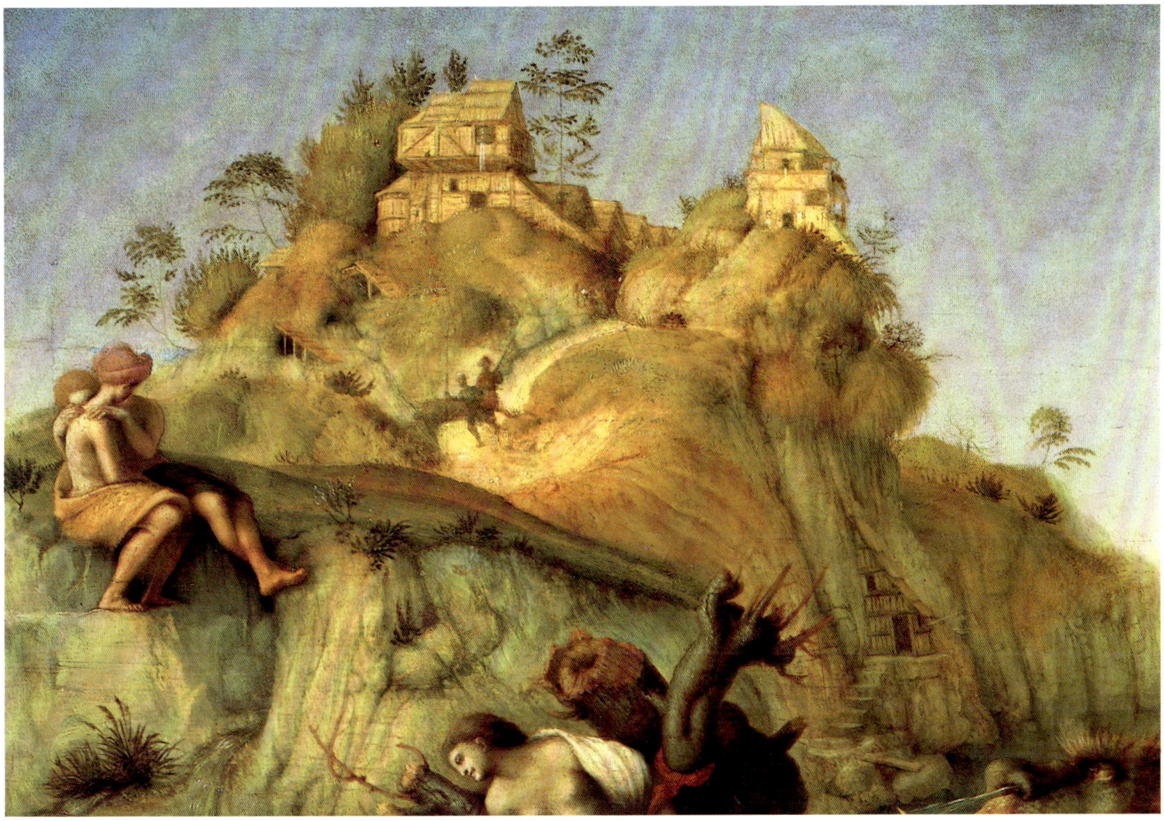

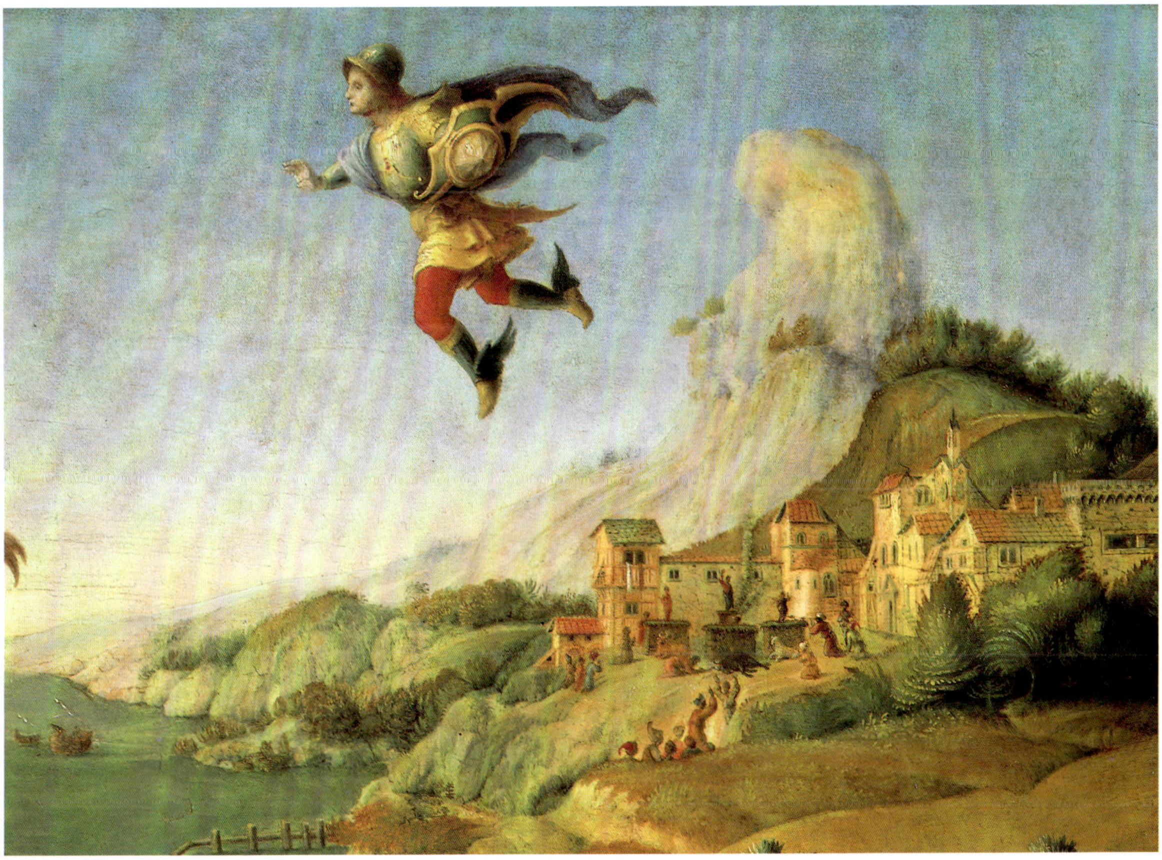

45 Landscape detail from *The Liberation of Andromeda*.

46 Perseus, and a landscape detail from *The Liberation of Andromeda*.

The Critical Terminology of Vasari's Life: the Fantastic and the Bizarre

As I explained in chapter One, Vasari's use of *fantasìa* is in line with, and derives much of its significance from, traditional faculty psychology. In this context *fantasìa* denoted a faculty of the mind, located between the senses and the intellect, the function of which was to produce mental images of the objects of sensory experience as the material for intellectual activity. It could also produce images of objects that do not actually exist, such as centaurs or flying men, based on a combination of objects and qualities observed in the natural world. While the location of *fantasìa* in the mind meant that it lacked the ability to abstract from particular images, and was tied to the individual objects of experience, its proximity to sight was thought to give a particular vividness and clarity to the images it produced, lending an apparent verisimilitude even to things we do not actually know.

Vasari's use of the term is consistent with this understanding of *fantasìa*. This is apparent, first, in the range and type of objects to which it is applied in the *Lives*. Rarely used in relation to the human figure, or to the overall composition of a work, it is used rather of its ornamental or decorative aspects, and applied to objects which thus partake of the particular rather than the general or abstract. Consequently, it is used with particular frequency of composite objects and images such as *grotteschi* or *spoglie*, which combined actual forms in unusual or amusing ways, or of hybrid creatures such as satyrs. *Fantasìa* denotes first and foremost the artist's ability to imagine such objects – often called *fantasìe* – in a vivid and convincing way.

Throughout the Life of Piero, Vasari emphasizes the extent and the quality of the artist's *fantasìa*, and with particular reference to objects of this kind. In his account of Piero's triumphal entries, for example, he mentions a 'chariot . . . full of ornaments and trophies and the most bizarre fantasies', while his painting of a sea-monster, given to Giuliano de' Medici, is described, 'by virtue of its deformity', as

> so extravagant, fantastic and bizarre, that it seems impossible that nature herself could produce such strangeness and such deformity in her works.[133]

Of the panels painted for Francesco del Pugliese, Vasari confessed that

> nor can one possibly describe the diversity of fantastic things which he delighted in painting in all these works, the buildings and animals, garments and different instruments, and other *fantasie*.[134]

Although Vasari does not use the term specifically in relation to *The Discovery of Honey* or *The Misfortunes of Silenus*, his account of them makes use of associated terms, such as 'variety', while the emphasis he places on the satyrs and wood-nymphs makes clear that they belong in the same critical context as products of the artist's *fantasìa*:

> He painted for Giovanni Vespucci . . . some bacchanals . . . in which he painted such strange fauns, nymphs and satyrs, and putti and bacchantes, that it is marvellous to behold the diversity of their garments and their implements, and the variety of goatlike forms, rendered with grace and in the most realistic manner.[135]

Piero's *fantasìa* is thus manifest in his ability to paint creatures such as the saytrs and centaurs of *The Hunt* and *The Discovery of Honey*, in the rich and unusual ornaments, instruments and strange garments of the *Liberation of Andromeda*, and the spoils, trophies and other ornaments that enrich his triumphs.

It is not simply a question of Piero's ability to imagine such forms or construct them in his mind, but his ability to represent them in a vivid and convincing way, and to lend them the particularity and concreteness that convinces us they actually exist. For Vasari, *fantasìa* also implies the ability to make the imaginary real, and to naturalize the improbable in a way that extends the limits of the viewer's own belief. That which, in psychological theory, is a natural attribute of the products of *fantasìa*, is here a particular achievement of the painter. This aspect of Piero's *fantasìa* is perhaps most evident in *The Discovery of Honey*, where the strangest and most improbable satyrs are endowed with the same reality and concreteness as the natural forms of the landscape (illus. 30 and 31). This is partly because they are themselves comprised of objects or parts of objects familiar from our experience, or which evoke vague reminiscences of things actually seen. In the satyr at the foot of the tree, for example, the legs of a goat are combined with a brightly coloured tail resembling that of an ostrich, or other exotic bird, while the head and ears appear to be composed of a mixture of horns and shells. At the same time, the satyr presents to the viewer an intensely human back and arms, but here decorated with a delicate frill of feathers running between the shoulders in parallel bands. To the right of the tree another satyr sports a loincloth made of a large shell above his shaggy thighs, while his hair and torso are adorned with conventional drapery and bows.

Piero renders these inventions credible by according each part of them the same detailed scrutiny, and by the care with which they are combined. In the satyr on the left, for example, he carefully juxtaposes the rough hair of the legs with the downy texture of the tail, which blends imperceptibly into the gleaming musculature of the back. These imaginative inventions are also painted with the same microscopic attention as the more conventional forms, whether the gnarled form of the tree, or the fully human maenads with which they intermingle. All are painted with equal scrupulosity and the same realistic technique, which makes their physical existence appear indisputable, just as they are bathed in the same crisp, almost hallucinatory, light, while the act of combining of the familiar and the exotic makes the latter easier to accept by apparently 'normalizing' its presence. Thus, while in terms of their content, so to speak, and their combination of forms, the figures stretch the bounds of credibility, Piero's technique gives them a degree of reality that makes their existence an irrefutable fact – a point signalled in Vasari's comment that the satyrs are here painted with an *imitazione verissima*.

In the *Hunt* panels and the *Battle of the Lapiths and Centaurs*, the same mixture of the familiar and the strange, and the same dispassionate and impartial rendering of detail, compels us to accept the existence of the centaurs and satyrs as fully as that of the naturalistic landscape. In the *Battle* the fabulous forms of the centaurs and the unusual details, such as the zoomorphic jug in the centre, are naturalized and made credible by their juxtaposition with more familiar objects, painted with remarkable realism, such as the richly patterned table-cloth in the centre, or the scattered shells and the basket of flowers in the foreground. It is this tension between fantasy and verisimilitude, and the incongruity it creates, that make Piero's works so compelling. This is particularly clear in details such as the figure of Hylonome in the *Battle* (illus. 13), whose animal face and grotesque ears are adorned with flowers and a conventional, ornate coiffure and whose body is draped in an elegant garment of skins. Her form renews in the observer a sense of wonder at the painter's own performance, at his adroitness in reconciling without strain the extremes of the imaginary and the real.

It is thus significant that in Vasari's accounts of Piero's work, the author associates the products of *fantasìa* with the experience by the observer of astonishment and awe, and that the diligence and realism of Piero's painting technique are stressed. The woodland creatures of *The Discovery of Honey* are said to engender wonder by their diversity, while Vasari states that it would be impossible to describe the wealth of *fantasie* included in the stories for Francesco del Pugliese. Likewise, the sea-monster painted for Giuliano de' Medici is said to be so convincing in its strangeness that it surpasses nature herself, and its effect is *stravagante*. Vasari also links *fantasìa* with the production of variety, and with the ornamentation or embellishment of the work of art, and this is quite consistent with the effect of Piero's works. As we have seen, his paintings are striking in their richness and seemingly inexhaustible detail, engaging the spectator not by a unified dramatic effect, but by leading the eye through a wealth of minutely observed objects, making us wonder at the fecundity of his imagination and the skill of his hand.

If *fantasìa* is that which enables the artist to produce such objects, the objects themselves are often described as 'bizarre', a term Vasari uses repeatedly in Piero's Life. In his account of the triumphs and processions designed by Piero in Florence, for example, Vasari notes that the chariots were 'full of decorative objects, and booty and the most bizarre fantasies', using the term particularly in relation to the Antique trophies and classicizing details with which Piero embellished these inventions.[136] 'Bizarre' is also used in this way in Vasari's Life of Filippino Lippi, a contemporary of Piero, where it appears with particular frequency. Describing Filippino's frescoes in the Strozzi Chapel in S. Maria Novella, Florence, Vasari makes the connotations of the term quite clear, noting that the Chapel

> astonishes everyone who sees it on account of the novelty and variety of the bizarre things (*bizzarrie*) that there are in it: armed men, temples, vases, helmet-crests, armour, trophies, spears, banners, costumes, stockings, headdresses, priestly garments, and other objects, executed in such a beautiful manner, that the whole deserves the greatest praise . . . [;] apart from this there are in it many *grottesche*, and other things painted in *chiaroscuro* so as to look like marble, and done in a strange manner (*stranamente*), with invention and the most beautiful design.[137]

Here too, 'bizarre' is used to describe inventive objects *all'antica* that engender wonder in the spectator by their novelty, and which bring beauty and variety to the work. The example of Filippino Lippi is important, not just because it helps to clarify the significance of the term, but because it also underlines the fact that, for Vasari, the production of the bizarre neither depended on nor implied an eccentric character. For while Piero is described by Vasari as strange and untamed, Filippino is a model of sociability, a 'modest and refined' person who is 'above all courteous and amiable'.[138] It is also implicit in Vasari's accounts of both Piero's and Filippino's works that 'bizarreness' demands discipline and control on the artist's part, so that the works remain both credible and pleasing to the eye.

In the Life of Piero, as elsewhere in the *Lives*, 'bizarre' is also used in relation to his paintings of exotic animals. The sea-monster for Giuliano de' Medici is described as 'by virtue of its deformity, so extraordinary, fantastic and bizarre, that it seems impossible that nature could employ such strangeness and such deformity', while Vasari describes as 'bizarre and very beautiful' a sketchbook of exotic animals, drawn by Piero 'with the utmost diligence and an indescribable patience'.[139] Of the sea-monster in the *Liberation of Andromeda*, which Vasari reckoned Piero's most pleasing and most finely executed work, he writes that 'one could not possibly see a more bizarre or capricious sea-monster than that which Piero contrived to paint'.[140] In each case, as in the Life of Filippino, 'bizarre' is thus associated with beauty and charm, and with the ornamentation of a work of art. It is also associated with diligence of execution, and Vasari constantly stresses Piero's painstaking technique. 'Bizarre' thus denotes a quality of the unusual and the strange that astonishes and delights by its novelty while avoiding the ugly or grotesque, and which, however exotic its objects, is made both credible and pleasing to the eye through a refinement of technique. For Vasari, the products of Piero's *fantasìa* are thus, on their own terms, the objects of unqualified praise, and he expresses whole-hearted enthusiasm of this aspect of his work. Throughout the Life, *fantasìa* and 'bizarre' are used in a positive way, one that also implies these qualities have been exercised with a proper sense of decorum. Piero's *fantasìa* is both appropriate to his subjects and rooted in the observation of nature: his imagination is disciplined and controlled by a profound understanding of the natural world, and by the diligence of his technique. At the same time, Piero's *fantasìa* was largely inimical to the qualities and achievements that Vasari considered fundamental to good art. Although this is never explicitly stated, the prevalence of *fantasìa* and related terms in his accounts of Piero's works, and the corresponding rarity of terms such as 'design', suggests that, in Piero's case at least, the two were mutually exclusive, a suggestion that is borne out by the experience of Piero's works.

Vasari also accorded the whole genre of *spalliera* panels a relatively low status, and saw them as considerably less important than large-scale dramatic narratives. In his Life of Dello Delli, an early-fifteenth-century artist who specialized in painting *cassone* and *spalliera* panels, he explains how

> At that time large wooden chests were used in the rooms of most citizens . . . and there was no artist who did not work at painting these chests . . . [;] in the same way, they [were] used to decorate not just chests, but bed-heads, *spalliere*, and the woodwork which ran around the rooms . . . And for

many years this practice continued, so that even the most excellent painters were not ashamed, as they would be nowadays, to paint such things, and ornament them with gold. And that this was truly the case one can see clearly in the number of *cassoni*, *spalliere* and *cornici* that survive amongst many others, in the rooms of Lorenzo de' Medici the Elder, on which are painted by artists of no little worth, but most excellent masters, all the jousts, tournaments, hunts, festivals and other spectacles of his time, executed with judgement, invention and the most marvellous art . . . But since none of the things of this world last for ever, or even for any time, however good and praiseworthy, this practice was discarded as men's minds became more subtle, and in recent years richer ornaments have been devised, with woodwork enriched with gold, and this and other furniture inset with paintings coloured in oils, depicting the most beautiful *istorie*, which made and continue to make known both the magnificence of the citizens who own them, and the excellence of those who paint them.[141]

As Vasari indicates, *spalliera* panels had begun to lose popularity as a form of interior decoration by the time he wrote the *Lives*, and were gradually being replaced by a combination of more ornate woodwork and independent oil paintings. To some extent this may be a reflection (as Vasari himself thought) of a growing resistance among painters to the execution of such works that, like Vasari, they saw as an inferior branch of art, one allied to the world of the craftsmen and unworthy of their own advancing status. As I have suggested, even in his own time Piero's concentration on *spalliera* panels was unusual among artists of standing, and those artists who worked on such commissions mostly attempted to dignify the activity by treating them in the same way as large-scale *istorie*, or by confining their input to that of the basic design.

Vasari's own reservations about such works almost certainly spring in part from the fact that they demanded small figures, and did not easily allow for the type of dramatic narrative, governed by the human figure, that he upheld as the achievement and the ideal object of Florentine art. Thus, not only were Piero's works deficient in this respect, but his ability and willingness to adapt his compositions to the small scale of the *spalliera* panel was something Vasari was not wholly equipped to admire. These same qualities are, however, essential to a proper understanding of Piero's works, and were clearly appreciated by numerous contemporary patrons. The design of his paintings is inextricable from their function as *spalliera* panels, and from their physical setting, just as their iconography may reflect their moral or didactic role. Similarly, the prevalence of landscapes in Piero's works and the way they are composed are fully in line with the emphasis placed on landscape as a subject for interior decoration in writings on art. Pliny and Vitruvius both make it clear that landscape played a major part in the decoration of private houses in Antiquity; their views were repeated by Alberti, who stressed the decorative and therapeutic value of such subjects, while also emphasizing the greater freedom and inventiveness that could be exercised in works for private apartments. Thus, while contemporary writers did not develop a theory relating to *spalliera* panels – and it would be a mistake to suggest that they were identified too rigidly as a genre – knowledge of their function, and of the expectations patrons had of them, helps clarify aspects of Piero's works that have been seen as problematic, and provides the proper framework for the appreciation of his *fantasia*.

CHAPTER THREE

Religious Works

While secular paintings made up an unusually large part of Piero's *oeuvre*, as was the case for most contemporary artists, it was religious works that constituted the bulk of his output and provided the major part of his income. Thirty-two of the works confidently believed to be Piero's are religious in nature, including small heads or half-lengths of saints, such as the *Young St John* (illus. 47) and the *Portrait of a Woman as the Magdalen* (illus. 53) to half-length Madonnas (illus. 37), altarpieces for family chapels, and tondi for domestic settings. As we have seen, his religious output does not appear to have included works in fresco, but comprised primarily small and medium-size works on panel or canvas, a fact that may reflect his lack of confidence in handling large-scale narratives and figure compositions and also, perhaps, the absence of a workshop such as could assist in the preparation of commissions of this kind. The large number, within this part of his *oeuvre*, of paintings designed for private devotion, as opposed to the more prestigious and competitive format of the altarpiece, is also significant in view of his particular interests and strengths.

Despite the number of religious works, this aspect of Piero's production is less well-known than his secular paintings, and has attracted relatively little discussion. This is partly due to the fact that in some ways they are more conventional and less difficult to interpret than the secular works, and thus less easy to link with the eccentric persona of Vasari's Life. Vasari himself devotes comparatively little space to this aspect of Piero's work, and makes no comment at all on the domestic tondi that comprise the most sophisticated part of his output, beyond noting that 'in Florence he (Piero) executed many paintings for other citizens, which are distributed throughout their houses, of which I have seen some that are very good'.[1] The difficulty of establishing a secure chronology for the religious works, and of locating them within a clear stylistic development may also account for their relative neglect by recent scholars, for it is in the religious works that we see most clearly that stylistic diversity signalled by Vasari in his statement that 'one can truly say that he changed his manner almost from one work to the next'.[2] Especially in his altarpieces, Piero demonstrated an unusual sensitivity and responsiveness to the artistic scene around him. Thus, while his *spalliera* panels are characterized by a pronounced individuality in both subject-matter and style, the religious paintings are marked rather by continual and diverse reminiscences of works by his contemporaries. In many respects, therefore, they differ notably among themselves, a feature which has engendered much confusion as regards both their dating and their attribution.[3]

This is not to say that as a painter of religious works Piero appears simply as an imitator, or as an eclectic in any straightforward way, for there are a number of

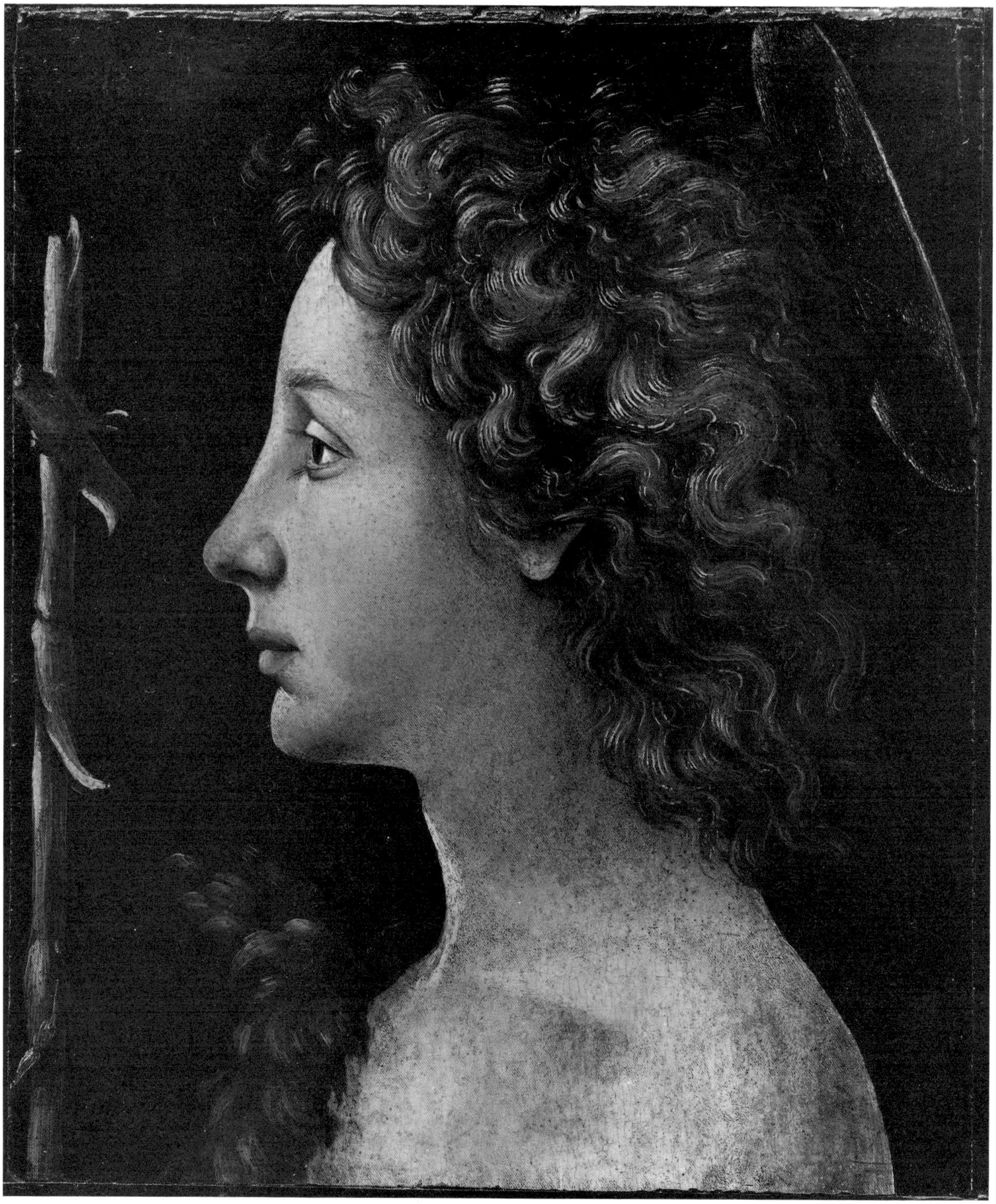

47 *The Young St John the Baptist*, *c.*1485, tempera on panel. Metropolitan Museum of Art, New York.

features that make the religious works distinctively his own. Furthermore, while Vasari had reservations about Piero's working procedure and constant change of manner, he did not disapprove of the practice of artistic emulation or imitation in itself. On the contrary, the notion that artists learn from one another and build on one another's achievements is central to his idea of artistic progress, as he makes clear in his Life of Raphael. Vasari's account of Raphael's career provides the *locus classicus* in the *Lives* of the way in which an artist can learn from the example of others, as Raphael's art develops through his successive emulation of Perugino, Leonardo, Michelangelo and Fra Bartolommeo, and his selection and synthesis of the best elements of each.[4]

In the case of Raphael, however, this process of selection is presented as systematic and selfconscious. It is also seen to result in the formation of a distinctive personal style, one that is manifest most clearly in Raphael's approach to the human form. For Vasari, however, Piero's response to and assimilation of the styles of his contemporaries does not appear to have followed a logical pattern, or to have resulted in a coherent or identifiable style on which later artists could build in their turn. It is significant that, as with the secular works, in the few comments he makes on Piero's religious paintings, Vasari rarely comments on the effect of the work as a whole, or on Piero's treatment of the figure, but focuses on details that appear to him praiseworthy, or on the technical execution of the work. The terms in which he does so, such as 'good' and 'diligent', are also very unspecific, and do not identify a distinctive quality of style. In describing Piero's altarpiece of the *Visitation* (illus. 87), for example, Vasari writes:

> There is within the painting a Visitation of Our Lady, with St Nicholas, and a St Anthony who is reading with a pair of glasses on his nose, a very lively figure. He also included in the painting a book of parchment, slightly aged, which appears real; and likewise some of the balls belonging to St Nicholas, which have a certain lustre, and each throws back the gleam and the reflections of the others in a way that truly revealed the strangeness of Piero's mind, and his desire to conquer the difficulties of his art.[5]

Of Piero's altarpiece of the *Madonna and Child with Saints* (illus. 57), painted for the Church of the Ospedale degli Innocenti, Vasari remarks only that 'in this work there are truly many good things', while an untraced *Coronation of the Virgin*, painted for S. Piero Gattolini, Florence, is described simply as 'a work carried out with such diligence that it earned him honour and praise'.[6]

Vasari's strongest commendation is reserved for Piero's altarpiece of the *Incarnation* (illus. 88) painted for the Tedaldi chapel in SS Annunziata, where he was particularly struck by the handling of light:

> he showed Our Lady standing and without the Christ Child, raised above the ground on a pedestal, with a book in her hand, lifting her eyes to Heaven, and above her is the Holy Spirit who bathes her in His light. And the artist wished it to appear that she and the figures around her were illuminated solely by the light emanating from the dove . . . apart from this he painted a landscape which is bizarre on account both of its strange trees, and of certain rocks which are in it.[7]

Vasari also accorded great praise to the predella of this altarpiece, in which, as in his *spalliera* panels, Piero could exploit his talent at painting on a small scale, and his mastery of unusual detail:

> He painted the predella of this work with certain little stories, very well done; and amongst other things there is in it a St Margaret emerging from the belly of the serpent; and he made the animal so convincing and so monstrous, rendering the venom in its eyes, its fiery breath, and the semblance of death in its truly fearsome appearance that I do not think one could find a better example of such a thing. And certainly I do not think that anyone painted things of this nature better than Piero, or imagined them so effectively.[8]

Of the work as a whole though, his conclusion is that

> in truth there are some very beautiful *parts* in this work, for example certain heads which reveal both grace and design, apart from the unified and harmonious colouring.[9]

For prospective patrons, however, less concerned with notions about the progress of art or the development of artistic style, the variability of Piero's approach may well have been an advantage, for his stylistic flexibility and his innovative approach to the rendering of standard themes guaranteed each an object of distinct originality. This must have been a particular attraction for patrons commissioning tondi for their homes, for such works were highly prized, not only as aids to devotion but, increasingly, for their aesthetic qualities, and as additions to the decoration of the domestic interior.[10] Furthermore, in this context the focus on naturalistic detail that Vasari saw as a distraction from the more important aspects of painting invariably added to the decorative potential of the works. Conversely, the private nature and less formal setting of the tondo allowed for a degree of flexibility and experimentation that the altarpiece did not, both in the interpretation of subject-matter, and in terms of composition.

It is in the altarpieces that we see most clearly Piero's response to the works of his contemporaries, especially those painted early in his career. This is not surprising, for altarpieces were among the most significant and prestigious commissions available to artists. They were also open to public scrutiny in ways that domestic paintings were not, and artists working on commissions of this kind must have felt a particular pressure to display their awareness of contemporary developments and techniques. This situation intensified during the middle and later years of Piero's career, when the altarpiece was a particularly innovative and dynamic genre, and underwent changes that were in some ways foreign to Piero's strengths. Inevitably, then, he turned to his contemporaries for guidance and inspiration in the design of such works.[11]

The Altarpieces

Piero's earliest surviving altarpiece is almost certainly the *Madonna and Child with SS Lazarus and Sebastian* (illus. 54) in the church of SS Michele and Lorenzo, Montevettolini. Nothing is known of the provenance of this work which, on stylistic grounds, can be dated to around 1480, shortly before Piero went to Rome and worked with Cosimo Rosselli in the Sistine Chapel. In view of its early date, it is quite likely that the painting was always destined for a church in a provincial location, before Piero became sufficiently established to secure comparable commissions in Florence itself. The presence in the painting of two saints associated with the plague also suggests that it may have been commissioned at the time of an epidemic, or in relation to a vow.[12]

The composition of the work, with the Madonna and Child enthroned symmetrically between the two Saints, is typical of the altarpieces produced in Florence by Ghirlandaio, Filippino Lippi, Cosimo Rosselli and other contemporary artists. Cosimo's specific influence is apparent in the robust, simplified form and blunt facial features of the Virgin, while the flanking Saints reveal the influence of Filippino in their slender, attenuated forms and elegant profiles (illus. 48). The neat and well-formed landscape is also of a type that appears in the works of both Filippino and Cosimo Rosselli, although its subdued colouring and unified *chiaroscuro* recall the works of Leonardo, as does the monochrome partition, pierced by biforate windows, that separates the landscape from the figures.

Soon after painting this work Piero executed the *Madonna and Child with SS Onofrius and Augustine* (illus. 55), an altarpiece now in a private collection in Toronto, the provenance of which is also unknown, although it seems likely that it too was destined for a provincial location. The painting can be dated with some certainty to around 1483–4, shortly after Piero's return from Rome, for while its composition is similar to that of the Montevettolini altarpiece, the figures are somewhat different. While the form of the Madonna has a certain similarity with that in the Montevettolini painting, the Saints are more solid and robust, revealing the renewed influence of Ghirlandaio, alongside whom Piero worked in the Sistine Chapel. This influence is particularly apparent in the figure of Augustine, which is given mass by means of large folds of drapery arranged in horizontal bands across his form. As in the previous work, however, the background architecture and the way the landscape is lit derive from Leonardo, although Piero begins to display his particular interest in landscape by extending the windows to the ground – a device unprecedented among his contemporaries – in order to reveal an extensive backdrop of hills, rivers and lush vegetation.

Following these works Piero painted three altarpieces for Florentine patrons, the provenance of which can be established with some certainty. The first was almost certainly the *Madonna and Child with SS John the Baptist, Peter, Nicholas and Dominic* – the '*Pala Pugliese*' – painted around 1485, the predella of which shows *St Dominic Burning the Books of the Albigensians*, the *Meeting of Christ and the Baptist* and *St Nicholas Destroying the Idols* (illus. 56). This altarpiece retains its original frame, which bears the

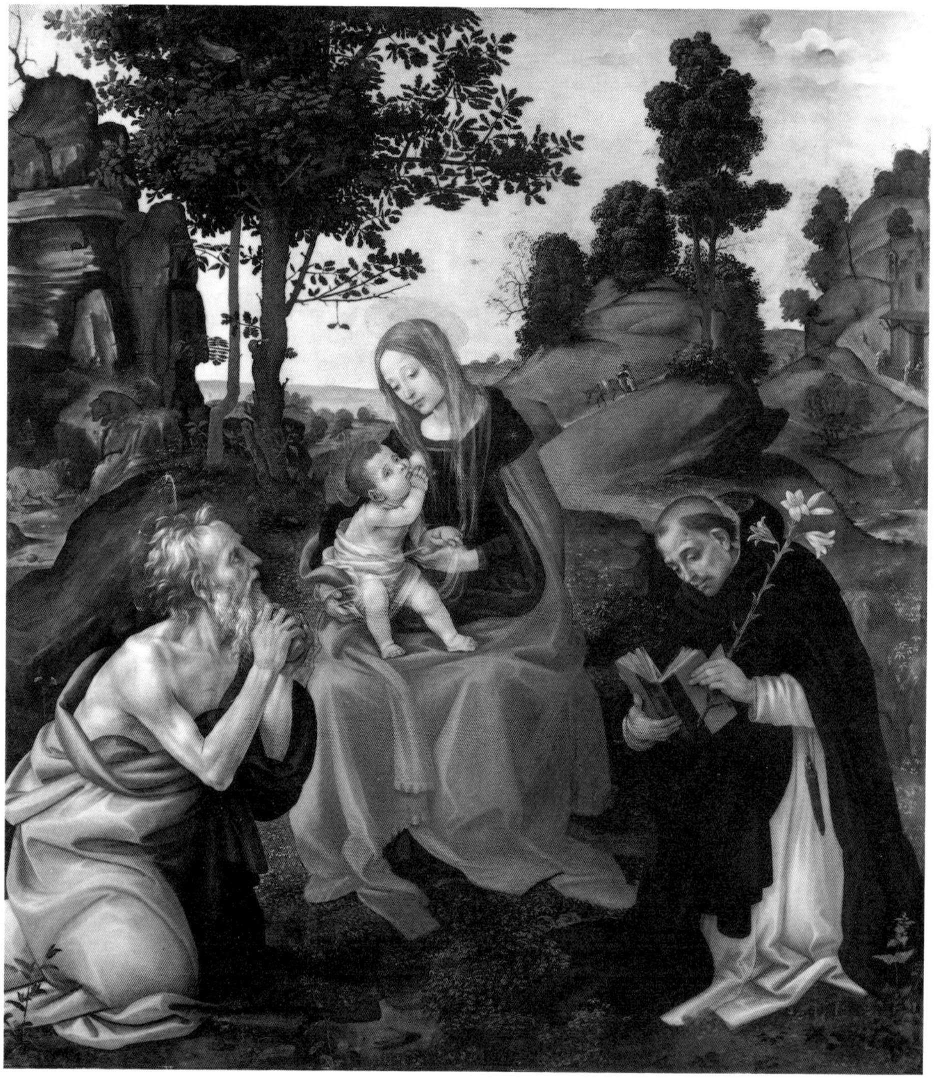

48 Filippino Lippi, *Madonna and Child with SS Dominic and Jerome*, *c.*1485, wood. National Gallery, London.

arms of the del Pugliese family, while the figure of Nicholas, probably a portrait of the donor, shows strong similarities with a donor portrait in Filippino Lippi's *Apparition of the Virgin to St Bernard* commissioned *c.*1485 by Piero del Pugliese for an altar maintained by his father in the church of La Campora near Florence. Although the identity of Filippino's figure has been debated by recent scholars, it is most likely to be Piero del Pugliese, who was probably also responsible for commissioning Piero's work.[13]

Like the two earlier altarpieces, the *Pala Pugliese* has a rigorously symmetrical composition of a type familiar from the workshops of Ghirlandaio, Cosimo Rosselli and Lorenzo di Credi. With the exception of the Madonna, the figures also suggest the continued influence of Ghirlandaio in their bulky, simplified forms and stocky proportions, although the Baptist appears more slender and delicate, recalling

Filippino Lippi. Filippino's influence is particularly clear, however, in the elegant form of the Madonna, in the exaggerated curve of her neck and the gesture of her free hand, and the intricate lines of her drapery, the fluidity of which contrasts notably with that of the Saints. The painting also registers Piero's growing awareness of Flemish art, not least Hugo van der Goes's *Portinari Altarpiece* (illus. 49), which had recently arrived in Florence, where it exerted a profound effect on numerous artists.[14] The disposition of the landscape in symmetrical peaks that frame the main figures, and the emphasis on naturalistic details, such as the *palle* of Nicholas and the meticulously rendered vase of flowers in the foreground, probably reflect van der Goes's influence.

The impact of van der Goes's work on Piero reached its peak in the latter's altarpiece of the *Visitation with SS Nicholas and Anthony Abbot* (illus. 87), one of the few

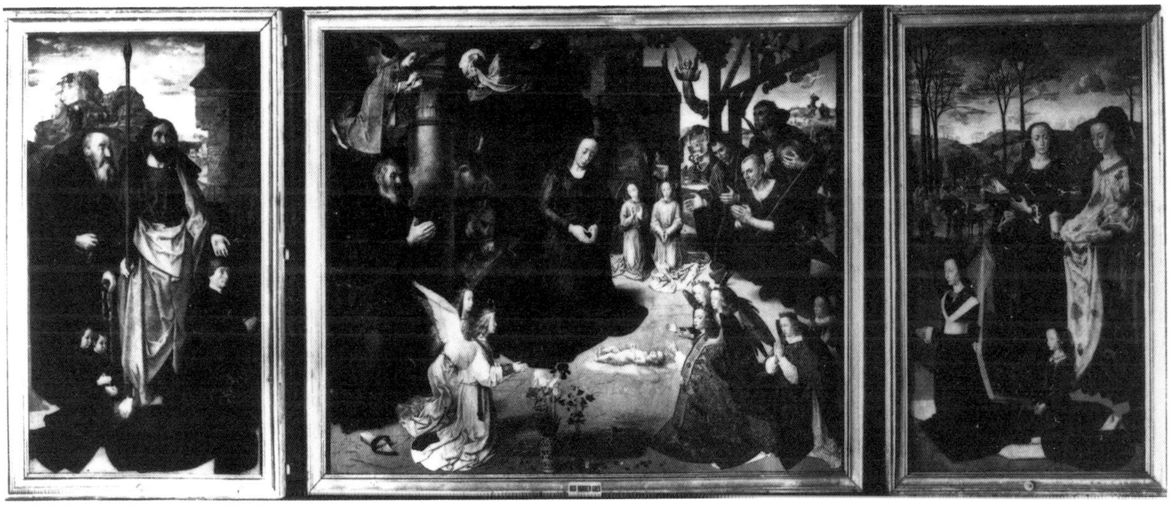

49 Hugo van der Goes, *Portinari Altarpiece*, *c.* 1473–5, oil on panel. Uffizi, Florence.

works by the artist for which secure documentation exists. Painted for one of the two chapels maintained by the Capponi family in Santo Spirito, it was probably commissioned by Piero Capponi in the late 1480s.[15] The subject was an unusual one for an altarpiece, and no obvious explanation has so far been adduced for its choice in this instance, or for the particular choice of saints. Piero also includes a number of subsidiary scenes, most notably the Massacre of the Innocents that occupies the middle ground. Two others are incorporated with characteristic subtlety, the Annunciation appearing on a distant church facade, while the left background includes the Adoration of the Shepherds and the Procession of the Magi. In certain details the painting maintains reminiscences of Filippino, as in the delicate profile and headdress of the Virgin, and also of Ghirlandaio, whose *Adoration of the Magi* (illus. 50) of 1488 for the church of the Ospedale degli Innocenti provided the model for the

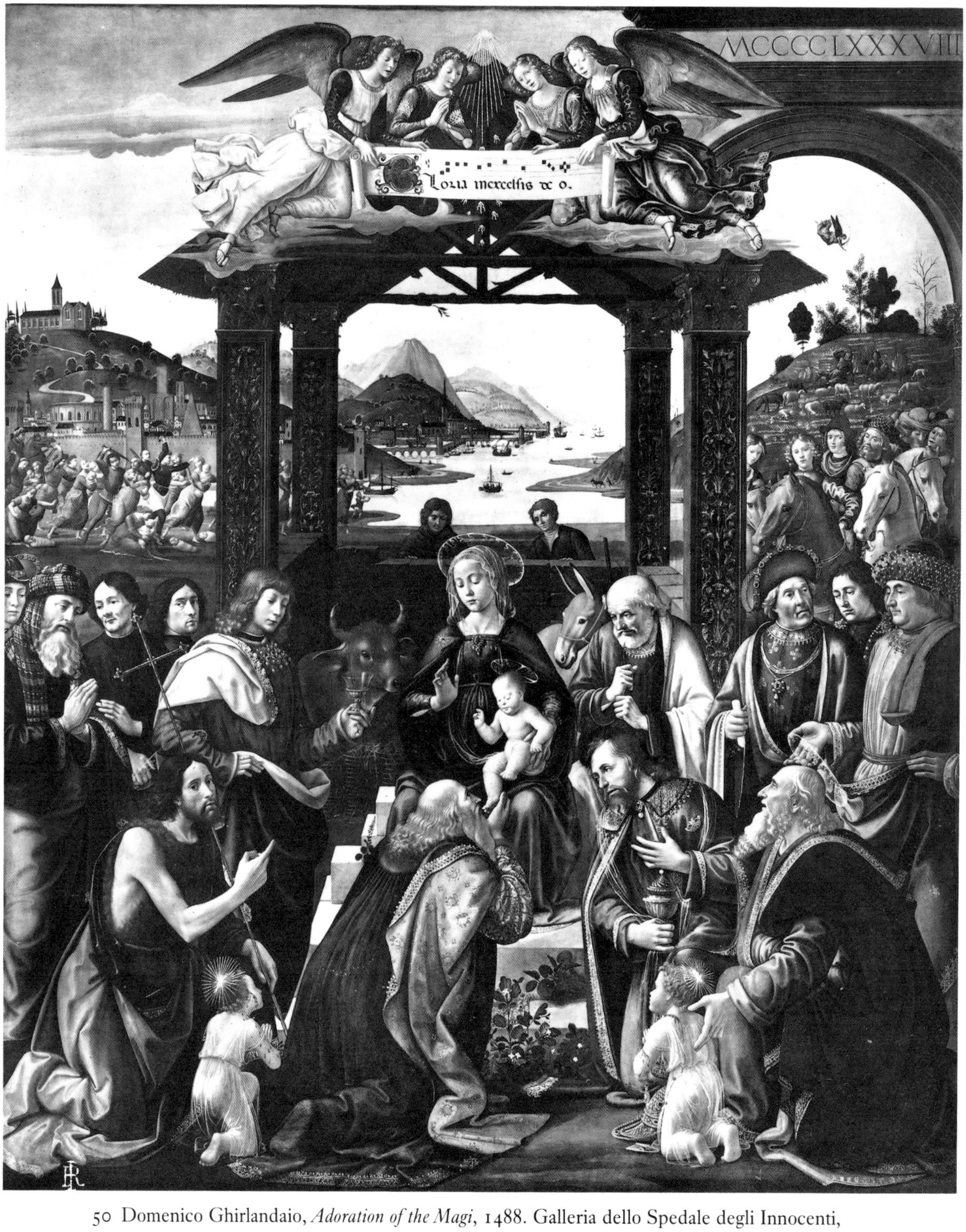

50 Domenico Ghirlandaio, *Adoration of the Magi*, 1488. Galleria dello Spedale degli Innocenti, Florence.

Massacre of the Innocents in Piero's work. It is, none the less, the influence of Flemish art that remains its most striking aspect: the rustic St Elizabeth, crisp light and the naturalistic details of the Saints and their attributes, painted with an almost hallucinatory clarity, to which Vasari accords rather ambivalent praise. At the same time, as in the *Madonna and Child with SS Onofrius and Augustine*, Piero displays his own inventiveness, in the careful integration of subsidiary scenes, the use of a window-like aperture as an interior frame for the main figures, and the placing of the seated Saints on a ledge in front of the narrative.

Piero probably completed the *Visitation* in the mid-1490s, and at some date after the installation of Ghirlandaio's *Adoration of the Magi* he executed his *Madonna and Child with SS Catherine of Alexandria, Rose of Viterbo, Peter, and John the Evangelist* (illus. 57) for the church of the Ospedale degli Innocenti. According to Vasari, this painting was also executed for the del Pugliese family, commissioned by the Prior of the Hospital for their chapel on the left of the entrance to the church.[16] In its general arrangement it resembles a conventional *sacra conversazione*, although it incorporates in the foreground the Mystic Marriage of St Catherine. Of all Piero's early altarpieces this is compositionally the most complex, and the least successful. A densely knit cluster of figures surrounds the Madonna, who is enthroned on a dais cut off from the landscape by a low wall, and fronted by a squared pavement. The throne is highly elaborate, incorporating both a canopy and ornate candelabra, and surmounted by putti. The landscape is full of incident and painted with great precision, while the figures, the treatment of details and the stark lighting reveal the continuing influence of Hugo van der Goes.

That Piero drew on the works of other artists is not in itself unusual. On the contrary, as Vasari implies in his Life of Raphael, this was accepted practice, and most Renaissance artists worked in this way to an extent, especially during their early years. There are, however, several features that make Piero's response to his contemporaries distinctive, and which had significant consequences for the appearance of his works. First, while the majority of artists developed their style around that of one other with whom they felt a particular affinity, Piero imitated a range of artists who are quite different among themselves. He did so, furthermore, not successively, as did Raphael, but simultaneously, in a way that engenders distinct differences between parts of the same work. This is particularly apparent in his rendering of figures, the forms and physiognomies of which can vary considerably within a single work. In the Montevettolini altarpiece, for example, the Lippiesque types of the two standing saints contrast markedly with the robust and foursquare figures of the Virgin and Child, the reverse being true in the *Pala Pugliese*. While to some extent these variations can be seen as a result of Piero's tendency to precise characterization, and his acute sense of decorum, they also result from his unusual eclecticism, and the closeness with which he imitated different styles. At the same time, as Vasari intimates, his emulation of the works of Filippino Lippi, Ghirlandaio, Leonardo and van der Goes did not result in a distinctive personal manner by which his works can be easily identified. What marks these images as peculiarly Piero's, in fact, is often their very diversity, and the subtle differences between their constituent parts.

It is also notable that Piero rarely appropriated entire compositions from the works of other artists, but drew on different artists for the figures and their settings. This is particularly interesting in view of the fact that, of all the aspects of a painting, it was the co-ordination of figures and background that appears to have presented him with the greatest difficulty. All the altarpieces display a tentative quality in the relationships of the figures to their surroundings, and of the figures to one another, making them appear unresolved. In the Montevettolini and Toronto altarpieces, for example, while the settings themselves are simple and uncluttered, and convincing in their spaciousness, the figures appear to be superimposed on them rather than inhabiting them freely, or occupying the space the settings imply. The more complex compositions of the *Pala Pugliese*, the *Visitation* and, in particular, the *Innocenti Altarpiece*, also appear as accumulations of separate motifs, rather than coherent wholes. The altarpieces also lack unity in the relationships between the figures, which appear formally and psychologically detached. In the Montevettolini and Toronto works, while the figures gesture towards one another, they are not oriented thus in space, and the gestures appear not to connect. In the *Visitation* there is a curious detachment between the main figures and the attendant saints, while in the *Innocenti Altarpiece* the sharply contrasting poses and angles of the figures act to separate rather than unite them. Even where the subject itself dictates a semi-narrative exchange, as here between St Catherine and the infant Christ, the two are only loosely bound together, for the infant appears to address Santa Rosa on the left, while presenting St Catherine with the ring.

It is here, perhaps, that we see most clearly Piero's limitations in the construction and disposition of figures on a large scale, limitations Vasari identified in his description of Piero's altarpiece of the *Immaculate Conception* (illus. 51), which he probably painted around 1520:

> He executed a small panel of the Immaculate Conception, in the transept of the church of San Francesco in Fiesole, and this is a very good little work, since the figures are quite small.[17]

The actual structuring of figures on a large scale, and the articulation of anatomy often appear to have posed problems for Piero, as also implied by Vasari's failure to discuss the artist's mastery of design. Although not all of Piero's drawings have survived, it may be significant here that those that remain do not include any anatomical studies, or preparatory sketches focusing on the structure of the body, or on its movement.[18] This uncertainty in the handling of the body in turn posed problems for Piero when it came to placing and interrelating his figures. It created particular difficulties for the positioning of figures in depth or at an angle to the picture plane, which involved foreshortening and thus a confident sense of the body's structure. It is significant that Piero avoided complex poses or twistings of the body, and that his figures do not extend far into depth, but are conceived in terms of broad and relatively simple planes, arranged as far as possible parallel to the surface of the work. Thus, with the exception

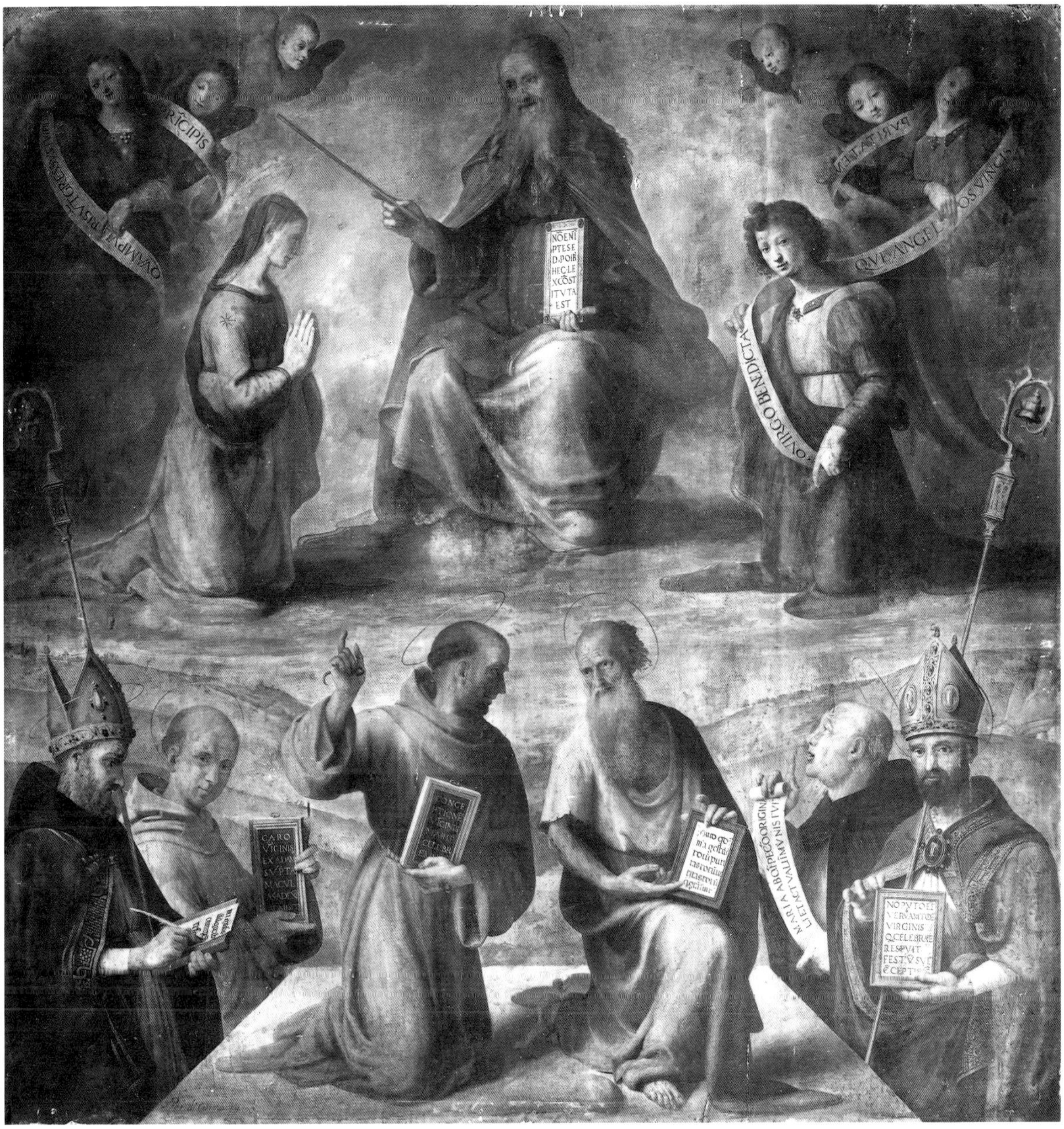

51 *The Immaculate Conception with SS Francis, Jerome, Bonaventure, Bernard, Augustine and Thomas Aquinas*, *c.*1520, oil on panel. S. Francesco, Fiesole.

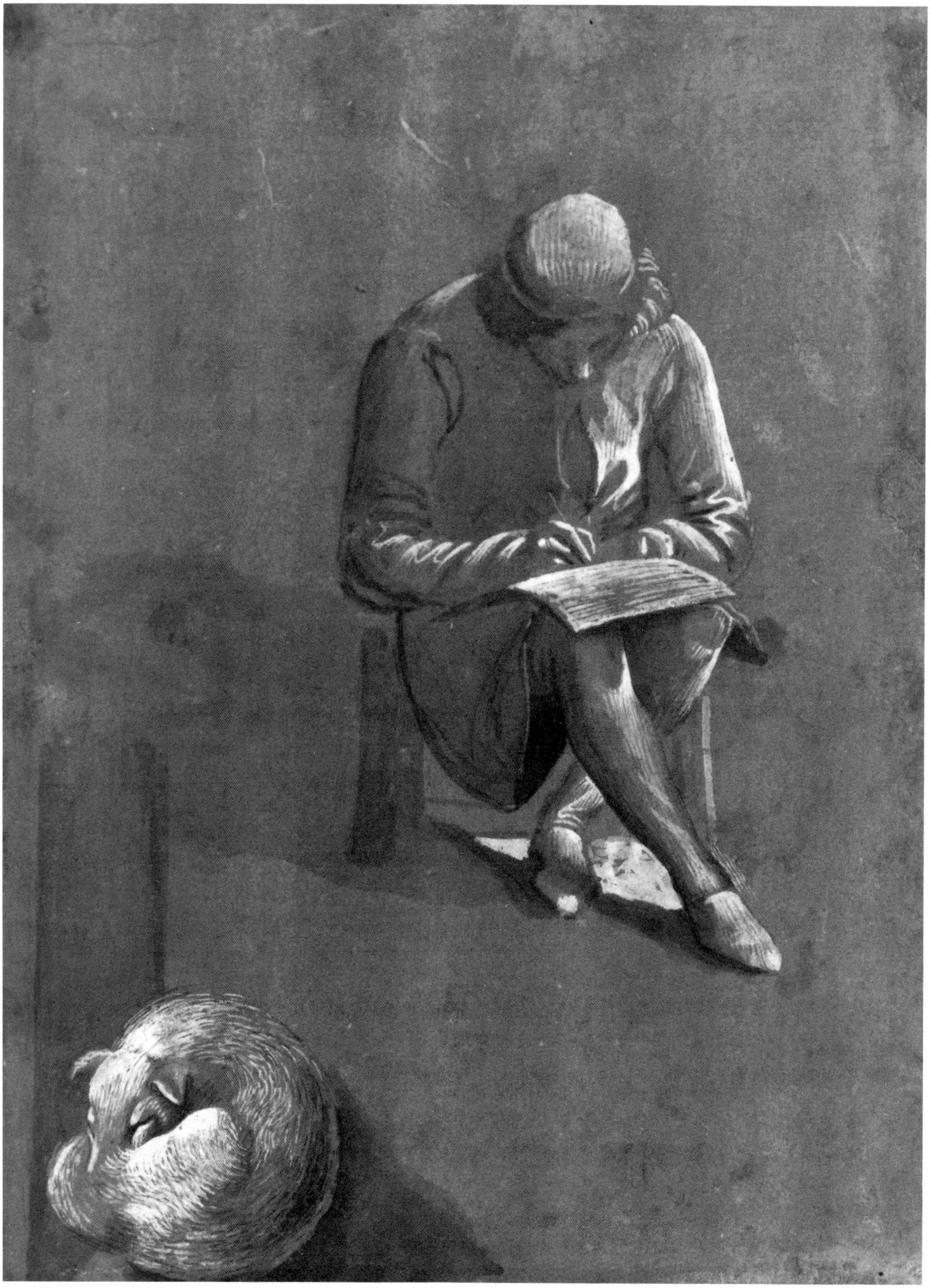

52 *Seated Youth with Dog*, brush and brown ink and white heightening. Royal Library, Windsor Castle.

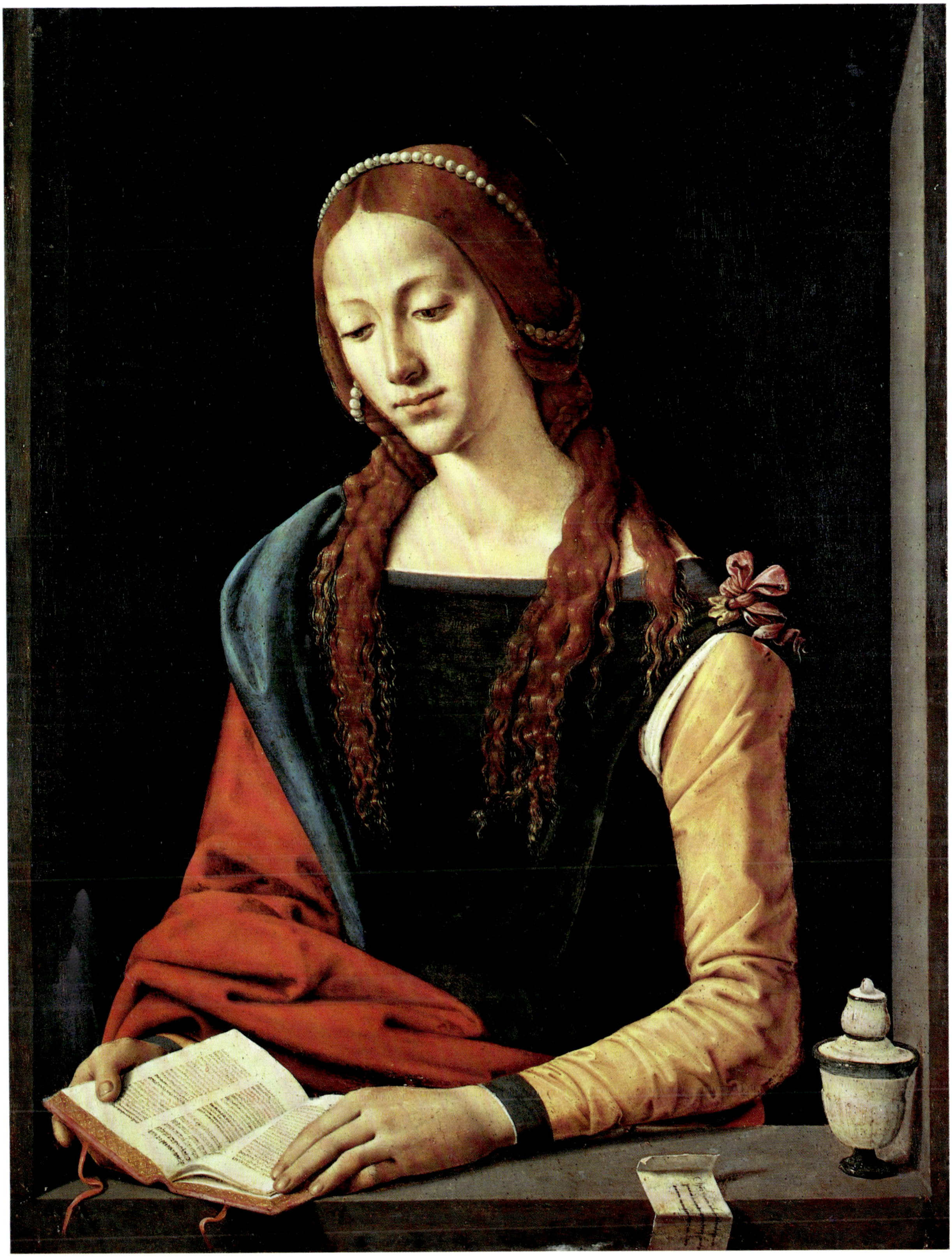

53 *Portrait of a Woman as the Magdalen*, *c*.1500–10, oil on panel. Galleria Nazionale d'Arte Antica, Rome.

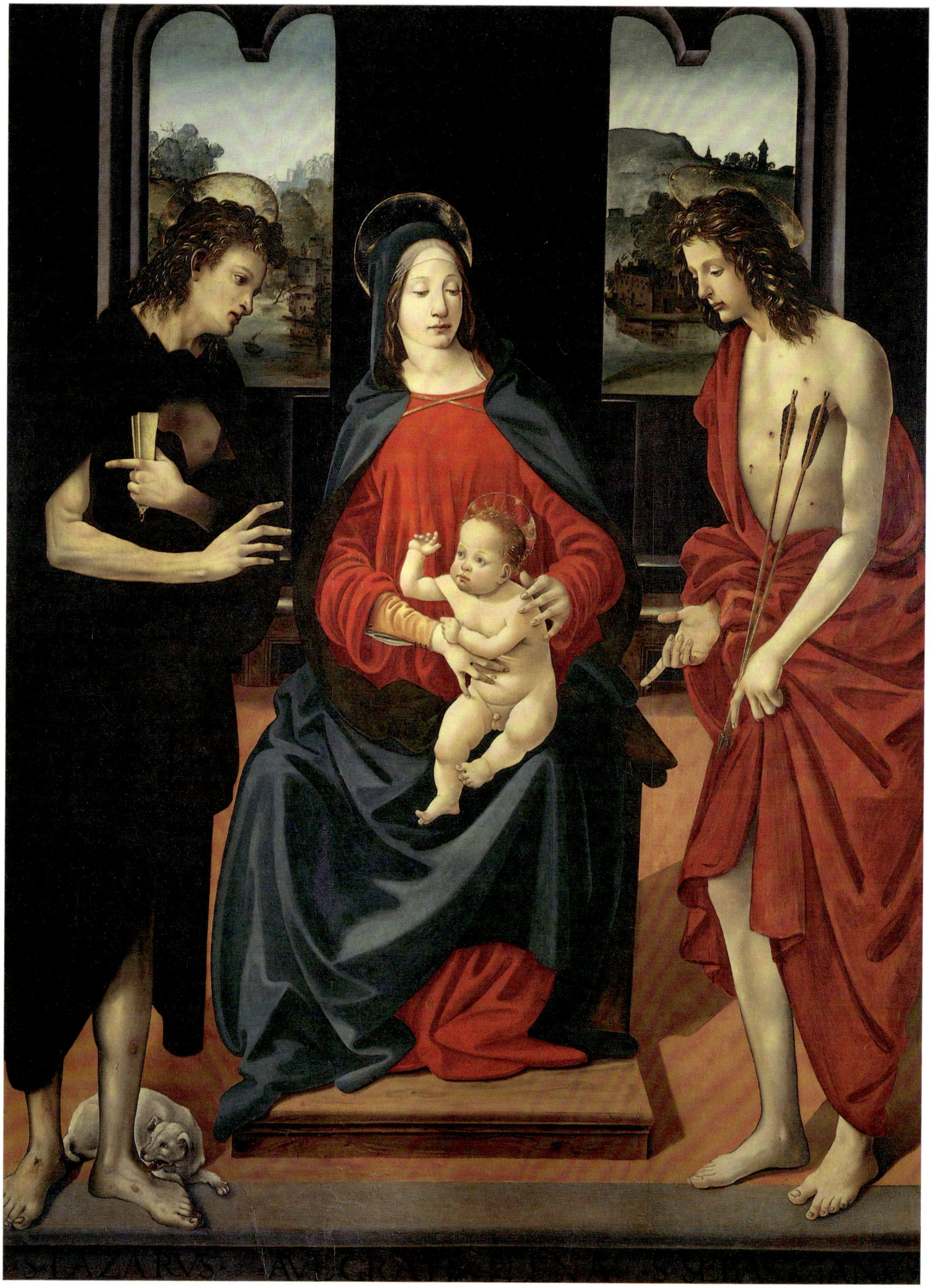

54 *Madonna and Child with SS Lazarus and Sebastian*, *c.*1480, tempera on panel. SS Michele Arcangelo and Lorenzo Martire, Montevettolini (Pistoia).

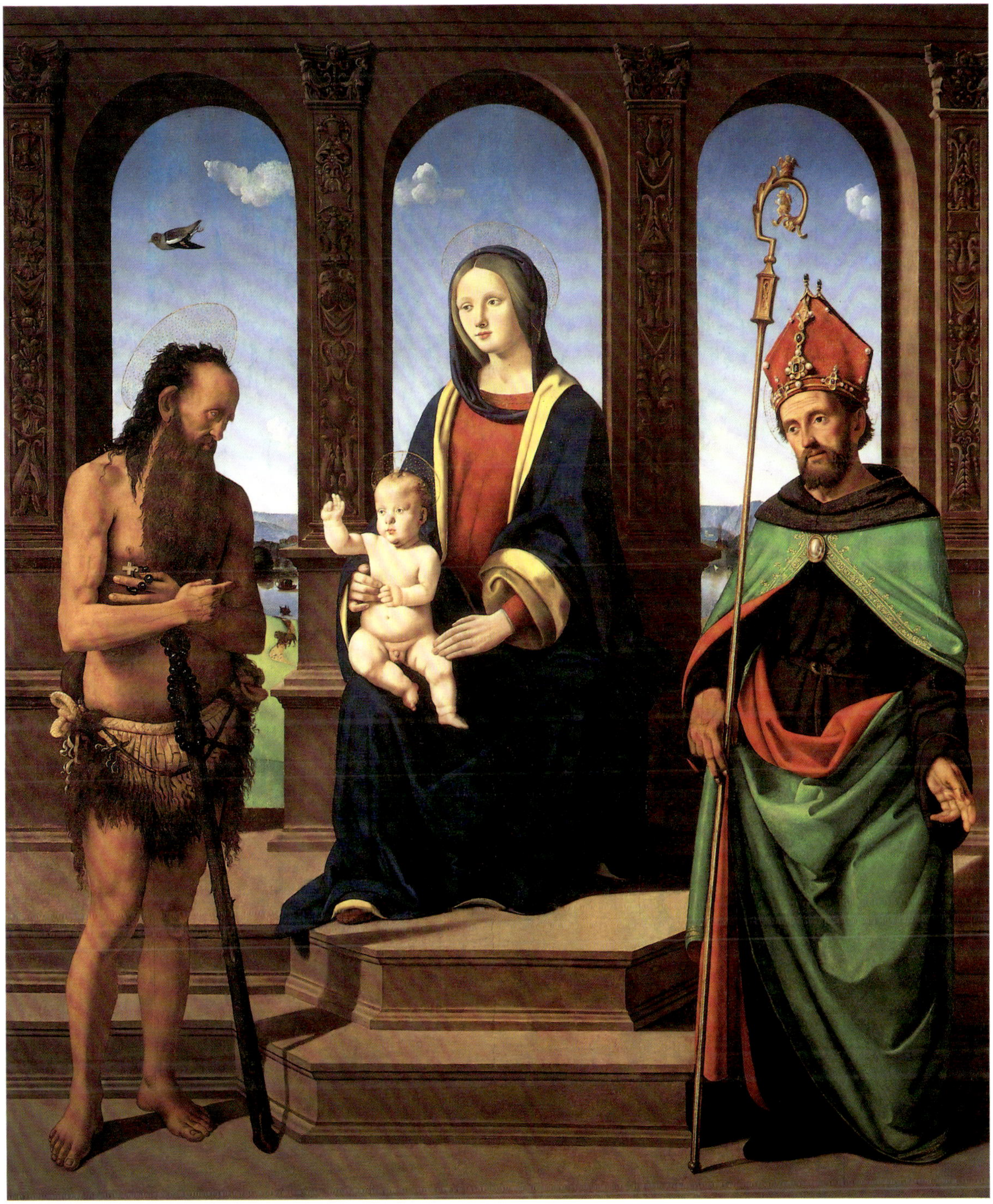

55 *Madonna and Child with SS Onofrius and Augustine*, *c.*1483–4, tempera on wood. Private collection, Toronto.

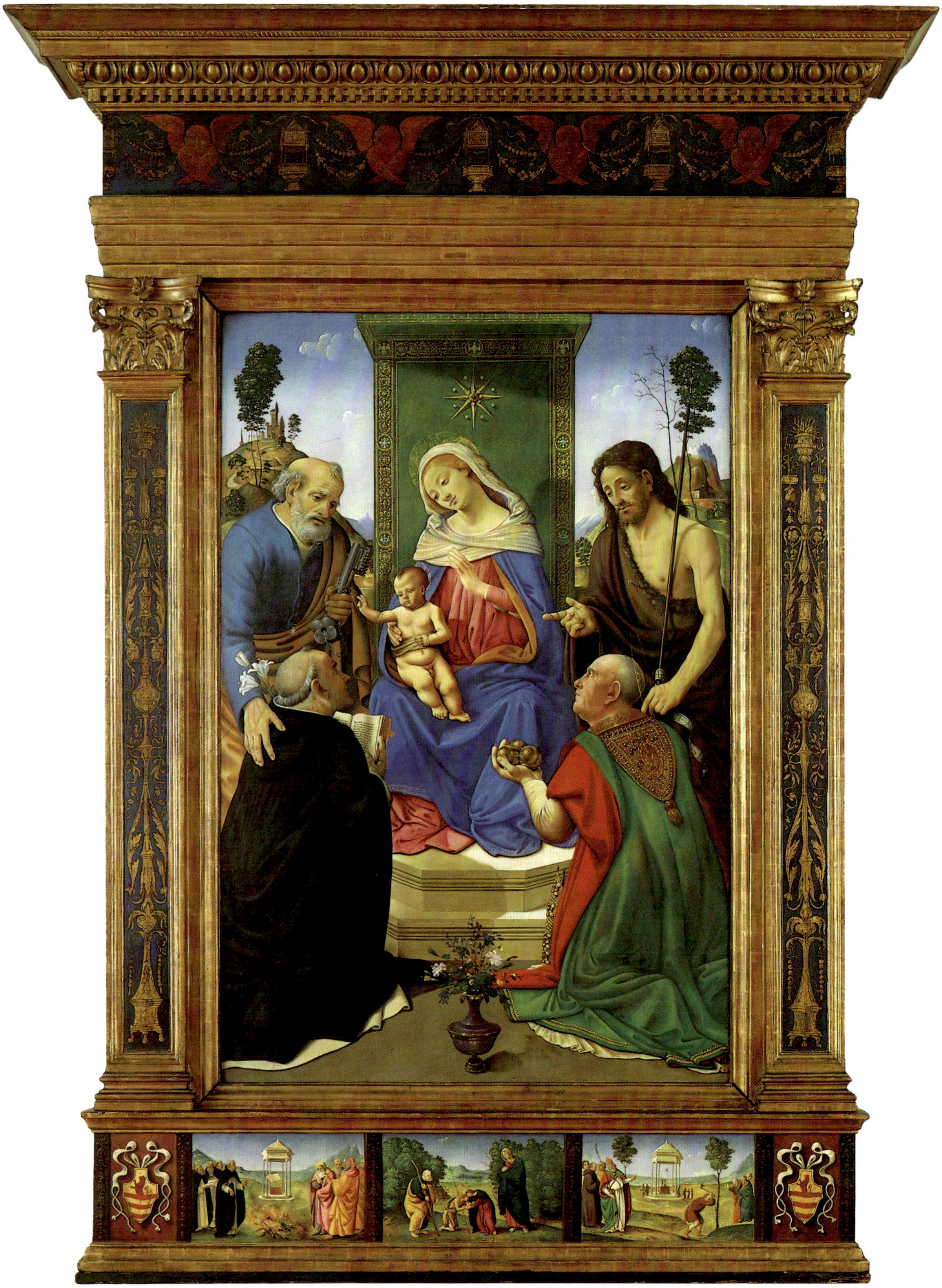

56 *Madonna and Child with SS Peter, John the Baptist, Nicholas of Bari and Dominic (*the *'Pala Pugliese')*, *c.*1485, tempera with oil glazes on wood. St Louis Art Museum, MO.

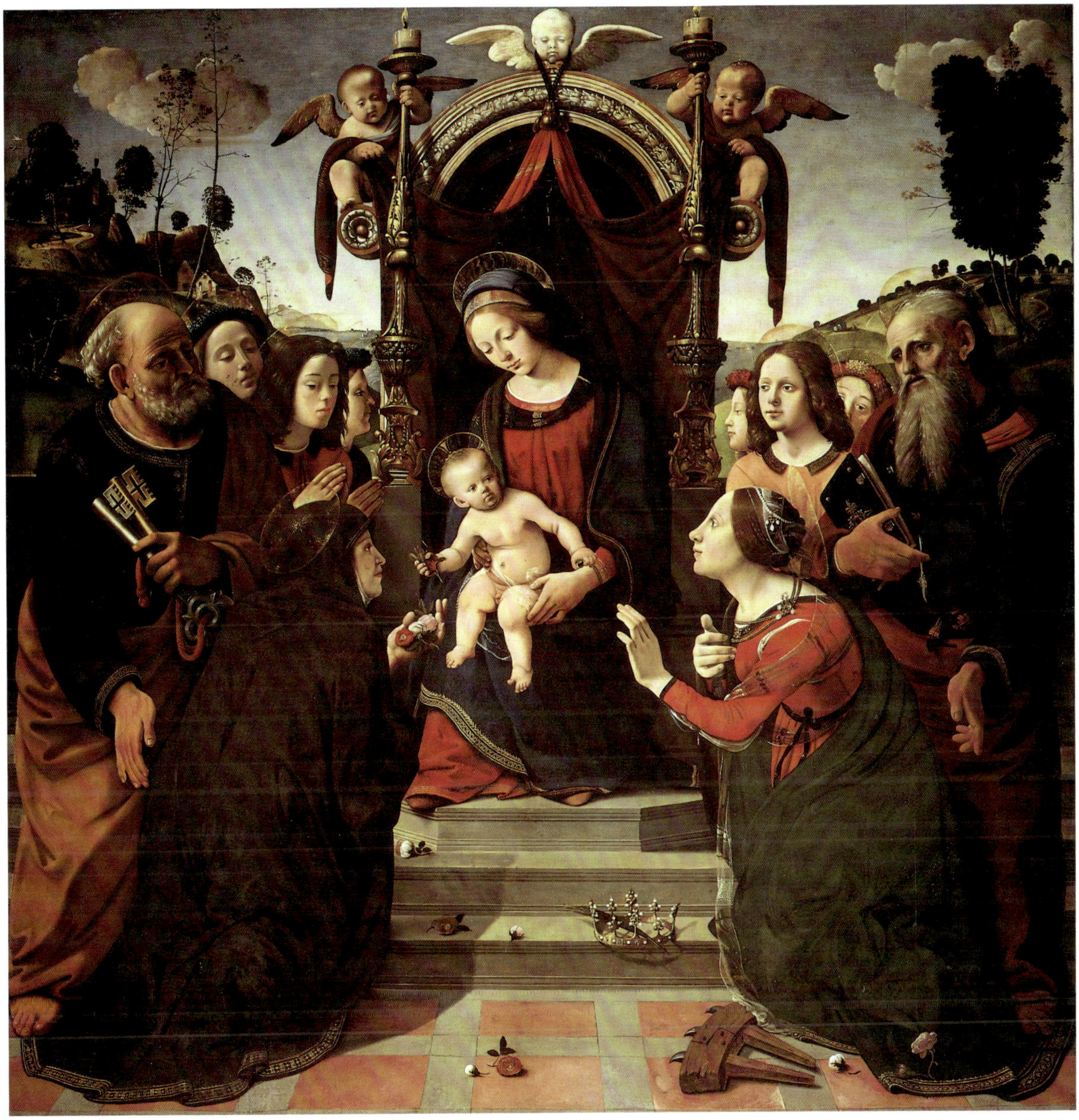

57 *Madonna and Child with SS Catherine of Alexandria, Rose of Viterbo, Peter, and John the Evangelist* (the *'Innocenti Altarpiece'*), *c.*1495–1500, oil on panel. Galleria dello Spedale degli Innocenti, Florence.

of the Tedaldi *Incarnation*, the least successful of the altarpieces are those involving the most figures, such as the *Innocenti* altarpiece, where the grouping and overlapping of figures in depth, and their relationship to the Madonna, are only partially resolved. At the same time, as in the other early works, the lack of formal unity between the figures, and the fact that they are not fully oriented towards each other, engenders a sense of psychological detachment that is accentuated by Piero's use of gesture, the characteristic reticence of which becomes particularly apparent in these larger works.

That Piero experienced problems in these respects is borne out by the relationship between the paintings and the preparatory drawings, which are invariably more dynamic and coherent than the finished works. As several scholars have noted, when rendering his figures in the smaller scale of the sketch Piero endowed them with a liveliness and sense of physical presence that are lacking in the paintings, particularly by his handling of drapery and his vigorous, fragmented use of line.[19] The drawings also display a thematic and compositional cohesion that the altarpieces do not. In the sketch (illus. 61) for the two main figures in the *Visitation*, the Virgin and St Elizabeth lean towards each other with an urgency that is absent from the painting, and which significantly intensifies the drama of their meeting. Their drapery also has considerable expressive force, and while barely revealing their underlying structure does lend the figures an energy and dynamism that Piero could not easily transfer into paint.[20] Similar differences are apparent in the case of the *Immaculate Conception* (illus. 51), one of Piero's latest surviving works.[21] A drawing for the top half of the composition (illus. 63) diverges notably from the painting, particularly in the relationship between the Virgin and God the Father. In the drawing this has the quality of a dramatic exchange. The attitude of the Virgin appears as one of fervent prayer, rather than the passive acceptance implied in the painting, her head and neck bowed and her hands clasped closely to her breast, while the sweeping curves of her drapery give her a sense of movement that is suppressed in the finished work. God the Father, who in the painting appears distant and remote from the Virgin, looks at her more directly, his body inclined towards her and his hand poised above her head. In the drawing, furthermore, both figures are placed at an angle, their bodies moving in and out of depth in a way that Piero does not reproduce in the painting, where the figures are clearly accommodated to the plane. The dynamism of the drawing is further accentuated by the lively figure of a saint on the right, probably St Jerome, which is replaced in the painting by a passively kneeling angel. Piero's drawing for the lower half of the composition (illus. 64) differs from the finished work in a similar way, creating a dialogue between the pairs of saints that is not apparent in the altarpiece.

Most revealing in this context, however, is Piero's altarpiece of the *Incarnation* (illus. 88), painted around 1505, and probably commissioned by Pierozzo di Baldo di Pierozzo Tedaldi, for the family chapel in SS Annunziata. The subject is not, in fact, entirely clear, although it is certainly not the Immaculate Conception, as has often been assumed.[22] It seems more likely that it is the Incarnation, and that it shows the Virgin at the moment when, after the angel's pronouncement of his message, an event

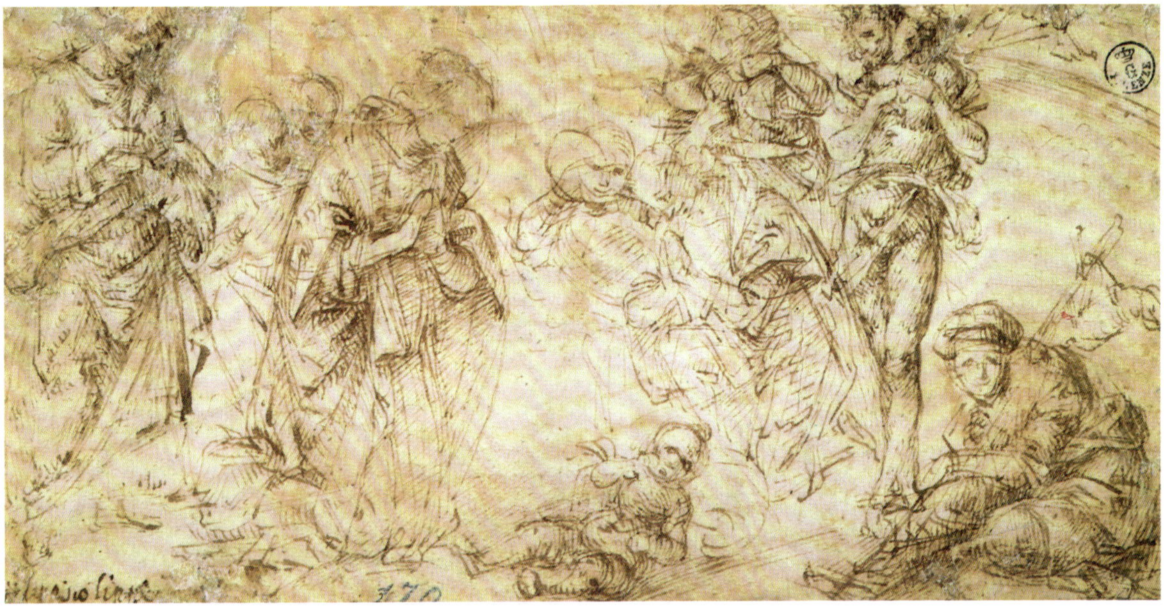

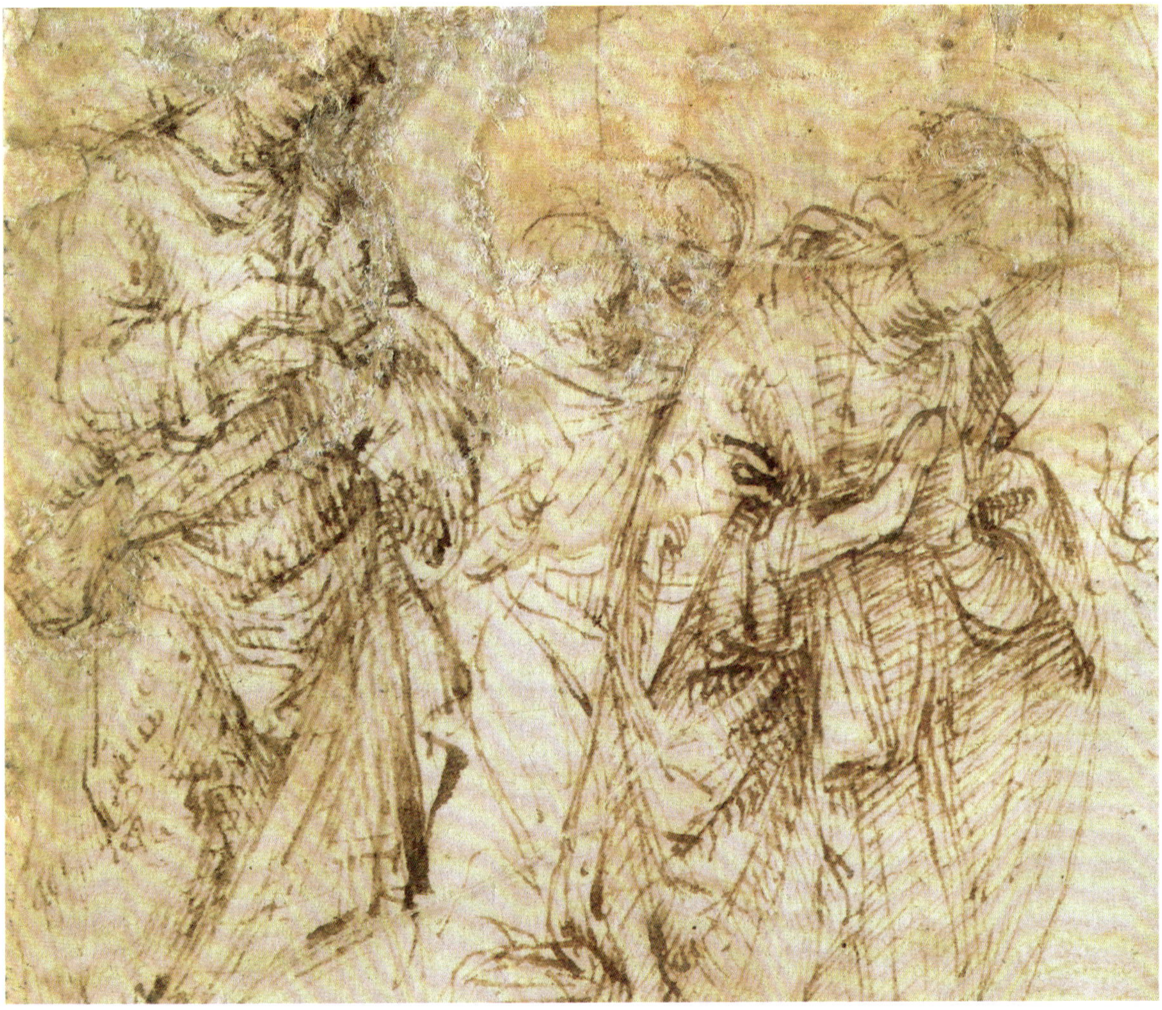

58 *Adoration of the Shepherds*, pen and ink on white paper. Uffizi, Florence.

59 Detail from the *Adoration of the Shepherds*.

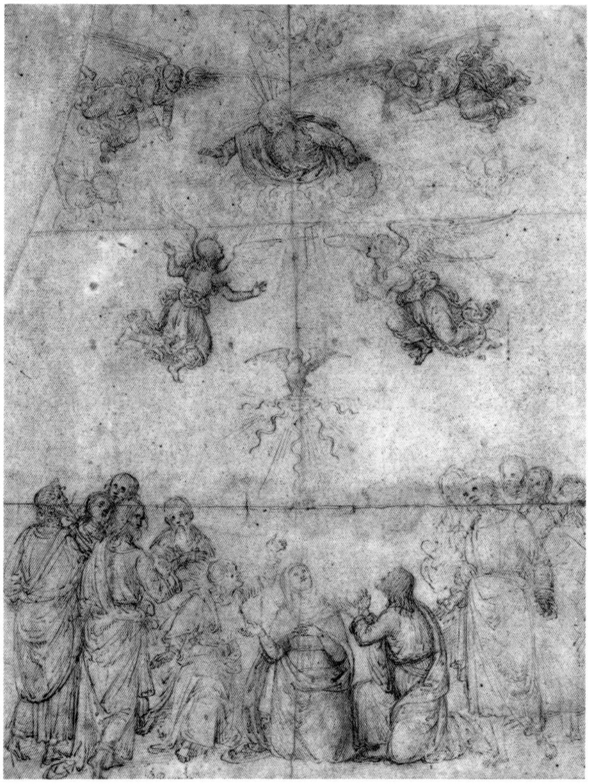

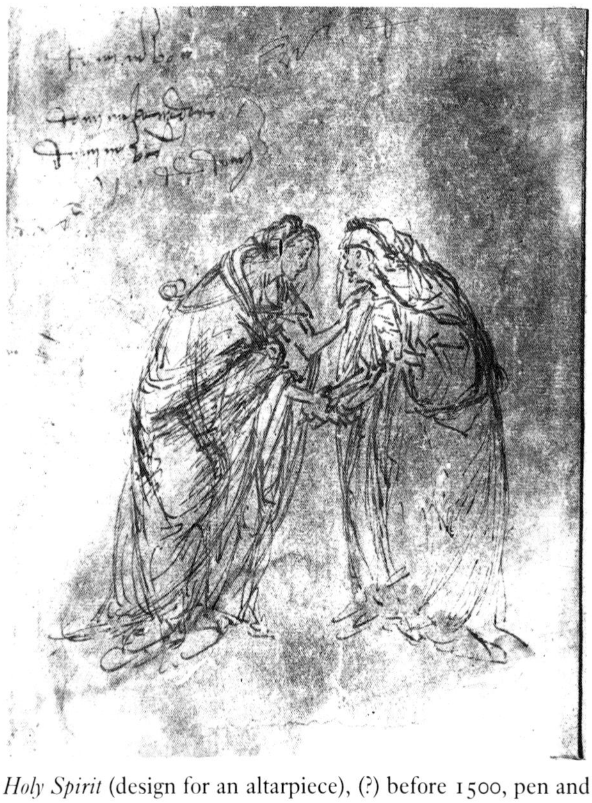

60 *Descent of the Holy Spirit* (design for an altarpiece), (?) before 1500, pen and ink over metalpoint. Fondation Custodia (Collection Frits Lugt), Institut Néerlandais, Paris.

61 *Virgin with St Elizabeth* (study for the Washington *Visitation*, illus. 87), pen and ink over chalk. Uffizi, Florence.

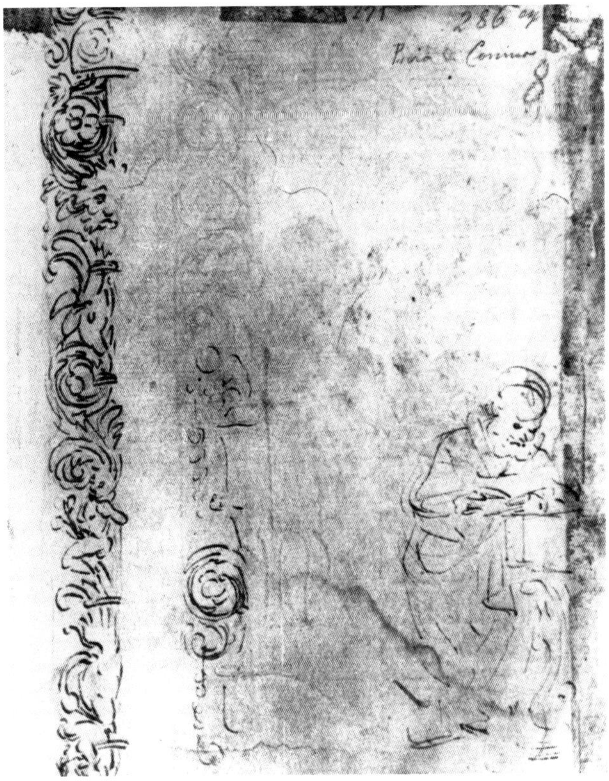

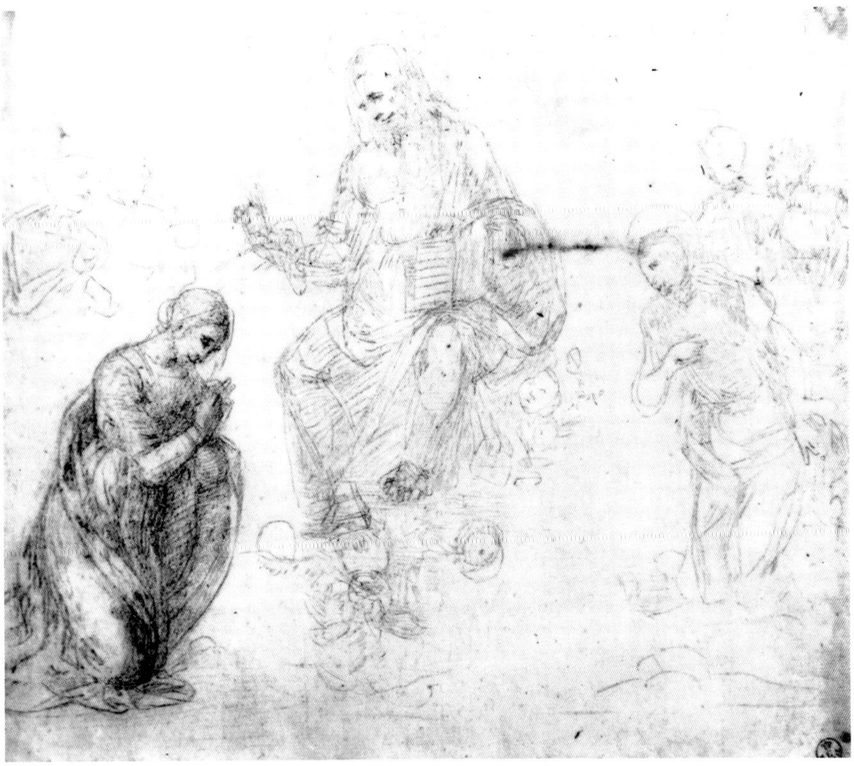

62 *Seated Figure at a Lectern and two Candelabra* (verso of illus. 61), pen and ink over chalk. Uffizi, Florence.

63 *Immaculate Conception* (study for the Fiesole *Immaculate Conception*, illus. 51), red and black chalk. Uffizi, Florence.

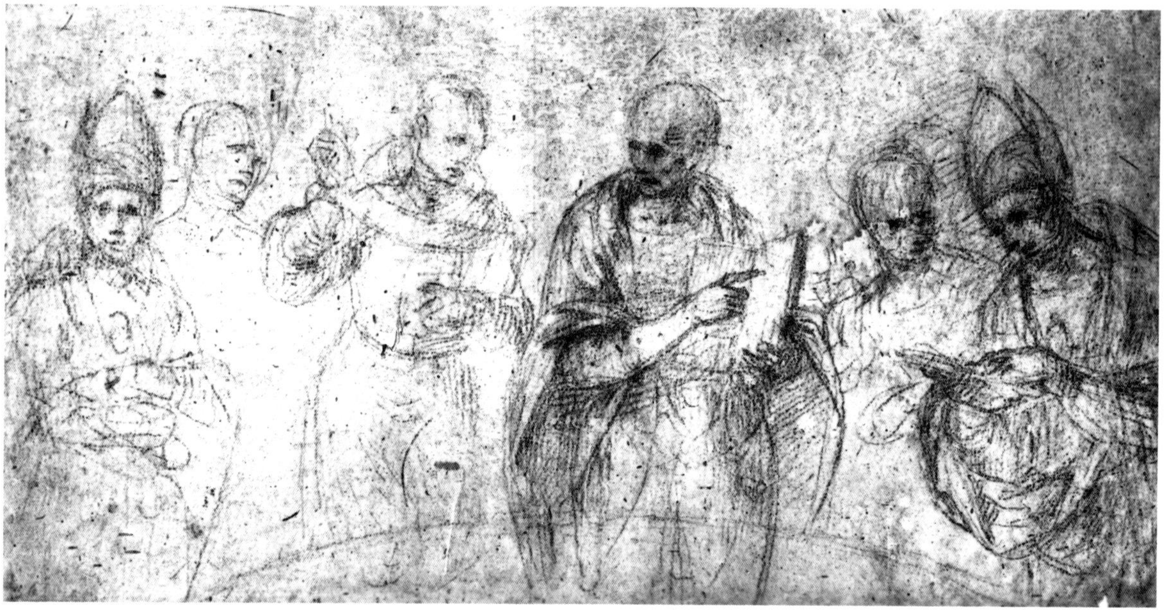

64 *Six Saints* (study for the Fiesole *Immaculate Conception*, illus. 51), chalk. Uffizi, Florence.

recorded on the dado beneath her, she accepts her destiny, 'extending her hands and raising her eyes to Heaven'. At that moment, according to the well-known medieval guide to ecclesiastical lore, *The Golden Legend*, 'the Son of God was conceived in her womb, perfect God and perfect man'.[23] But it has recently been suggested that the painting actually represents the Virgin Annunciate, accompanied by saints.[24] This would certainly be unusual, as there was an established iconography for the theme of the Virgin in contemplation after the departure of the angel. In such cases the Virgin is almost invariably shown alone, often reading, and without the conspicuous presence of the Holy Spirit. At the same time, as has been pointed out, an expanded image of the Virgin Annunciate would not have been inappropriate, given that the work was painted for the church of the Santissima Annunziata.[25] Nor does there appear to have been a particularly well-established iconography for the Incarnation, and it is possible that the distinction between the two subjects was not clear-cut. Piero may thus have been asked to paint an image of the Virgin Annunciate, which he interpreted in an unorthodox and imaginative way, showing the Virgin at the moment when she acknowledges her destiny, and the child is conceived within her.

Whatever the precise implications of the subject, the differences between the sketch and the painting in this instance are particularly striking. The painting shows the Virgin poised serenely on a pedestal beneath the dove of the Holy Spirit, surrounded by SS Catherine of Alexandria, Margaret, John the Evangelist, Peter, Philip Benizzi and Antoninus. In contrast, the sketch (illus. 65) presents the moment – and the descent of the Holy Spirit – as a dramatic event, perhaps stressing more overtly the notion of incarnation. The Virgin stands in vigorous *contrapposto* in the centre of a wide dais, her body twisted and hands raised as she looks up at the hovering dove. The female saints to either side of her are also highly animated, turning towards

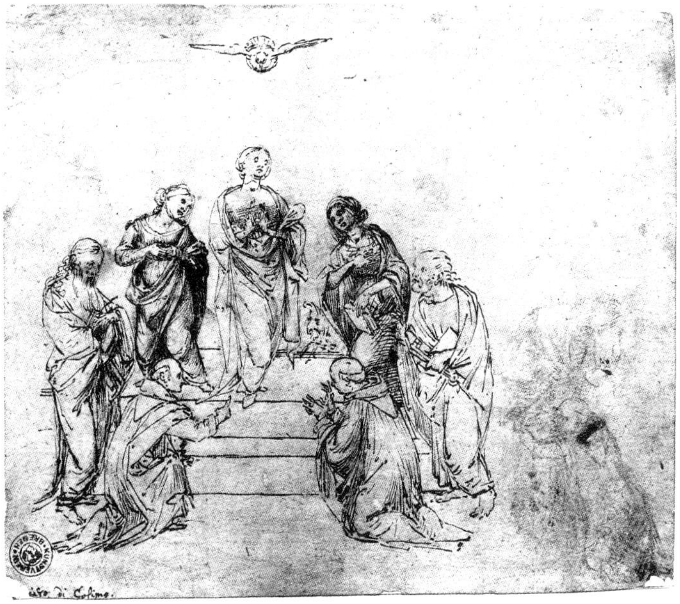

65 *Incarnation with Six Saints* (study for the Uffizi *Incarnation*, illus. 88), *c.*1505, pen and ink. Location unknown, formerly Bremen Kunsthalle.

her in attitudes of fervent devotion, as if directly witnessing a miraculous event. The immediacy and dynamism of the scene are further accentuated by the kneeling figures of SS Philip and Antoninus, who turn sharply inwards, and gesticulate towards the Virgin in wonderment and awe. It is hard to imagine how Piero could have translated this dynamic, narrative conception of the Incarnation into the larger format of the painting. Not only would the composition have appeared cumbersome and diffuse on a larger scale, but the dynamism of the figures, engendered largely by Piero's drawing technique and use of broken line, would inevitably have been lost. The *contrapposto* of the figures is also quite distinct from the type of posture Piero was able to construct on a large scale. For the painting, he thus altered the composition substantially, in ways that not only circumvented these problems but led to the production of one of his finest and most coherent works.

First, the conception of the theme is made more iconic, the Virgin being shown frontally oriented, and in a more static pose, while the narrative and symbolic implications of the theme are clarified by the relief of the Annunciation on her pedestal. The saints are also more passive, their movements and postures becoming simplified and less dynamic. In addition, Piero simplifies the whole composition by altering the positions of the figures, and showing the Virgin alone on a pedestal, which replaces the sketch's wide dais. He thus elevates her above the other figures, isolating her in space in a way that creates a clear formal and dramatic focus, accentuated by the fact that she is framed between the background hills. The reduction of the dais, and the use of an open landscape background, unencumbered by architectural devices, also allowed Piero to exploit his skill in using natural forms to articulate the composition. The Virgin is marked out by her placement against the river bed, the positions of the standing saints are echoed by the hills, and those of the kneeling saints, as well as the form of their profiles, follow the slopes of the valley. The subject allowed Piero to use light, *chiaroscuro* and his increasing mastery of subtle colour harmonies as a means of unifying the composition while underlining the symbolic content of the scene, something that Vasari noted with great enthusiasm.

In the light of this discussion it is significant that the most complex compositions in Piero's religious works are not to be found in the altarpieces, but in smaller works intended for private devotion, such as the *Madonna and Child with Angels* of 1505–10 in the Cini Collection, Venice (illus. 67), the *Holy Family with St John the Baptist* of *c.* 1520, in the same collection (illus. 68), and a small tondo of the *Madonna and Child with Saints*, painted during the period 1495–1505 (illus. 69).[26] The *Madonna and Child with Angels* and the tondo both draw on Leonardo's experiments with overlapping figures and interlocking patterns of gestures. The spiralling figure of the angel-musician in the former, for example, is taken from that of Leda in Leonardo's untraced *Leda and the Swan*, known from a preparatory drawing (illus. 66), and is co-ordinated with those of the Virgin and Child with a facility and refinement quite

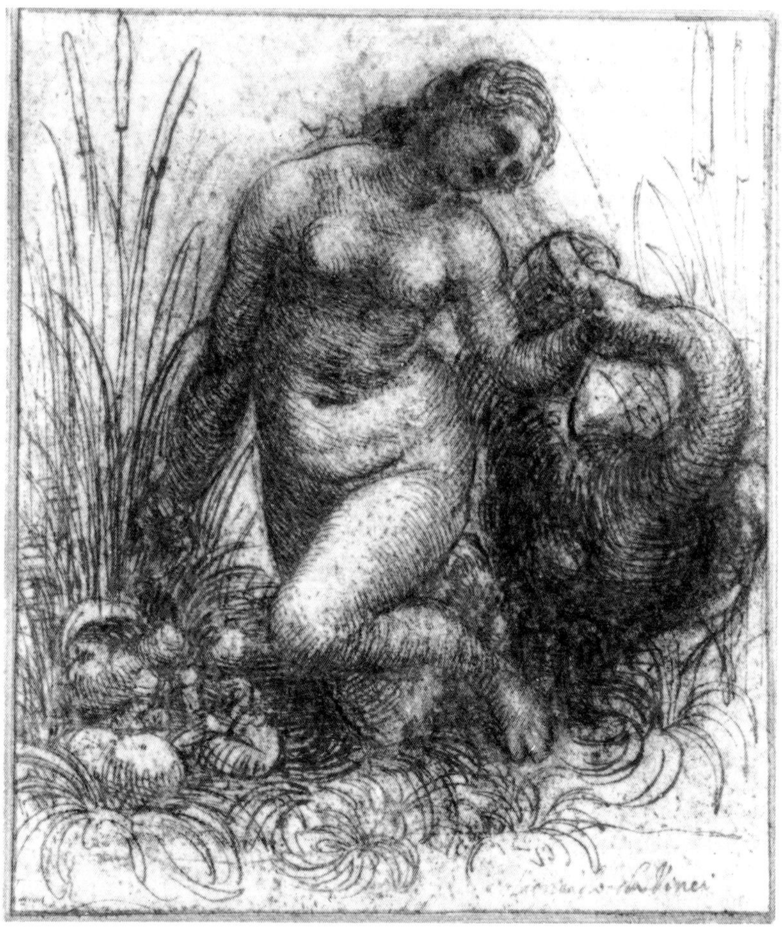

66 Leonardo da Vinci, *Leda and the Swan*, *c.*1505–7, pen and ink with chalk. Boymans–van Beuningen Museum, Rotterdam.

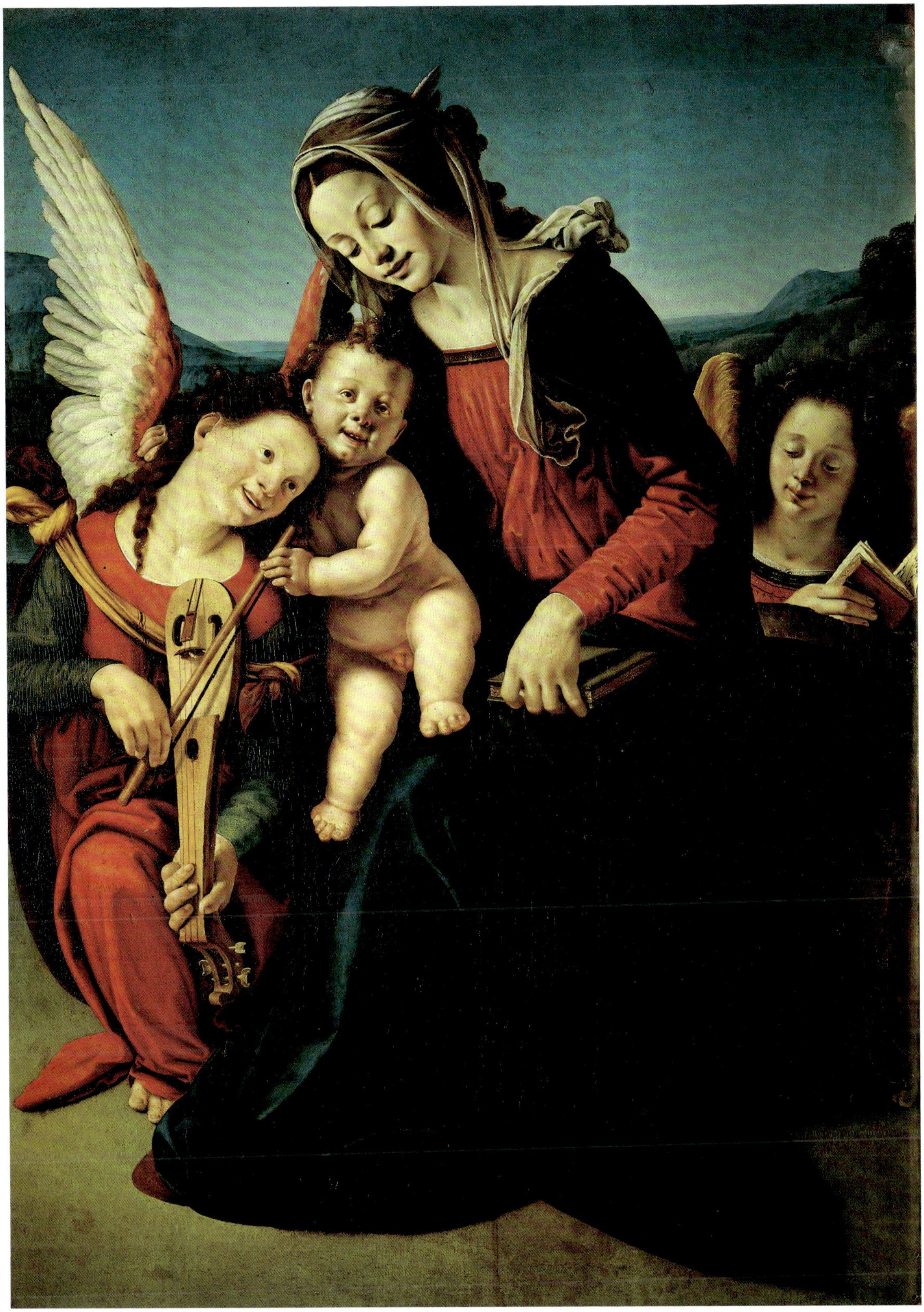

67 *Madonna and Child with Angels*, *c.*1505–10, oil on panel. Galleria di Palazzo Cini, Venice.

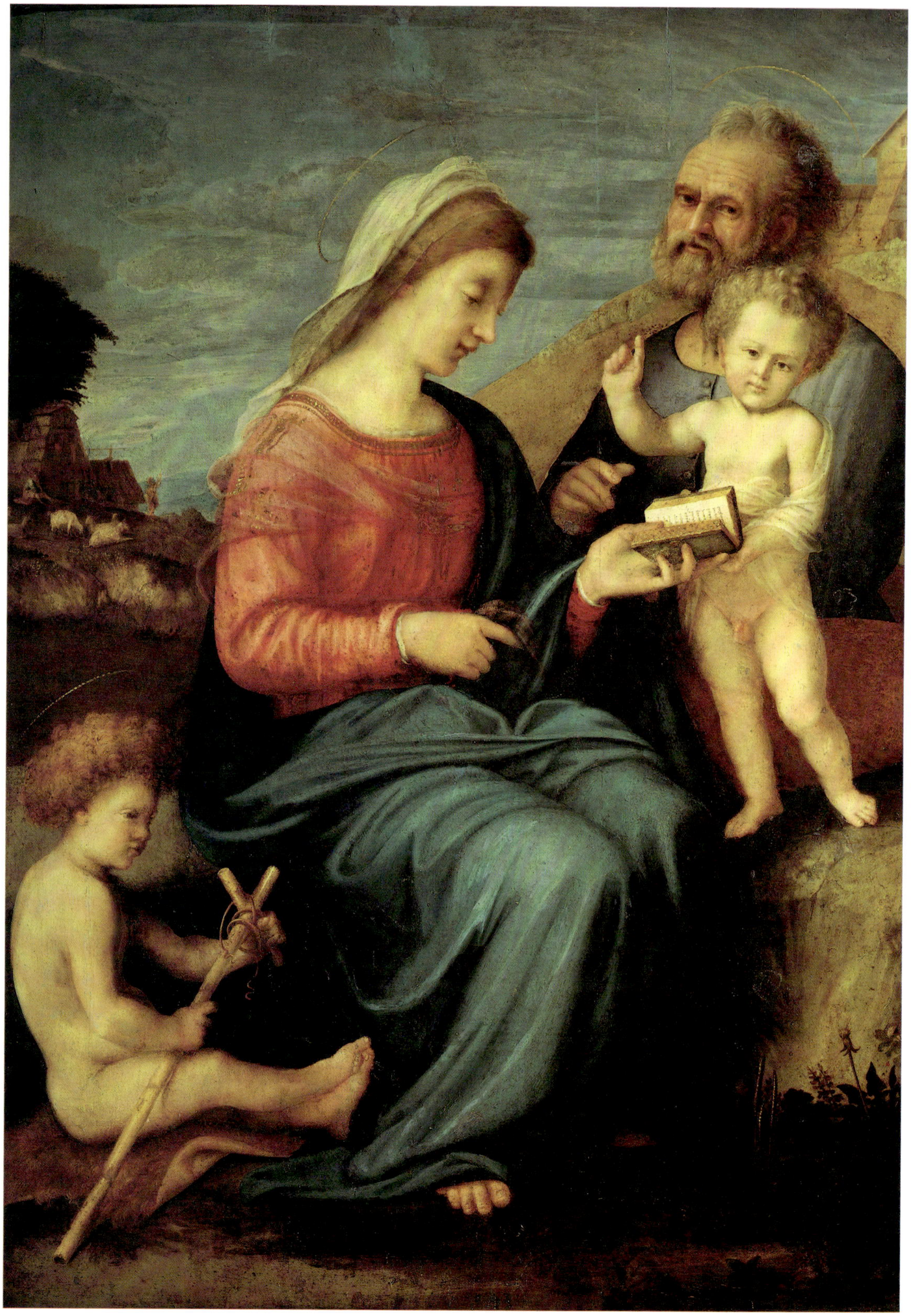

68 *The Holy Family with the young St John the Baptist*, *c.*1520, oil on panel. Galleria di Palazzo Cini, Venice.

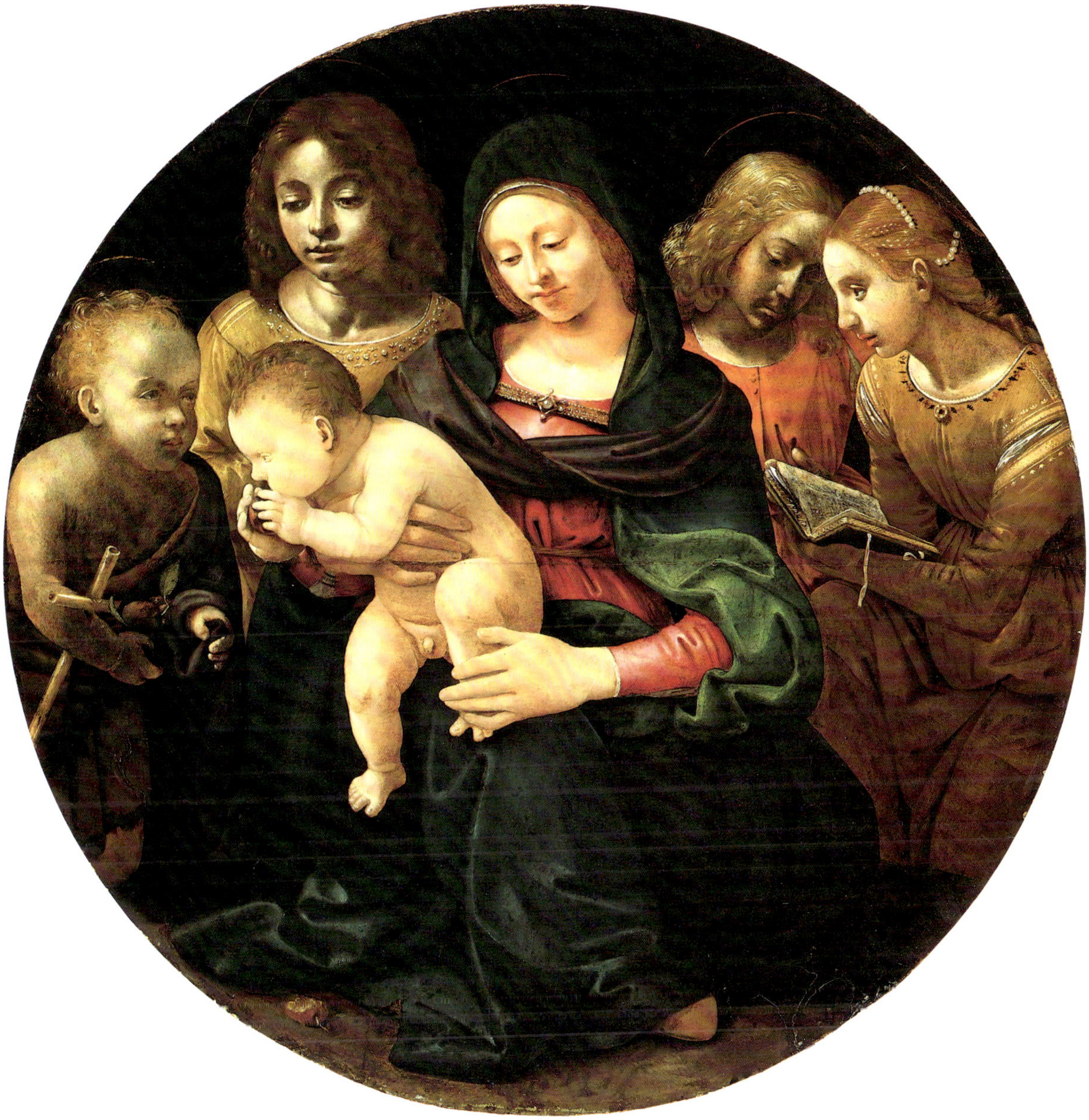

69 *Madonna and Child with Saints and Angels*, *c.*1495–1505, oil on panel. Private collection, New York.

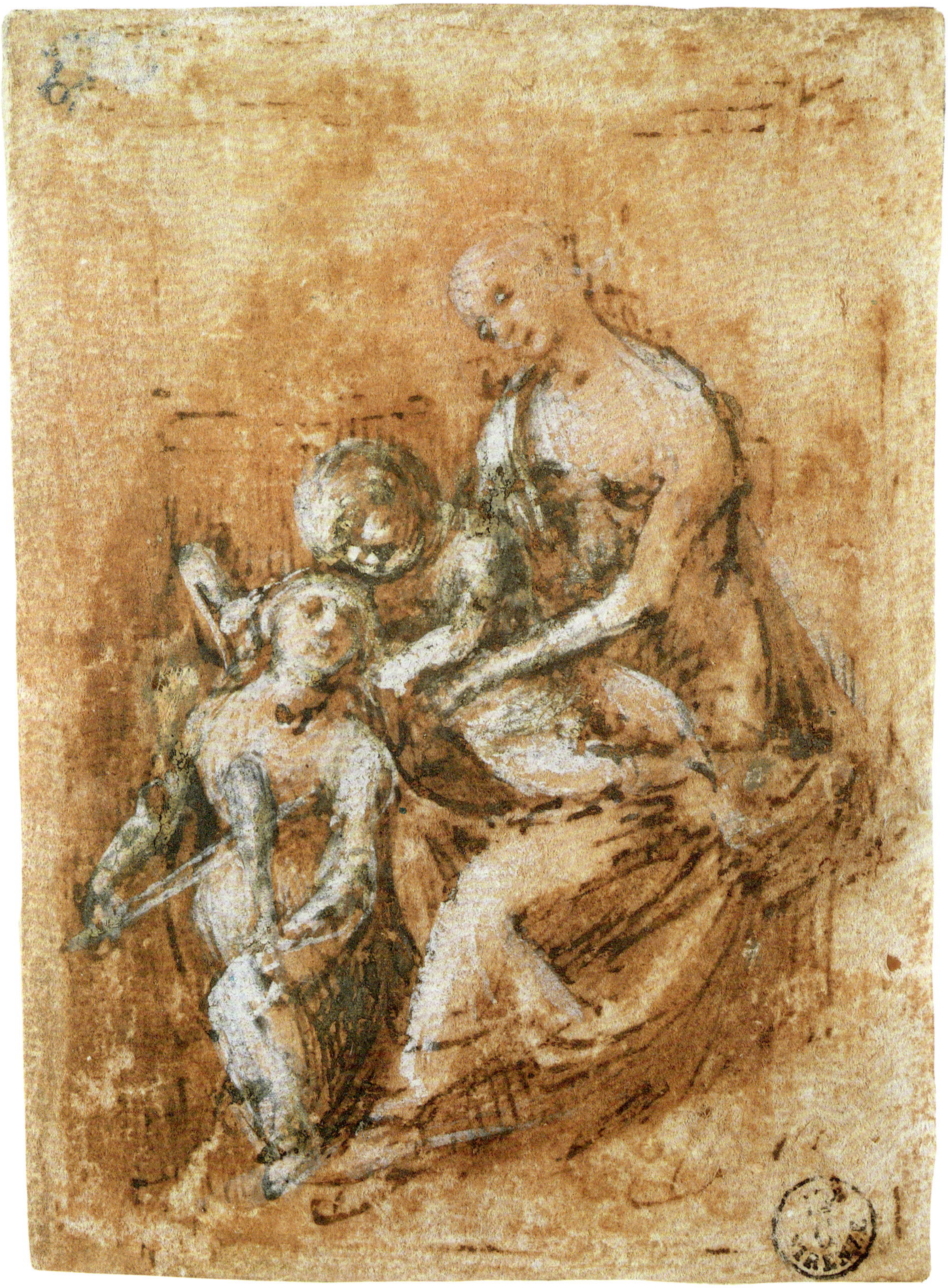

70 *Virgin and Child with a Musician Angel* (study for the Venice *Madonna and Child with Angels*, illus. 67), pen and ink with wash. Uffizi, Florence.

absent from the larger works. In this instance, unusually, the finished painting also has a greater fluency than Piero's preliminary study for the work (illus. 70), which shows him experimenting with the arrangement of figures. In the tondo, the tightly knit grouping of overlapping figures may refer in a general way to Leonardo's *Madonna and Child with St Anne* (illus. 91), and the work displays a density and concentration in the arrangement of figures that Piero rarely attempted on a larger scale.[27] In the *Holy Family with St John the Baptist*, the figures are successfully placed at varying angles to the picture plane, and that of the seated Virgin is one of Piero's most accomplished. It may also be significant that Piero's altarpieces are, for the most part, on a modest scale, and that he was not commissioned for works of the size produced by Raphael, Fra Bartolommeo or Andrea del Sarto, for example, suggesting that his patrons recognized the scope of his talent and the nature of his limitations. That is not to say that Piero's altarpieces do not have distinctive features, and they all possess considerable visual appeal. Generally speaking, however, their distinctive qualities reside less in the figures than in other aspects of the works, such as use of landscape and still-life details, the handling of light and the colour range.

In all the early altarpieces the landscapes are strikingly anecdotal, and while the colouring and use of light owe much to Leonardo, the individual features of the settings are unusual in their familiarity, and quite different from Leonardo's fantastic landscape forms. In the Montevettolini and Toronto altarpieces, for example, the backgrounds are formed of ordinary hills and valleys, dotted with vernacular buildings and peopled by shepherds and fishermen whose activities are observed with scrupulous precision. Piero also incorporated symbolic details and subsidiary scenes into his works in an unusually subtle way, integrating them unobtrusively with their surroundings. In the Toronto altarpiece the homely countryside beyond St Onofrius is patrolled by two lions (a reference to those that reputedly helped dig his grave), whose presence seems wholly natural, while above him flies a raven, for it was said that one fed him during his sojourn in the desert. In the *Incarnation*, a rustic but strangely anthropomorphic landscape accommodates with only slight incongruity the Annunciation to the Shepherds and the Nativity on the left, and the Flight into Egypt on the right, where fleeing figures wind their way up the hillside into a typical Tuscan town.

Piero's treatment of detail in these works is also highly inventive, and enhanced by the clear, limpid light that illuminates the foreground, defining textures and casting shadows that are rendered with painstaking exactness. In the Toronto altarpiece the clothing of both saints, and the crozier of St Augustine, are distinctive in the imaginative eye for detail they reveal, and the precision with which they are observed. St Onofrius is dressed in a loin-cloth of dried palm leaves, a reference to the tree that fed him in the desert and shrivelled at his death, each part of which is carefully distinguished and rendered. In the dress of St Augustine, Piero carefully contrasts the crude, inelegant form of the monastic habit, its rough fabric pulled in by an untidy leather belt, with the fineness of his episcopal cope, adorned with pearls and trimmings of gold, while his crozier is surmounted by a delicate figure of an angel poised in prayer.[28]

In each work Piero skilfully combines the clear, well-defined light of the foreground with other, less direct sources of lighting, some seemingly natural, some apparently divine, which subtly point up the symbolic content of the work. In the *Incarnation*, for example, a ray of sunlight striking the church on the right, and the supernatural light falling on the shepherds on the left are both eclipsed in intensity by the brilliant illumination cast by the Holy Spirit. While in general terms the bright, rather metallic colouring of these early works is typical of that used by Piero's contemporaries, the particular colour harmonies are original and distinctive, as in the red, orange and grey tones of the Montevettolini altarpiece, the glowing green and scarlet of the Toronto painting, and the vivid note of emerald green that dominates the *Pala Pugliese*.

By *c.* 1505, however, when the *Incarnation* was painted, the skills Piero brought to such commissions were in many ways outmoded, and in the hands of artists such as Raphael, Andrea del Sarto and Fra Bartolommeo the altarpiece was changing in ways that were foreign to Piero's talents.[29] First, perhaps under the influence of Alberti's emphasis on the narrative *istoria* as the artist's most elevated task, altarpieces were conceived in an increasingly dramatic way. One of the earliest and best-known manifestations of this development is Leonardo's *Adoration of the Magi*, begun in 1481, for the monastery of S. Donato a Scopeto near Florence, which transformed the conventional, relatively iconic, representation of the theme into a form of dramatic narrative.[30] Even subjects such as the *sacra conversazione*, which did not obviously demand or lend themselves to a narrative interpretation, were treated by many artists in a semi-dramatic way, with vigorous, overtly expressive gestures, and with an emphasis on the formal and psychological unity of the figures. Partly in order to accommodate these developments, and partly as a result of an increased emphasis on the figure as an object of skill, altarpieces also grew in size, with the figures themselves occupying more of the pictorial field. In many cases, these developments also prompted a suppression of the kind of background detail at which Piero excelled, which risked detracting from the figures. These developments almost certainly posed problems for Piero, and the number of altarpieces he carried out does appear to have decreased after the *Incarnation*. While the only partial survival of his works makes it difficult to establish the pattern of his commissions with any certainty, he appears to have been less in demand for altarpieces during this period of change. His remaining works also suggest that, during this time, he sought to establish himself rather as a painter of tondi for domestic use, and of *spalliera* panels, both of which were better suited to his talents.

There are, none the less, a few altarpieces that survive from the last years of Piero's career, which indicate his response to these transformations, and in a particularly interesting way. The most notable of these, apart from the late *Immaculate Conception*, are the *Madonna and Child with SS Thomas and John the Baptist* (illus. 71) in the Chiesa del Crocifisso, Borgo San Lorenzo, and the *Madonna and Child with SS Dominic and Jerome* (illus. 95) in the Yale University Art Gallery, New Haven, both of which Piero

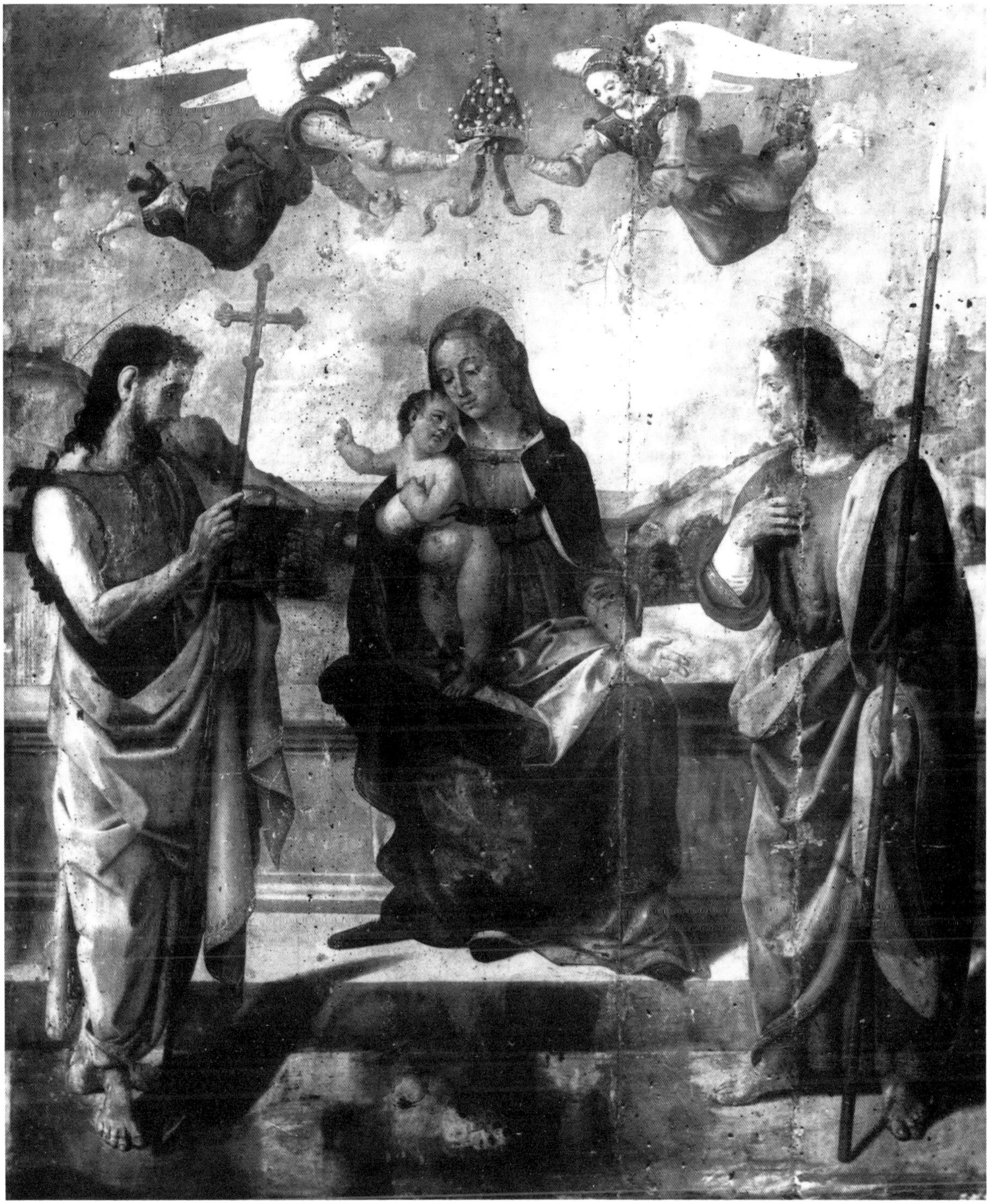

71 *Madonna and Child with SS Thomas and John the Baptist*, *c*.1510–20, oil on panel. Chiesa del Crocifisso, Borgo San Lorenzo, Florence.

must have painted between 1510 and 1520, that is, in the last decade of his life. They are on a large scale, and the original size of the New Haven work, which has been cut down, would have made it Piero's most sizeable commission of this kind.[31] In both paintings, the figures are large in relation to the pictorial field, especially compared to Piero's earlier works. They are also placed close to the picture plane, and have a presence and forcefulness that those in the earlier altarpieces lack, accentuated by the fact that they are simply structured, and their drapery is less complex. Their gestures are also more forceful and emphatic, and made more effective by being isolated against the background, or against the broad planes of the figures themselves. The impact of the figures is further accentuated by the plainness of their settings and the simplification of the landscape backgrounds, which in this respect contrast markedly with those of the earlier works. While Piero still uses the shapes of the landscape to underline the figures' positions, and to structure the composition as a whole, the shapes themselves are notably less complex. At the same time, while the backgrounds are still full of incident, especially in the case of the New Haven painting, the details are spread out, and the main expanses of the landscape are painted in relatively generalized terms.

To this extent Piero signals his awareness of recent developments, and these late works have something of the breadth and grandeur achieved by contemporary artists such as Fra Bartolommeo in *God the Father with SS Mary Magdalen and Catherine of Siena* (illus. 93), an altarpiece that Piero almost certainly knew.[32] But in other ways they retain features that link them clearly with Piero's earlier works. Piero does not utilize the depth of the painting, but places the figures in the foreground, as far as possible parallel to the surface of the work. They do not turn in and out of depth, and Piero does not attempt complex foreshortenings so that, despite their size, the figures have little sense of mass, and do not appear to displace or fully occupy the space in which they stand. The compositions are rigorously oriented towards the plane, relying for their effect on the intervals between figures and shapes arranged parallel to the surface. In their spaciousness and simplicity, their two-dimensional appearance and the plain but eloquent gestures of the figures, the works thus recall those of Perugino at the end of the fifteenth century, as much as those of Piero's immediate contemporaries. The comparison with Perugino is significant, for his works enjoyed great popularity in the late fifteenth and early sixteenth centuries, although in the *Lives* Vasari implies strong criticism of the simplicity and repetitive nature of his works.[33] Their spacious compositions, generalized figures and simple yet deliberate gestures appear to have made them especially effective as aids to devotion. It is partly for this reason, perhaps, that his works appear to have been particularly popular at the time when the influence of Savonarola was at its height.[34]

For Piero, whatever the devotional potentialities of Perugino's works, they appear to have provided him with a model of a plain but monumental compositional style compatible with his own talents, and which combined the spaciousness and grandeur of Fra Bartolommeo with a simple and relatively two-dimensional approach to the figure and its gestures.[35] The gentle, undulating shapes of Perugino's landscape, and the composition of works such as his *Pietà* (illus. 79) of 1495 find clear echoes in Piero's late altarpieces, such as the *Pietà* (illus. 83) in Perugia painted around 1510, and the altarpieces in Borgo San Lorenzo and New Haven. The works have the same open, airy feel, and rely in a similar way on simple but contrasting poses, and on the opposition between flat but imposing figures and areas of empty space.

Private Devotional Works

If the altarpiece demanded skills outside Piero's range, religious paintings for private devotion allowed him to exploit his talents to the utmost. While it would be a mistake to overemphasize the distinction between the two, especially in iconographic terms, religious works for the home appear to have allowed artists a greater freedom and flexibility than altarpieces, both in the treatment of subject-matter, and in terms of composition.[36] At the same time, the subjects favoured for such works, such as the Holy Family, or the Adoration of the Child, themselves allowed a less formal and hierarchical arrangement of figures, minimizing the difficulties Piero encountered in co-ordinating figures on a large scale. In addition, the emphasis on fine detail, at which Piero excelled, and which was progressively eliminated from altarpieces, remained a feature of private religious works for a considerable time, reflecting their different religious role as well as their decorative function.

This is particularly true of the tondo, the type of commission that features most frequently among Piero's religious works. Recent research has shown that tondi were particularly highly prized as aids to devotion and for their aesthetic appeal, and were often the most costly objects in a patron's private collection, commanding higher prices even than secular works.[37] In part this may reflect the fact that, of all the objects a patron could commission for the home, the tondo was potentially one of the most decorative, the circular format accentuating and enhancing its ornamental function, while encouraging artists to take an inventive approach to the problem of composition.[38] In many respects, therefore, the tondo was more amenable to Piero's skills than the altarpiece, and his works in this genre comprise the most distinguished and sophisticated part of his religious output. The number by his hand that survive suggests he was highly sought after for such works, and that the combination of psychological subtlety and intricate detail that characterizes this aspect of his output was appreciated by many sorts of patron.

Piero's tondi mostly comprise variations on the theme of the Virgin and Child or the Holy Family, with the exception of a small *St Jerome* (illus. 96). Unlike some artists working in the genre, such as Botticelli or Lorenzo di Credi, he did not attempt such subjects as the Adoration of the Magi, which demand large numbers of figures and more complex compositions. He did, however, approach his limited subject-matter with an unusual freshness and sensitivity, elaborating both its thematic and decorative potential through the use of subsidiary scenes and a wealth of symbolic detail.

The earliest of Piero's surviving tondi is almost certainly that in the Toledo Museum of Art, probably painted in the late 1490s, and showing the Virgin in adoration before the Child (illus. 72). The subject is a conventional one, which derived in general terms from an account of the Nativity in the *Revelations* of the fourteenth-century saint, Bridget of Sweden. The *Revelations* relate that the Virgin gave birth kneeling and without pain, and instantly began worshipping the Child as he lay before her on the ground.[39] Piero depicts this moment of adoration, while St Joseph who, according to St Bridget, withdrew during the birth, sleeps under a rudimentary shelter in the left background. The references to the Nativity are completed by the ox and ass beside him; on the right a lone shepherd tends his flocks. Among the plants surrounding the Virgin is lady's bedstraw, pieces of which were thought to have been mixed with the straw on which she lay in the stable at Bethlehem.[40] Piero, however, amplifies the theme in a variety of ways, elaborating on its implications of new life and introducing portents of the Child's eventual death. The Virgin has before her a book inscribed with verses taken from the Letter to the Hebrews, in which God is said to have praised his Son with words beginning 'It is you, Lord, who laid earth's foundations in the beginning, the heavens are the work of your hands . . .'.[41] Unusually within depictions of the Nativity or the Adoration of the Child, Christ is shown sleeping, in a pose which foreshadows that of the *Pietà*, thus alluding to his death and the Virgin's mourning of his adult body. These allusions are continued in the dandelions among the grass, often used as a symbol of the Passion, and in the form of the bird, a common symbol of the human soul – although it may act here as a symbol of fertility.[42] References to death and new life are also implicit in the tree-stump budding with new growth beside Christ's head, while a spring of clear water tumbles into a pool teeming with tadpoles and winged insects.[43] The ground beneath the figures is lush and fertile and dotted with various flowers, while behind the Child rises an ominous outcrop of barren rock.

The subject of a tondo in Dresden, painted around the same time, or shortly after that in Toledo, is more obviously the Holy Family (illus. 73). The Virgin kneels before the Child within the shelter of a rock, cradling him protectively, with St Joseph and the young St John the Baptist completing the group. If a wider narrative context is implied here it is probably that of the Rest on the Flight into Egypt rather than the Nativity. An ass grazes alone in the right background, while two singing angels watch over the family. The Virgin's cloak and head-dress are knotted as if for travelling, and the immediate foreground includes objects often found in scenes of the Rest on the Flight. These include a water-flask, here encased in wicker, and pairs of cherries, conventional symbols of Heaven, but possibly also a reference to the fruit that miraculously fed Christ during the journey.[44] Piero also constructs within the group of figures a complex web of gestures and glances that enriches and amplifies the thematic connotations of the scene, and invites us to contemplate the full range of its significance. The Virgin responds to the Child's lively attention with a solemn glance, suggestive of foreboding, in a manner that is repeated by the angel in pink above her.

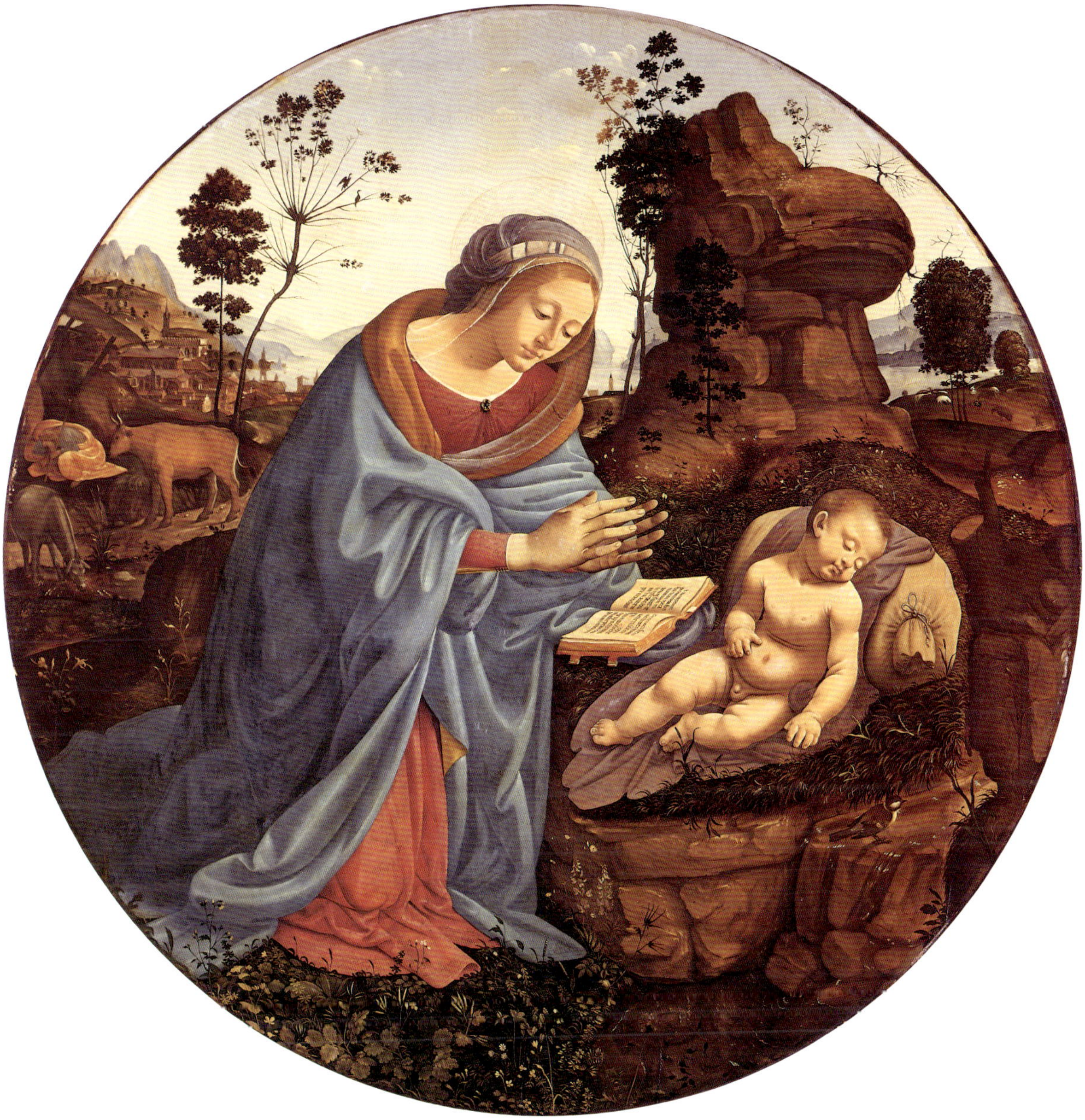

72 *Adoration of the Child*, *c.*1495–1500, oil on wood. Toledo Museum of Art, OH.

The Baptist rests his hand protectively on the Child's head, his cross raised portentously behind it, whilst St Joseph indicates the Child with a gesture that, for Piero, is unusually overt.

Piero's allusive approach to his subjects reaches its most complex in a tondo of the *Adoration of the Child* (illus. 74) painted around 1500–5, now in the National Gallery of Art, Washington. As in the Toledo tondo the Virgin kneels in adoration of the Child, although here she is more distant from him and her action is amplified by the addition of an angel and the young St John, their hands clasped in prayer. The immediate narrative context is again that of the Nativity, made more explicit than in the Toledo painting by the conspicuous presence of the ox and the ass, the hay on which the Child lies, the saddle behind the kneeling angel and the imaginatively rendered shelter, whose steps Joseph descends. The Child is shown awake, as was customary in such scenes but, unusually, rather than gazing at or reaching toward his mother he turns towards the viewer, commanding as much attention as the Virgin's silent prayer. The scene is made more complex by the inclusion of subsidiary figures and scenes. At the top of the shelter are three magnificent angels, one poised commandingly on the steps, and two in flight, each bearing a flowering branch. The latter two appear to guide the steps of three horsemen in the left background who, although they lack their customary retinue, are almost certainly the Magi, and must thus refer to Epiphany. Less clear is the significance of the two haloed figures on the extreme left, one standing, the other seated holding a cross of the type conventionally carried by the Baptist. It seems likely they are intended to represent Christ and the Baptist as adults. While the specific nature of their encounter, and the reason for their inclusion, are by no means certain, and may reflect some particular interest or object of devotion on the part of the patron, it is possible that they allude to the occasion on which Christ came to St John to be baptized, since, according to *The Golden Legend*, this took place on the same day of the year as the Epiphany.[45]

There can be little doubt that the latest surviving tondo by Piero is the one in the Philbrook Museum of Art in Tulsa, painted between 1515 and 1520, where the subject is again subtly different (illus. 75). Here, the focus of attention is the Madonna and Child, accompanied by St John and two angels. The figure on the right is usually identified as St Margaret, while in the background is a vignette of St Martin dividing his cloak with a beggar. Once again references to the Passion are built into the work, with St John handing the Christ Child a lamb, the implications of this being underscored by the strategic placing of two crosses on the rock, and the crown of thorns hanging casually on the tree-stump to the left.[46]

For the patron, the primary focus of all these works was almost certainly the Virgin and Child, and the paintings would have been commissioned as such, as images of the Virgin and Child. The patron is also likely to have specified the saints to be included in each case.[47] Beyond this, however, the particular formulation of the figures and their relationships, and the devising of subsidiary scenes, must in most cases have been left to the artist. In Piero's case the additional details, and the allusion to other events in the life of Christ included in the tondi, were almost certainly his own invention, and he may well have been sought after particularly for his abilities in this respect, for the inventiveness of his secondary scenes and for the subtle but suggestive way in which he was able to amplify the narrative and symbolic connotations of his subjects.

Piero's tondi are distinguished primarily by the imaginative nature of the subsidiary scenes and objects he employs, and the way in which they are incorporated into the image. The figures he uses in this respect are often unusual in themselves, and frequently lack their conventional attributes or distinguishing features. In the Washington tondo, for example, we see the Magi without their customary retinue or the rich garments by which they are normally identified. They appear as ordinary travellers in undistinguished attire, while their gifts are only hinted at by the small gold object held by the foremost figure. They approach without ceremony, winding their way through ordinary plains and hills, rather than through the kind of mountainous landscape that most artists employed as a setting for their journey. At the same time, rather than being clearly identified as subsidiary or incidental by being placed in a different setting, or set apart from the main focus of the picture, they are set within the same spatial continuum as the Virgin and Child, as if present in the same place and time. The adult Christ and Baptist also form part of the scene, as if simultaneously present with their infant selves, the two parts of the painting being further connected through the placing of the ox and the ass. Likewise, the angels who guide the Magi inhabit the same setting as St Joseph, one poised quite casually at the top of the steps Joseph descends. These continuities are accentuated by the gestures linking the figures: the leading Magus addresses the seated figures on the left, while the Magi as a group are united with the Adoration scene by the gestures of the angels.

In a tondo of the *Madonna and Child with St John* (illus. 76) that dates from the late 1490s, now in the Musée des Beaux-Arts in Strasbourg, the Virgin and Child in the foreground are linked, in an analogous way, with St Bernard and St Jerome in the background. While the two infants are isolated on a parapet, the Virgin and the Saints occupy a shared landscape that also subtly combines the familiar and the exotic, unobtrusively linking natural and symbolic forms. St Bernard looks up towards the Virgin, his pen poised in one hand as if seeing her in a vision, while St Jerome is transfixed before his cross.[48] Piero thus gives a semi-narrative quality to a conventional image of the Virgin and Child with Saints. Likewise, in the Tulsa tondo, St Martin and the beggar move through the landscape towards St Margaret, who in turn connects them with the foreground as she watches the children wrestle with the lamb.

Piero also incorporates symbolic objects and attributes into each image in a unusually unobtrusive and naturalistic way, eliding the distinction between the symbolic and the real in a manner that accentuates the unrhetorical quality of the work as a whole. In the Strasbourg tondo the different parts of the landscape are in fact quite distinct, and function in part as attributes of the saints. Yet they also appear to be continuous, the wilder landscape around the penitent Jerome, behind whom fishermen and labourers go quietly about their business, blending almost imperceptibly into

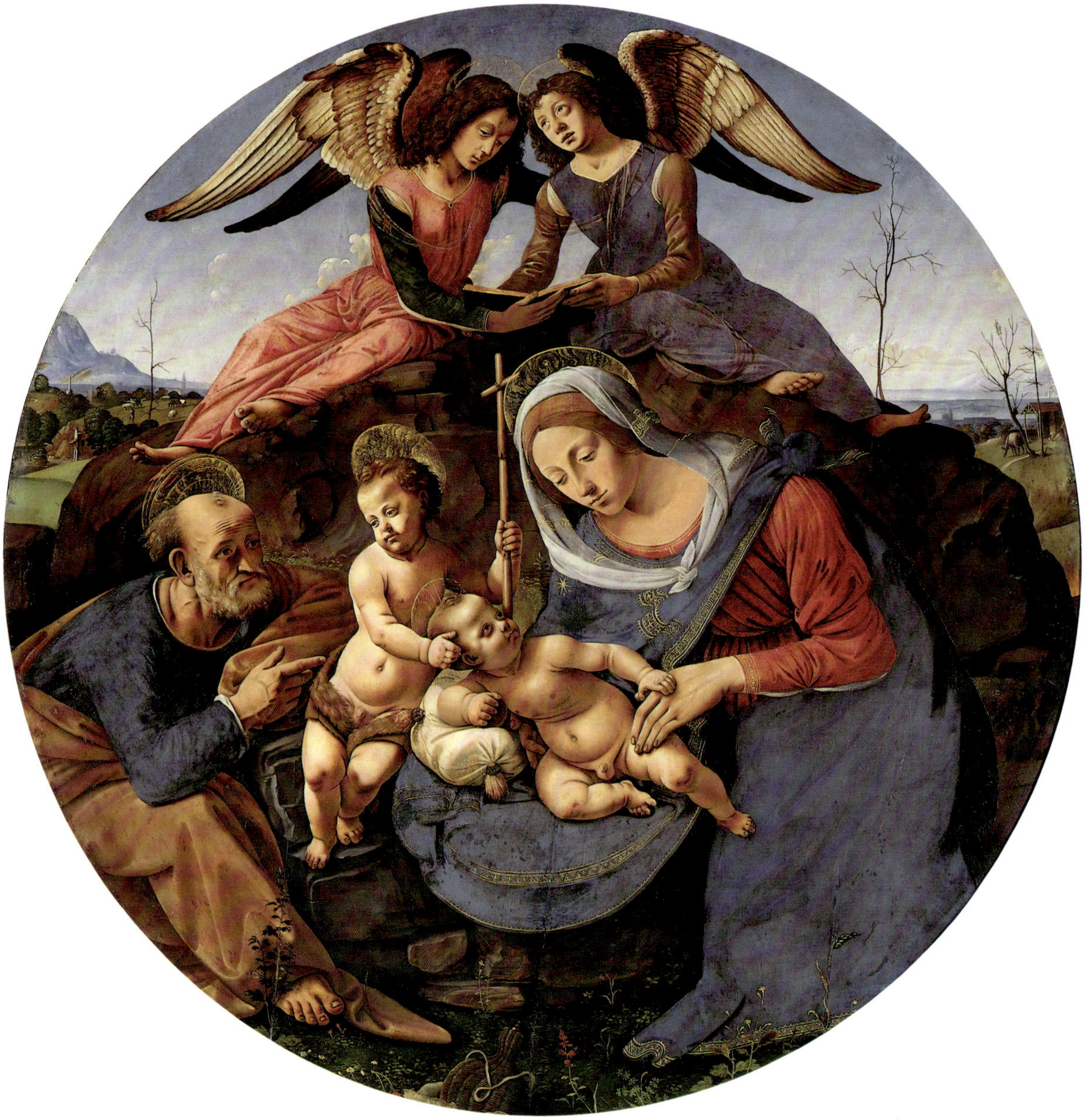

73 *Holy Family with the young St John and Angels*, *c.*1495–1500, oil on panel. Gemäldegalerie Alte Meister, Dresden.

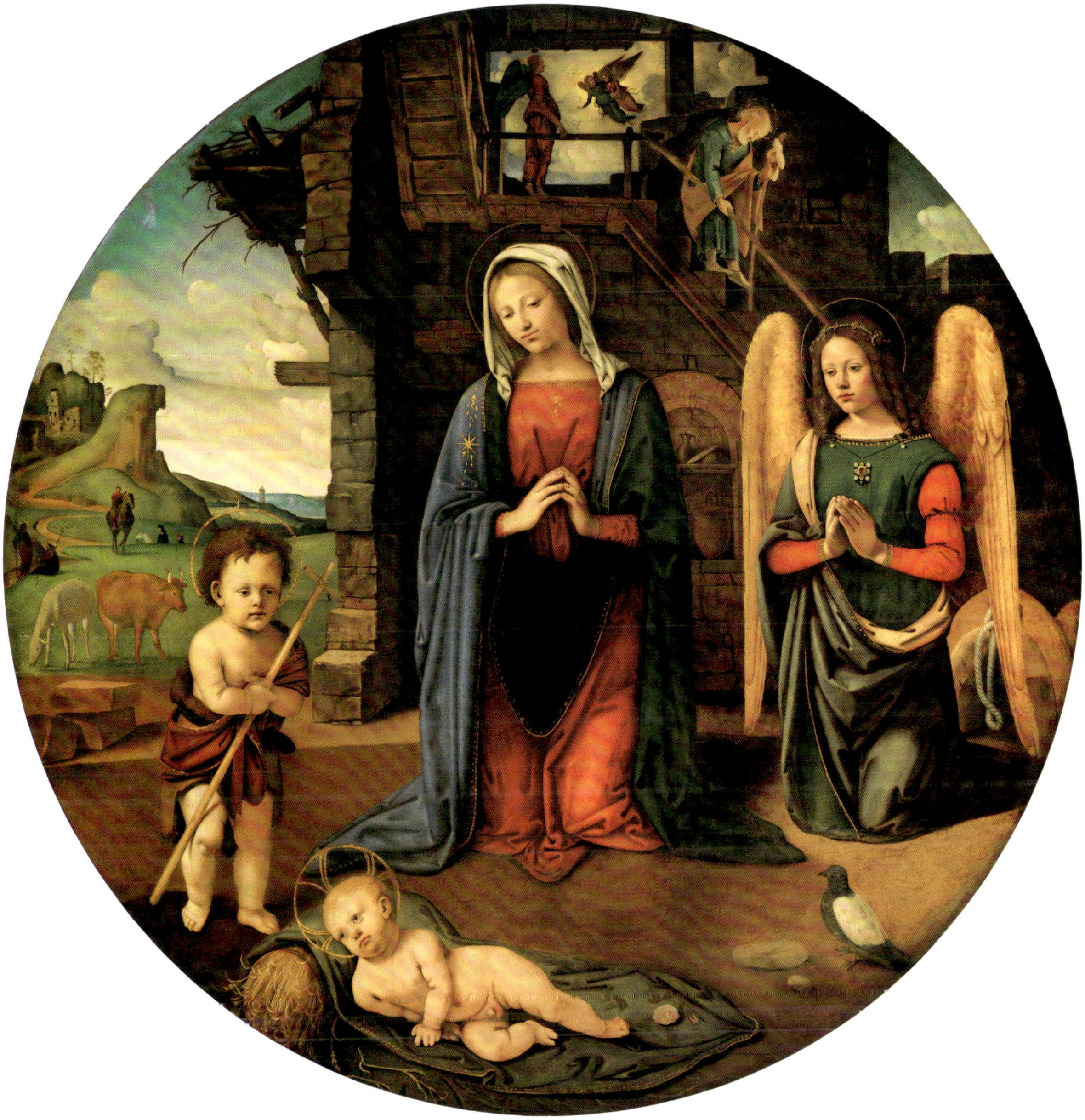

74 *Adoration of the Child with the young St John*, *c.*1500–5, oil on canvas. National Gallery of Art, Washington DC.

the ordered, cultivated setting in which St Bernard sits, against the backdrop of a Cistercian monastery. At the same time, Jerome's lion and cross, and the chained demon that functions as a symbol of St Bernard conquering heresy, appear as natural inhabitants or products of the landscape itself, rather than symbolic objects superimposed on or introduced into it. In the same way, in the Toledo tondo, the bird, the spring and the pond life, all of which have clear symbolic connotations, form part of the naturalistic setting in a seemingly unaccented way, while in the Tulsa tondo the crown of thorns alluding to the Passion hangs almost carelessly over the tree-stump on the left.

Thus, while none of the images is narrative in any strict sense, Piero weaves around the central figures a range of narrative contexts or references that are richly allusive, without being strictly defined or made explicit through conventional symbols or motifs. The allusions he sets up in this way are enhanced by his characteristically reticent use of gesture, the subtlety with which he implies the pyschological links between figures and the continuities between them, and the unobtrusive way symbolic objects are introduced. There is no doubt that these devices lead to a certain diffusion of interest: like the *spalliera* panels, the tondi often lack a clear focus of attention. As in the *spalliera* panels, this is further accentuated by the fact that Piero does not give the figures clear priority over the background, and paints both with similar attention to detail. To some extent this dispersal of interest may have been less apparent to a viewer who was culturally attuned to focus on the Virgin as the main subject of the work, and the object of his devotion, and whose attention was probably predisposed in a way that is now difficult to grasp. At the same time, Piero's approach to the tondi was not inappropriate to their function, for while it is difficult to be certain about the manner in which such objects were used, they are likely to have been the focus of more prolonged and more individual contemplation than altarpieces, and were probably not expected to be didactic in the same way, or as clear-cut and explicit in their content. The effectiveness of the tondi, in fact, may well have depended on the scope they offered for sustained meditation and the extent to which they elaborated on the implications of the main figures, and their relationship to one another. In this respect Piero's works may have been particularly effective, providing a range of narrative and symbolic allusions that offered scope for contemplation without being over-explicit, thus leaving room for the viewer's own imaginative projections. The inventive use of detail, such as the ruined shelter in the Washington tondo, with the unusual motif of St Joseph descending the steps, and its meticulous still-life of domestic utensils, must also have served to make the scene more vivid, while adding to the decorative potential of the work.

The tondi are also distinctive in the way in which Piero utilizes the circular format. It was a format which coincided particularly well with his preference for organic forms as a means of structuring his compositions, and with his tendency to compose on the surface of the image, rather than in depth. The frame of a tondo tends naturally to limit the field of vision and one's inclination to look into depth, and itself draws attention to the surface of a work, a tendency Piero subtly but consistently exploits by echoing the shape of the tondo within the actual image. In the Toledo and the Dresden examples, the top arch of the frame is repeated in the curve of the rock mass that serves as a backdrop for the figures. In the former this device serves as a means of bringing the Madonna closer to the surface, emphasizing her separateness from the sleeping Joseph, and the private nature of her moment of devotion. The semicircular shape, accentuated by crevices and striations in the rock, also serves to unite the composition: it is systematically echoed in Joseph's huddled form, in the lines of the Virgin's drapery and in the curves of the background landscape.

In the Dresden tondo a similar arch of rock again provides an internal echo of the frame, accentuated by the sweep of the angels' wings that closely follows its lines, bringing the figures forward and curbing the eye's movement into depth. In the Washington tondo the composition is given focus and stability by the shape of the shelter, whose rigorous verticals and horizontals are repeated in the clouds and in the upright postures of the kneeling figures. This rigidly geometric base is, however, softened, and brought into relation with the frame by the body of the Christ Child, which follows its lower curve, by the lines of the cloak on which he lies and by the winding path on the left. The arch of the frame of the Tulsa painting is reiterated throughout the composition, with a subtlety and attention to detail that recall the *Liberation of Andromeda*, which Piero produced about the same date. It is echoed most obviously in the sweep of the angels' wings, but also in the smooth lines of their profiles and rounded physiognomies, the parallel strands of their hair and the rippling folds of their garments.

As in his *spalliera* panels, Piero thus devises compositions that function on the surface rather than in depth, held together by curving lines that run throughout the image and subtly align it with the frame. This enhances the decorative quality of the works, preventing the eye from wandering too far into depth, and focusing attention on the figures in a way that compensates in some measure for their relatively modest scale and quiet, unemphatic gestures. This approach to the composition of the tondo marked Piero out to an extent among his contemporaries, many of whom approached such commissions in a rather different way. As with *spalliera* panels, and increasingly with altarpieces, many artists treated tondi in ways that stressed their inventiveness in other areas, seeking equivalents to that dramatic unity and immediacy that Alberti advocated in the narrative *istoria*. This is evident in the works of artists such as Raphael and Michelangelo who, in their private devotional images, as in their altarpieces, stress the emotional and dynamic interaction of the figures as well as their plasticity and movement in three dimensions, as in Michelangelo's *Doni Tondo* (illus. 77). They also give less prominence to the background, painting it in relatively generalized ways in order to emphasize the figures, while subsidiary scenes and figures are clearly relegated to the background. The symbolic connotations of the scenes are also made more overt than in Piero's works, as for example in Raphael's *Madonna del Belvedere* (illus. 78), where, under the Virgin's watchful eye, the children

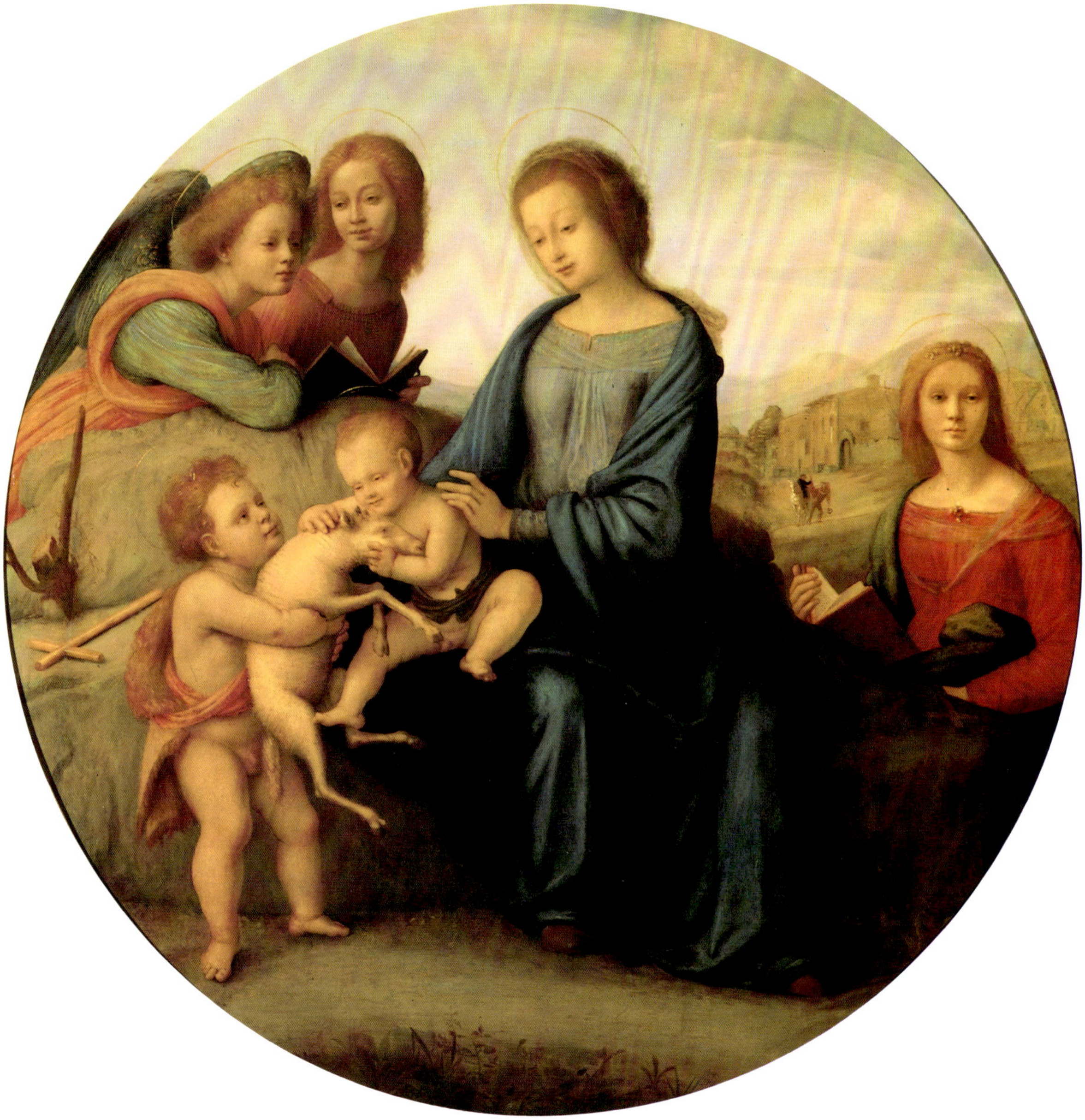

75 *Madonna and Child with Saints*, *c.*1515–20, oil and tempera on panel. Philbrook Museum of Art, Tulsa.

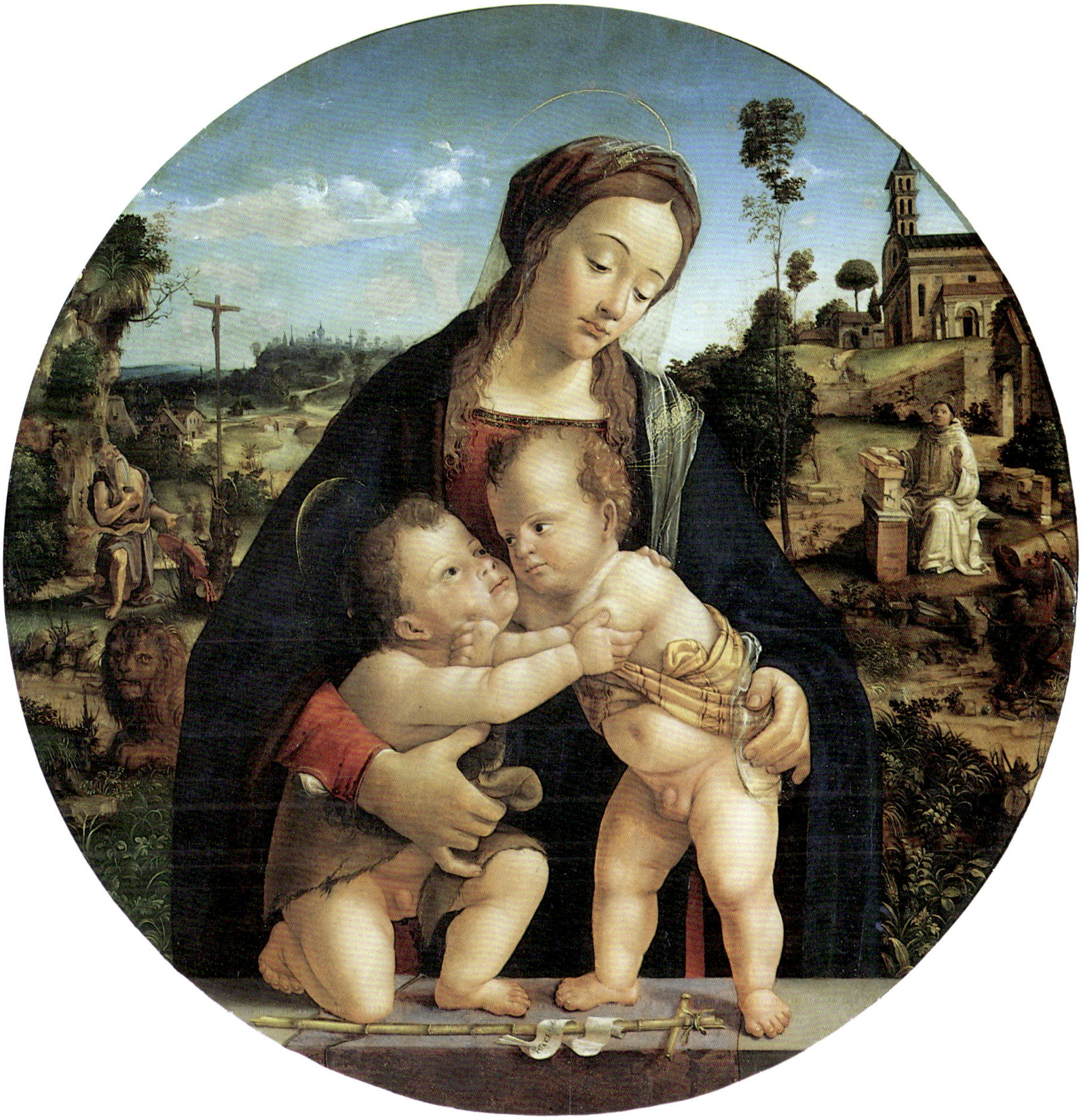

76 *Madonna and Child with the young St John the Baptist*, *c*.1495–1500, oil on panel. Musée des Beaux-Arts, Strasbourg.

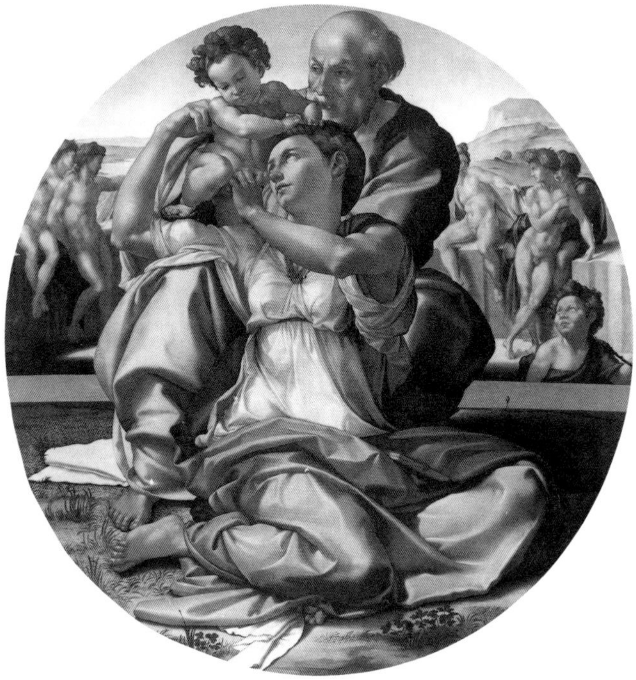

77 Michelangelo, *The Holy Family* (the '*Doni Tondo*'), 1503–4, tempera on panel. Uffizi, Florence.

ostentatiously grasp the Baptist's cross. In the works of many artists the distinction between altarpieces and private devotional works, and between narrative and non-narrative subjects, thus became progressively less clear. Yet while some patrons evidently responded to such developments, and valued their innovative quality from an artistic point of view, Piero's approach may well have been better suited to the function of the tondo as a devotional tool, while also possessing a greater decorative potential.

The Patronage of Piero's Religious Works

While no information exists regarding the provenance of Piero's tondi, or their original patrons, the large number of commissions that he received for such works, and the existence of numerous copies after his compositions for private devotional works, make clear his popularity in this respect, underlining the fact that the more selfconscious experimentation apparent in the works of Raphael, Leonardo and Michelangelo – too often seen as typical of the period as a whole – was only one of a number of options. It is also difficult to draw conclusions about the patronage of Piero's altarpieces, for while three of the families for whom he worked can be identified, for the most part the provenance of the paintings remains unknown. Furthermore, while the interests and tastes of these families can be reconstructed in a general way, it is difficult to be precise about the nature of their interest in Piero, or their motives for offering him such commissions.

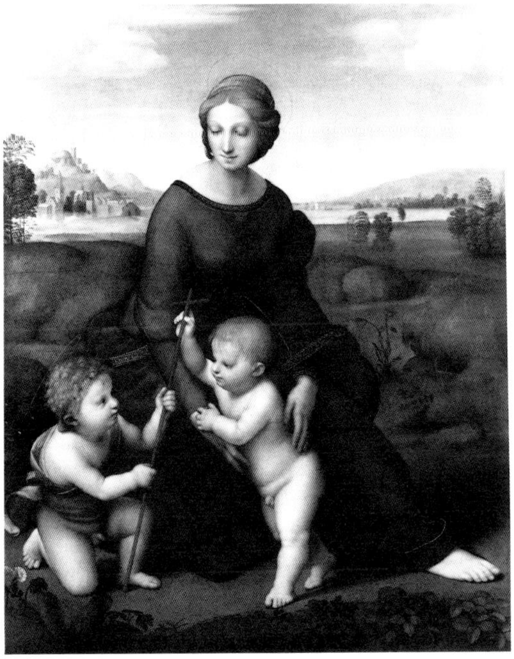

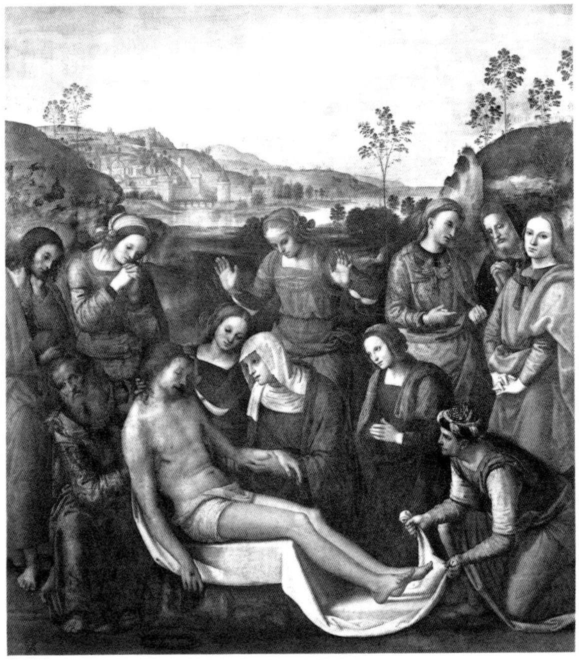

78 Raphael, *Madonna del Belvedere* (the '*Madonna of the Meadow*'), 1505/6, poplar panel. Kunsthistorisches Museum, Vienna.

79 Perugino, *Pietà*, 1495, oil on panel. Palazzo Pitti, Florence.

In the case of the *Pala Pugliese*, and the *Innocenti Altarpiece* which, according to Vasari, was also linked with the same family, the precise identity of the donor remains unclear, although it seems likely that it was Piero del Pugliese. This patron had connections with a number of churches belonging to the Cistercian order, including La Campora and the Badia in Florence, where Filippino Lippi's *Apparition to St Bernard*, which he probably also commissioned, is now housed. Piero del Pugliese also endowed the chapel at La Campora with a chalice, vestments and an illuminated manuscript of the sermons of St Bernard. Like his nephew Francesco del Pugliese, who, as mentioned earlier, had close links with Savonarola, Piero thus appears to have been interested in religious reform, and the predella of the *Pala Pugliese* includes two subjects – *St Nicholas Destroying the Idols* and *The Burning of the Books* – that make specific reference to the combating of heresy. Despite extensive research in recent years, however, scholars have found it difficult to establish conclusive links between Reformist ideas, and the patronage of a particular artist, or a preference for a particular style. Where the views and interests of patrons involved with Reformist trends or movements can be discerned in the works they commissioned, this is almost invariably a question of iconography – as in this instance – rather than of a style or pictorial mode. While the fact that Piero del Pugliese appears to have patronized both Filippino Lippi and Piero di Cosimo might suggest a certain consistency in his taste, it is less clear that this can be connected with his religious sympathies or ideas.[49]

It may well have been Piero del Pugliese who brought Piero's work to the attention of his nephew Francesco, for during the Renaissance various members of a family often employed the same artist, maintaining a family tradition of patronage. What may be significant, however, is that Francesco, a considerable connoisseur of painting and sculpture and a collector of some distinction, appears to have commissioned secular rather than religious works from Piero. Francesco owned religious works by a number of distinguished artists, including Fra Bartolommeo, Botticelli, Fra Angelico and several Flemings. According to Vasari he also attempted to acquire Perugino's *Pietà* (illus. 79), painted for the nuns of S. Chiara, Florence, in 1495, offering them three times the price they had paid the artist for the work.[50] Clearly, his tastes were quite eclectic, and he appears to have acquired works on the basis of their artistic value and interest, as well as for their function, for he owned far more religious works than would normally have been required for strictly devotional purposes. It appears to be in keeping with this that, while his uncle may have considered Piero's religious works quite serviceable, Francesco valued the artist rather for his *spalliera* panels, perhaps recognizing that Piero's strengths lay more in this aspect of his work.

Like Piero del Pugliese, Piero Capponi, who commissioned Piero's *Visitation*, appears to have been quite pragmatic as a patron, and to have viewed the acquisition of religious works in relatively functional terms. The family's patronage seems to have been confined largely to the furnishing of their chapels in S. Spirito, which was their parish church. It also seems likely that their original plan for the setting of Neri Capponi's tomb, in the chapel which housed Piero's altarpiece, and which was to incorporate a bronze grille, was influenced as much by their desire to emulate the Medici tombs in S. Lorenzo, than by their own personal taste.[51] It thus seems likely that, in terms of altarpieces, Piero was regarded as a competent practitioner, attuned to some extent with contemporary trends, who produced works that were attractive without being controversial, in either formal or iconographic terms. It is in the production of private devotional works that he excelled, and commissions for these appear to have remained fairly constant throughout his career, while his altarpieces were less in demand towards the end of his life, as stylistic developments to some extent overtook him. The inventive treatment of subject-matter, exquisite detail, and striking use of colour make the tondi compelling in both visual and psychological terms, while the element of *fantasìa* that allowed Piero to bring such conviction to both natural and symbolic forms makes them at once highly decorative and rich in thematic significance.

CHAPTER FOUR

Piero and the Depiction of Landscape

Of all the aspects of Piero's work we have considered, his painting of landscape is one of the most original. I have already suggested that Piero was unusual among his Florentine contemporaries in the space he allotted to landscape in his tondi and *spalliera* panels, in the particular balance he creates between the figures and their settings and in the way he uses landscape as a compositional device. Equally unusual, however, are the range and variety of landscape backgrounds he employs, the forms that compose them and the meticulous attention to detail. In all these respects Piero's landscapes are highly distinctive, and while they never became 'pure' landscapes (and cannot, therefore, be considered apart from the works in which they appear), their singularity warrants a separate and more extended discussion. This is particularly important since previous discussions of Piero's landscapes, while brief, have tended to focus on works such as the *Hunt* panels and *The Forest Fire*, drawing links between their 'primitive' backgrounds and the uncultivated, *selvatico* character described in Vasari's Life of Piero. Indeed, in many cases, the wild and inhospitable settings of these works have been seen as the clearest manifestation in Piero's art of his allegedly primitive nature, while the strange, anthropomorphic backgrounds of the *Incarnation* or the *Liberation of Andromeda* have been seen as direct expressions of his supposed love of the bizarre, and of the freaks and accidents of nature.[1]

Such an emphasis on the paintings of primitive man, and on the more obviously exotic forms in Piero's repertory is wholly misleading, for his approach to landscape was extremely varied, and the setting of *Mars and Venus* or the less idiosyncratic landscapes of his religious works are equally revealing of his attitude to this aspect of his art. Nor can his landscapes be seen simply as spontaneous or unmediated expressions of his own sympathies and interests, for in all his landscapes Piero shows an acute awareness of the requirements of decorum and of the appropriateness of his chosen motifs to both the subject and the function of a work – an issue that looms large in discussions of landscape in Renaissance art criticism and theory. He also shows a clear sense of contemporary conventions for depicting the natural world, and only in one instance – that of the *Incarnation* – could his own interests and inclinations be said to have held sway at the expense of the subject. For the most part, the interest of Piero's landscapes lies not only in their variety and inventiveness but in the delicate balance he achieves between the demands of convention and decorum and his desire to explore new and unusual forms.

My aim in this chapter is thus to re-examine Piero as a painter of landscape by considering the whole range of his landscape backgrounds, and the diverse functions landscape performs within his works in different genres. I also wish to re-evaluate

Vasari's appraisal of Piero's landscapes, and to consider more closely the implications in this respect of his description of both Piero and his work as 'uncultivated' and 'bizarre'. Vasari's brief comments on Piero's landscapes and his description of the artist's attitude to nature are precise and highly revealing. They are also extremely subtle, and to some extent his views on this aspect of Piero's work are apparent as much through what he fails to say as in his actual words. This part of the Life thus needs to be approached with caution, and to be set within the context of the *Lives* as whole. As with other aspects of his account Vasari's assessment of Piero can only be fully understood against the background of his own wider aims, and of his broader attitude to landscape as revealed in the biographies of artists such as Uccello, Michelangelo or Raphael.

It is perhaps not surprising that, for the most part, Piero's most conventional essays in landscape depiction appear in his altarpieces, especially those painted at the beginning of his career. In these works, as in the landscape background that he painted in Cosimo Rosselli's fresco of the *Sermon on the Mount* (illus. 1), Piero shows quite clearly his awareness of late-fifteenth-century conventions and techniques for the depiction of natural settings. As is well-known, the concept of landscape for its own sake, or as itself the subject of painting, was as yet undeveloped in Italian art criticism or theory.[2] Drawing largely on the discussion of Classical authors, particularly Pliny and Vitruvius, writers on art from Alberti onwards invariably assigned landscape a subordinate role in painting.[3] For Alberti and Vasari, its main function was to support and underline the narrative of a work by providing an appropriate setting for the figures, or by adding symbolic detail.[4] They also acknowledged the decorative potential of landscape, and its ability to give pleasure through a variety of carefully chosen and well-ordered elements – an aspect of landscape painting that was particularly emphasized by Pliny. Accordingly, for writers on art, landscape motifs should be chosen on the basis of their narrative or visual potential. Overall realism in landscape was rarely a prime concern, and painters were not expected to produce accurate renderings of specific or observed locations.

Most painters in the late fifteenth and early sixteenth centuries approached landscape in this functional way, and few of them were interested in topographical views, or in accurate renderings of particular sites or forms. Antonio and Piero Pollaiuolo's panorama of the Arno Valley in the *Martyrdom of St Sebastian* of 1475 (illus. 80) and Leonardo da Vinci's well-known drawing of a Tuscan landscape, dated 1473 (illus. 81), are thus exceptions rather than the rule.[5] Furthermore, while some of Leonardo's paintings include landscapes similar to that in the drawing, or backgrounds that depend on a close observation of nature, in others his landscapes are conventional and formulaic. In his *Annunciation* (illus. 82), for example, of *c.* 1472–3, the landscape is divided up in strict relation to the figures, with the foreground dominated by the conventional *hortus conclusus*, symbolizing the Virgin's chastity. The angel kneels against a background of dark cypress trees, and is separated quite methodically from the Virgin by a tunnel of space giving onto the horizon, which also

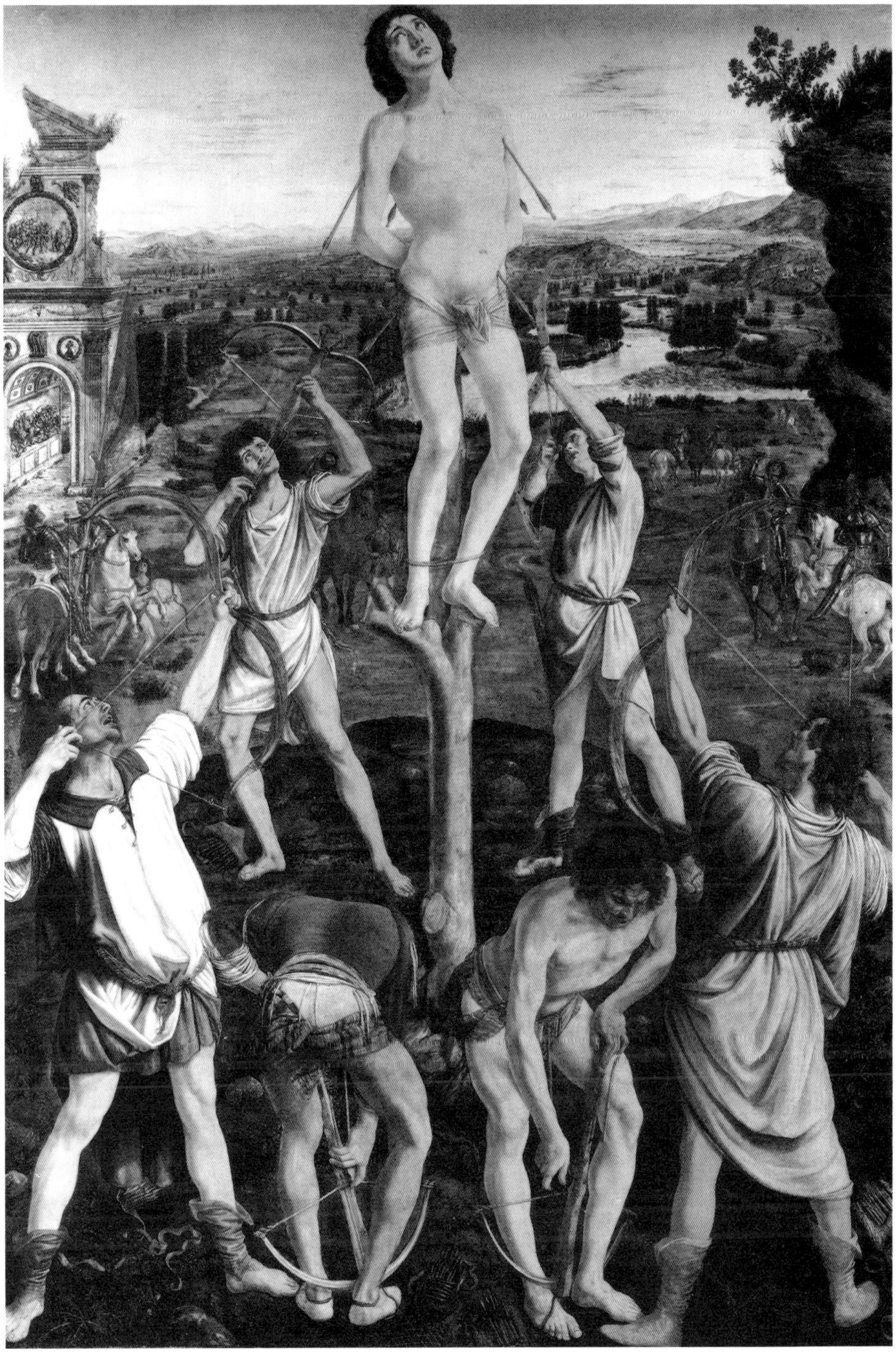

80 Antonio and Piero Pollaiuolo, *The Martyrdom of St Sebastian*, 1475, tempera on wood. National Gallery, London.

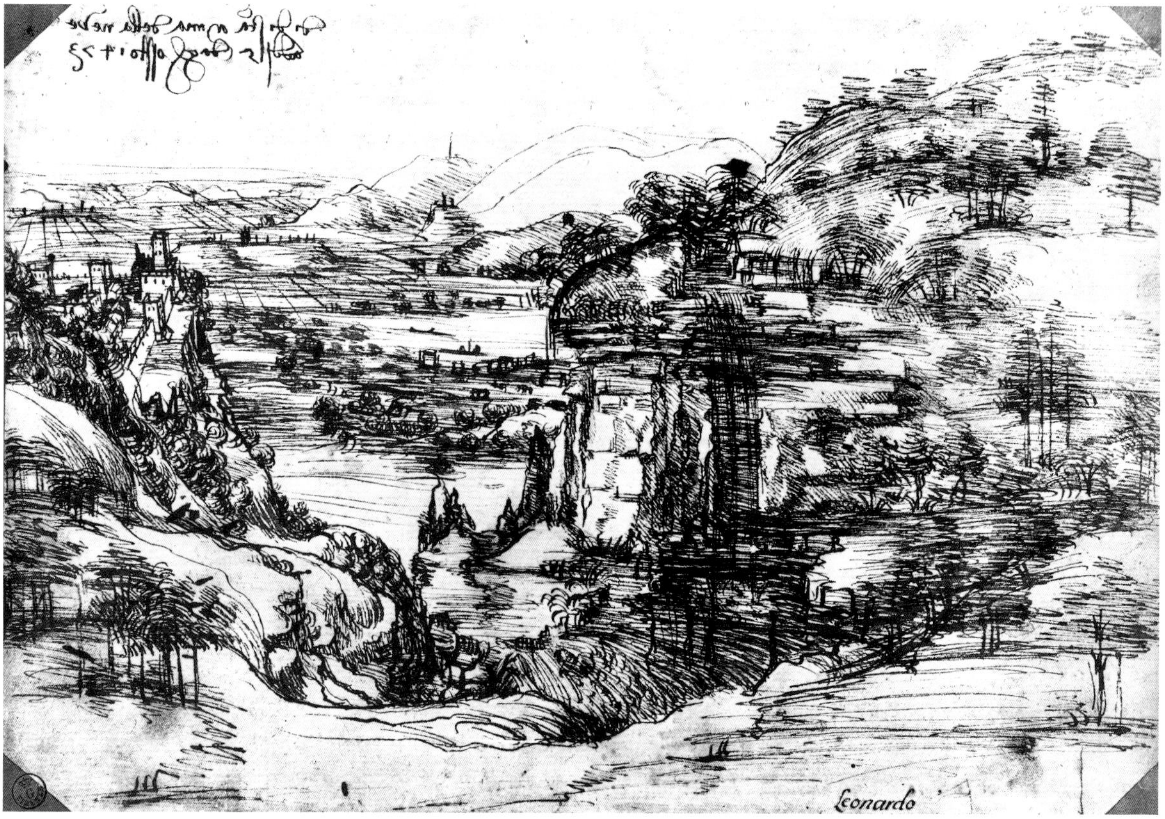

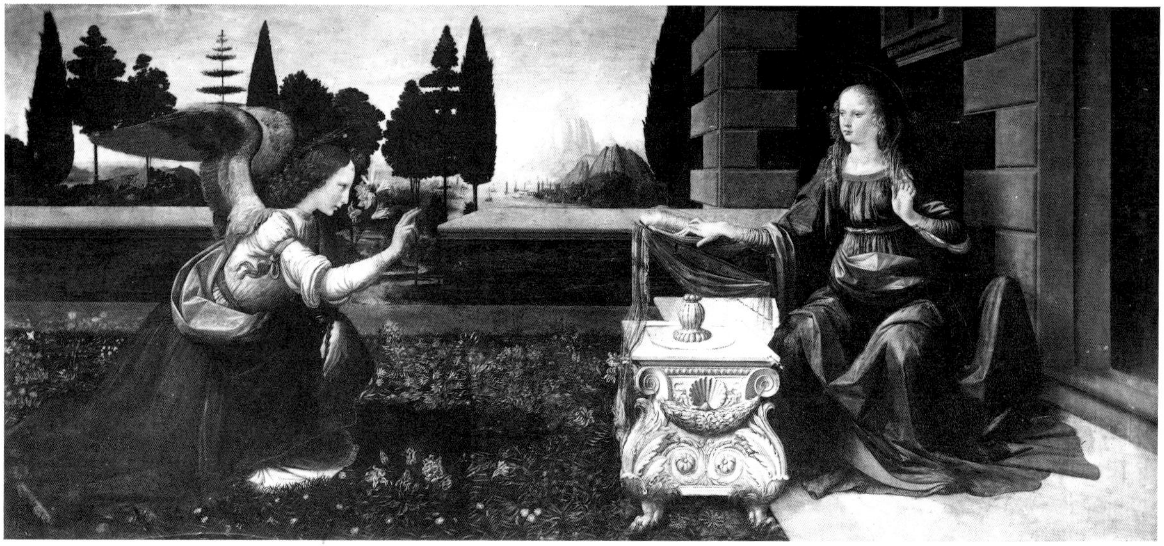

81 Leonardo da Vinci, *Study of a Tuscan Landscape*, 1473, pen and ink. Uffizi, Florence.

82 Leonardo da Vinci, *Annunciation*, *c.*1472–3, oil on wood. Uffizi, Florence.

serves to accentuate the angel's significant gesture. At the same time, while the individual flowers may appear realistic, they are laid out quite separately on the grass, each distinguished as if it were a botanical specimen, and arranged with a close eye for the decorative effect. Furthermore, the breeze ruffling the vegetation on the ground is to be understood less as a 'natural' phenomenon than as an indication of the angel's unearthly, and unsettling, descent.

For the most part, therefore, landscape backgrounds of the period consisted of motifs drawn not only, or even primarily, from observation, but from a variety of different sources, including religious texts, poetic descriptions of gardens and rural settings in the works of Petrarch and Boccaccio, botanical prints and Books of Hours.[6] The selection and arrangement of these were dictated primarily by the nature and activities of the figures in a work, and by formal and aesthetic considerations, as well as by the need to establish a clear pictorial structure.[7]

Piero's landscape in the Sistine Chapel, painted in 1481–2, is no exception to this, although, as for the other artists working in the Chapel, the construction of the setting was an unusually complex task in view of the scale of the frescoes and the number of incidents that were to be included in each one. In the case of Rosselli's fresco of the Sermon on the Mount, this subject had rarely been depicted on a large scale, and the construction of the landscape appears to have been dictated primarily by practical and iconographical considerations.[8] Like that in Leonardo's *Annunciation*, the landscape comprises a range of different settings determined primarily by the action they contain. Thus, the centre of the painting is dominated by a mountain on which Christ appears alone, before joining the disciples on a separate plateau to the right; his position on the mountain, and the shape of his body, are repeated by the church on the summit, whose function is both formal and symbolic. This section, and that in the left background, are probably intended to allude to Christ's progress through Galilee before the Sermon, as described in the Gospels, while the mountain setting connects the scene with that of Moses receiving the Ten Commandments on Mount Sinai, shown on the opposite wall. In the foreground Christ delivers the Sermon from a hillock that repeats the form of the mountain. The clustered buildings on the left-hand side of the painting serve to emphasize the isolation and remoteness of the figures on the mountain, while providing a formal contrast with the thickly wooded, uninhabited slopes on the right.

Each aspect of the landscape is thus constructed in relation to the narrative and the figures within it, while also providing variety in a formal sense. At the same time, its sections are envisaged as relatively separate entities, rather than parts of a continuous natural space or environment, and are related only in a somewhat schematic way, serving first and foremost to clarify the narrative and the sequence of events. The individual motifs also appear isolated, and sometimes randomly combined, as in the area to Christ's right, where buildings, bridges and neatly formed bushes seem to jostle for space in the narrow valley. The landscape is also dictated in part by the demands of compositional structure and balance; the central mountain, while it aids the narrative, provides a clear focal point to the composition, while the valleys on either side are a conventional method of establishing movement into depth, approximating the effect of linear perspective and creating the illusion of recession.

This is not to say that there are not distinguishing features in the landscape, and elements that are characteristically Piero's. The meticulous detail with which the buildings are rendered, and the variety and contrast in their different functions and types; the mossy growth that hangs from the edges of the mountain; the birds and the face of the wind that punctuate the sky, and the brilliant sunset on the left all point to his own distinctive interests, and particularly his concern with the varying effects of light. Beyond this, however, and in more general terms, there is relatively little in the landscape to distinguish it from those by Cosimo Rosselli, who was a highly competent painter of standard types of landscape background. It is quite likely, then, that Piero was assigned the landscape in the fresco because this was commonly the job of an assistant or apprentice – a fact itself indicative of the importance attached to this aspect of a painting – rather than because he displayed any particular distinction in this area at this point in his career.

The landscapes in Piero's early altarpieces display his awareness of conventional types and formulas in a similar way, although his originality becomes increasingly apparent. In both the Montevettolini and Toronto altarpieces, for example, and also in the *Pala Pugliese*, all painted between 1480 and 1485, the landscape remains strictly subordinate to the figures, although its extent is steadily increased by devices such as the full-length windows that give onto the landscape in the painting in Toronto. Furthermore, while some of their individual elements are unusual in their ordinariness and anecdotal quality, the landscapes are used for thematic and symbolic purposes in a straightforward and conventional way, each part of the landscape alluding in some manner to the subject of the whole, or to the figures within it. In the Toronto altarpiece, (illus. 55), for example, Piero makes a clear, though subtle, distinction between the landscapes behind the two saints. The landscape behind the hermit St Onofrius is empty and extensive, inhabited only by the lions that came to dig his grave, while that behind St Augustine is more confined, and marked by signs of human activity and habitation in the forms of the distant buildings. It is also dominated by the sea, a possible reference to the legend of the vision Augustine experienced while walking along the shore. The landscape in the *Pala Pugliese* (illus. 56) is divided in a similar way, as bare mountains rise up behind St John the Baptist, a reference to his sojourn in the wilderness, while behind St Peter appears a more gentle and verdant hill, surmounted by a church. The rendering of individual forms in these works is also quite formulaic. For example, the trees in the *Pala Pugliese* are neat and regular, and outlined against a uniformly clear sky, and do not suggest a particularly close study of nature, while the landscape overall is conceived less as a continuous or integrated whole than as a collection of separate symbolic motifs or sites, their placement dictated primarily by the figures.

In the predella of the *Pala Pugliese*, however, we gain some insight into Piero's own particular interests and skills, especially when it is considered in relation to the main panel. In the main panel the forms are crisp, detailed and precisely delineated, from the trees in the background to the foreground vase of flowers, while the way the landscape frames and complements the figures is rigidly schematic. The predella panels, though, are free and highly impressionistic studies of rather bare stretches of land, the contours of which frame the figures and echo their movements, in a manner more familiar from Piero's *spalliera* panels. At the same time, each panel reveals an intense interest in the fleeting effects of light, in the variations of clouds and sky and in the illusion of distance created by aerial perspective. Light and shade are depicted with a refinement quite absent from the schematic sky and stark shadows of the main panel, and serve to unite rather than separate the different parts of the landscape. In the central part of the predella, for example, the landscape shifts seamlessly from the patchy grass in the foreground to a stony expanse in the middle, and thence to a hazy blue distance, the transitions from one to the other, and the gradual recession into depth subtly underlined by the dissolving forms of three fleeing deer. In each of the two side panels a relatively featureless foreground melts into an apparently limitless distance, brought alive only by the flecks of white that suggest scattered buildings. Thus, while many artists used predella panels to display their skill in the rendering of fine detail, Piero appears rather to explore the possibility of painting a small surface in the broadest possible terms, presenting a minimum of detail to the scrutiny of the viewer, and experimenting with the spatial and colouristic effects of light.

The landscape background of the *Visitation* (illus. 87), painted around five years later, is probably Piero's most conventional, in terms of both content and structure. It is also the one that reveals most clearly the influence of Flemish art, and of other late-fifteenth-century Florentine artists, such as Ghirlandaio, particularly his *Adoration of the Magi* (illus. 50), with its busy accumulation of different motifs, orderly composition and precise and regular forms. In the *Visitation*, recession into depth is created by means of linear perspective, in a manner unusual in Piero's work, primarily by the foreshortened buildings that frame the composition in a similar manner to Ghirlandaio's 'stable', and which provide a platform for two of the background scenes – the Massacre of the Innocents on the right and the Adoration of the Shepherds on the left. While architectural settings of this kind were slightly unusual as locations for these scenes, Piero combines them with more conventional motifs, such as the mountain on the left, which provides a context for the Journey of the Magi, and suggests, in a rudimentary way, the distance and the dangers of their travels. As in the *Pala Pugliese*, the rest of the landscape is also related to the figures within it and filled with symbolic allusions. On the left, for example, a tree in full leaf rises above the Virgin and new-born Child, while the denuded branches behind the Massacre of the Innocents are backed by gathering clouds, references to life and death respectively. A similar contrast is set up in the foreground, between the strip of lush grass behind the Virgin and St Nicholas and the waste land behind the hermit St Anthony, patrolled by his attribute, a pig. Here again the landscape is dictated primarily by the narrative and by the need to provide significant and appropriate contexts for the figures, although within this Piero aims at maximum variety and contrast, including, like Ghirlandaio, a mixture of hills and plains, water and land, buildings and mountains, and trees in different stages of growth.

In these altarpieces, therefore, and in the Sistine Chapel fresco, Piero adheres clearly to the demands of the narrative and to the requirements of decorum, using landscape for symbolic and thematic purposes in relatively conventional ways. Nor can the individual forms in these landscapes be described as particularly naturalistic; similar, rather schematic, motifs appear in the works of numerous contemporary artists and do not suggest a very close study of nature. At the same time, while the space given over to landscape is quite extensive, especially in the *Visitation*, the figures in the altarpieces are clearly the focus of attention, and are also set apart from their settings by architecture or, as in the *Pala Pugliese*, by the Madonna's throne.

One exception to this among Piero's altarpieces is the *Incarnation* (illus. 88) painted *c.* 1505, in which the landscape plays a far greater part, and commands almost as much attention as the figures. Not only is the landscape more extensive, and not separated from the figures in any way, but the forms within it, some of which are highly unusual, are painted with enormous attention to detail, and with a scrutiny that instantly compels the gaze. While there are elements of conventional symbolism in the work, Piero combines these with forms that have no clear narrative or symbolic function, while subtly interweaving the fantastic and the mundane. In the left background, for example (illus. 89), above the scene of the Nativity, stands a palm tree, a conventional symbol of the Virgin and also of Christian sacrifice, and thus quite appropriate to the narrative. The tree is rendered with meticulous precision, and convincing in every detail. It is, however, juxtaposed with an ominous and skeletal black trunk, the significance of which is less clear, and which springs oddly from an isolated rock. Similarly, behind the trees rises a hillock which, while its vegetation is painted in a highly naturalistic way, seems precarious and ill-put together, overhanging the valley in vigorous curves with no apparent support and bearing on its peak a group of robust buildings crammed up against a rock. The eerie, moss-like growth that cascades like water over the cliff-face also contrasts strangely with the homely detail of the fence, while above loom finger-like excrescences of cloud, at once uncannily alive and, in their contours, unnaturally regular and contrived.

In the right background (illus. 90) Piero abandons the deserted and inhospitable setting that more usually served as a background for the Flight into Egypt, to show the Holy Family ascending the valley into a peaceful hill-town, alive with normal activity. The path of their approach is, none the less, dotted with gnarled and menacing tree-stumps, the roots of which assume the shape of claws, while the rocks appear on the verge of engulfing the figures as they echo the shapes of their movements. Figures and landscape are thus assimilated to each other in a manner familar from the *spalliera* panels, and which appears to convey the implications of the narrative and the trials of the Flight in an unusually abstract way. At the same time, while the trees and bushes seem to assume animal characteristics, the rock-faces framing the central figures take on the appearance of human profiles, while in the area of landscape immediately surrounding the Virgin, Piero appears to abandon conventional symbolism: the background contains no obvious allusions to her purity, or to the miraculous event of the Incarnation, which is signalled almost exclusively by Piero's use of light. The landscape thus mixes unremarkable objects and motifs with zoomorphic and anthropomorphic forms, and combines conventional symbols and settings with others whose presence has no obvious rationale. Despite this, however, when considered as a whole the landscape appears highly naturalistic, and in contrast to the other works we have considered, these different and sometimes anachronistic motifs appear as part of a continuous and integrated whole, bound together in part by the subtle *chiaroscuro*. In this instance, therefore, the balance between tradition and innovation, and between the demands of the subject and Piero's interest in particular types of form, appears especially delicate and fine. More precisely, perhaps, there is a tension between the two that, while making the picture extremely compelling, led Vasari to feel that Piero had allowed his own interests to take over at the expense of the whole, a point to which I shall return.

In his later altarpieces, and in works such as the *Volto Santo* (illus. 94), Piero moved towards a simpler, less detailed type of landscape that gives clearer precedence to the figures, perhaps signalling his awareness of the growing emphasis on figural content among his early-sixteenth-century contemporaries. The *Volto Santo*, painted between 1505 and 1510, depicts an oriental statue of Christ crucified, housed in the city of Lucca, and thought to work miracles. Here Christ stands out clearly against the sky, towering above a landscape pushed down to the lower part of the panel. At the same time, within a relatively small space, Piero includes a wealth of meticulously rendered detail, including the bell-tower of the Duomo in Florence, and a shining expanse of water, whose highlights are painted with the same scrupulous care as the glowing chalice at Christ's foot and the jewels of his clothing. The relatively small scale of the landscape, and the juxtaposition of the chalice with the buildings in the middle ground emphasize in turn the scale of the miraculous image. In the Perugia *Pietà* (illus. 83) *c.* 1510, which also reflects the clear, balanced structures of Perugino's painting of the same subject (illus. 79), the precise description of detail is largely confined to the foreground, which includes a pool of water and abundant growth of wild flowers. Here too, however, precedence is given to the hammer and pliers, and the ointment jar of the Magdalen, which form a poignant still-life in front of the grieving figures. The stark shapes of the background serve primarily to echo the figures and throw them into relief, and Piero emphasizes only the most telling narrative detail, such as the crosses silhouetted against the sky. In the Borgo S. Lorenzo and New Haven altarpieces (illus. 71 and 95), both painted after 1510, this simplification is taken further, and the landscape is also made less prominent by a more subdued range of colours. At the same time, while on close observation the background of the New Haven altarpiece yields a wealth of inventive detail, this is focused as much on figures

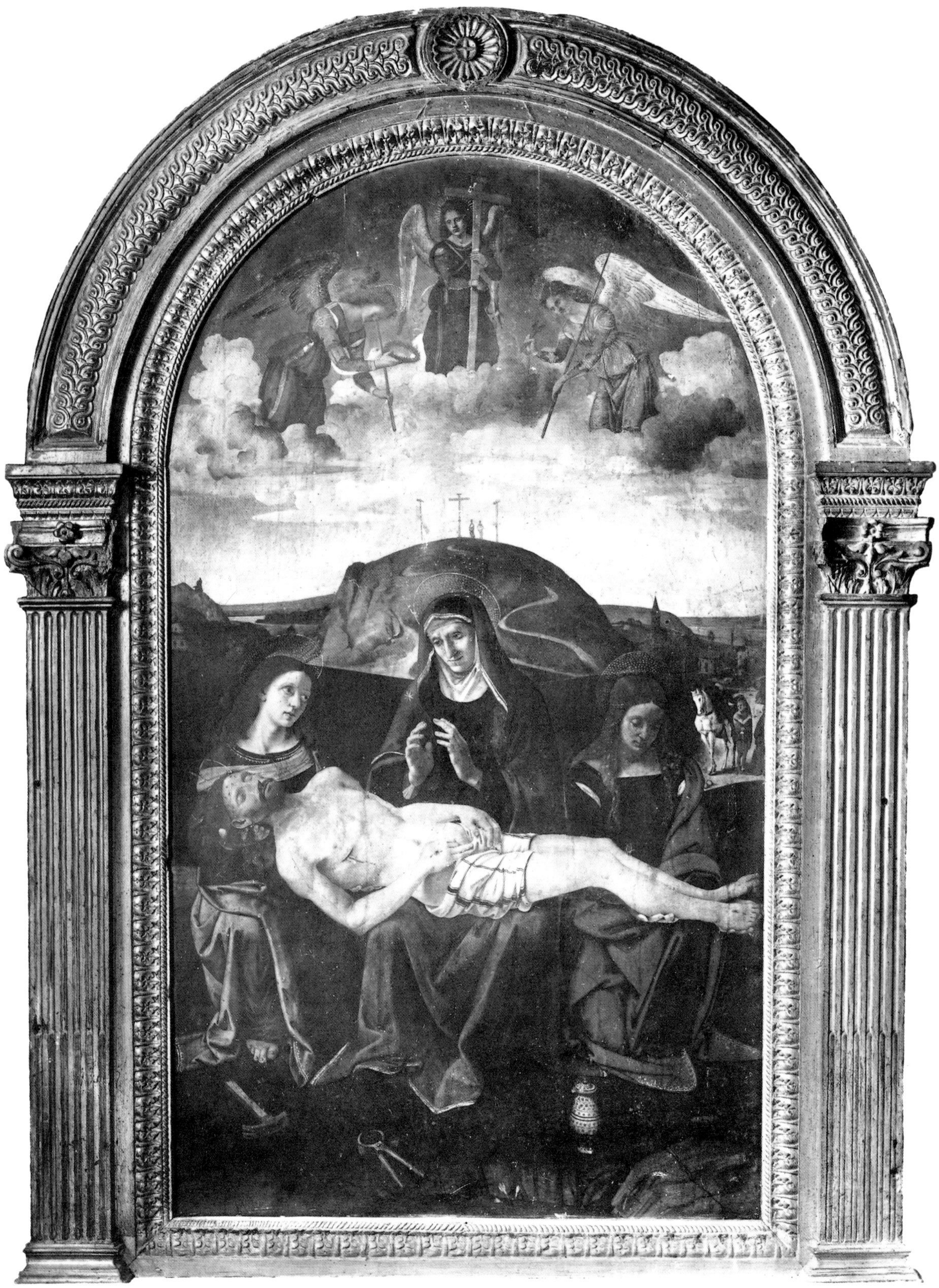

83 *Pietà with Saints*, *c.*1510, oil on panel. Galleria Nazionale dell' Umbria, Perugia.

as on the description of flora or fauna, and on details such as the penitent St Jerome on the right and the delightful procession of cardinals behind St Dominic on the left.

Like those in the altarpieces, the landscapes in Piero's tondi display a delicate balance between conventional iconography and symbolism, and an innovative approach to detail, although the tondo allowed him greater freedom, and it seems likely that the decorative potential of landscape was here allowed a more substantial role. In the Toledo tondo (illus. 72), for example, painted in the late 1490s, Piero places the adoring Virgin in a conventional flowery meadow, ignoring the temporal context of the Nativity in favour of a symbolic landscape setting rich in allusions to the purity of the Virgin, and to the death and resurrection of Christ. The carpet of colourful and minutely rendered flowers, which gives the painting much of its decorative charm, contains dandelions, a symbol of the Passion, daisies, pinks, poppies and white campion, all associated with love, and lilies that refer to the Virgin's purity.[9] The spring of clear water, the birds, tadpoles and water-boatman underline the sense of fertility engendered by the foreground setting, and together with the abundant flora may also serve as an echo to the references to the Creation contained in the open book. The limpid blue sky is perfectly in keeping with the dominant message of the landscape, although the barren and craggy rock behind the sleeping Child, and the cormorants in the tree above the Madonna may also serve as reminders of the suffering to come, for while the latter may have been included simply as fish-eating birds appropriate to the marine setting, they are described in several books of the Old Testament as unclean, and as harbingers of evil.[10] The landscape in the background is also composed in accordance with the figures. Joseph sleeps peacefully on a plain against a sweeping panorama of land and sea, conspicuously marked by a church, which may have been modelled on Old St Peter's in Rome, while on the right a more pastoral landscape of rolling fields provides a fitting backdrop for the shepherd tending his sheep.[11] Here again, while the symbolic motifs are incorporated in the setting in an apparently natural way, the different parts of the landscape remain formally and thematically comparatively distinct, each fulfilling its separate allotted function in relation to the figures within it, and to the wider implication of the theme. At the same time, as in his *Visitation* altarpiece, Piero aims for maximum variety and contrast in the motifs that he includes, although he exploits the aesthetic potential of the landscape to a greater extent than in his altarpieces. The spiky, umbrella-like form of the tree on the left, silhouetted against the sky, the vigorous striations and crevices of the rock and the colouristic range of the carpet of flowers give the painting a decorative quality appropriate to its function, and offer a wealth of charming and significant detail for the viewer's contemplation.

In the Strasbourg tondo (illus. 76), painted around the same date, the landscape is more distinctive, and the contrast between the two works illustrates clearly the range and variety of Piero's natural settings, and the flexibility with which he approached this aspect of his work. In this instance, in fact, the subject itself may have allowed him a greater inventive freedom since, unlike the Toledo tondo, it does not have a narrative context, even though Piero treats the figures in a semi-narrative way. In this instance the type and construction of landscape appear to have been determined primarily by the identity of the saints in the background, the two sides being subtly differentiated in accordance with their respective positions. Thus, behind St Jerome stretches an extensive vista of rich but uncultivated land, while above him towers a craggy rock, overhung with foliage and bristling with bare twigs. St Bernard, on the other hand, is seated before the neatly trimmed precinct of a church, adorned with shapely trees in full leaf, where monks of his Cistercian order go about their business. In front of him a tall leafy tree forms a parallel to the crucifix before St Jerome, and a clump of dense bushes emphasizes his seclusion, while the chained demon below him appears as the natural inhabitant of the rough and rock-strewn ground.

Yet, while in broad terms the backgrounds are appropriate to the figures, in contrast to the Toledo tondo, the individual motifs are unusual, and in the case of St Jerome depart from traditional iconography.[12] While the terrain behind him is unworked, it is also lush and full of life, and a far remove from the more barren desert setting in which he is more often placed in contemporary art, even if the dead trees at his back could be construed as a token reference to the aridity of the wilderness to which he withdrew. The ground is thick with plants and traversed by a wide and flowing stream, while the land is full of signs of human habitation, including a stone bridge, a watermill and numerous rustic dwellings, among which peasants go about their work in a kind of secular parallel to that of the monks behind St Bernard. At the same time, this homely and rustic landscape contrasts oddly with the blue horizon, above which rises a string of spires, given a fairy-tale aspect by the fineness and delicacy of their execution.

The forms of the landscapes are also different from those in the Toledo picture in their lack of obvious pictorial appeal. While their combined effect is not unpleasing, the forms do not appear to have been chosen for their intrinsic charm or their colouristic effects, and Piero does not exploit the decorative potential of the setting in such an obvious way. Despite the subtle distinctions between its parts, the landscape also appears as a coherent and integrated whole, rather than a collection of different and distinct symbolic sites. All the figures, including the Virgin, appear part of the same environment, inhabiting a continuous and seemingly realistic setting that has a convincing consistency, both in its detail and in its underlying structure and illusion of space.

This same use of an integrated landscape setting is apparent in the Washington *Adoration of the Child* (illus. 74) of *c.* 1500–5, which includes the most original of the landscapes in Piero's tondi. Here, not only is the landscape conceived as a continuous whole, but there is little trace of the locations or motifs conventionally used in scenes of the Nativity or the Journey of the Magi. The figures co-exist in a landscape remarkable rather for its lack of distinctive or symbolic features and for its overall plainness and lack of detail. The Magi thus wind their way, not through the conventional mountains or through a distant panorama that implies their journey, but over ordinary grassy plains devoid of any trace of the exotic, the perilous or the strange, while the grassy crag behind them is domesticated by its cluster of buildings adorned with airing linen. The Virgin watches over her Child in a smooth, hospitable patch of earth, and the only trace of the dramatic or unusual appears in the unearthly lighting emanating from the angels within the otherwise homely shelter.

Here, in fact, Piero's concern appears to be less with the symbolic potential of the landscape than with the formal and compositional balance of the image as a whole, and with finding forms that would complement the figures in a different, less specific way. He appears to have sought a landscape that, in its plainness and tranquillity, and in its subtle but insistent pattern of verticals and horizontals, repeated in land and sky, would underline the silent prayer of the foreground figures, echoing in a formal way their attitudes of quiet contemplation. Precise landscape detail and the scrutiny of individual parts, are here sacrificed to formal balance and to the larger structural requirements of the work, in a manner more reminiscent of the works of Piero della Francesca than of any of Piero's Florentine contemporaries.

In the particular motifs he uses, therefore, and the combination of conventional types and frameworks with innovative detail, the landscape backgrounds of Piero's religious works are highly original, as are his scrupulous attention to detail and the resulting particularity of his forms. They are also unusual in their variety and in the subtle diversity with which Piero exploits their symbolic, narrative and compositional functions, ranging from the conventional setting of the Toledo tondo, dense with religious symbolism, to the spare, formal balance of the Washington tondo, and the quirky detail of the *Incarnation*. While most of his contemporaries adopted a set of standard forms for the depiction of landscape, which they used in all their works, and which were mostly quite schematic, Piero visualizes each setting in an individual way, employing both different forms and a different composition.

Piero, in the oddity of some of his landscape forms, and their particularity, is thus closer in some ways to artists working in Northern Italy, such as Mantegna in Mantua (illus. 41 and 99), Giovanni Bellini in Venice (illus. 85 and 86), or Cosimo Tura in Ferrara, while there are also echoes in his works of the landscapes of Flemish artists such as Hans Memling and Hugo van der Goes (illus. 49). Among his Florentine contemporaries, only Filippino Lippi in the late fifteenth century, and later Leonardo, show a comparable interest in the less common forms of nature and in exploring the particularity of individual forms. In altarpieces, Filippino Lippi's for example, and in his *spalliera* panels, we find a comparable interest in the vernacular and anecdotal, in misshapen rock forms, and in extensive landscapes not entirely regularized by art, as in his altarpiece of the *Madonna and Child with SS Dominic and Jerome*, painted *c.* 1485 (illus. 48). On the other hand, Leonardo displays a similar preoccupation with the details of individual species, and with atmospheric effects. In his writings, however, Leonardo reveals a certain ambiguity towards the inclusion in painting of the ugly and grotesque parts of nature, and of forms such as those in Piero's *Incarnation*. While the freaks and accidents of nature formed part of the material of the universal artist, and Leonardo sees their importance within the painter's mastery of the visible world, he

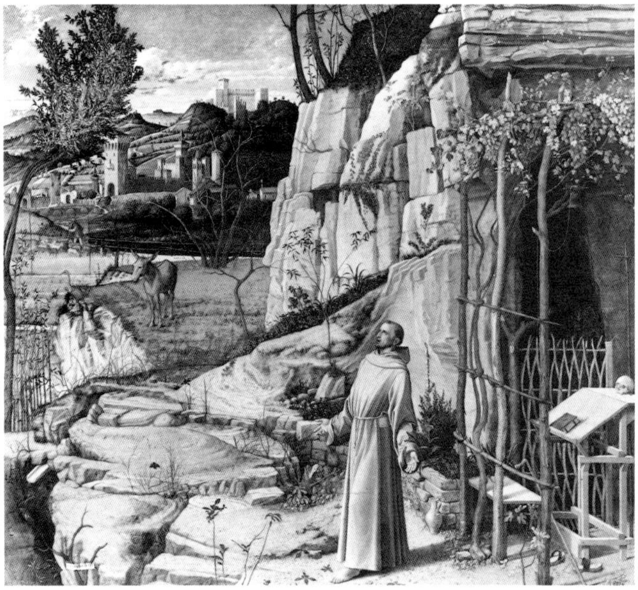

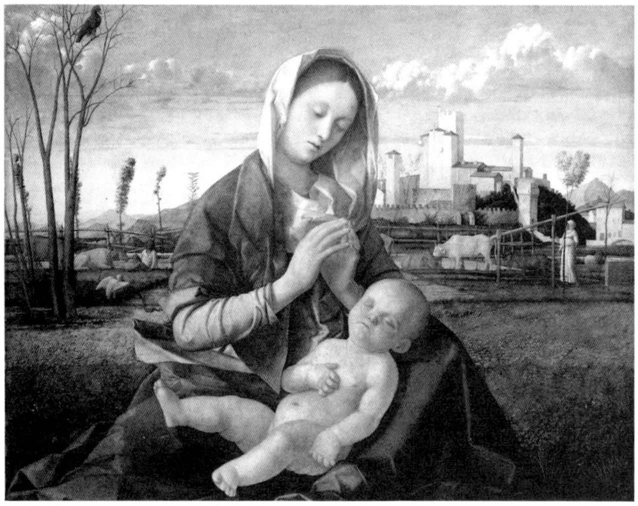

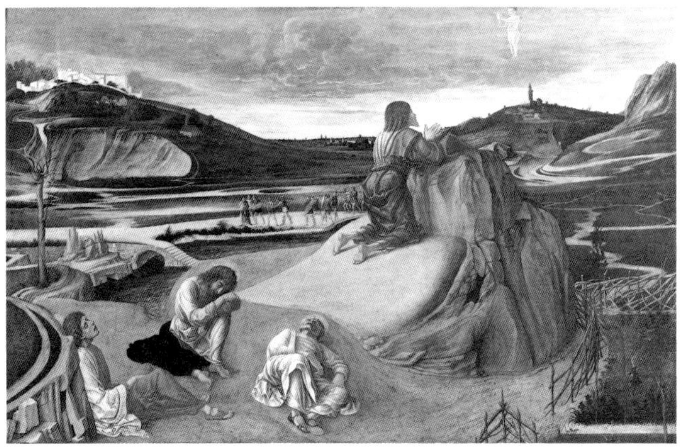

84 Giovanni Bellini, *The Ecstasy of St Francis*, *c.*1480, tempera and oil on poplar panel. The Frick Collection, New York.

85 Giovanni Bellini, *Madonna and Child* (the '*Madonna of the Meadow*'), *c.*1505, canvas transferred from wood. National Gallery, London.

86 Giovanni Bellini, *The Agony in the Garden*, *c.*1459. National Gallery, London.

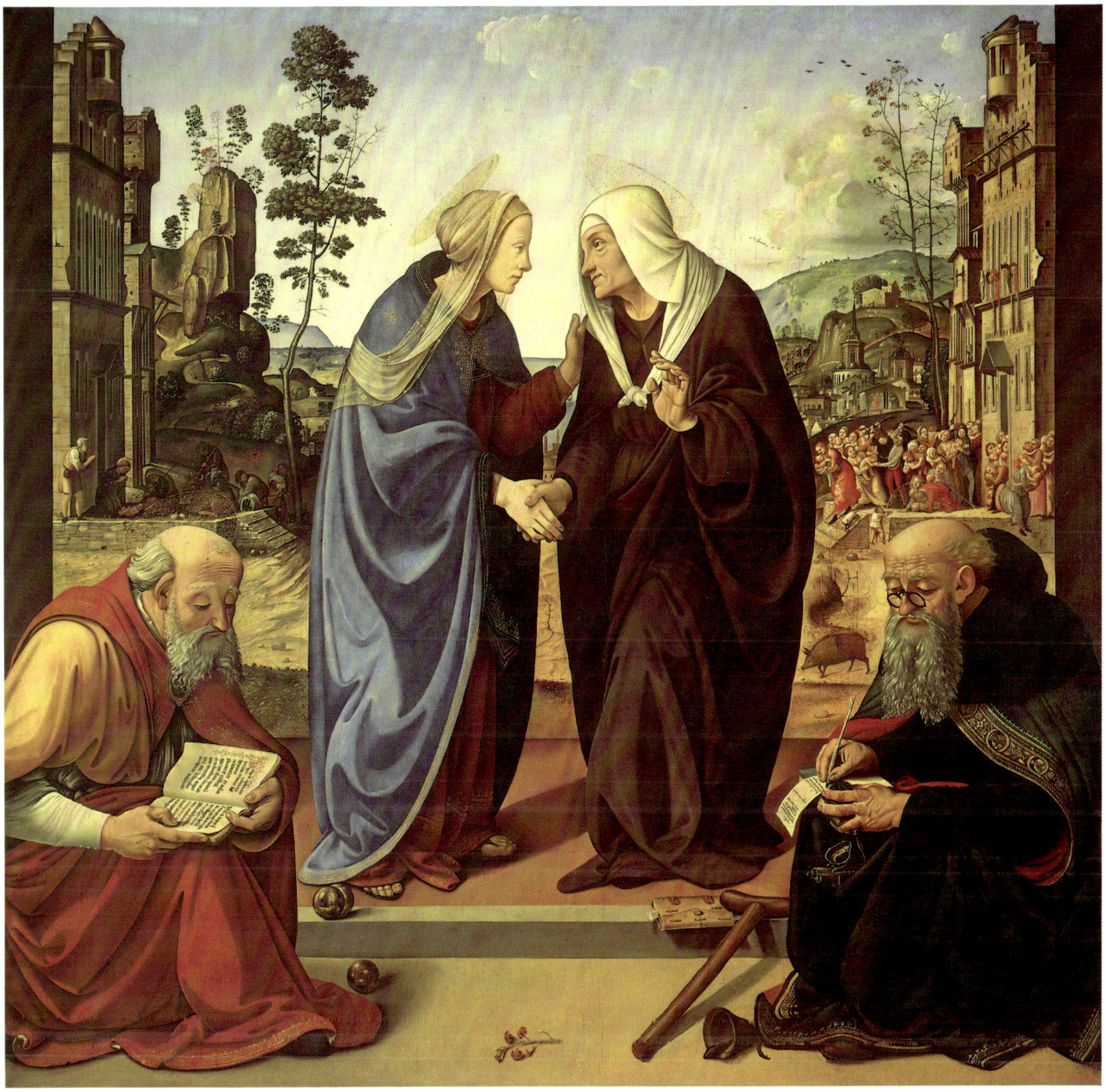

87 *The Visitation with SS Nicholas of Bari and Anthony Abbot*, *c.*1490, oil on wood. National Gallery of Art, Washington DC.

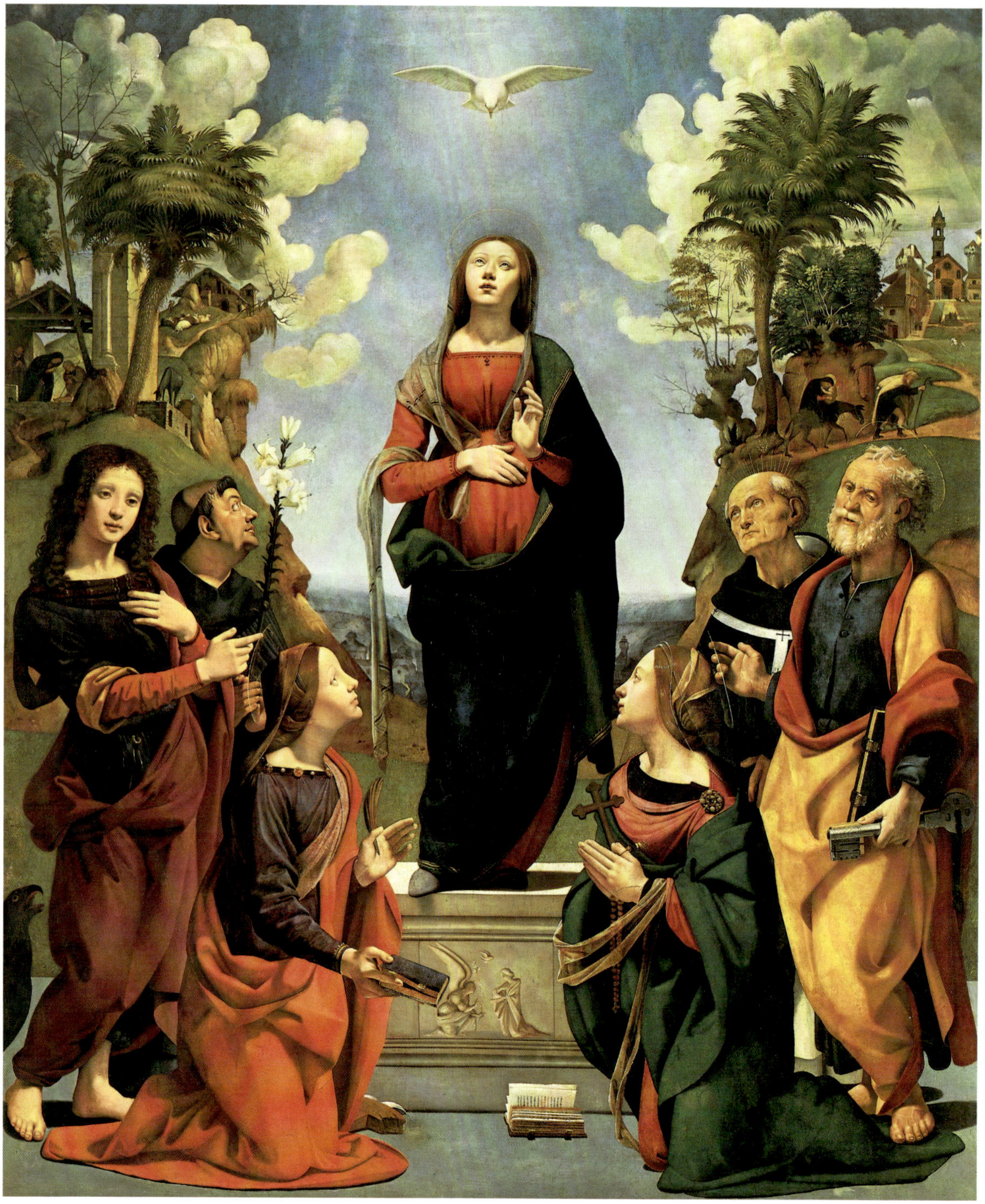

88 *Incarnation with SS Catherine of Alexandria, Margaret, John the Evangelist, Peter, Philip Benizzi and Antoninus*, *c.*1505, oil on panel. Uffizi, Florence.

89 Left background detail from the *Incarnation with Saints*.

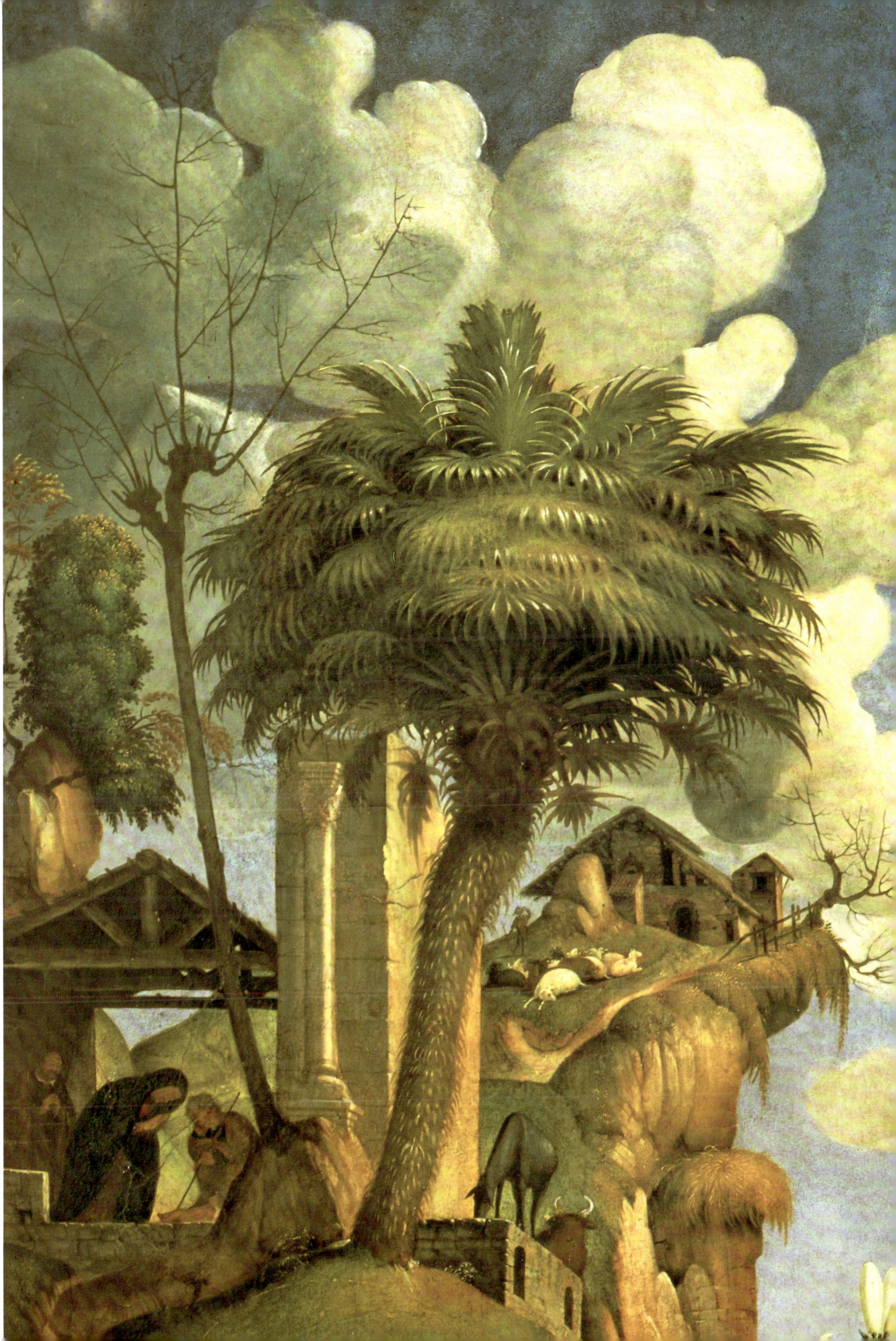

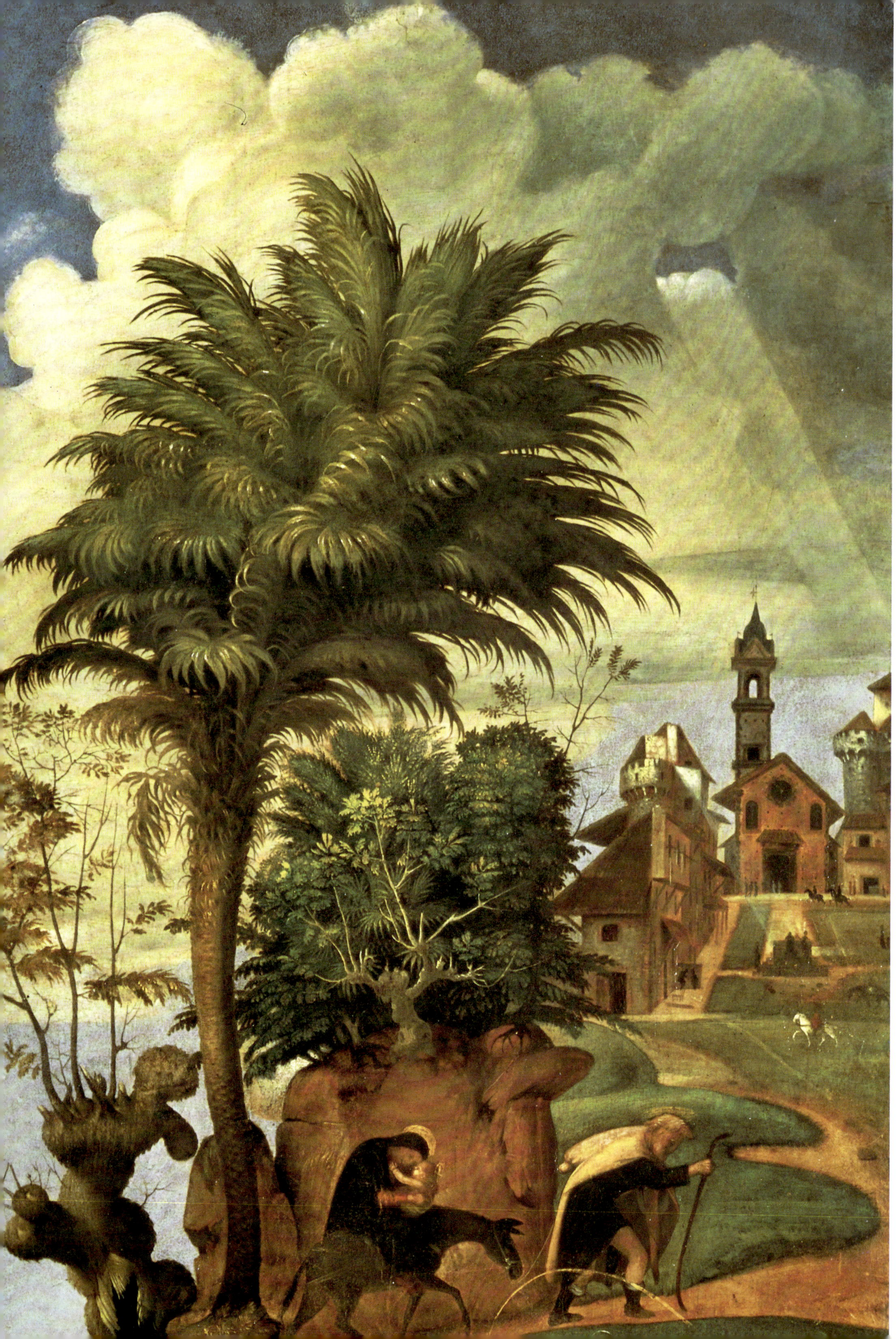

also stresses the importance of decorum in landscape, and of the appearance of beauty, which serves to instil harmony in the viewer. In his paintings, furthermore, while the landscape forms are often unusually dramatic, and especially his mountainous panoramas, they are invariably selected and arranged so as to look pleasing, and endow the work with beauty. Detail is suppressed in order to give clear precedence to the figures, while the irregularities of his rocky settings are made unobtrusive by his delicate *sfumato*, as in the *Madonna and Child with St Anne and a Lamb* (illus. 91).[13] In this respect his works are often distant from those of Piero, although works such as the latter's *Liberation of Andromeda* show clearly the influence of Leonardo's experiments with aerial perspective.[14]

The majority of Piero's contemporaries in Florence sought the typical and unobtrusive in landscape, imposing a degree of regularity and order both on individual motifs, and on the landscape as a whole, as in Botticelli's *Nastagio degli Onesti* panels of *c.* 1482–3 (illus. 10 and 11) or Ghirlandaio's *Adoration of the Magi* (illus. 50); few, if any, approached the diversity and range of Piero's landscape backgrounds. Nor can this diversity be explained simply in terms of Piero's changing interests or priorities, or his gradual mastery of a particular technique – although these were certainly contributory factors – for an element of diversity is apparent at all stages in his career, so that he produces within the same space of time works with different settings and types of landscape motif. The variety of his landscapes springs rather from his intrinsic interest in landscape as a subject, and in its expressive possibilities, and from his acute awareness of the demands of decorum in a painting, in both functional and thematic terms. Even where he could be said to have breached the limits of decorum and extended his originality too far, as in the *Incarnation*, his sense of convention is none the less apparent, and to some extent continues to govern both the structures and the content of the setting.

It is with the *Incarnation* that we can turn to Vasari, and his response to Piero's landscape, for not only is his account of this painting particularly informative, it also provides a useful framework within which to examine the landscapes in several other key works. In considering Vasari's perception of the artist in this respect it is important to note at the outset that his comments on Piero's landscapes, while revealing, are few and relatively brief, and he only comments specifically on three works – the *Incarnation*, the *Liberation of Andromeda* and *Mars and Venus*. Most significant, and most striking in view of the interest which they hold for modern viewers, Vasari rarely praises Piero for his landscapes, and at no point in the Life does he commend them in general terms, or suggest that Piero was especially distinguished in this aspect of his art. He appears to have had particular reservations about the background of the *Incarnation*, which he describes as 'a landscape which is bizarre on account of the strange trees, and of certain caves'.[15]

The significance of Vasari's response here lies in his use of the term 'bizarre', which he relates specifically to the strange trees, and the caves, or *grotte*. It seems likely that he is alluding to zoomorphic trees with their fleshy, bulbous trunks, claw-like roots

90 Right background detail from the *Incarnation with Saints* (illus. 88).

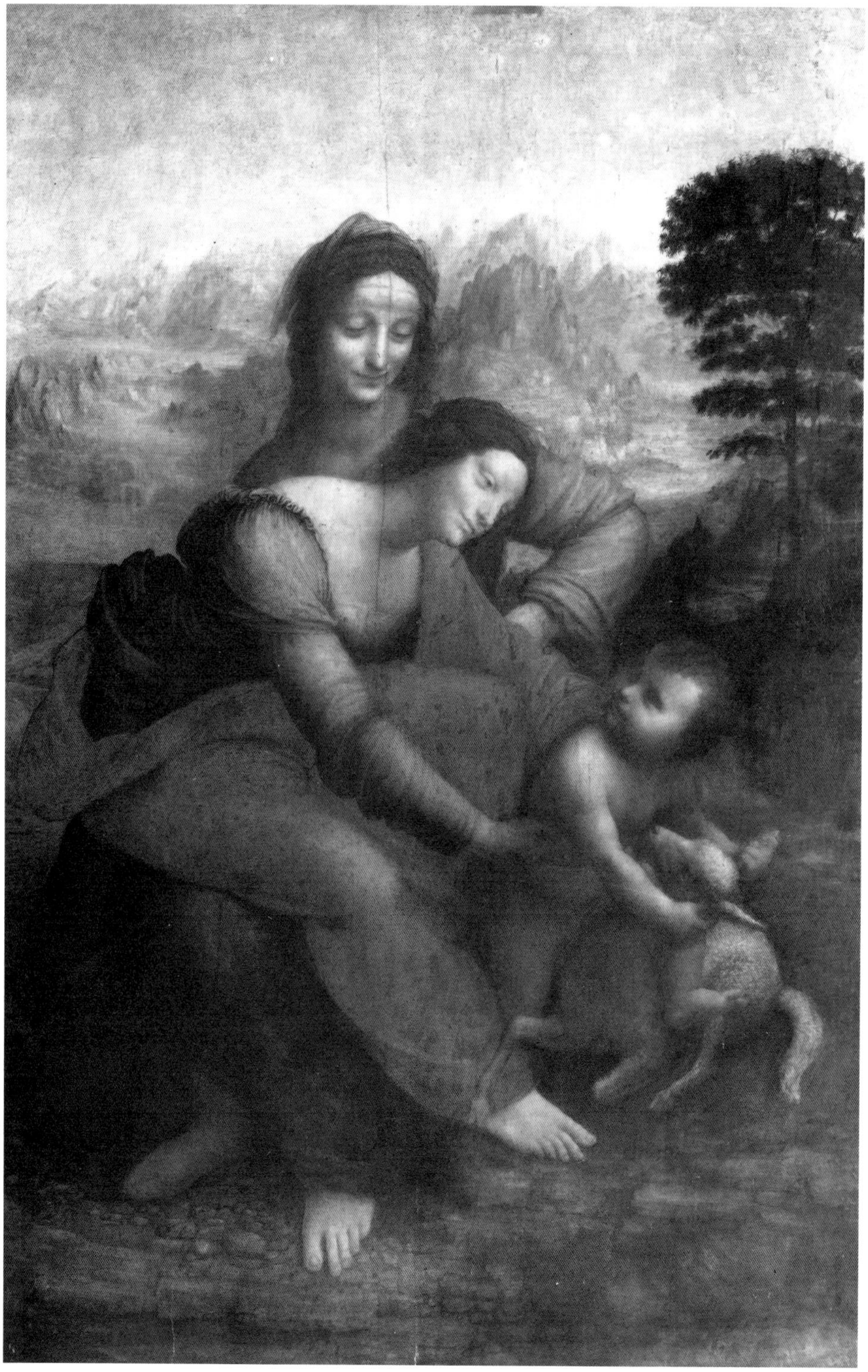

91 Leonardo da Vinci, *Madonna and Child with St Anne and a Lamb*, *c.*1508–10, oil on panel. Musée du Louvre, Paris.

and skeletal branches, and, perhaps, to the rocky recess that houses the Nativity, surrounded by rocks and boulders arranged in an apparently random way, and interspersed with areas of lush growth. As we saw in chapter Two, for Vasari, 'bizarre' is usually a term of praise, associated with a desirable element of inventiveness and *fantasìa* found most often in artists of the Third Age. We also saw that it was used most often with reference to a particular repertory of forms, such as armour or vessels *all'antica*, fanciful costumes, exotic animals, motifs of fruit and foliage and forms of a hybrid nature, such as *grotteschi*, which generally belonged to the more decorative elements of a work. In describing Piero's own works, Vasari applies it to the sea-monster that the artist gave to Giuliano de' Medici, to that in the *Liberation of Andromeda*, and to a book of drawings of fantastic animals, described as 'very beautiful and bizarre, executed most diligently in pen, and carried out with inestimable patience'. As in the last instance, the term is often grouped with others such as 'patience', 'refinement' and 'diligence', which imply a minuteness and delicacy of execution and a pleasing attention to detail.[16]

Vasari's use of the term to describe the landscape of the *Incarnation* is in keeping with this. Yet, while in other contexts 'bizarre' is a term of praise, its use here is more problematic and more equivocal, and it is significant that Vasari does not actually commend Piero for the 'bizarre' quality of the landscape, and omits the latter from his list of those parts of the work that he considered beautiful and worthy of praise. It thus seems likely that in this instance the semblance of the bizarre was not entirely fitting in Vasari's eyes, and that the grotesque and fantastic forms of the landscape were out of keeping with the function and seriousness of the image. While the monstrous and grotesque in nature were acceptable as decoration, particularly in a secular context, or in the garden of a villa, for Vasari they appear to have had little place in an altarpiece. Not only did the presence of such forms constitute a breach of decorum but, in their very novelty, they tended to draw undue attention to an aspect of a work to which he assigned a subsidiary role, while also detracting from the figures. His reservations were almost certainly compounded by the detail with which Piero renders the forms, by that particularity often associated with the bizarre, and which makes the landscape so fascinating. As I have suggested, Piero's attention to detail lends an uncanny reality and peculiar vividness even to forms that in other ways are unremarkable, endowing even the prosaic with a touch of the grotesque. Seen with his unflinching eye, details such as the rough trunk of the palm tree, the vegetation on the cliff-top, and the oddly placed fence become almost as fantastic as the zoomorphic trees and humanized rock-faces, while the comparable treatment of the exotic and the mundane adds a disconcerting tension to the whole.

For Vasari, a scrupulous attention to detail, and a focus on the particularity of individual forms, were undesirable in any aspect of painting, including the rendering of the figure. They ran contrary to the abstracting or idealizing process that was integral to his notion of design, and which raised the artist above a mere copyist or transcriber of nature. They also suggested a certain obsessiveness and lack of judgement on the artist's part, while creating in the work itself an appearance of effort and labour that was inimical to the facility and grace Vasari saw as fundamental to good art. It is thus a characteristic that Vasari attributes particularly to the artists of the Second Age, such as Uccello, who he criticises for an excessive diligence that rendered their manner difficult and dry.[17]

Close attention to detail was particularly problematic in the depiction of landscape, and Vasari's comments on the issue are focused most often on the painting of the natural world. Not only could close scrutiny of nature make the painter's manner laboured, it also constituted effort misspent, since landscape was only secondary in importance. Furthermore, and particularly important as regards the *Incarnation*, a detailed landscape could compete with and detract from the figures in a work. Thus, while he recognized the importance of landscape in the overall task of representation, and was quick to appreciate the skill involved in the fine description of nature, Vasari's attitude to this aspect of painting was ambivalent, and an assiduous study of nature is not always seen as desirable in the *Lives*. In the light of this, his observation that Piero's works reveal 'a spirit quite different and remote from those of other painters, and . . . a certain subtlety and refinement in the study of the certain minute details of nature, which he dwelt over with no heed for the time or effort involved' – while it might at first reading seem complimentary, it appears more ambiguous in its implications.[18]

While Vasari does not present an actual theory of landscape in his writings, it is clear from a number of passages in the *Lives* that, like Alberti in the fifteenth century, he saw it as a secondary aspect of art. Although it was necessary for the mastery of representation as a whole, and could serve as a demonstration of skill, it should not be an end in itself. Thus, as we saw in chapter One, a fascination with the natural world was acceptable in the case of Leonardo, as one part of the artist's interests and a sign of his universal talent. Artists who concentrate extensively on landscape, however, invariably invite Vasari's censure. At the end of his Life of Dosso Dossi, for example, a Ferrarese artist of the Third Age who also included extensive landscapes in his works, Vasari writes critically of Dossi's contemporary, the Milanese painter known as 'il Bernazzano', whom he describes as 'the most excellent of all in painting landscapes, grass, animals and other things'. So, Vasari continues, 'because he spent little time on the figure, like one who knows his talent to be imperfect he kept company with Cesare da Sesto, who painted the figure very well, and with a beautiful manner'.[19] Conversely, Michelangelo is praised for having put such things aside. His *Last Judgement*, and his frescoes in the Pauline Chapel are praised precisely for their absence of landscape, and the artist is commended for his refusal to demean his talent by painting anything other than the figure:

> As has been said elsewhere, Michelangelo concentrated his energies on achieving absolute perfection in what he could do best, so there are no landscapes in these scenes, nor any trees, buildings, or other embellishments and variations, for he never spent his time on these things, lest perhaps he should degrade his genius.[20]

In the Life of Raphael, Vasari suggests that landscape, like charming drapery, while not unimportant, is one of the things that adorn and enrich the *istoria*, rather than being fundamental to it, or constituting an end in itself. Recognizing that he could never rival Michelangelo in the depiction of the figure, Raphael,

> like a man of the greatest judgement, considered the fact that painting does not consist solely in painting nude men, but that it has a wide field, and among the best painters can also be included those who know how to express well and with facility the invention of the *istoria* . . . to this . . . should be added the ability to *enrich* the *istoria* with the variety and the wonder of perspectives, and buildings and of landscapes, and to dress figures with charm . . . he also reflected on the importance of being able to paint the flight of horses in battle, the ferocity of soldiers, and of the knowledge of all sorts of animals and an infinite number of other things, such as arrangements of drapery, stockings, armour and weapons, women's coiffures, hair, beards, vases, *trees, caves, rocks, fire, stormy and clear skies, clouds, rain, thunderbolts, brightening skies, nights, the lights of the moon and the brightness of the sun*, and an infinity of other things that are necessary to the art of painting . . . [21]

Vasari's relative lack of interest in landscape is also implicit in the fact that in his descriptions of works that, for the modern scholar, appear remarkable for their landscapes and constitute key points in the development of the field, Vasari omits any mention of the setting. In his account of Antonio and Piero Pollaiuolo's altarpiece of the *Martyrdom of St Sebastian* (illus. 80), for example, a painting he clearly knew well, and which includes an unusually extensive panoramic landscape based partly on a study of the Arno Valley outside Florence, Vasari confines his remarks exclusively to the figures. While he commends the work for its imitation of nature, this is seen solely in terms of the rendering of anatomy, and does not include the description of the environment:

> in order to imitate nature as well as he could, he showed one of the archers pressing his crossbow to his chest, leaning towards the ground to load it and putting into the task all the strength of his arm, so that one can see in the figure the swelling of the veins and muscles, and the way he is holding his breath to increase his strength.[22]

Likewise, in works of the Third Age which are now considered remarkable for their landscapes, such as Leonardo's *Mona Lisa*, Vasari makes not even a passing reference to the setting, Leonardo's mastery of the natural world being revealed solely through his depiction of the sitter's face:

> in which . . . whoever wishes to see to what extent art can imitate nature, can readily do so, since there are reproduced in it, with great attention and precision, all the subtleties and fine details that one can paint.[23]

Against this background, it is less surprising that Vasari rarely mentions Piero's landscapes, and that in his account of the Vespucci *Bacchanals* (illus. 28 and 29), for example, he makes no mention of the setting. As regards *The Discovery of Honey*, the delightful landscape that has generated so much discussion among scholars, and which appears so integral a part of the work, seems to play no part in the variety and charm Vasari finds in the painting, and which he relates solely to its figural content –

the 'fauns, satyrs and woodland creatures, and putti and bacchantes . . . rendered with grace and in a most lifelike manner.'[24]

As we saw earlier, for Vasari, as for Alberti, the role of landscape was two-fold. First, and most important, it could support and underline the figural content, adding symbolic detail and emphasizing the theme of the *istoria* without, of course, becoming obtrusive. It could also embellish the image, and give pleasure through its beauty and charm. It followed from this that the choice and nature of landscape elements should be governed by the demands of the narrative, and that they be painted in a generalized rather than in a particular way, so as not to command undue attention. It also followed that the emphasis should be on the pleasing aspects of nature, and on those that add beauty to a picture, rather than on the grotesque, the misshapen or the idiosyncratic. Vasari makes this last point particularly clear in the Life of Uccello, where he censures this artist for his indiscriminate rendering of the natural world:

> Paolo continued to paint landscapes in perspective and in foreshortening, showing them receding into the distance, and just as they appear, and including in them everything that he saw, green fields and ploughed fields, ditches and other intricacies of nature, in that sharp and dry manner that he had; whereas, if he had chosen only the best of things, and put in his works those things which actually look well in a painting, they would have been the most perfect of all.[25]

Even more revealing of Vasari's views is a passage from the Life of Polidoro da Caravaggio, an artist of the Third Age whose landscapes he particularly commends, and one of the few in the Modern Age who he praises in this respect. Describing Polidoro's frescoes of saints in landscape settings that adorn the church of S. Silvestro in Rome, he writes:

> he painted there two *storie* in colours of St Mary Magdalen, in which there are the marks (*macchiati*) of some landscapes painted with all possible grace and discretion, for truly Polidoro painted landscapes, and the outlines and blotches (*macchie*) of trees and rocks better than any other artist; and he was the cause of that facility in the art which modern artists bring to their works.[26]

The significance of this passage lies in Vasari's use of terms, and his description of Polidoro's landscapes as executed with 'grace' and 'discretion'. For while 'grace' suggests that facility and apparent absence of effort that Vasari found lacking in the landscapes of artists such as Uccello, 'discretion' suggests an element of selection and restraint both in the forms the artists chose, and in the way they are painted. Most significant of all is his description of Polidoro's landscapes in terms of 'marks' (*macchiati*) and 'blotches' (*macchie*), suggesting a roughness and imprecision, an indistinctness and sketch-like quality in the rendering of forms. Indeed, these terms, which are unusual in the actual biographies in the *Lives*, are used in the Technical Preface on Painting precisely in the context of the making of a preliminary sketch.[27] It is this imprecision, I suggest, and the mere blotches of trees and rocks, that prevent the landscape from becoming obtrusive and drawing excessive attention to itself, whilst imparting to it a facility and grace, and a *semblance* of naturalness, which should be the artist's ultimate aim.

To some extent, Vasari is alluding here to qualities that are most easily achieved in fresco; in the works of Polidoro he approves a breadth of handling and vagueness of form that were less appropriate to the medium of oil paint. He must also have been struck by their classicizing, *all'antica* appearance, for of all early sixteenth-century landscapes Polidoro's approximate most closely to the style of Antique Roman landscape depiction as it was then understood. None the less, his account of Polidoro also establishes general principles for the depiction of landscape, namely that the artist should exercise judgement and discretion, aiming for the grace and beauty that come from selection and refinement, and from a generalized treatment of forms. It is these qualities that Vasari praises in the landscapes of Raphael, which he invariably describes as 'very beautiful', and which, as in the *Madonna del Belvedere* (illus. 78), display a lightness of touch and symmetry of form that renders them wholly unobtrusive, in spite of their obvious charm.

In the light of these observations it is particularly significant, and fully consistent, that the only one of Piero's landscapes to earn Vasari's praise is that in the *Liberation of Andromeda* (illus. 43), and the terms in which he describes it are extremely telling:

> Piero never painted a more pleasing work than this, or one that was more finely finished, seeing that one could not possibly see a more bizarre or capricious sea monster than that which Piero imagined . . . The landscape is very beautiful, and done with a soft and graceful colouring, and the colours are as harmonious and well-blended as they could possibly be, and he carried out the work with extreme diligence.[28]

The landscape in this painting is, in fact, one of Piero's most generalized, and that in which he achieves the most subtle use of colour and *chiaroscuro*. While the foreground is relatively detailed, and forms such as the shells on the shore and the anthropomorphic tree, are rendered with precision, the background is painted in softer terms, and the landscape becomes progressively less distinct as it recedes into the distance. The banks that frame the main action and accommodate the subsidiary scenes, and details such as the looming mountain on the right are painted less precisely, and with subtle gradations of light and shade, even though, on close scrutiny, they reveal a wealth of natural detail. In this instance, then, Piero's soft and graceful colour, and the less minute and finicky rendering of landscape could be seen to impart to the work that facility and apparent absence of effort Vasari sought among the artists of the Third Age, and which he considered incompatible with too close a scrutiny of nature. It is these qualities, furthermore, that give the landscape its beauty, and lend the work its charm. At the same time, the relative indistinctness of the setting, and of the landscape beyond the foreground plane, allows the viewer to focus more clearly on the figures, while facilitating the distinction between the main action and the subsidiary scenes.

In addition, the subtlety of the aerial perspective renders it one of Piero's most successful works in terms of the illusion of distance, a skill that Vasari sought particularly in the artists of the Third Age, and which he considered one of their most important achievements in landscape. In the Preface to part Three of the *Lives* he lists those things that the artists of the Third Age added to those of the Second, including 'an abundance of beautiful costumes, the variety of so many *bizzarrie*, a charming use of colour, and distance (*lontananza*) and variety of landscapes', while in the passage discussed above from the Life of Raphael he stresses the importance of 'fire, stormy and clear skies, clouds, rain, thunderbolts, brightening skies, nights, the lights of the moon and the brightness of the sun'.[29] Thus, in so far as he acknowledged landscape as a forum for the display of skill, it was particularly the illusion of depth and the mastery of atmospheric effects that Vasari valued among the artists of his own time, partly because they were less of a distraction from the figure than the detailed rendering of the earth that he associated more with artists of the Second Age. Such devices were also a means of achieving realism in landscape, and of rendering the setting convincing in an unobtrusive way.

Last, it is worth recalling that, like the one in the *Incarnation*, the landscape of the *Liberation of Andromeda* contains a number of zoomorphic and anthropomorphic forms, and it too could justifiably be described as 'bizarre', a term that Vasari uses here of the sea-monster. Yet it is precisely in this context, that of a mythological painting intended partly for decorative purposes, and for the adornment of a private space, that the bizarre finds its place, and there is no suggestion here that the fantastic forms of the landscape are other than appropriate or beguiling. Not only, in fact, is this the proper forum for the exercise of such skills, but in this context the fantastic landscape, like the whimsical monster, can be seen to enhance and support the narrative in a way that is perhaps less apparent in the *Incarnation*.

It was not only the more bizarre of Piero's landscapes that posed problems for Vasari, however, for these were acceptable in their place, and he may also have had reservations about the artist's more prosaic landscape motifs. But this is implied less in his comments on individual works than in his account of the artist's lifestyle:

> He did not wish his rooms to be cleaned, he wished to eat only when he was hungry, and he did not want the fruit trees in his garden to be pruned, or the ground hoed, and likewise he let the vines grow and the shoots trail over the ground; and he never pruned the figs or the other trees, for he took delight in watching everything run wild (*selvatico*), as was his own nature, claiming that nature should be left to take care of herself, without interference.[30]

While, as I suggested in chapter One, this account of Piero's life and his love of untamed nature could be seen as a metaphor for his uncontrolled talent and the lack of discipline he exercised over his natural inclinations and gifts, it may also constitute a subtle comment on the nature of his landscapes, suggesting that they are similarly uncultivated or *selvatico*, and that in his art, as in his daily existence, Piero showed a preference for the uncultivated and the wild. Vasari also relates Piero's specific delight in the forms that nature had made 'by accident, or from whim', implying the artist showed an interest in the imperfect or malformed.[31]

It is important, none the less, to be clear about the implications of the term *selvatico* here, for it certainly does not imply that his landscapes are alien or exotic. Indeed, as we have seen, the content of Piero's landscapes is distinguished more often by its ordinariness, and by his scrutiny of the mundane, rather than by any overt strangeness or by the exploration of odd or unfamiliar species. In terms of Renaissance attitudes to landscape, however, it is here that their unconventionality resides, for within this context, a natural, seemingly unmediated landscape had no obvious function or place, since it could neither aid the narrative nor give pleasure to the viewer through its beauty. For if the effectiveness of landscape as a narrative device depended to a large extent on the use of conventional or recognizable types, symbols and motifs, whose choice and disposition were governed by the figures, its function as a source of pleasure relied on a process of selection and refinement. As we saw when considering the Lives of Uccello and Polidoro, there is an assumption in Vasari's writings that, in the rendering of landscape, nature should be governed by artifice, tamed and refined through the exercise of art. Its inherent disorderliness and irregularities should be eliminated by the discretion and judgement of the artist, just as its charms should be enhanced by a subtly inventive use of colour. To a large extent, therefore, the concept of a wholly natural or untamed landscape was quite foreign, and if Piero's landscapes struck his viewers as odd or unusual, this strangeness probably lay less in any obvious exoticism than in their appearance of unmediated nature – of a nature that was not, in fact, naturalized or made familiar through reference to formal or iconographic convention.

It is in this sense, I suggest, that we may understand Vasari's use of the word *selvatico* in relation to Piero's paintings, for his landscapes appear untamed and ungoverned, either by convention or by the demands and resources of art. *Selvatico* may thus denote less a positive quality than a lack of order and symmetry and a pervasive unruliness in Piero's landscapes, which appear uncontrolled by the exercise of art. Like the figs and the vines in his garden, and like his own talent, his landscapes are uncultivated; by implication, therefore, they are not fully harnessed to their role, either of imparting beauty, or of supporting, in a subordinate way, the activities of the figures within them. For Vasari, like the untrimmed plants that comprise them, reproduced in all their accidental detail, Piero's landscapes overrun their proper bounds, and the demands of pictorial order and, in some cases, of narrative decorum.

Piero's more immediate contemporaries had similar reservations about the notion of a natural landscape, and it was only Leonardo who recognized the possibility of a landscape painting that took in every element of the visible, observable world. In his *Notebooks*, he discusses the range of landscape elements that the painter should master if he is to be truly universal and a proper master of nature. As has been noted, the range of landscape elements that he admits is far more inclusive than those listed by other fifteenth-century writers, such as Alberti, Lorenzo de' Medici, Ficino, Poliziano or Giovanni Santi, or by Boccaccio or Petrarch in the fourteenth century.[32] Like the Classical writers on whom they drew, particularly Pliny and Vitruvius, but also Virgil and Horace, these writers stressed above all the pleasing aspects of landscape painting, those that could give delight to the viewer and bring calm and refreshment to the spirit. Most common among these were features associated with the motif of the *locus amoenus*, such as abundant greenery, flowery meadows, shady groves, running streams and woods redolent with bird-song.[33] They also stress the importance of human activity in a landscape, such as dancing or singing, fishing and hunting, while the fantastic or the monstrous in nature is largely eliminated, considered appropriate only for the decoration of villas or places of leisure, or in the construction of gardens.

In his *De Re Aedificatoria*, for example, completed in the early 1450s and first printed in 1485, Alberti discusses the landscape decoration of interiors, seen as particularly appropriate for villas and garden buildings, and the list of elements he includes is clearly derived from Pliny. He stresses the pleasing and restorative effects of landscape, and the importance of variety, while also emphasizing that different types of landscape are appropriate to different sites and to the different temperament of the viewer. Thus, villas and rural dwellings are best adorned with 'paintings of pleasant landscapes or harbours, scenes of fishing, hunting, bathing or country sports, and flowering or leafy views', and Alberti also notes that

> paintings of springs and streams may be of considerable benefit to the feverish. It is possible to verify this: if some night as you lie awake in bed, unable to sleep, you visualise in your mind the clearest springs and streams you have ever seen, that dryness of insomnia will be quenched immediately, and sleep will steal you away into the sweetest slumber.[34]

In his *Comento sopra alcuni de' suoi sonetti*, Lorenzo de' Medici discusses the requirements of panel paintings designed for private decoration. Most of the subjects considered suitable include landscape, and Lorenzo stresses that the elements to be included must all be attractive in themselves, and in harmony with the temperament of the viewer. Among these he includes 'pleasing and delightful things such as animals, greenery, dancing and similar things', a list that recalls both literary accounts and also, perhaps, the repertory of landscape elements familiar to him from Northern tapestries, which were much prized for the decoration of private buildings.[35] Fifteenth-century descriptions of landscape, whether real or painted, and recommendations to painters for the rendering of landscape were thus heavily influenced by the classical literary tradition, and humanists sometimes suggested that artists should look to poets, such as Homer and Virgil, for the invention of landscape elements.[36] The ability of landscape to give pleasure, both in its individual elements and through a certain variety, is invariably a prime consideration. Within these writings, as for Vasari, there is also an assumption that the artist should improve on nature, rather than merely transcribe it, and that in order to give pleasure and to instil harmony in the viewer, landscapes, like well-planned gardens, should be ordered and tamed, and rendered beautiful and harmonious through the exercise of art.

In his own discussions of landscape painting, and in his drawings, Leonardo casts his net wider, particularly in his inclusion of rock forms and odd geological configurations (illus. 92), and his interest in atmospheric effects, deluges and stormy skies. In his discussion of the *paragone* debate, he also stresses the artist's ability to reproduce

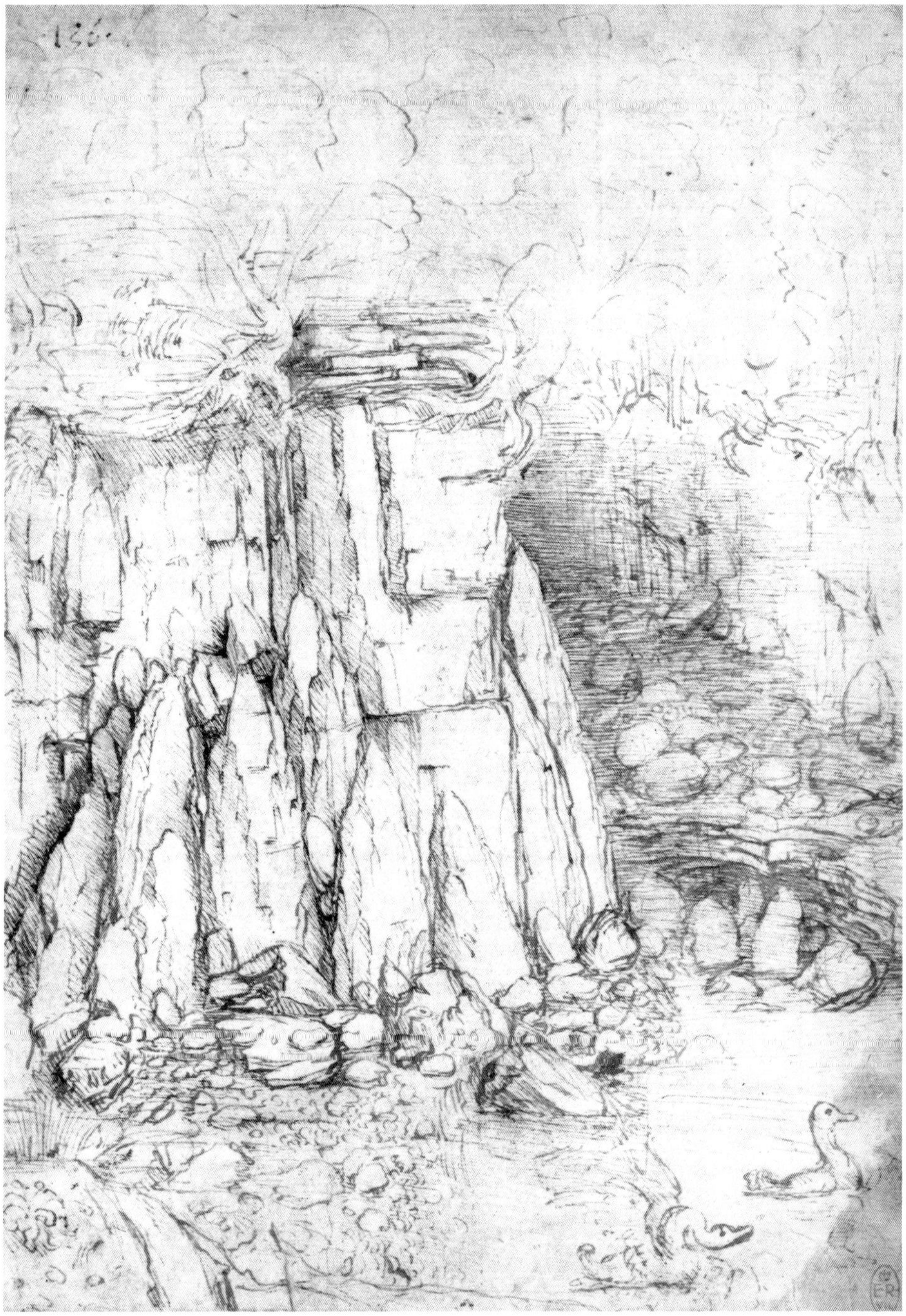

92 Leonardo da Vinci, *A River Running through a Rocky Ravine*, *c.*1483, pen and ink. Royal Library, Windsor Castle.

all the objects of nature, including the ugly, misshapen and grotesque, implying that landscape painting should be more inclusive and, like painting as a whole, an equivalent to or form of natural philosophy.[37] He stops short, however, of recommending these aspects of nature as objects of representation, and in his own paintings creates landscapes that, while unusual, are invariably pleasing in their effect, especially in their colouring and their overall harmony of parts. Nor does Leonardo suggest that the artist should reproduce nature exactly, rather he should be selective and 'look now at this thing and now at that, making a compound of different things chosen and selected from among those of less value'. The artist should also embellish and supplement the forms of nature through the exercise of his own inventive powers.[38]

Piero is thus conspicuous among contemporary artists, and to some extent at odds with contemporary writings on landscape, in the extent to which he focuses on the prosaic and the accidental, on his refusal always to select the pleasing in nature, and in his efforts to preserve rather than eliminate the irregularities of its structure. As we saw in chapter Two, Piero rarely attempted, especially in his mature works, to regularize the forms of nature or subject them to a geometric order, nor did he select his motifs on the basis of their intrinsic beauty. Indeed, he tried to preserve the imperfections of the natural world and the asymmetry of its shapes, and in building his compositions appeared to follow and extend the contours of the landscape rather than suppress or impose order upon them.

This is clearest, perhaps, in the Early Man panels, whose landscapes could be described as *selvatico* precisely by virtue of their disordered and uncultivated forms. In *The Hunt* (illus. 22), for example, the most intense scrutiny is reserved for the rough tree-trunks in the foreground, and for their broken branches and clusters of spiky twigs, while a misshapen rock is outlined against the horizon, its profile made more jagged by the skeletal trees that protrude from it at a variety of odd angles. Similarly, in the *Return from the Hunt* (illus. 23), the most striking motif is the boulder on the right, adorned with leafless trees, while the foreground is an uneven expanse of barren and stony ground, broken only by a blasted tree-stump deliberately aligned with the frame. In both works, furthermore, Piero avoids an obvious semblance of order in the overall structure in favour of a subtle asymmetry that seems to preserve the integrity of nature herself.

Furthermore, seen as a whole, the landscapes in both works are barren and stark, and relatively devoid of distinguishing detail. Their impact derives largely from their blunt, irregular forms, and from the bareness of both the trees and the land, and it is interesting to note that in this respect Piero chose not to follow the suggestions of Lucretius in his *De Rerum Natura*, for Lucretius describes the earth in the early stages of existence as lush and fruitful, and teeming with growth. It is an account that has obvious pictorial potential in a conventional sense, and it is thus significant that Piero ignored the opportunity offered by the text in favour of bleak, relatively featureless expanses of land, more in line with his own conception of the theme, and which provide the proper setting for his brutal and hybrid figures in their desperate struggle for survival.

Even in *The Forest Fire* (illus. 19), while the landscape is full of strange and exotic animals, the trees and plants are not particularly distinctive in terms of their species or the use of detail, and the landscape itself appears relatively mundane. Its untamed quality resides primarily in the twisted tree-trunks in the foreground and in the bare, uncultivated ground. As in the *Incarnation*, however, these ordinary, 'natural' landscapes are made strange by the intensity with which Piero scrutinizes their unremarkable forms, and by the tension between the prosaic nature of the objects themselves and the attention they command from the artist. What gives the landscapes their fascination, in fact, and which must have struck contemporary viewers with particular force, is the absorption and intense scrutiny with which Piero paints the ordinary detail of a denuded tree or a featureless expanse of grass.

Despite the emphasis scholars have placed on the landscapes in these paintings, Piero's interest was clearly as much in the depiction of light and shade as in the details of the trees or rocks, and in those atmospheric effects that, for Vasari, were as much a component of landscape as the features of the earth, and the distinguishing achievements of the artists of the Third Age. Even in the fifteenth century writers occasionally admitted the category of skies and clouds as an addition to the landscape painter's repertory. Angelo Decembrio, for example, writing in the 1450s, includes skies and clouds as objects on which the painter can exercise his skill, while in a contract drawn up in 1495 for Pintoricchio's painting of S. Maria de' Fossi in Perugia, the artist is specifically asked to include 'landscape and skies'.[39] As we have seen, Leonardo discusses at length the painting of stormy skies, a notion for which there was at least one Classical precedent in Pliny's praise for the painter Apelles, and his ability to 'paint the unpaintable, thunder, lightning and thunderbolts . . . '.[40] To a limited extent, therefore, writers and artists had begun to display an awareness of the attraction of skyscapes and atmospheric effects and their value as demonstrations of skill, a trend reflected in the rich, tempestuous sky of Piero's *Cleopatra* (illus. 34), the intricate clouds of the Stockholm *Madonna* (illus. 37), and the milky distance of *The Death of Procris* (illus. 6).

I noted in chapter Two that the depiction of fire could itself be seen as a humanist conceit – a demonstration of skill sanctioned in Classical texts – and it is clear that this was one of Piero's main concerns, rather than the abundance of colourful flora and fauna pervading contemporary descriptions of landscape. Yet, his interest in light effects in the Early Man panels extends far beyond the rendering of fire itself, to the subtle variations in colour and light caused by different times of day, the effects of drifting smoke and its mingling with the clouds, the casting of shadows and the manifold reflections of firelight on both water and the earth, all of which are made more apparent precisely by the bareness of the landscape itself and the relative lack of detail in its individual forms.

Even the more unconventional of Piero's landscapes are constructed with a close eye to the demands of the narrative. In his secular paintings, as in the religious works, Piero varies his approach to landscape in relation to his subject, and the forms he uses in these are as diverse as those in the altarpieces and the tondi. The landscape backgrounds of the Vespucci *Bacchanals*, for example, are in keeping with Piero's conception of the subject as a whole, while being quite different from those in the *Hunt* panels. In *The Discovery of Honey* (illus. 28), the maenads and attendants of Bacchus on the left, unusual in their rusticity, proceed through a pleasant and sunny landscape that is similarly undistinguished and non-classical, and full of ordinary flora and fauna, and which, as much as the figures, adds to the joyfulness and spirit of delight that Vasari perceived in the whole. In the centre, by contrast, the fantastic tree, half-animal, half-plant, provides a natural setting or focus for the hybrid creatures surrounding it, while the satyrs on the right search frantically in a dark inhospitable forest for the sweet gift of honey. As I pointed out in chapter Two, in this way the landscape also follows the pattern of a traditional *paysage moralisé*, the differences between its parts underlined in the contrast between light and darkness, and between the clear and stormy skies.

There are also more conventional landscapes among Piero's secular works, and backgrounds that follow traditional types more closely. The most obvious example of this is the *Mars and Venus* (illus. 5), where the lovers lie in the *locus amoenus* conventionally associated with such themes, although Piero achieves in it a consummate variety and a contrast of different parts that appears consciously to recall Pliny's account of the landscape repertory of the Classical painter Studius.[41] The conventionality of the setting is also indicated in Vasari's account of the work, which was in his own possession. In describing the painting he notes that the figures recline 'upon a meadow full of flowers', adding that 'there is there a grove of myrtle, and a Cupid who is frightened of a rabbit, and there are also the doves of Venus and the other appurtenances of love'.[42] His account of the landscape is purely factual and descriptive and involves no qualifying terms, underlining the fact that it is unremarkable in formal or iconographic terms and constitutes a natural and appropriate part of such a scene. Like the doves, the Cupid and the rabbit, in fact, the landscape is seen simply as an attribute of Venus, a natural part of the paraphernalia of love.

In the *Death of Procris* (illus. 6), however, Piero could exercise a greater degree of freedom, since the subject had not previously been depicted on a large scale. He was thus at greater liberty, perhaps, to create his own landscape setting although, as I suggested in chapter Two, he stayed close to the text of Correggio's play. But he did not do so by drawing on the text for a specific setting or for the description of a location, but for the way in which the landscape and all the details of nature take part in the scene of mourning. Here again the landscape is striking by virtue of its familiarity, for the unremarkable beach or estuary serving as a backdrop (roamed by a trio of dogs), the boats in the middle distance, and the blunt shapes of the buildings on the far shore. These are combined, however, with a foreground that is disarmingly natural as well as richly expressive and symbolic in its carpet of flowers and herbs and in the overhanging plants that seem to join in the lament. Among the plants we can identify with reasonable certainty are daisies (symbols of the trials of love), forget-me-nots and periwinkles (sweet remembrance and fidelity), the crocus (a symbol of love in marriage) and narcissi, anemones and sage, all of which had funereal associations. The pelican, and the standing birds resembling cranes, may also be symbolic, although their significance is less clear, since cranes generally symbolized watchfulness while the pelican is more familiar as a religious symbol denoting piety or charity towards others.[43] Yet the effectiveness of the landscape depends primarily on the way in which it echoes the positions and movements of the figures, underlining the expressive lines of their limbs, and on its distant emptiness and lack of human presence, the palpable tranquillity and silence it creates, and its sense of abandonment and seclusion.

To see Piero's landscapes as direct and straightforward expressions of his own interests, or reflections of his supposedly primitive nature is thus both misleading and a gross over-simplification, for it is by no means the case that his secular panels consist solely of 'primitive' landscapes. As we have seen, his landscapes are extremely diverse, to an extent and in a manner that argue clearly against the notion of his personal identification with a particular type of landscape or vision of nature, or a nostalgia for the primordial, uninhabited world. At the same time, even if his interpretation of what was appropriate differed from Vasari's, his landscapes are marked by a strong sense of decorum and of the demands of the subject that both determine their content and control the exercise of his own inventive powers.

This does not mean that Piero's landscapes fit neatly into standard types or genres, for they frequently depart from the conventional frameworks or schemata suggested by religious or literary texts, or by artistic tradition. It is probably for this reason that he had no successors as a painter of landscape, even in centres such as Venice where landscape played a greater part in contemporary art, and which in the works of artists like Giorgione and Titian came to assume almost equal importance to the figures. The so-called *poesie* of Titian, with their seemingly pure and natural landscapes, also appear to have followed set formulas, often suggested by pastoral literature and descriptions of rural life, while the individual forms they use are often quite idealized.[44] Conversely, in Florence, the majority of artists came to favour the generalized landscape types of Raphael, with their broad and regularized forms, and Piero's idiosyncratic forms and strange combinations of motifs had little impact on artists working there or elsewhere.

That is not to say that Piero was entirely alone among Florentine artists in the use of vernacular motifs, or in the anecdotal quality of his landscapes. As we have seen, in the late fifteenth century comparable motifs appear in the works of Filippino Lippi (illus. 48), while in the early sixteenth century the works of Fra Bartolommeo appear close to Piero's, and his *God the Father with SS. Mary Magdalen and Catherine of Siena* (illus. 93), painted in 1508, provides an interesting point of comparison with Piero's near-contemporary *Incarnation*. As in Piero's work, the landscape in Fra Bartolommeo's

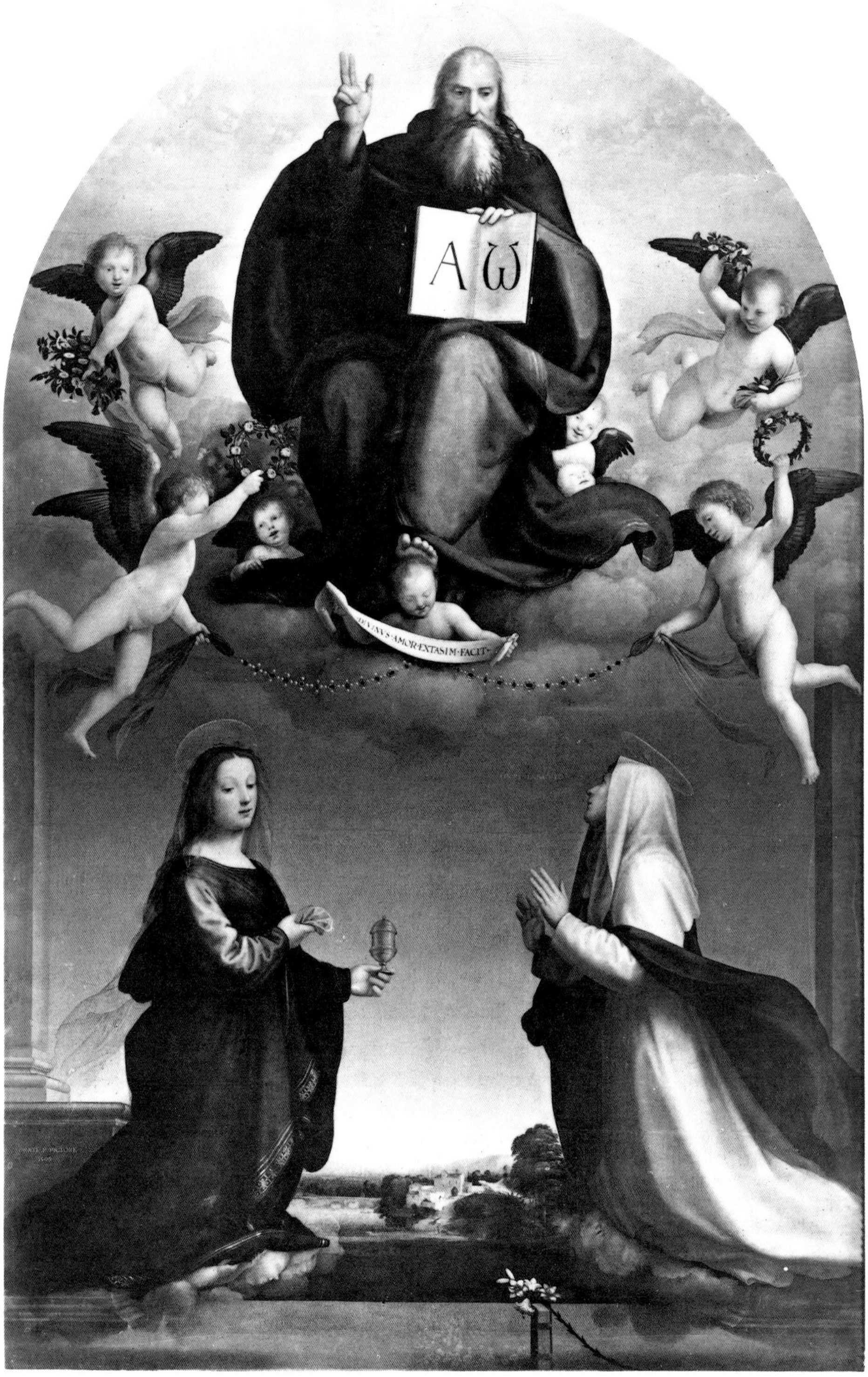

93 Fra Bartolommeo, *God the Father with SS Mary Magdalen and Catherine of Siena*, 1508, oil on canvas. Museo Nazionale di Villa Guinigi, Lucca.

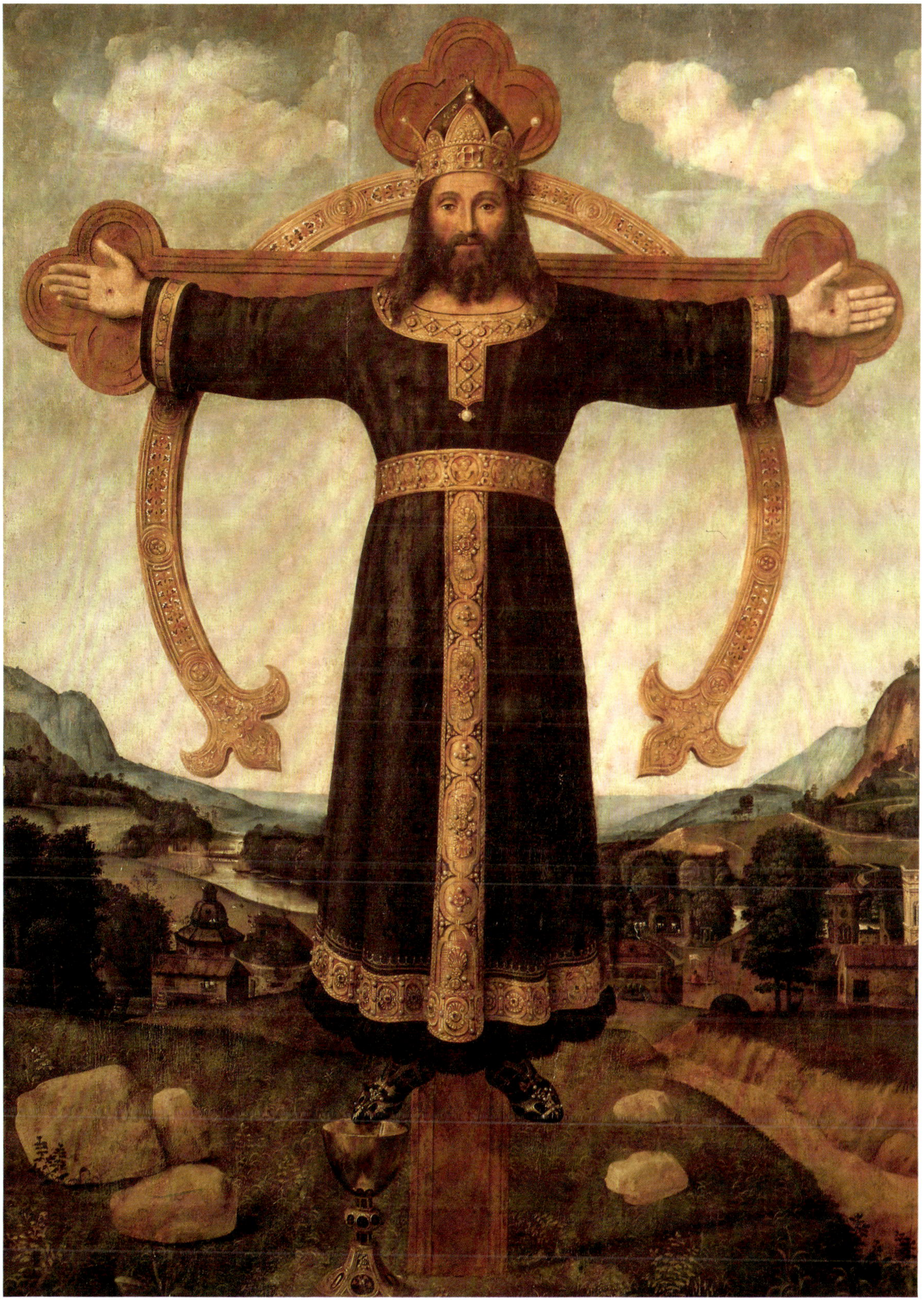

94 *The Volto Santo of Lucca*, *c.*1505–10, oil on panel. Szépmüveszéti Múzeum, Budapest.

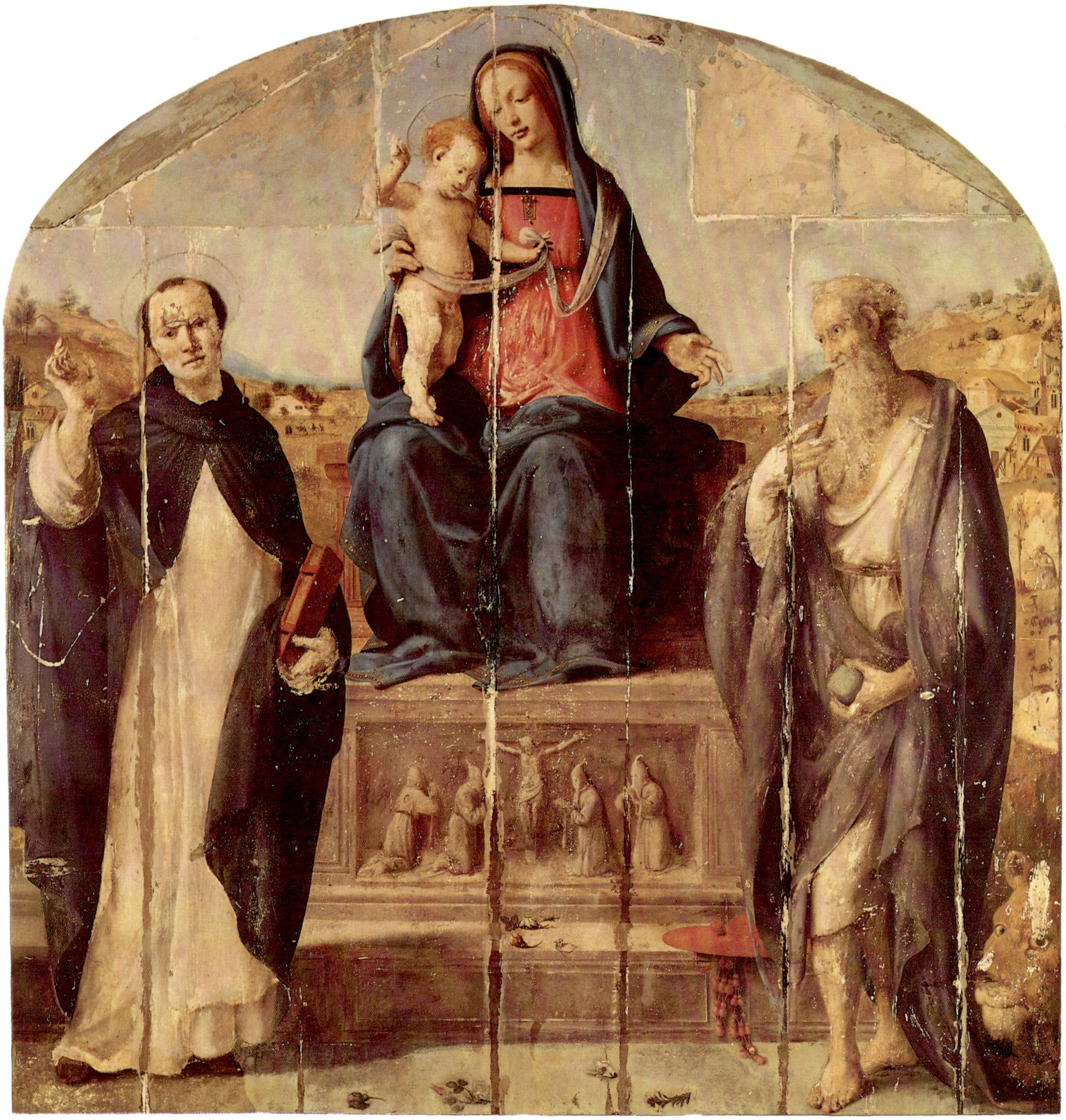

95 *Madonna and Child with SS Dominic and Jerome*, *c.*1510–20, oil on panel. Yale University Art Gallery, New Haven.

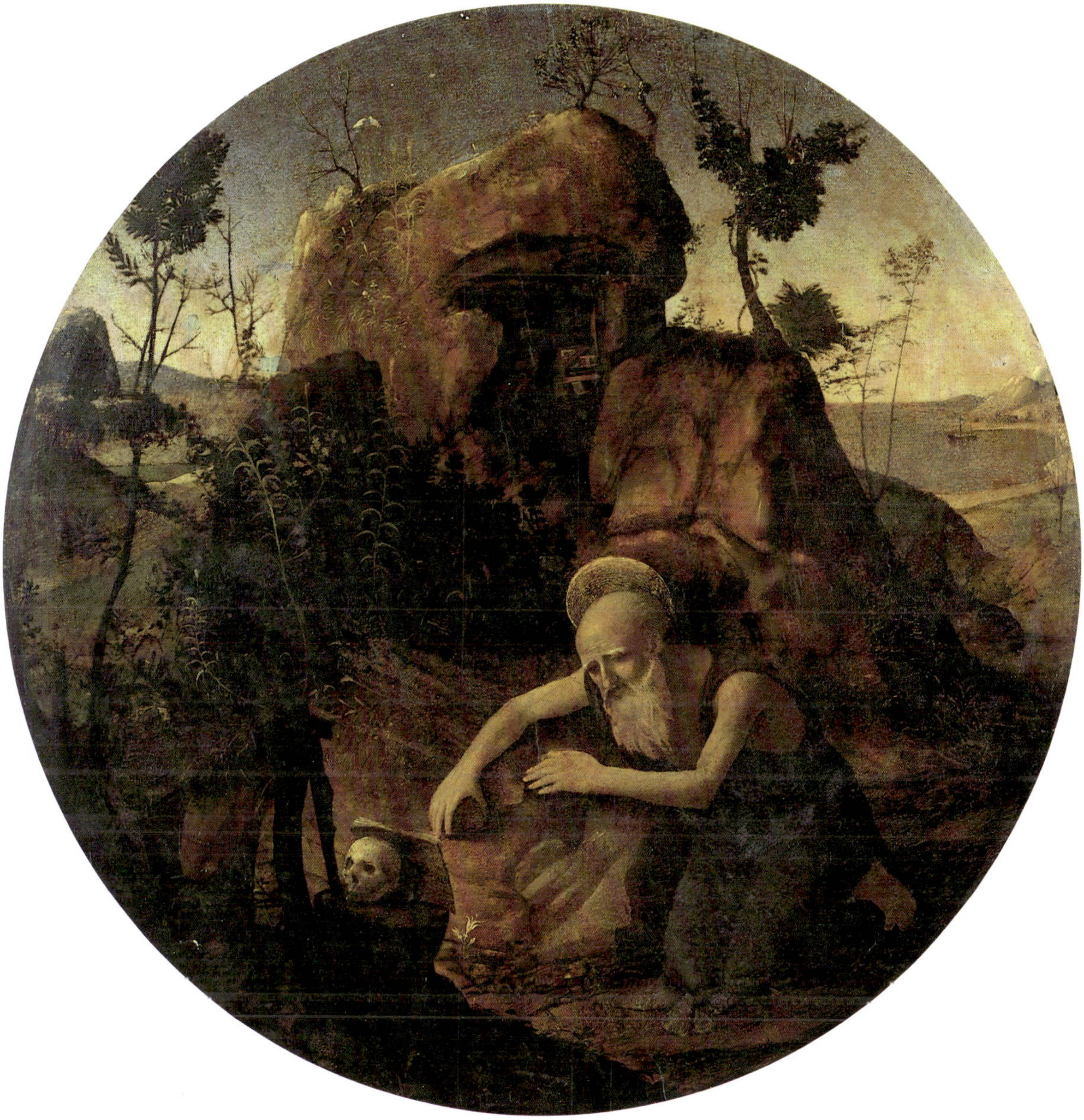

96 *The Penitent St Jerome*, *c.*1495–1500, oil on panel. Museo Horne, Florence.

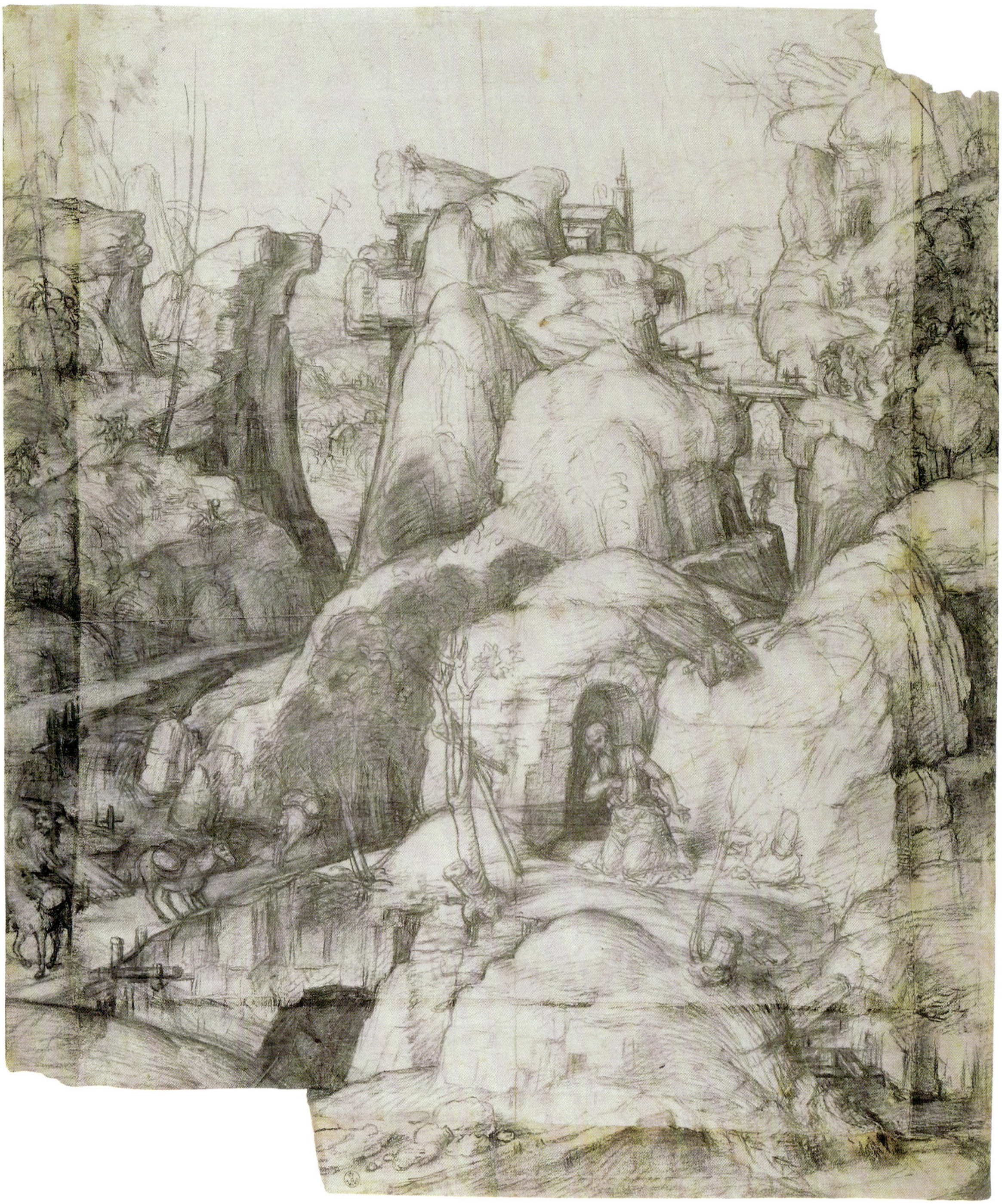

97 *St Jerome in a Panoramic Landscape*, black chalk. Uffizi, Florence.

altarpiece is homely and familiar; it contains rural dwellings whose smoking chimneys offer signs of life, as well as peasants going about their daily work. The flora and fauna are both highly naturalistic and painted with great attention to detail, and the radiant autumn light of the background is painted with consummate attention and skill. Here, however, the landscape is kept at a distance from the figures and rendered on quite a different scale, so that the figures remain clearly the focus of attention. Furthermore, while Piero makes no distinction between the symbolic and the 'real' in his landscape, Fra Bartolommeo carefully contrasts and subordinates the distant 'natural' landscape to the foreground detail of St Catherine's symbolic lily, rendered with greater precision, the presence of which is more palpable and compelling. The landscape, while it presents a background of infinite variety and charm and, in the nature of its contents is not far removed from Piero's, remains secondary to the figures, serving also to emphasize the unearthly nature of the subject and the spirituality of the Saints.

Vasari, as we have seen, judged Piero's landscapes in largely negative terms, primarily because in several respects they constituted a diversion and distraction from the more important subject of the figure. At the same time, the quirky, anecdotal quality of his landscapes and the close exploration of individual forms were of a type that he associated with the Second Age, and with Uccello's indiscriminate surveys of nature, exercised without discretion, or without due regard for the overall beauty of a work of art. In some respects, in fact, Piero's works do occupy an awkward place in the development of landscape, and the *Liberation of Andromeda* combines the detailed rendering of the earth and emphasis on the accidental and the odd, with the simplified background, refined exploration of light, and atmospheric effects and subdued colouring that were to become characteristic of Florentine painters in the following decade.

As in other respects, however, the attitude of patrons towards landscape painting appears to have been more flexible, and it would be a mistake to assume that they were always conscious of or concerned with the ideas expressed in literary works or texts of art criticism and theory. Contemporary inventories of picture collections, and of the contents of town and country houses, list landscapes of different sorts with some regularity, as well as paintings of animals, making clear that there was a market for such works. And while Flemish paintings may have been valued primarily for their devotional qualities, the strong interest contemporary Italian patrons showed in them also suggests a certain receptiveness to the use of naturalistic detail. The tondi and *spalliera* panels that include Piero's most adventurous essays in landscape were also clearly in demand, while the surviving tondo of *St Jerome* (illus. 96) and two drawings (illus. 97 and 98) that must be preparatory studies for works of a similar kind suggest that he was recognized precisely for his landscape skills. In all three of these works it is clearly the landscape that forms the focus of attention, even if its contents are dictated by the actions and identity of the Saint, although it is worth noting that the figure of St Jerome in the tondo is more dominant than in the drawings. In the painting the setting is comprised of a central mass of rock, its top covered with stubby branches and rough grass, while in the foreground the artist describes with meticulous care a collection of grasses, bullrushes and tiny white flowers inhabited by birds, the details of each plant standing out against a denser mass of brambles behind. Behind the rock itself, the landscape gives way to a distant sea and thence to the snowy peaks of a mountain range, and includes both boats and buildings.

Of all Piero's landscapes this is probably the most detailed and the most continuous, although its damaged state conceals the true extent of his description of particular species, and the painting's original colour range. It is also the most naturalistic, and is devoid of any of the more idiosyncratic features that appear in certain other works. In this case, it would seem, the interest of the tondo resided in the range of plausible naturalistic detail, rendered with almost scientific precision, which the owner of such a work could scrutinize at leisure and at close range. At the same time, like most of Piero's landscapes, it shows a subtle and varied handling of light – the brilliant sunlight that floods the background and the light dancing on the sea contrasting with the shadowy recess in which Jerome kneels. He is, however, illuminated and picked out from the surrounding vegetation by a shaft of light falling from the left, which also highlights details of the plants.

In the drawing of *St Jerome in a Rocky Landscape* (illus. 98), Piero uses a similar rock mass as a central device, its crags and crevices roughly sketched in alongside shapes that seem to indicate clouds on the left and distant mountains on the right, although he includes relatively little detail. The drawing of *St Jerome in a Panoramic Landscape* (illus. 97) is more detailed, in a manner that suggests it may be a cartoon made for a second painting of the same subject. It is, in fact, the largest and most detailed drawing of a landscape to have survived from the period and is thus of particular significance, suggesting at the same time the extent of Piero's own interest in the natural world. Inevitably, given its medium and scale, this drawing includes relatively little detail of flora and fauna, although the forms of some trees – most of them quite bare – are indicated in the foreground, and Piero also includes a number of tree-stumps. In the middle ground, areas of shading seem to indicate patches of denser growth, while isolated lines around the edges of the rocks recall the spiky, denuded forms that Piero usually includes in such places. The more varied shading on the plateau on the left may also indicate a carpet of moss such as appears in certain works, for example the *Incarnation*, while below the mountain-top church are patches of the familiar hanging vegetation.

Piero's main interest here appears, however, to be in the rock-forms themselves, the shapes of which are notably more varied and idiosyncratic than those in the other works, ranging from the horizontal, ovoid forms on the right to the tall rounded peaks in the centre, and the square protuberances that almost meet above a sheer gorge on the left. More precisely, Piero appears to be interested in the expressive effects of these motifs, their awe-inspiring appearance, and the way in which they dwarf the tiny figures. The perilousness of the setting, and its remoteness are emphasized, for example, by the inclusion of the fragile bridge spanning the gorge on the right, and by

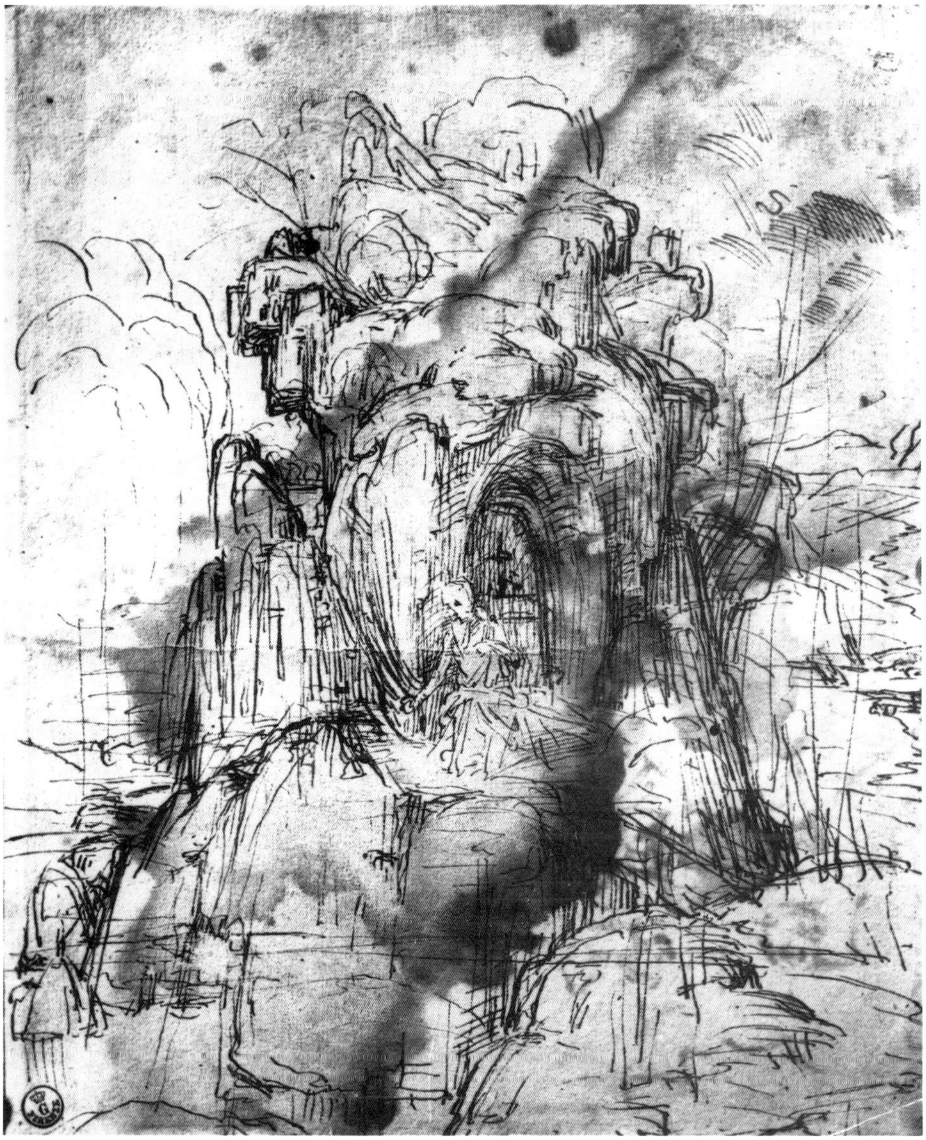

98 *St Jerome in a Rocky Landscape*, *c*1495–1500, pen and ink. Uffizi, Florence.

the appearance of several laden donkeys on the left that, taking fright on seeing the lion, flee into the dark recesses of the rocks. The church and monastery at the summit, and placed directly above St Jerome, offer the only apparent haven, and in the peaks and crevices around it the diminutive figures of the Saint's fellow monks seem engulfed by their stony setting. Even here, therefore, in a drawing that on first sight suggests a study of nature and a spontaneous response to an awesome panorama, the individual motifs are carefully considered and controlled, and the whole put together in strict accordance with the figural subjects and the implications of the theme.

This discussion inevitably raises the question of the sources of Piero's landscapes, and the extent to which they were based on direct observation. As we have seen, there

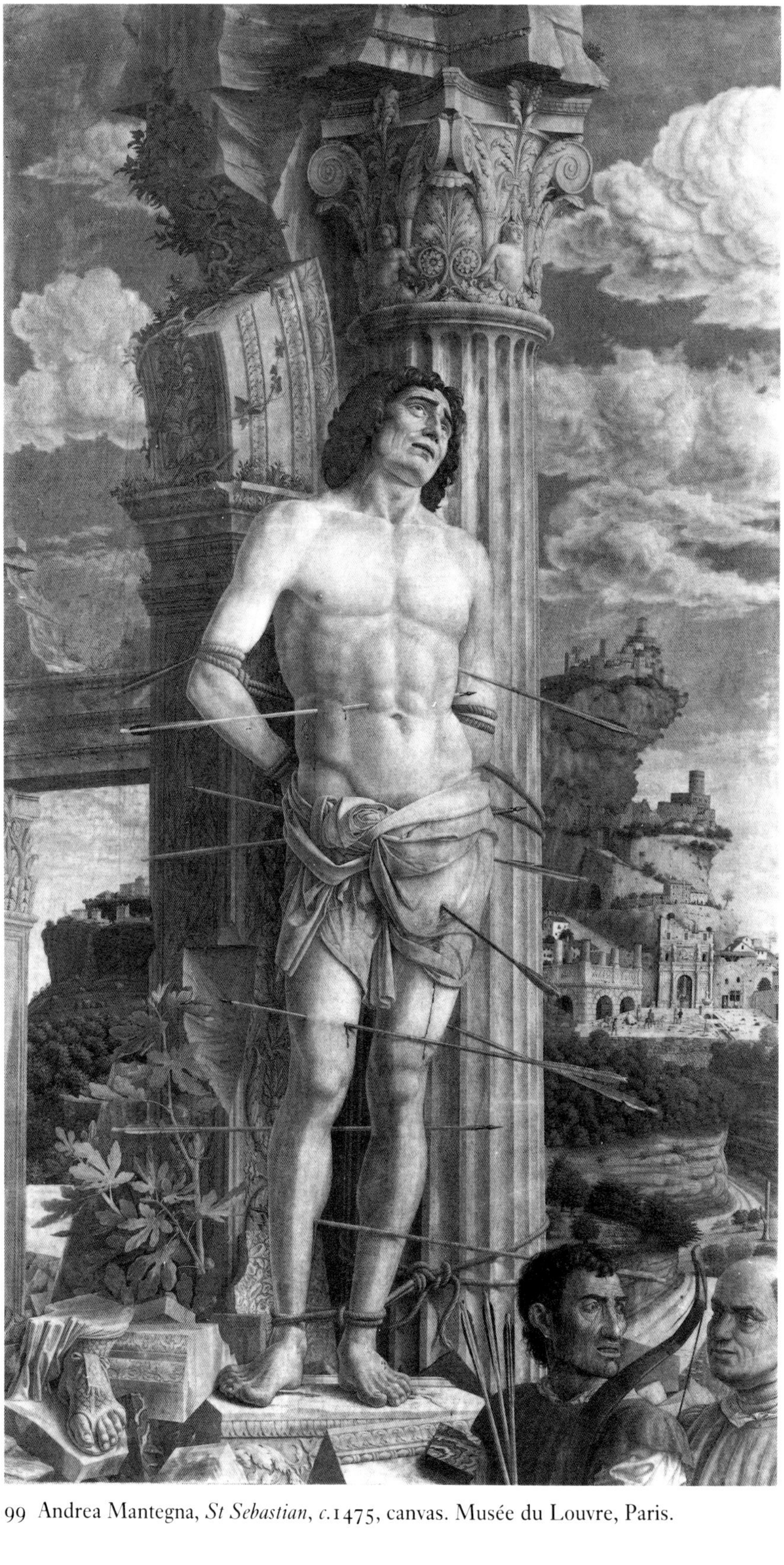

99 Andrea Mantegna, *St Sebastian*, *c.*1475, canvas. Musée du Louvre, Paris.

are relatively few instances of contemporary artists painting accurate topographical views, and no writer recommends that artists should make literal depictions of specific sites. Piero was no exception to this, and while there is among his drawings one townscape apparently based on observation, and believed by some scholars to be a view of Prato, this kind of literal transcription is not to be found in his paintings.[45] Nor do his surviving drawings include studies of plants or trees, and while the plants in the *Death of Procris*, for example, suggest a close observation of nature, like other artists he may also have made use of botanical treatises in some instances, rather than relying solely on observation. Likewise, in his depiction of rocks and mountains, it is probable that he drew partly on Northern prints, as did Mantegna for his own depiction of fantastic rock-forms (illus. 99 and 41). Thus, while there is no doubt that Piero looked at nature closely, this was not a sole or a direct source of his landscapes, and a careful consideration of the works themselves makes clear they can hardly have been taken from specific sites. In general terms his landscapes may also reveal the influence of Flemish art, in their use of ordinary or vernacular motifs, the subtlety with which he incorporates symbolic details and his emphasis on the texture of the real. His works are also closer to Flemish than to Florentine examples in their approach to landscape composition, in which the structure is instinctual and held together by light, rather than by linear perspective, and based around the irregularities of nature. In other respects, however, in their combination of the ordinary and the bizarre, their range and variety, and their feel for the formal and expressive possibilities of the natural world, his landscapes are remote from those of Flemish art.

To a large extent, in fact, to search for the sources of and inspiration for Piero's landscapes seems a futile endeavour, for they are both highly individual and extremely varied. Nor would the discovery of models for individual motifs in his works prove particularly illuminating, for the way in which he combines them is wholly distinctive and original, and it is this as much as the specific forms that gives his landscapes their power. In the Life of Piero, we recall, Vasari relates that the artist used the shapes of clouds and spit-marks on walls as a source of inspiration, a procedure that Leonardo also recommends as a starting-point for interesting landscape forms.[46] Vasari writes:

> He would often stop to consider a wall against which sick people had spat repeatedly, and he extracted from the marks on it battles of horses, and the most fantastic cities and the most extensive landscapes that one could ever hope to see: he did the same with the clouds in the sky.[47]

While, as I suggested in chapter One, the significance of this passage from the Life is complex, on one level it offers an apt account of the sources and nature of Piero's landscapes, of the accidental quality and irregularity of his forms, which pervade both earth and sky, and of their foundation in observed nature, made wondrous by his unique *fantasia*.

References

INTRODUCTION

1 – Vasari's Life of Piero is in G. B. Vasari, *Le Vite de' più eccellenti pittori, scultori ed architettori*, ed. G. Milanesi, 9 vols, Florence, 1875–85, IV, pp. 131–44. Unless otherwise stated, all references to the *Lives* will be to Milanesi's edition, which is based on the revised version that was first published in 1568.

2 – W. H. Wackenroder, *Herzensergeissungen eines kunstliebenden Klosterbruders*, Berlin, 1797, p. 78. For a translation of and commentary on Wackenroder's writings see W. H. Wackenroder, *Confessions and Fantasies*, translated and annotated by M. Hurst Schubert, London, 1971. For the passage on Piero see pp. 121–5.

3 – George Eliot, *Romola*, 2 vols, Philadelphia, 1890, I, pp. 303–11 and p. 414ff.

4 – G. Pudelko, 'Piero di Cosimo, Peintre Bizarre', *Minotaure*, XI, May 1938, pp. 19–26.

5 – E. Battisti, *L'Antirinascimento*, Milan, 1962, p. 101.

6 – R. and M. Wittkower, *Born Under Saturn: The Character and Conduct of Artists; A Documented Study from Antiquity to the French Revolution*, London, 1963, p. 71; M. Bacci, *Piero di Cosimo*, Milan, 1966, p. 9.

7 – For a general guide to Vasari's life, and the writing of the *Lives*, see T. S. R. Boase, *Giorgio Vasari: The Man and the Book*, Princeton, NJ, 1979. More detailed analyses can be found in *Il Vasari storiografo e artista: Atti del congresso Internazionale nel IV centenario della Morte: 1974*, Florence, 1976, and in P. Barocchi, ed., *Studi Vasariani*, Turin, 1984.

8 – Alberti's views on the ideal artist are most clearly stated in Book III of his *De Pictura*, written in 1435. The best edition is C. Grayson, *Leon Battista Alberti: On Painting and On Sculpture*, London, 1972. For a brief discussion of Alberti and Vasari on the artist see also A. Blunt, *Artistic Theory in Italy 1450–1600*, Oxford, 1940, pp. 1–22, 48–57 and 86–102.

9 – See, for example, A. Chastel, *Art et humanisme à Florence au temps de Laurent le Magnifique*, Paris, 1959, pp. 61–2 and 176–7.

10 – A good, short account of Vasari's approach to biography is P. Rubin, 'What Men Saw: Vasari's Life of Leonardo da Vinci and the Image of the Artist', *Art History*, XIII, 1990, pp. 34–46. See also Rubin's forthcoming book on Vasari as biographer and, more tangentially, C. M. Soussloff, 'Lives of Poets and Painters in the Renaissance', *Word and Image*, VI, 1990, pp. 154–62, and the same author's 'Imitatio Buonarroti', *Sixteenth-Century Journal*, XX, 1989, pp. 581–602. Also useful are P. Barolsky, *Why Mona Lisa Smiles and other Tales by Vasari*, London, 1991, and the same author's *Giotto's Father and the Family of Vasari's 'Lives'*, London, 1992.

11 – The dating of Piero's works is extremely complex and few of them are documented. Since it is not the purpose of this book to rehearse or review this aspect of his *oeuvre*, unless stated otherwise I have accepted the datings proposed in Bacci (1966), with which I am largely in agreement. For discussions of the dating and provenance of Piero's works, the reader should refer to this work in the first instance, together with F. Zeri, 'Rivedendo Piero di Cosimo', *Paragone (Arte)*, CXV, July 1959, pp. 36–50. Bacci did, however, revise some of her opinions in her *L'Opera Completa di Piero di Cosimo*, Milan, 1976, most significantly with reference to the Uffizi *Liberation of Andromeda*. A further reliable account of the chronology of Piero's works is in W. Griswold, *The Drawings of Piero di Cosimo*, PhD dissertation, Courtauld Institute, University of London, 1988, pp. 18–32.

12 – The best and most complete account of Vasari's critical language is R. Le Mollé, *Georges Vasari et le vocabulaire de la critique d'art dans les 'Vite'*, Université Stendhal Grenoble 3, 1988.

CHAPTER ONE

1 – The documentation concerning Piero's life and work is fragmentary and complex, and only the major points are given here. For a fuller account see Bacci, 1966, p. 21ff, and 1976, p. 83ff; S. J. Craven, 'Three Dates for Piero di Cosimo', *The Burlington Magazine*, CXVII, 1975, pp. 572–6, and Griswold, *The Drawings of Piero di Cosimo*, pp. 18–22, 33–5. The most recent book in English on the artist is R. Langton Douglas, *Piero di Cosimo*, Chicago, 1946. I am greatly indebted to Patricia Rubin for her comments on this chapter.

2 – G. Vasari, *Le Vite de' più eccellenti pittori, scultori ed architettori nelle redazioni del 1550 e 1568*, ed. R.

Bettarini and P. Barocchi, Florence, 1966–87, IV, p. 60.
3 – Vasari–Milanesi, IV, p. 132.
4 – Vasari–Milanesi, III, p. 189 and IV, p. 132. The frescoes in the Sistine Chapel were painted between 1481 and 1482, and are discussed fully in L. Ettlinger, *The Sistine Chapel before Michelangelo*, Oxford, 1965. The attribution to Piero of the landscape is accepted by most scholars. The portraits in the *Crossing of the Red Sea* cannot be securely identified.
5 – Craven, 'Three Dates', p. 574.
6 – For the deliberations over the site of the *David*, and Piero's inclusion on the committee see M. Wackernagel, *The World of the Florentine Renaissance Artist*, trans. A. Luchs, Princeton, NJ, 1981, pp. 67–70.
7 – The relevant documents are transcribed by F. Melis, 'Un'opera di Piero di Cosimo per Napoli', *Commentari*, XIX, 1968, p. 154.
8 – Craven, 'Three Dates', p. 575.
9 – Vasari–Milanesi, IV, pp. 135–7.
10 – Piero was paid 56 fiorini for his work on painting a triumphal arch made by the sculptor Baccio Bandinelli and others. For a full account see J. Shearman, 'The Florentine Entrata of Leo X, 1515', *Journal of the Warburg and Courtauld Institutes*, XXXVIII, 1975, pp. 136–54; the payment to Piero is mentioned on p. 147.
11 – Craven, 'Three Dates', pp. 575–6.
12 – On the dating of this panel see particularly Craven, 'Three Dates', p. 576; Bacci 1976, pp. 98–9; Zeri, 'Rivedendo Piero di Cosimo', pp. 41–2, and L. Berti *et al*, eds, *Firenze et la Toscana dei Medici nell'Europa del Cinquecento: Il primato del disegno*, exhibition catalogue, Florence, 1980, p. 163.
13 – Bacci, 1966, p. 22.
14 – Wackernagel, *op. cit.*, p. 302.
15 – Vasari–Milanesi, V, p. 7.
16 – Vasari owned Piero's *Mars and Venus*, now in Berlin, as he attests in the second edition of the Life. He also records that works by the artist were in the possession of Cosimo I de' Medici, one of Vasari's own patrons: Vasari–Milanesi, IV, p. 140 and 138.
17 – On the copies after Piero's works see F. Abbate, review of Bacci's *Piero di Cosimo*, 1966, in *Paragone (Arte)*, XIX, 1968, pp. 77–8.
18 – Vasari names Andrea del Sarto as a pupil both in the Life of Sarto, and in that of Piero: Vasari–Milanesi, V, p. 7 and IV, p. 144. Pontormo's apprenticeship is noted in his Life of Pontormo: Vasari–Milanesi, VI, p. 246. For Ridolfo Ghirlandaio's drawings after Piero see W. Griswold, 'Early Drawings by Ridolfo Ghirlandaio', *Master Drawings*, XXVII, 1989, pp. 215–23.
19 – The drawings are discussed in Griswold, *The Drawings of Piero di Cosimo*, p. 74ff and p. 170ff.
20 – The portraits were almost certainly executed between 1500 and 1504, and are discussed in Bacci, 1966, pp. 39–40 and p. 83. A drawing of the head of an old man, now in the Louvre (illus. 4), may possibly be related to the posthumous portrait of Giamberti. For a discussion see Griswold, *The Drawings of Piero di Cosimo*, pp. 264–6.
21 – Vasari arrived in Florence from Arezzo at the age of twelve, only two years after Piero's death, and began collecting material for the *Lives* around 1540. On this see Boase, *Giorgio Vasari*, p. 43ff.
22 – For the Classical models used by Vasari see Rubin, 'What Men Saw', pp. 34–5. Vasari's concept of biography and its origins are discussed in more general terms by Z. Wazbinski, 'L'idée de l'histoire dans la première et la seconde edition des vies de Vasari', in *Il Vasari storiografo e artista*, pp. 1–26.
23 – Vasari–Milanesi, IV, p. 134. Translations of passages from Vasari are my own unless otherwise stated.
24 – Vasari revised the *Lives* on the advice of his friend Borghini, on which point see Wazbinski *op. cit.*, *passim*, and Boase, *op. cit.*, pp. 60–72. The different openings to the Life are given together in the Bettarini and Barocchi edition of the *Lives*, IV, p. 59, and in Bacci, 1966, p. 12ff, where the reasons for the alterations are also discussed.
25 – *Leonardo on Painting*, selected and translated by M. Kemp and M. Walker, London, 1989, p. 205.
26 – Vasari–Milanesi, VI, p. 280.
27 – Ascanio Condivi, *Michelangelo: La vita raccolta dal suo discepolo Ascanio Condivi*, ed. A. Maraini, Florence, 1928, pp. 94–5; Francisco de Hollanda, *Four Dialogues on Painting*, trans. A. F. G. Bell, London, 1928. Michelangelo's reputation for solitude is discussed by D. Summers, *Michelangelo and the Language of Art*, Princeton, NJ, 1981, pp. 103–19.
28 – *Four Dialogues*, pp. 11–12.
29 – Vasari–Milanesi, VII, p. 270.
30 – On this point see R. and M. Wittkower, *Born Under Saturn*, pp. 63–6, and Summers, *Michelangelo*, pp. 103–19.
31 – Vasari establishes Michelangelo's Christ-like persona at the opening of the Life: Vasari–Milanesi, VII, pp. 135–6.
32 – For the Life of Uccello see Vasari–Milanesi, II, pp. 203–17, and for that of Pontormo, VI, pp. 245–89. Vasari divided the *Lives* into three parts, or Ages, according to the progress he felt had been made by the artists in each.
33 – Vasari–Milanesi, IV, p. 139.
34 – Vasari–Milanesi, VII, p. 210, trans. G. Bull,

Lives of the Artists, Harmondsworth, 1965, pp. 378–9.
35 – Vasari–Milanesi, IV, pp. 315–16, trans. G. Bull, *Lives*, p. 284.
36 – Vasari–Milanesi, IV, p. 316.
37 – For the Life of Leonardo see Vasari–Milanesi, IV, pp. 17–52. For a discussion of the Life see particularly Rubin, *op. cit.*, *passim*.
38 – Vasari–Milanesi, IV, p. 24.
39 – *Op. cit.*, p. 25.
40 – *Op. cit.*, p. 138.
41 – Ibid.
42 – *Op. cit.*, p. 17.
43 – *De re publica*, I, XXV, 40. For discussion of this passage, and Cicero's place in theories of primitivism, see A. Lovejoy and G. Boas, *A Documentary History of Primitivism and Related Ideas, I: Primitivism and Related Ideas in Antiquity*, Baltimore, 1935, p. 243ff. Lovejoy and Boas trace the origins of Cicero's ideas to Aristotle and the Stoics, but stress his importance in the transmission of ideas.
44 – Cicero, *De officiis*, I, iv, 11.
45 – For the Life of Sodoma see Vasari–Milanesi, VI, pp. 370–99.
46 – For examples of contemporary uses of the terms *bestiale* and *selvatico* see the relevant entries in the *Dizionario della Lingua Italiana nuovamente* compiled by N. Tommaseo and B. Bellini, Turin, 1865–79.
47 – The most accessible accounts of the notion of *fantasia* in the Renaissance are E. Ruth Harvey, *The Inward Wits: Psychological Theory in the Middle Ages and the Renaissance*, Warburg Institute Surveys VI, The Warburg Institute, University of London, 1975; M. Kemp, 'From "mimesis" to "fantasia": The Quattrocento Vocabulary of Creation, Inspiration and Genius in the Visual Arts', *Viator*, VIII, 1977, pp. 347–98; and Summers, *Michelangelo*, p. 103ff. See also M. Bundy, 'Invention and Imagination in the Renaissance', *Journal of English and Germanic Philology*, XXIX, 1930, pp. 535–54, and *The Theory of Imagination in Classical and Medieval Thought*, University of Illinois Studies 12, 1927.
48 – Aristotle, *De memoria*, 449b 31; *De anima*, 3.3. 428af.
49 – Avicenna, *Canon*, I, 176–82. *Cf.* Kemp, *op. cit.*, p. 362.
50 – Augustine, *Epistolae*, 7. *Cf.* Summers, *op. cit.*, pp. 109–11.
51 – On this see particularly Kemp, 'From "mimesis" to "fantasia"', p. 361ff.
52 – Cennino Cennini, *Il Libro dell'Arte: The Craftsman's Handbook*, trans. D. V. Thompson, New Haven, 1933, p. 2, where the term is translated as 'imagination'. Cennini's source was probably *Ars Poetica*, 1–13.
53 – See E. Verheyen, *The Paintings in the Studiolo of Isabella d'Este at Mantua*, New York, 1971, pp. 22–9, and Kemp, *op. cit.*, pp. 357–9 and p. 374.
54 – Vasari–Milanesi, III, p. 519. See also J. Schulz, 'Pintoricchio and the Revival of Antiquity', *Journal of the Warburg and Courtauld Institutes*, XXV, 1962, pp. 35–55.
55 – For a good analysis of these terms in the *Lives*, see Le Mollé, *op.cit.*, pp. 154–208.
56 – Vasari–Milanesi, VII, p. 193, trans. Bull, p. 366.
57 – Vasari–Milanesi, VII, p. 210, trans. Bull, p.379.
58 – Vasari–Milanesi, I, pp. 168–9. The Technical Prefaces to the *Lives* are published separately in an English translation by L. Maclehose, *Vasari on Technique*, New York, 1960. For the passage on design see p. 205.
59 – For Dolce's definition of the parts of painting see M. Roskill, *Dolce's 'Aretino' and Venetian Art Theory of the Cinquecento*, New York, 1968, p. 117ff.
60 – Vasari–Milanesi, IV, p. 8, trans. Bull, p. 249.
61 – Vasari–Milanesi, I, p. xx, trans. Bull, p. 25.
62 – The best discussion of this phenomenon is H. W. Janson, 'The "Image Made by Chance" in Renaissance Thought', *Sixteen Studies*, New York, 1973, pp. 53–75. See also Kemp, 'From "mimesis" to "fantasia",' p. 366ff, and E. H. Gombrich, 'Leonardo's Method for Working out Compositions', *Norm and Form*, London, 1966, pp. 58–63.
63 – Lucretius, *De rerum natura*, IV, p. 129ff.
64 – Philostratus, *Life of Apollonius of Tyana*, II, 22.
65 – Janson, *op. cit.*, p. 60ff, and Summers, *op. cit.*, p. 491 n. 56.
66 – *Leonardo on Painting*, ed. Kemp, p. 222. *Cf.* Gombrich, *op. cit.*, *passim*.
67 – For Vasari's use of these terms in relation to Pontormo see, for example, Vasari–Milanesi, VII, pp. 271–2. *Cf.* also Le Mollé, pp. 154–208.
68 – Vasari–Milanesi, IV, p. 134.
69 – On this see particularly M. Kemp, 'Equal Excellences: Lomazzo and the Explanation of Individual Style in the Visual Arts', *Renaissance Studies*, I, 1987, pp. 1–27, and by the same author 'Ogni dipintore diping se: A Neoplatonic Echo in Leonardo's Art Theory?', in C. H. Clough, ed., *Cultural Aspects of the Italian Renaissance: Essays in Honour of Paul Oskar Kristeller*, Manchester, 1976, pp. 311–23. For a general discussion of the relationship drawn between artists' characters and their works in writings on art from Antiquity onwards see R. and M. Wittkower, *Born under Saturn*, especially pp. 281–92.
70 – For the Life of Parmigianino see Vasari–Milanesi, V, pp. 217–238, and particularly pp. 235–8.
71 – On Sodoma's figures see particularly Vasari–Milanesi, VI, p. 383.

72 – Vasari–Milanesi, IV, p. 133.
73 – *Op. cit.*, p. 138.

CHAPTER TWO

1 – The best discussion of *spalliera* panels is A. B. Barriault, *Florentine Paintings for 'spalliere'*, PhD dissertation, University of Virginia, 1985. Barriault discusses Piero's works in this context on pp. 24–5, p. 36, pp. 45–7, pp. 50–51, pp. 71–2, pp. 97–9, pp. 112–3, p. 159ff and pp. 268–9. On paintings for domestic settings more generally, see particularly K. J. Lydeker, *The Domestic Setting of the Arts in Renaissance Florence*, PhD dissertation, Johns Hopkins University, Baltimore, 1987. The most useful discussions in published works are A. Schiaparelli, *La casa fiorentina ed i suoi arredi nei secoli XIV e XV*, Florence, 1908; Wackernagel, *The Renaissance Artist at Work*, pp. 146–79; P. Thornton, *The Italian Renaissance Interior, 1400–1600*, London, 1991, and E. Callmann, 'Apollonio di Giovanni and Painting for the Early Renaissance Room', *Antichità Viva*, XXXVI, 1988, pp. 5–18.
2 – On the division of labour in the making of *spalliera* panels, see in particular, Barriault, *op. cit.*, pp. 46–7, and Wackernagel, *op. cit.*, p. 299ff. *Cf.* also E. H. Gombrich, 'Apollonio di Giovanni: A Florentine Cassone Workshop through the Eyes of a Humanist Poet', *Norm and Form*, London, 1966, pp. 11–28.
3 – Alberti's views on narrative paintings are to be found in book Two of *De Pictura*. For a brief discussion see M. Baxandall, *Giotto and the Orators*, Oxford, 1971, pp. 121–39, and Blunt, *Artistic Theory in Italy*, pp. 1–22.
4 – Lydeker, *op. cit.*, p. 251ff; Wackernagel, *op. cit.*, pp. 220–87, and E. Callmann, *Beyond Nobility: Art for the Private Citizen in the Early Renaissance*, exhibition catalogue, Allentown Art Museum, Allentown, PA, 1981.
5 – The narrative conventions of *spalliera* panels, and their relationship to works in other media are discussed by Barriault, *op. cit.*, p. 69ff and p. 136 ff.
6 – Vasari–Milanesi, IV, p. 140. Vasari does not mention the painting in the first edition of the *Lives*. Bacci suggests that his acquisition of the work may account in part for the more laudatory tone of the Life in the second edition: *Piero di Cosimo*, 1966, p. 10. For full discussions of the dating and provenance of works discussed in this chapter, the reader is again directed to Bacci's monograph.
7 – Lucian, *Herodotus (Aetion)*, 4–6.
8 – The story of Mars and Venus is recounted in Ovid, *Metamorphoses*, IV, 171–89, and in Homer, *Odyssey*, VII, 266–365.
9 – On this see particularly Lydeker, *op. cit.*, p. 61ff, and Barriault, pp. 123–7, p. 168ff and p. 136 ff.
10 – Botticelli's painting has been extensively discussed. See particularly E. H. Gombrich, 'Botticelli's Mythologies: A Study in the Neo-Platonic Symbolism of his Circle', *Symbolic Images*, Oxford, 1972, p. 31ff, especially pp. 66–9, and R. Lightbown, *Botticelli: Life and Work*, New York, 1989, pp. 164–8. For an alternative view of the two paintings, and of Piero's as a generic image of Venus and a knight, see P. Holberton, 'Botticelli's "Hypnerotomachia" in the National Gallery, London: A Problem in the Use of Classical Sources in Renaissance Art', *Illinois Classical Studies*, IX, 1984, pp. 149–82.
11 – For a discussion of Eros and Anteros see E. Panofsky, 'Blind Cupid', *Studies in Iconology: Humanistic Themes in the Art of the Renaissance*, New York, 1939, pp. 95–128, and E. Verheyen, 'Eros et Anteros: L'Education de Cupidon et la prétendue "Antiope" du Corrège', *Gazette des Beaux-Arts*, LXV, 1965, pp. 321–40, with an extensive bibliography.
12 – It is possible that this is meant to suggest the approach of Vulcan, and the lovers' imminent discovery, a theme that, according to Vasari, Piero illustrated in another work, now lost: Vasari–Milanesi, IV, p. 139.
13 – See, for example, the stories of Parrhasius's curtain, and Zeuxis's grapes, in Pliny, *Natural History*, XXXV, 65–6.
14 – Gombrich, *op. cit.*, pp. 68–9.
15 – E. Panofsky, 'The Early History of Man in Two Cycles of Paintings by Piero di Cosimo', *Studies in Iconology*, pp. 33–67, p. 63n., and *Renaissance and Renascences*, 2nd edn, Uppsala, 1965, pp. 179–81.
16 – For example, A. Chastel, *Art et humanisme*, p. 176, and E. Battisti, *L'Antirinascimento*, pp. 101–2.
17 – On this see also C. Hope, 'Artists, Patrons and Advisers in the Italian Renaissance', *Patronage in the Renaissance*, ed. G. Fytch Lytle and S. Orgel, Princeton, NJ, 1981, pp. 329–30.
18 – Chastel, *op. cit.*, pp. 60–61 and Bacci 1966, pp. 32–3.
19 – *Cf.* Gombrich, 'Botticelli's Mythologies', p. 36, and p. 200 n. 1–11, where the author lists key works in the historiography of Botticelli's paintings. See also Gombrich, *Aby Warburg*, 2nd edn, Oxford, 1986, pp. 1–67, and M. Levey, 'Botticelli and Nineteenth-century England', *Journal of the Warburg and Courtauld Institutes*, XXIII, 1960, pp. 291–306.
20 – For a similar argument regarding the interpretation of *cassone* panels see J. Pope-Hennessy and K. Christiansen, 'Secular Painting in Fifteenth-century Tuscany: Birth Trays,

Cassone Panels and Portraits', *Bulletin of the Metropolitan Museum of Art*, XXXVIII, 1980. Different responses to the Antique among fifteenth-century artists are also discussed in Panofsky, *Renaissance and Renascences*, p. 162ff; E. H. Gombrich, 'The Style "all'antica": Imitation and Assimilation', *Norm and Form*, pp. 122–8, and F. Saxl, 'Jacopo Bellini and Mantegna as Antiquarians', in *A Heritage of Images*, Harmondsworth, 1970, pp. 57–71.

21 – On the Classical sources of Botticelli's painting see Lightbown, *op. cit.*, pp. 168–70, and Holberton, *op. cit.*, *passim*. Piero's awareness of Classical models is also made clear in two drawings of unidentified mythological subjects, one of which may represent Ariadne asleep in a landscape (illus. 8), and another that has tentatively been interpreted as Mars and Rhea Silvia (illus. 9). Both of these use motifs from Classical sarcophagi. For a discussion see Griswold, pp. 86–9, 215–8, 244–7.

22 – In contrast to this it is interesting to note that Leonardo, at least, considered Botticelli to be a dull landscape painter: *Leonardo on Painting*, ed. Kemp and Walker, pp. 201–2.

23 – The connection between Correggio's play and Piero's panel was first made by P. Schubring, *Cassoni*, Leipzig, 1915, p. 52ff. For a more recent discussion see I. Lavin, 'Cephalus and Procris: Transformation of an Ovidian Myth', *Journal of the Warburg and Courtauld Institutes*, XVII, 1954, p. 260ff.

24 – The interpretation of the painting as the *Death of Procris* is still disputed, for example, in the *National Gallery General Illustrated Catalogue*, 2nd edn, London, 1986, p. 477.

25 – *Metamorphoses*, VII, ll. 690–865.

26 – *Cf.* Lavin, *op. cit.*, pp. 264–5.

27 – Lavin, *op. cit.*, pp. 271–2. Lavin's interpretation is accepted by Bacci, 1966, p. 82 and 1976, p. 90.

28 – On the date of the first performance see Lavin, p. 267, and for the play's numerous editions, p. 270. The play exists in a modern edition in A. Tissoni Benvenuti, ed., *Niccolò da Correggio: Opere*, Bari, 1969, pp. 7–45.

29 – *Cefalo*, edn *cit.*, pp. 39–40; my translation.

30 – There is a growing literature on the function and ideology of panels commissioned in relation to marriage. See particularly Barriault, *op. cit.*, pp. 123–7, p. 168ff and p. 178ff. Lydeker, *op. cit.*, p. 145ff; E. Callmann, 'The Growing Threat to Marital Bliss as seen in Fifteenth-century Florentine Painting', *Studies in Iconography*, V, 1979, pp. 73–92, and most recently R. M. San Juan, 'Mythology, Women and Renaissance Private Life: The Myth of Eurydice in Italian Furniture Painting', *Art History*, XV, 1992, pp. 127–45, which was in press at the time of writing.

31 – On this shift in imagery see Callmann, 'The Growing Threat to Marital Bliss', *passim*; San Juan, *op. cit.*, *passim*; and P. Watson, *Virtue and Voluptas in Cassone Painting*, Ann Arbor, 1970. Changing attitudes to marriage during the Renaissance and their effects on the visual arts are also discussed in *Saints and She-devils: Images of Women in the 15th and 16th Centuries*, London, 1987.

32 – On Botticelli's Nastagio degli Onesti panels see Barriault, chapter 5, and C. Olsen, 'Gross Expenditure: Botticelli's Nastagio degli Onesti Panels', *Art History*, XV, 1992, pp. 146–69.

33 – *Cf.* Lavin, *op. cit.*, *passim*.

34 – *Cefalo*, edn. *cit.*, p. 35.

35 – The treatment of fauns in Renaissance art and literature is discussed in L. F. Kaufmann, *The Noble Savage: Satyrs and Satyr Families in Renaissance Art*, Ann Arbor, 1984.

36 – *Metamorphoses*, XII, 208–536.

37 – *Metamorphoses*, XII, trans. F. Miller, Loeb Classical Library, London and New York, 1926, pp. 199ff.

38 – *Metamorphoses*, edn *cit.*, pp. 209–11.

39 – *De Pictura*, ed. Grayson, p. 77.

40 – *De Pictura*, edn. *cit.*, p. 83.

41 – *Leonardo on Painting*, ed. Kemp and Walker, pp. 217–8, p. 220, 225 and 227ff. Leonardo's views on composition are discussed in M. Kemp, *Leonardo da Vinci: The Marvellous Works of Nature and Man*, London, 1981, pp. 239–47, and in Barriault, *op. cit.*, p. 69ff and p. 138ff. See also E. H. Gombrich, *Means and Ends: Reflections on the History of Fresco Painting*, London, 1976, p. 7ff.

42 – *Cf.* Wackernagel, *op. cit.*, p. 154ff; Chastel, *op. cit.*, pp. 168–77; and P. Emison, 'The Word Made Naked in Pollaiuolo's Battle of the Nudes', *Art History*, XIII, 1990, p. 261–75.

43 – The head of the Lapith hurling a vase above the head of Hippodame appears to have been derived from a sketch for Leonardo's fresco, now in the Museum of Fine Arts in Budapest. On Michelangelo's cartoon see H. Hibbard, *Michelangelo*, 2nd edn, Harmondsworth, 1985, p. 79–84.

44 – *Cf.* Gombrich, *op. cit.*, pp. 69–72. The identity of the female figure is discussed at greater length by Lightbown, *Botticelli*, pp. 146–52.

45 – Hibbard, *op. cit.*, pp. 22–5.

46 – On the subject-matter of *cassone* panels, whose function was to some extent taken over by *spalliera* panels, see E. Callmann, *Apollonio di Giovanni*, Oxford, 1974, pp. 7–24 and 39–56.

47 – Bacci, 1966, pp. 89–90.

48 – The story of Theseus is also told in Ovid, *Metamorphoses*, VIII, 259ff and 548ff, and Book XII, 208ff. He appears in the right foreground of

Piero's painting, clubbing a kneeling centaur, as described by Ovid, XII, 340–5.
49 – That this is an unusual combination was pointed out by E. Fahy, 'Some Later Works by Piero di Cosimo', *Gazette des Beaux-Arts*, CVII, 1965, pp. 202–6. Fahy suggests, however, that the panels should be grouped with the Vespucci *Bacchanals*, a suggestion convincingly refuted by Bacci, pp. 89–90, but supported by Barriault, pp. 159–60 and p. 204 n. 35.
50 – There exist numerous small panels, particularly of secular subjects, that were clearly designed for domestic settings, but whose precise function and location remain unclear. *Cf.* Wackernagel, *op. cit.*, pp. 153ff, and Barriault, *op. cit.*, pp. 24–5.
51 – For Strozzi patronage more generally, see S. J. Craven, *Aspects of Patronage in Florence, 1494–1512*, PhD dissertation, Courtauld Institute, University of London, 1973, p. 89ff, A. Lillie, *Florentine Villas in the Fifteenth Century: A Study of the Strozzi and Sassetti Country Properties*, PhD dissertation, Courtauld Institute, University of London, 1987, especially chapter 7, and Wackernagel, *op. cit.*, p. 271ff.
52 – Berti *et al.*, eds, *Il Primato del Disegno*, pp. 27–8 and p. 163n, and S. J. Freedberg, *Painting in Italy, 1500–1600*, 2nd edn, Harmondsworth, 1983, p. 98 and p. 675 n.66a. On the Medici festivals, and the symbolism of the *broncone* see J. Cox-Rearick, *Dynasty and Destiny in Medici Art*, Princeton, NJ, 1984, pp. 15–40.
53 – *Cf.* Barriault, pp. 123–7, p. 168ff and p. 176ff, and Lydeker *op. cit.*, p. 145ff, 235ff. For an extended discussion of one such example, the famous panels executed for Pierfrancesco Borgherini, see A. Braham, 'The Bed of Pierfrancesco Borgherini', *The Burlington Magazine*, CXXI, 1979, pp. 754–65.
54 – On this, see Hope, 'Artists, Patrons and Advisers', *passim*.
55 – *Metamorphoses*, IV, 665–739.
56 – The dating of all five works is the subject of considerable controversy, although most scholars agree that they belong to the same period of Piero's career, probably between *c.* 1490 and 1505. For a full account see Bacci, 1966, pp. 74–8.
57 – Panofsky, 'The Early History of Man', *passim*. Important discussions and reappraisals of Panofsky's ideas are Bacci, 1966, pp. 74–8; C. Cieri Via, 'Per una revisione del tema del primitivismo nell'opera di Piero di Cosimo', *Storia dell'Arte*, XXIX, 1977, pp. 5–14; K. Christiansen, 'Early Renaissance Narrative Painting in Italy', *Bulletin of the Metropolitan Museum of Art*, XLI, 1983, pp. 38–47, and Barriault, *op. cit.*, pp. 159–64.
58 – Vasari–Milanesi, IV, p. 139.
59 – *De rerum natura*, V, 780–792. For a discussion of theories of primitivism in Antiquity and their later influence see Lovejoy and Boas, *Primitivism and Related Ideas*, *passim*, and for Lucretius, pp. 222–42.
60 – *De rerum natura*, V, 925ff. I have followed the translation of Lovejoy and Boas, *op. cit.*, p. 228.
61 – *De rerum natura*, V, 1011–1027. *Cf.* Lovejoy and Boas, pp. 228–9.
62 – *De rerum natura*, V, 1028–90. Piero may also have known Vitruvius's account of the origins of fire in *De Architectura* (II i.ff), either at first hand, or as cited in Boccaccio's *Genealogia Deorum* (XII. lxx). *Cf.* J. G. Frazer, *The Myths of the Origins of Fire*, London, 1930.
63 – For a full discussion of *The Forest Fire*, see *Piero di Cosimo's 'The Forest Fire'*, Ashmolean Museum, Oxford, 1984.
64 – *De rerum natura*, V, 821–924; *cf.* Lovejoy and Boas, p. 223. The possible sources for Piero's animals are discussed in *Piero di Cosimo's 'The Forest Fire'*. Vasari records Piero's drawings of fabulous beasts in the Life: Vasari–Milanesi, IV, p. 138. Two sheets of drawings, both featuring oxen (illus. 24 and 25), may be related to the painting in a general way, and illustrate Piero's close attention to natural detail, as does a studio drawing of a youth with a sleeping dog (illus 52).
65 – *Fragments*, 61. *Cf.* Lovejoy and Boas, p. 82.
66 – Wackernagel, p. 154 and p. 167, and particularly Lillie, *Florentine Villas*, I, pp. 278–9, who records that the paintings kept at the Strozzi villa at Santuccio included 'a burning house with several "fantasie"'. Pesellino's paintings of animals are recorded by Vasari in his Life of the artist: Vasari–Milanesi, III, p. 37.
67 – See the Life of Francia: Vasari–Milanesi, III, p. 544.
68 – 'The Early History of Man', p. 33ff.
69 – Piero would probably have taken this from Boccaccio's relating of it in the *Genealogia Deorum*, XII, IXX.
70 – On this see particularly Hope, 'Artists, Patrons and Advisers', *passim*.
71 – On this see Barriault, op. cit., passim, Callmann, 'Apollonio di Giovanni and Painting for the Early Renaissance Room', and the same author's *Beyond Nobility*, pp. xiv–xxii, and Schiaparelli, *La casa fiorentina*, pp. 162–8, and p. 301. *The Hunt* and the *Return from the Hunt* measure 70.5 × 169.5 cm and 70.5 × 168.9 cm respectively, and *The Forest Fire* measures 71 × 202 cm. The dimensions of *The Finding of Vulcan on Lemnos* and *Vulcan and Aeolus* are 155 × 174.5 cm and 155.5 × 166.5 cm.
72 – Hope, 'Artists, Patrons and Advisers', pp. 342–3.

73 – 'The Early History of Man', pp. 57–8.
74 – On Pugliese and his patronage see also Christiansen, 'Early Renaissance Narrative Painting', pp. 12–13, and Craven, *Aspects of Patronage*, p. 140ff.
75 – Chastel, *op. cit.*, p. 177.
76 – The terms 'hard' and 'soft' primitivism were formulated by Lovejoy and Boas, *op. cit.*, who discuss the myth of the Golden Age in relation to other theories of primitivism. The Golden Age myth is also discussed in Cieri Via, *op. cit.*, *passim*, and H. Levin, *The Myth of the Golden Age in the Renaissance*, Indiana UP, 1969.
77 – The manuscript of Lucretius was rediscovered in 1418 by Poggio Bracciolini, sent to Florence and copied by Niccolò Niccoli, who owned it until 1434. It was not printed, however, until 1473, shortly before the execution of Piero's panels. *Cf.* J. Sandys, *A History of Classical Scholarship*, II, New York, 1958, p. 29 and p. 103, and Panofsky, *Renaissance and Renascences*, pp. 177–8.
78 – Vasari–Milanesi, IV, p. 141.
79 – *Cf.* Gombrich, *Symbolic Images*, p. 216, n. 139.
80 – Ovid, *Fasti*, III, 735ff, trans. J. G. Frazer, Loeb Classical Library, London 1931, pp. 175–7.
81 – Aristotle, *Historia Animalium*, ix, 40.
82 – Virgil, *Georgics*, iv, 64–66.
83 – *Cf.* Panofsky, *Renaissance and Renascences*, pp. 175–6, Chastel, *op. cit.*, pp. 58ff, and Gombrich, *Aby Warburg*, p. 43ff.
84 – Panofsky, 'The Early History of Man', pp. 63–7, and *Renaissance and Renascences*, pp. 181–3, and Chastel, *op. cit.*, p. 176.
85 – Lucian, *Dionysus*, 1–3, in *The Works of Lucian*, trans. A. M. Harmon, Loeb Classical Library, London, 1913, I, pp. 49–50.
86 – 'The Early History of Man', pp 64–5.
87 – H. W. Janson pointed out the presence in right of the *Discovery* of an ape-like figure eating grapes, suggesting that this might constitute a reference to the discovery of the wild grape – a 'burlesque analogue to the discovery of honey': *Apes and Ape-Lore in the Middle Ages and Renaissance*, Studies of the Warburg Institute XX, London, 1952, p. 257, n.28. As Janson also points out, however, this idea is not substantiated in any known text.
88 – *Genealogia Deorum*, IV, 45. Barriault, pp. 165–6, suggests Boccaccio as a source, as does Panofsky, *Studies in Iconology*, p. 50. For an account of the main incidents see also Bacci (1966), p. 100.
89 – *Cf.* Bacci, *loc. cit.*
90 – On the Prometheus myth generally see particularly K. Borinski, 'Die Deutung der Piero di Cosimo zugeschriebenen Prometheus-Bilder', in *Sitzungsberichte der Bayerischen Akademie der Wissenschaft*, VII/2, 1920, and G. Habich, 'Ueber zwei Prometheus-Bilder angeblich von Piero di Cosimo', in *Sitzungsberichte der Bayerischen Akademie der Wissenchaft*, XXI/1, 1919. *Cf.* also *sub voce* 'Prometheus' in Lovejoy and Boas, *A Documentary History of Primitivism.*
91 – *Cf.* Lovejoy and Boas, pp. 200–02.
92 – *Op. cit.*, p. 120 and p. 132.
93 – *Cf.* Panofsky, *op. cit.*, p. 50.
94 – *Op. cit.*, pp. 49ff.
95 – The painting has been extensively discussed. The main arguments concerning its iconography are summarised in Bacci, 1966; M. Warton Vanderzani, *"Simonetta Vespucci": A Fantasy Portrait*, MA dissertation, Michigan State University, 1983, and E. de Boissard, *Chantilly, Musée Condé: Peintures de l'Ecole italienne*, Paris, 1988, pp. 118–19. The identification of Simonetta Vespucci in Botticelli's paintings is discussed by Gombrich, *op. cit.*, pp. 37–8, and by H. P. Horne, *Alessandro Filipepi, commonly called Sandro Botticelli, Painter of Florence*, London, 1908, reprinted Princeton, NJ, 1980, pp. 52–4 and p. 141, with much that is relevant for Piero.
96 – See, for example, R. Langton Douglas, *Piero di Cosimo*, Chicago, 1946, pp. 74–5, and Battisti, *L'Antirinascimento*, pp. 61–2.
97 – Recent technical examination of the painting suggests that the coloured strip bearing Simonetta's name may be original, but the lettering is almost certainly a later addition, possibly later even than de Boissard's suggestion of the late 16th century. For a discussion of the inscription see de Boissard, *op. cit.*, p. 118, and Vanderzani, *op. cit.*, pp. 32–40.
98 – For a discussion of the drawing see Griswold, *The Drawings of Piero di Cosimo*, pp. 264–6.
99 – The connection was suggested by Eve Borsook in a verbal communication to Mina Bacci, on which see Bacci, 1966, p. 67. For the symbolism of the snake in Piero's picture see Vanderzani, *op. cit.*, pp. 41–2. For its use as a Medici emblem and the symbolism attached to it see E. Wind, *Pagan Mysteries in the Renaissance*, 2nd edn, London, 1968, p. 126n and pp. 265–7, and Gombrich, p. 66 and p. 214–15.
100 – For a discussion of this romantic view of Renaissance landscape, and the concept of mood, see A. Cole, *Aspects of Quattrocento Landscape Depiction*, M.Phil. Dissertation, the Warburg Institute, University of London, 1981, pp. 4–13.
101 – Piero would only have been fifteen years old when Simonetta died.
102 – There is a growing literature on female portraiture. Useful discussions, in addition to Vanderzani's specific remarks on Piero's work, are

J. Lipman, 'The Florentine Profile Portrait in the Quattrocento', *Art Bulletin*, XVIII, 1936, pp. 54–102; P. Simons, 'Women in Frames: the Gaze, the Eye, the Portrait in Renaissance Portraiture', *History Workshop Journal*, XXV, 1989, pp. 4–30, and M. Rogers, 'Sonnets on Female Portraits from Renaissance North Italy', *Word and Image*, II, 1986, pp. 291–9, and by the same author, 'The Decorum of Women's Beauty: Trissino, Firenzuola, Luigini and the Representation of Women in Sixteenth-century Painting', *Renaissance Studies*, II, 1988, pp. 47–89.

103 – On the erotic connotations of hair and hairstyles see particularly Rogers, 'Decorum', p. 63ff.

104 – *Cf.* Lipman, 'The Florentine Profile Portrait', pp. 83–92.

105 – On this see particularly Simons, 'Women in Frames', *passim*.

106 – Lipman, *op. cit.*, See also J. Pope-Hennessy, *The Portrait in the Renaissance*, Princeton, NJ, 1979, pp. 205–56, and L. Campbell, *Renaissance Portraits: European Portrait-Painting in the 14th, 15th and 16th Centuries*, New Haven, 1990, pp. 109–39.

107 – Vasari–Milanesi, IV, p. 144. It is probable that, at some point after the death of Francesco's son in 1586, intestate and without an heir, the painting was acquired by the Vespucci family, in whose possession it is recorded from the late eighteenth century, and who may have added the inscription to identify the painting with an ancestor who had by then acquired almost mythical status. On the provenance of the panel see E. de Boissard, p. 118 and p. 120.

108 – Boccaccio, *De Claris Mulieribus*, LXXXVIII.

109 – Cleopatra appears in canto V of Dante's *Inferno*, among the souls of the carnal, and is described as *Cleopatra lussuriosa*. Like the other inhabitants of the second circle of Hell, she is seen to have betrayed reason to her appetites. In Petrarch's *Trionfi*, she is the luxurious conqueror of generals, with a talent for rendering soldiers effete (*Trionfo d'Amore* I, 90; *Trionfo della Fama*, III, 106.).

110 – *De Claris Mulieribus*, LXXXVIII, in *Tutte le Opere di Giovanni Boccaccio*, ed. V. Branca, X, 2nd edn, Milan, 1970, pp. 344–57; my translation.

111 – Ibid.

112 – This episode is also described by Boccaccio, *loc. cit.*

113 – For Boccaccio, the snakes were not the actual cause of Cleopatra's death, but a means of speeding up the loss of blood from her veins.

114 – On this see chapter Four.

115 – On this see particularly J. Guillaume, 'Cleopatra Nova Pandora', *Gazette des Beaux-Arts*, 6th series, LXXX, 1972, pp. 185–94. In addition, as Gombrich has noted, the legend of Simonetta Vespucci has exerted an irresistible appeal for scholars since the nineteenth century, who have been tireless in their attempts, invariably inconclusive, to identify her likeness in contemporary art: *Symbolic Images*, p. 37 and pp. 201ff.

116 – Michelangelo's *Cleopatra* was probably made as a presentation drawing for his friend Tommaso Cavalieri. See M. Hirst, *Michelangelo and his Drawings*, London, 1988, p. 111.

117 – The significance of the profile view is discussed by Simons, *op. cit.*, *passim*.

118 – *Cf.* Vanderzani, *op. cit.*, pp. 50–60; H. Diane Russell, *Eva/Ave: Women in Renaissance and Baroque Prints*, National Gallery of Art, Washington DC, 1990, pp. 13–35, and *Saints and She-devils*, pp. 129–56.

119 – Lydeker, p. 200 and p. 295. Cf. Vasari–Milanesi, IV, p. 465.

120 – On this see particularly *Saints and She-devils*, p. 129ff.

121 – Alberti's theory of composition is in Book II of *De Pictura*. For a discussion see Baxandall, *Giotto and the Orators*, pp. 121–39.

122 – A possible exception to this among Piero's works is a panel in the Ringling Museum, showing the *Construction of a Building* (illus. 38), which I have been unable to see at first-hand. It seems likely, however, that it can be ascribed to Piero, although the subject remains unclear. For a discussion see Bacci, 1966, pp. 104–5.

123 – See particularly Barriault, *op. cit.*, pp. 6–7, pp. 23–4 and p. 92ff.

124 – On the use of landscape in the Renaissance see particularly Cole, *Aspects of Landscape Depiction, passim*. For a more general discussion see R. Turner, *The Vision of Landscape in Renaissance Italy*, Princeton, NJ, 1966. The use of landscape in Early Renaissance painting and the problems of composition are also discussed in Christiansen, *Early Renaissance Narrative Painting in Italy*, pp. 31–8. This aspect of Piero's work is discussed in more detail in chapter Four.

125 – For a recent discussion of Uccello's *Hunt*, see M. Kemp and A. Massing, 'Paolo Uccello's "Hunt in the Forest"', *The Burlington Magazine*, CXXXIII, March 1991, p. 164ff. On the *Battle of San Romano* see V. Gebhardt, 'Some Problems in the Reconstruction of Uccello's Rout of San Romano cycle', *The Burlington Magazine*, CXXXIII, March, 1991, p. 179ff.

126 – *Cf.* Christiansen, *op. cit.*, p. 46.

127 – See, for example, E. H. Gombrich, 'Norm and Form', *Norm and Form*, edn *cit.*, pp. 94–5.

128 – Vasari–Milanesi IV, p. 315ff.

129 – *Vasari On Technique*, ed. L. Maclehose, p. 210.

130 – On the use of these terms, see also L. Mollé, *op. cit.*, pp. 154–208.

131 – A drawing (illus. 42) on the back of the panel of the *Death of Procris* may be a study for one of the painting's framing elements, taking the form of a classically inspired candelabra, and illustrates the kind of framework in which such images may have been placed. For a full discussion see Callmann, 'Apollonio di Giovanni and Painting for the Early Renaissance Room', where Piero's sketch is considered in some detail.
132 – *Cf.* Lydeker, *op. cit.*, chapter I.
133 – Vasari–Milanesi, IV, p. 138.
134 – *Op. cit.*, p. 139.
135 – *Op. cit.*, p. 141.
136 – *Op. cit.*, p. 135.
137 – *Op. cit.*, p. 471.
138 – *Op. cit.*, p. 176.
139 – *Op. cit.*, p. 138.
140 – *Op. cit.*, p. 139.
141 – *Op. cit.*, II, pp. 148–9. For a discussion of this passage see Barriault pp. 13–14, 49–50, 218–9, and Lydeker, pp. 259–60.

CHAPTER THREE

1 – Vasari–Milanesi, IV, p. 133.
2 – *Op. cit.*, p. 134.
3 – The diverse stylistic influences on Piero's works are reviewed by Bacci, 1966, pp. 23ff, to which the reader is directed for further discussion, and by Griswold, *The Drawings of Piero di Cosimo*, pp. 18–32.
4 – Vasari's discussion of Raphael's artistic education, which was added to the revised edition of the *Lives*, did not feature in the 1550 edition.
5 – Vasari–Milanesi, IV, p. 133.
6 – *Op. cit.*, p. 141.
7 – *Op. cit.*, pp. 137–8.
8 – *Op. cit.*, p. 138.
9 – Ibid.
10 – On this see particularly Lydeker, *op. cit.*, pp. 65–6. For a full discussion of the tondo as a genre see M. Hauptmann, *Der Tondo*, Frankfurt-am-Main, 1936.
11 – Good general discussions of the altarpiece and its development are J. Burckhardt, *Das Altarbild*, trans. as *The Altarpiece in Renaissance Italy*, ed. P. Humfrey, Oxford, 1988; C. Hope, 'Altarpieces and the Requirements of Patrons', *Christianity in the Renaissance*, ed. T. Verdon and J. Henderson, Syracuse NY, 1989, pp. 537–71, and the essays in *The Altarpiece in the Renaissance*, ed. P. Humfrey and M. Kemp, Cambridge, 1990.
12 – This may be borne out by Mina Bacci's suggestion that the St Lazarus was originally St Roch, transformed at a later date through the addition of the rather crude inscription: *L'Opera Completa di Piero di Cosimo*, 1976, p. 85.
13 – On the patronage of the Pugliese, see particularly Craven, *Aspects of Patronage*, p. 140ff; Bacci, 1966, p. 69–70, and Christiansen, *Early Narrative Painting*, pp. 12–13.
14 – The *Portinari Altarpiece* arrived in Florence on 28 May 1483. See B. Hatfield Strens, 'L'arrivo del trittico Portinari a Firenze', *Commentari*, XX, 1968, pp. 315–19. More general discussions of the influence of Flemish art on Piero's contemporaries are P. Hills, 'Leonardo and Flemish Painting', *The Burlington Magazine*, CXXIII, 1980, pp. 609–15, with an extensive bibliography, and F. Ames-Lewis, 'On Domenico Ghirlandaio's Responsiveness to North European Art', *Gazette des Beaux-Arts*, Oct 1989, p. 1ff.
15 – The painting can probably be dated to *c.* 1490, on which see Craven, 'Three Dates', p. 574. For a general discussion of the Capponi's patronage see Craven, *Aspects of Patronage*, p. 7ff.
16 – Vasari–Milanesi, IV, p. 140.
17 – Vasari–Milanesi, IV, p. 141.
18 – For a discussion of the drawings see Griswold, *op. cit.*, *passim*.
19 – On the relationship between paintings and drawings in Piero's work see particularly Griswold, p. 61ff. A drawing in the Frits Lugt collection, Paris (illus. 60), of the *Descent of the Holy Spirit*, also shows Piero attempting to resolve in different ways the arrangement of large numbers of figures, probably in preparation for a lost altarpiece, and drawing on a range of influences, including Perugino, and possibly also Signorelli. The top half of the drawing demonstrates the degree of vitality and dramatic movement that he could achieve on a small scale. For a discussion see Griswold, pp. 261–3.
20 – The verso of this drawing (illus. 62) shows a monk seated at a lectern, which may represent Piero's first thought for the arrangement of the attendant saints, and a delightful sketch for a classically inspired candelabra, incorporating bound nude figures and acanthus scrolls. This may have been related to the decoration of the original frame.
21 – On the iconography of the Immaculate Conception in general see Hope, 'Altarpieces', pp. 554–64, and M. Carmichael, *Francia's Masterpiece: An Essay on the Beginnings of the Immaculate Conception in Art*, London, 1909.
22 – *Cf.* A. Chastel, 'Fra Bartolomeo's Carondolet Altarpiece and the theme of the "Virgo in nubibus" in the High Renaissance', in *The Altarpiece in the Renaissance*, ed. Kemp and Humfrey, pp. 129–40, who maintains that the Immaculate Conception is the subject of the painting. This is rightly disputed by Bacci, 1976, p. 92, and by Hope, 'Altarpieces and the Requirements of Patrons', pp. 536.

23 – J. de Voragine, *The Golden Legend*, trans. G. Ryan and H. Ripperger, London, 1941, p. 207.
24 – Hope, *loc. cit.*
25 – Ibid.
26 – For a discussion of the Cini paintings see F. Zeri *et al.*, *Dipinti Toscani e Oggetti d'Arte dalla Collezione Vittorio Cini*, Vicenza, 1984, pp. 31–3. The tondo is currently in a New York private collection. I am most grateful to the owner for allowing me to examine the work at close quarters.
27 – X-rays of the painting also reveal that Piero originally envisaged the background of the painting as a rocky grotto, almost certainly modelled on that in Leonardo's *Madonna of the Rocks*.
28 – For the iconography of the saints see the relevant entries in G. Kaftal, *Iconography of the Saints in Tuscan Painting*, Florence, 1952.
29 – On the experimental and innovative nature of the altarpiece in the late fifteenth and early sixteenth centuries see Martin Kemp's introductory essay to *The Altarpiece in the Renaissance*, ed. Kemp and Humfrey, p. 1ff, and Hope, 'Altarpieces', pp. 547–9 and p. 564.
30 – For a discussion of Leonardo's painting see Kemp, *Leonardo da Vinci*, p. 66ff.
31 – The altarpiece in Borgo San Lorenzo measures 202 × 165 cm. That in New Haven is 208.9 × 205.7 cm. This painting was cut at some unknown date, and filled in to create the oval shape at the top.
32 – For a discussion of Fra Bartolommeo's painting see P. Humfrey, 'Fra Bartolommeo, Venice and St. Catherine of Siena', *The Burlington Magazine*, CXXXII, 1990, pp. 476–83, and Chastel, *op. cit.*, pp. 136–40.
33 – Vasari–Milanesi, III, pp. 586–7.
34 – The effectiveness of Perugino's 'devout' style is discussed briefly in M. Baxandall, *Painting and Experience in Fifteenth-century Italy*, Oxford, 1972, p. 27, 46–7, 66–7 and 110. On the Savonarolan connection see Craven, *Aspects of Patronage*, chapter V. The possible influence of Savonarola on artistic styles has been extensively discussed, although such discussions have invariably proven inconclusive. See, for example, R. M. Steinberg, *Fra Girolamo Savonarola: Florentine Art and Renaissance Historiography*, Athens, OH, 1977; Chastel, *Art et Humanisme*, p. 397ff, and Wackernagel, p. 50, 128, 133, 293–4, 321, and 355.
35 – On Piero's Peruginesque or 'neo-Quattrocento' style see particularly Zeri, 'Rivedendo Piero di Cosimo', pp. 41–3.
36 – On the distinction between types of religious image see Hope, 'Altarpieces', *passim*, and S. Ringbom, *Icon to Narrative: The Rise of the Dramatic Close-up in Fifteenth-Century Devotional Painting*, 2nd edn, Davaco, Doornspijk, 1984, chapter I, pp. 11–71, where the emergence of types of private religious painting is discussed in detail. On the particular qualities of private religious works, and the expectations of patrons see also Lydeker, *op. cit.*, pp. 175–83.
37 – *Cf.* Lydeker, *op. cit.*, pp. 65–6.
38 – For a discussion of this point in relation to the works of Raphael see E. H. Gombrich, 'Raphael's "Madonna della Sedia"', *Norm and Form*, edn *cit.*, pp. 64–80.
39 – On this see particularly H. Cornell, *The Iconography of the Nativity of Christ*, Uppsala, 1924.
40 – *Cf.* Mirella Levi d'Ancona, *The Garden of the Renaissance: Botanical Symbolism in Italian Painting*, Florence, 1977, pp. 199–200.
41 – *Hebrews* I, 10–11. The inscription in Piero's work is discussed by D. Covi, *The Inscription in Fifteenth-century Florentine Painting*, New York, 1986, p. 245 and 458. *Cf.* also A. H. Van Buren, 'The Canonical Office in Renaissance Painting: Raphael's Madonna at Nones', *The Art Bulletin*, LVII, 1975, p. 44 n. 24.
42 – On the dandelion, see Levi d'Ancona, *op. cit.*, pp. 126–8.
43 – The precise identity of the bird in the foreground remains a matter of debate. One might expect Piero to have included a goldfinch, often used as symbol of the Crucifixion, and frequently held by the Christ Child in images of the Holy Family. Yet Piero's bird lacks the red spot on the head by which the goldfinch is normally identified, and it is possible that the artist intended the bird as a more general symbol of the human soul, and of its flight or resurrection at the moment of death. *Cf.* H. Friedmann, *The Symbolic Goldfinch*, Bollingen Series VII, Washington DC, 1946, p. 29, where the bird is identified as a coal-tit and a symbol of fertility. A note in the file of the Toledo museum identifies the bird as a bunting. The landscape of the painting is discussed in more detail here in chapter Four.
44 – According to the Gospel of Pseudo-Matthew, a palm tree bent down during the Flight into Egypt to feed the Christ-Child with dates. In some paintings of the Flight and the Rest on the Flight these are replaced by cherries. *Cf. sub voce* 'cherry' in Levi d'Ancona, *op. cit.*
45 – *The Golden Legend*, edn *cit.*, pp. 84–5.
46 – *Cf.* L. Steinberg, *The Sexuality of Christ in Renaissance Art and in Modern Oblivion*, New York, 1983, p. 49, where it is suggested that the exposure of Christ's genitals, touched by the lamb, alludes to the impending pains of Circumcision and Crucifixion. An alternative view is proposed by C. W. Bynum, 'The Body of Christ in the Later Middle Ages: A Reply to Leo Steinberg', *Art Quarterly*, XXXIX, 1986, pp. 349–99, where the

exposed genitalia are seen as a reference rather to the Incarnation of Christ, and his taking of human form.

47 – On the definition and identification of subject-matter and the instructions of patrons see Ringbom, *Icon to Narrative*, p. 11ff, and more generally Hope, 'Altarpieces', *passim*.

48 – For the iconography of the saints see Kaftal, *op. cit.*, and for St Jerome see also Eugene F. Rice Jr, *St Jerome in the Renaissance*, London, 1985.

49 – On this, and on the patronage of the Pugliese, see particularly Craven, *Aspects of Patronage*, chapter V, p. 133ff. It seems likely that, had Piero had any personal involvement with Savonarola, Vasari would have made mention of this in his Life, as he does in the case of Botticelli amongst others.

50 – Vasari–Milanesi, III, pp. 569–70.

51 – *Cf.* Craven, p. 22.

CHAPTER FOUR

1 – Chastel, *Art et Humanisme*, p. 318, and Pudelko, 'Piero di Cosimo: Peintre Bizarre', *passim*, where the author proposes a psycho-analytical reading of the landscapes.

2 – There is no satisfactory comprehensive account of Renaissance landscape. For an excellent discussion of the depiction of landscape in fifteenth-century art and theory see particularly A. Cole, *Aspects of Quattrocento Landscape Depiction*, *passim*. My remarks on fifteenth-century landscape in this chapter are much indebted to this study, and to Ms Cole's comments on my text, although our conclusions often differ. Other discussions of Renaissance landscape are R. Turner, *The Vision of Landscape in Renaissance Italy*, Princeton, NJ, 1966, and E. H. Gombrich, 'The Renaissance Theory of Art and the Rise of Landscape', *Norm and Form*, edn *cit.*, pp. 107–61. *Cf.* also G. Pochat, *Figur und Landschaft: Eine historiche Interpretation der Landschaft malerei von der Antik bis zur Renaissance*, Berlin, 1973.

3 – Pliny's enumeration of the repertory of the Classical landscape painter Studius was highly influential on fifteenth-century writers (*Natural History*, XXXV, 116–19). Vitruvius discusses landscape painting in his *De Architectura*, VII, 5, 1–7.

4 – Alberti's most extensive discussion of landscape painting is in his *De Re Aedificatoria*, IX, iv. The text was completed in the early 1450s, and first published in 1485. Landscape is mentioned only briefly in *De Pictura*, edn *cit.*, p. 79.

5 – For a discussion of Leonardo's drawing see Kemp, *Leonardo da Vinci*, pp. 51–2. On Leonardo and landscape see Hills, 'Leonardo and Flemish Painting', and the bibliography to this article, and Cole *op. cit.*, pp. 34–43.

6 – For the literary influences on fifteenth-century landscape see particularly Cole, p. 17ff. On the influence of manuscript illustrations see O. Pächt, 'Early Italian Nature Studies and the Calendar Landscape', *Journal of the Warburg and Courtauld Institutes*, XIII, 1950, pp. 13–47.

7 – On the problems of landscape and pictorial structure see Cole, p. 60ff and Christiansen, 'Early Renaissance Narrative Painting', pp. 31–8.

8 – On the programme for the frescoes and the compositional problems involved see Ettlinger, *The Sistine Chapel*, *passim*, and for the *Sermon on the Mount*, p. 55 and pp. 89ff.

9 – For the floral symbolism see the relevant entries in Levi d'Ancona, *The Garden of the Renaissance*.

10 – Among biblical references to the cormorant are Leviticus 11:17 and Deuteronomy 14:17.

11 – For the identification of the church building see R. Krautheimer and A. Fraser, *Corpus Basilicarum Christianorum Romae*, V, Vatican City, 1977, p. 169.

12 – *Cf.* Rice, *St Jerome in the Renaissance*, pp. 1–23, 84–115.

13 – For a discussion of the depiction of nature in Leonardo's Madonna see Kemp, *Leonardo da Vinci*, pp. 343–6.

14 – On Leonardo's use of light see J. Shearman, 'Leonardo's Colour and Chiaroscuro', *Zeitschrift für Kunstgeschichte*, XXV, 1962, pp. 13–47, and Cole, pp. 82ff.

15 – Vasari–Milanesi, IV, p. 138.

16 – Ibid.

17 – See for example Vasari–Milanesi, II, p. 204.

18 – Vasari–Milanesi, IV, p. 142.

19 – Vasari–Milanesi, V, pp. 101–2.

20 – Vasari–Milanesi, VII, p. 216, p. 384.

21 – Vasari–Milanesi, IV, pp. 375–6, p. 317.

22 – Vasari–Milanesi, III, pp. 292–3. Vasari ascribes the painting to Antonio alone.

23 – Vasari–Milanesi, IV, pp. 39–40.

24 – *Op. cit.*, p. 141.

25 – Vasari–Milanesi, II, p. 209.

26 – Vasari–Milanesi, V, p. 147.

27 – *Cf.* Maclehose, *Vasari on Technique*, p. 212.

28 – Vasari–Milanesi, IV, p. 139.

29 – *Op. cit.*, p. 9 and p. 376.

30 – *Op. cit.*, pp. 133–4.

31 – Ibid.

32 – On fifteenth-century views of landscape see particularly Cole, *op. cit.*, *passim*.

33 – On the tradition of the *locus amoenus* in Classical literature, and its influence, see E. Curtius, *European Literature and the Latin Middle Ages*, London, 1953, p. 183ff. On the motif in art see P. Watson, *The Garden of Love in Tuscan Art of the Early Renaissance*, Philadelphia, 1979.

34 – Leon Battista Alberti, *On the Art of Building*

in Ten Books, trans. J. Rykwert, N. Leach and R. Tavernor, London, 1988, pp. 299–300.
35 – In Lorenzo de' Medici, *Opere*, ed. A. Simioni, I, Bari, 1913, p. 68.
36 – M. Baxandall, 'A Dialogue on Art from the Court of Leonello d'Este', *Journal of the Warburg and Courtauld Institutes*, XXVI, 1963, pp. 304–26 (p. 318). *Cf.* also F. Saxl, 'A Humanist Dreamland', *Lectures*, I, London, 1957, pp. 215–27.
37 – See, for example, *Leonardo on Painting*, trans. A. P. McMahon, 2 vols, Princeton, NJ, 1956, I, p. 24.
38 – *Notebooks, Leonardo on Painting*, edn *cit.*, I, pp. 48–9, and p. 51.
39 – For Decembrio see Baxandall, 'A Dialogue on Art', p. 314 and p. 320. The contract for Pintoricchio is in G. B. Vermogli, *Bernardino Pinturicchio*, Perugia, 1837, Appendix II, p. vi.
40 – *Natural History*, XXXV, 96.
41 – *Natural History*, XXXV, 116–17.
42 – Vasari–Milanesi, IV, p. 140.
43 – On the botanical symbolism see the relevant entries in Levi d'Ancona, *op. cit.* Lavin discusses the Christianization of the Procris myth in the Middle Ages, and it is not inconceivable that a Christian allegory was intended here in the case of the pelican: 'Cephalus and Procris', *passim*. It seems equally likely, however, that Piero included the birds simply as interesting landscape details.
44 – D. Rosand, L. Gowing and R. Cafritz, *Places of Delight: The Pastoral Landscape*, London, 1988.
45 – Gabinetto Disegni e Stampe, Rome, F.C. 1305.07, but attributed to Albertinelli. The drawing is attributed to Piero by Griswold, *op. cit.*, pp. 272–4.
46 – *Notebooks*, ed. Kemp and Walker, pp. 201–2.
47 – Vasari–Milanesi, IV, p. 134.

Select Bibliography

L. B. Alberti, *De Pictura*, ed. C. Grayson as *Leon Battista Alberti: On Painting and on Sculpture*, London, 1972

– *De Re Aedificatoria*, trans. J. Rykwert, N. Leach and R. Tavernor as *On the Art of Building in Ten Books*, London, 1988

M. Bacci, *Piero di Cosimo*, Milan, 1966

– *L'Opera Completa di Piero di Cosimo*, Milan, 1976

A. B. Barriault, *Florentine Paintings for 'spalliere'*, PhD dissertation, University of Virginia, 1985

E. Battisti, *L'Antirinascimento*, Milan, 1962

T. S. R. Boase, *Giorgio Vasari: The Man and the Book*, Princeton, NJ, 1979

K. Borinski, 'Die Deutung der Piero di Cosimo zugeschriebenen Prometheus-Bilder', *Sitzungsberichte der Bayerischen Akademie der Wissenschaft*, VII, 2, 1920

E. Callmann, 'Apollonio di Giovanni and Painting for the Early Renaissance Room', *Antichità Viva*, XXVII/3–4, 1988, pp. 5–18

– 'The Growing Threat to Marital Bliss as seen in Fifteenth-century Florentine Painting', *Studies in Iconography*, V, 1979, pp. 73–92

– *Beyond Nobility: Art for the Private Citizen in the Early Renaissance*, exhibition catalogue by E. Callmann; Allentown Art Museum, Allentown, PA, 1981

A. Chastel, *Art et Humanisme à Florence au temps de Laurent le Magnifique*, Paris, 1959

K. Christiansen, 'Early Renaissance Narrative Painting in Italy', *Bulletin of the Metropolitan Museum of Art*, XLI/2, 1983, pp. 3–48

C. Cieri Via, 'Per una revisione della tema del primitivismo nell'opera di Piero di Cosimo', *Storia dell'Arte*, XXIX, 1977, pp. 5–14

K. Clark, *Landscape into Art*, London, 1949

A. Cole, *Aspects of Quattrocento Landscape Depiction*, M.Phil. dissertation, Warburg Institute, University of London, 1981

S. J. Craven, *Aspects of Patronage in Florence, 1494–1512*, PhD dissertation, Courtauld Institute, University of London, 1973

– 'Three Dates for Piero di Cosimo', *The Burlington Magazine*, CXVII, 1975, pp. 572–6

E. Fahy, 'Some Later Works by Piero di Cosimo', *Gazette des Beaux-Arts*, CVII, 1965, p. 201ff.

Firenze e la Toscana dei Medici nell'Europa del Cinquecento: Il primato del disegno, exhibition catalogue; Palazzo Strozzi, Florence, 1980

C. Gamba, 'Piero di Cosimo e i suoi quadri mitologici', *Bolletino d'Arte*, XXX, 1936–7, p. 45ff.

E. Gombrich, 'Botticelli's Mythologies: A Study in the Neo-Platonic Symbolism of his Circle', *Symbolic Images*, Oxford, 1972, p. 31ff.

– 'The Renaissance Theory of Art and the Rise of Landscape', *Norm and Form*, London, 1966, pp. 107–21

W. Griswold, *The Drawings of Piero di Cosimo*, PhD dissertation, Courtauld Institute, University of London, 1988

– 'Early Drawings by Ridolfo Ghirlandaio', *Master Drawings*, XXVII, 1989, pp. 215–23

J. Guillaume, 'Cleopatra Nova Pandora', *Gazette des Beaux-Arts*, 6th series, LXXX, 1972, pp. 185–94

G. Habich, 'Ueber zwei Prometheus-Bilder angeblich von Piero di Cosimo', *Sitzungsberichte der Bayerischen Akademie der Wissenschaft*, XXI/6, 1919

C. Hope, 'Altarpieces and the Requirements of Patrons', *Christianity in the Renaissance*, ed. T. Verdon and J. Henderson, Syracuse, NY, 1989, pp. 537–71

– 'Artists, Patrons and Advisers', *Patronage in the Renaissance*, ed. G. Fytch Lytle and S. Orgel, Princeton, NJ, 1981, p. 329–30

H. P. Horne, 'Piero di Cosimo's Battle of Centaurs and the Lapithae', *The Architectural Review*, XII, 1902, pp. 61ff.

P. Humfrey and M. Kemp, *The Altarpiece in the Renaissance*, Cambridge, 1990

H. W. Janson, 'The "Image Made by Chance" in Renaissance Thought', *Sixteen Studies*, New York, 1973, pp. 53–75

M. Kemp, 'From "mimesis" to "fantasia": The Quattrocento Vocabulary of Creation, Inspiration and Genius in the Visual Arts', *Viator*, VIII, 1977, pp. 347–98

R. Langton Douglas, *Piero di Cosimo*, Chicago, 1946

– 'Letters to the Editor', *The Art Bulletin*, XXIX, 1947, p. 143ff.

I. Lavin, 'Cephalus and Procris: Transformation of an Ovidian Myth', *Journal of the Warburg and Courtauld Institutes*, XVII, 1954, p. 260ff.

R. Le Mollé, *Georges Vasari et le vocabulaire de la critique d'art dans les 'Vite'*, Université Stendhal Grenoble 3, 1988

Leonardo on Painting, selected and trans. by M. Kemp and M. Walker, London, 1989

Leonardo on Painting, trans. A. P. McMahon, 2 vols, Princeton, NJ, 1956

M. Levi d'Ancona, *The Garden of the Renaissance: Botanical Symbolism in Italian Painting*, Florence, 1977

H. Levin, *The Myth of the Golden Age in the Renaissance*, 1969

J. Lipman, 'The Florentine Profile Portrait in the Quattrocento', *The Art Bulletin*, XVIII, 1936, pp. 54–102

A. Lovejoy and G. Boas, *A Documentary History of Primitivism and Related Ideas, I: Primitivism and Related Ideas in Antiquity*, Baltimore, 1935

K. J. Lydeker, *The Domestic Setting of the Arts in Renaissance Florence*, PhD dissertation, Johns Hopkins University, Baltimore, 1987

F. Melis 'Un'opera di Piero di Cosimo per Napoli', *Commentari*, XIX, 1968, p. 154

E. Panofsky, 'The "Discovery of Honey" by Piero di Cosimo', *Worcester Art Museum Annual*, II, 1936–7, p. 33ff.

– 'The Early History of Man in Two Cycles of Works by Piero di Cosimo', *Studies in Iconology: Humanistic Themes in the Art of the Renaissance*, New York, 1939, pp. 33–67

– 'Letters to the Editor', *The Art Bulletin*, XXVIII, 1946, p. 286ff.

Piero di Cosimo's 'The Forest Fire', Ashmolean Museum, Oxford, 1984

G. Pudelko, 'Piero di Cosimo: Peintre Bizarre', *Minotaure*, XI, May 1938, pp. 19–26

O. Raggio, 'The Myth of Prometheus: Its Survival and Metamorphoses up to the 18th Century', *Journal of the Warburg and Courtauld Institutes*, XXI, 1958, p. 44ff.

S. Ringbom, *Icon to Narrative: The Rise of the Dramatic Close-up in Fifteenth-century Devotional Painting*, 2nd edn, Davaco, Doornspijk, 1984

P. Rubin, 'What Men Saw: Vasari's Life of Leonardo da Vinci and the Image of the Artist', *Art History*, XIII, 1990, pp. 34–46

A. Schiaparelli, *La casa fiorentina ed i suoi arredi nei secoli XIV e XV*, Florence, 1908

P. Schubring, *Cassoni*, Leipzig, 1915

J. Shearman, 'The Florentine Entrata of Leo X, 1515', *Journal of the Warburg and Courtauld Institutes*, XXXVIII, 1975, pp. 136–54

D. Summers, *Michelangelo and the Language of Art*, Princeton, NJ, 1981

R. Turner, *The Vision of Landscape in Renaissance Italy*, Princeton, NJ, 1966

M. W. Vanderzani, *'Simonetta Vespucci': A Fantasy Portrait*, MA Dissertation, Michigan State University, 1983

G. Vasari, *Le Vite de' più eccellenti pittori, scultori ed architettori*, ed. G. Milanesi, 9 vols, Florence, 1875–85

W. Wackenroder, *Confessions and Fantasies*, trans. M. Hurst Schubert, London, 1971

M. Wackernagel, *The World of the Florentine Renaissance Artist*, trans. A. Luchs, Princeton, NJ, 1981

Z. Wazbinski, 'L'idée de l'histoire dans la première et la seconde edition des vies de Vasari', *Il Vasari storiografo e artista: Atti del congresso Internazionale nel IV centenario della Morte: 1974*, Florence, 1976

R. and M. Wittkower, *Born Under Saturn: The Character and Conduct of Artists; A Documented Study from Antiquity to the French Revolution*, London, 1963

F. Zeri, 'Rivedendo Piero di Cosimo', *Paragone (Arte)*, CXV, July 1959, pp. 36–50

List of Illustrations

All measurements are given in centimetres

1 Cosimo Rosselli and Piero di Cosimo, *The Sermon on the Mount and the Healing of the Leper*, 1481–2, fresco. Sistine Chapel, Rome. Photo: Foto Scala, Florence.

2 *Giuliano da Sangallo*, *c.*1500–4, oil on panel, 47.5 x 33.5. Rijksmuseum, Amsterdam.

3 *Francesco Giamberti*, *c.*1500–4, oil on panel, 47.5 x 33.5. Rijksmuseum, Amsterdam.

4 *Head of a Bearded Old Man Wearing a Cap* (verso of illus. 35), pen and brown ink, brown wash and white heightening over preliminary indications in black chalk on yellow-brown tinted paper, 23.9 x 17.8. Cabinet des Dessins, Musée du Louvre, Paris (RF 1870/1439). Photo: Service Photographique de la Réunion des Musées Nationaux.

5 *Mars and Venus*, *c.*1500–5, oil on panel, 72 x 182. Gemäldegalerie, Berlin. Photo: Jörg P. Anders.

6 *The Death of Procris*, *c.*1500–10, oil on panel, 65.4 x 184.2. National Gallery, London.

7 Botticelli, *Mars and Venus*, *c.*1483, tempera on panel, 69.2 x 173.4. National Gallery, London.

8 *Ariadne Asleep in a Landscape*, pen and ink and brown wash, heightened in white, 14.1 x 24.8. British Museum, London (1902–8–22–6).

9 An unidentified mythological subject (possibly 'Mars and Rhea Silvia'), pen, brown ink and wash over chalk, 15.8 x 37.2. Gabinetto Disegni e Stampe, Uffizi, Florence (1257 F). Photo: The Witt Library, Courtauld Institute of Art, University of London.

10 Botticelli, *Episodes from the Story of Nastagio degli Onesti* (first panel), *c.*1482–3, tempera on panel, 83 x 138. Prado Museum, Madrid.

11 Botticelli, *Episodes from the Story of Nastagio degli Onesti* (second panel), *c.*1482–3, tempera on panel, 82 x 138. Prado Museum, Madrid.

12 *The Battle of the Lapiths and Centaurs*, *c.*1505–7, oil on panel, 71 x 260. National Gallery, London.

13 Detail from *The Battle of the Lapiths and Centaurs*, illus. 12.

14 Michelangelo, *Battle of the Centaurs*, 1491–2, marble relief, 84.5 x 90.5. Casa Buonarroti, Florence. Photo: Alinari.

15 *Tritons and Nereids*, *c.*1505–10, oil on panel, 37 x 158. One of two panels, this one is in the S. J. Freedberg Collection, Washington DC. Photo: Witt Library, Courtauld Institute of Art, University of London.

16 Detail from *The Forest Fire*, *c.*1500–5, oil on wood, illus. 19.

17 Detail from *The Forest Fire*, *c.*1500–5, oil on wood, illus. 19.

18 Detail from *The Forest Fire*, *c.*1500–5, oil on wood, illus. 19.

19 *The Forest Fire*, *c.*1500–5, oil on wood, 71 x 202. Ashmolean Museum, Oxford.

20 *The Finding of Vulcan on Lemnos*, *c.*1495–1505, oil and tempera on canvas, 155 x 174.5. Wadsworth Athenaeum, Hartford, CT, Ella Gallup Sumner and Mary Catlin Sumner Collection.

21 *Vulcan and Aeolus*, *c.*1495–1500, oil and tempera on canvas, 155.5 x 166.5. National Gallery of Canada, Ottawa.

22 *The Hunt*, *c.*1495–1505, tempera and oil on wood, 70.5 x 169.5. Metropolitan Museum of Art, New York, gift of Robert Gordon.

23 *Return from the Hunt*, *c.*1495–1505, tempera and oil on wood, 70.5 x 168.9. Metropolitan Museum of Art, New York, gift of Robert Gordon.

24 *A Bear and Cub; Two Deer; Head of an Ox*, pen and brown ink over metalpoint on rose-salmon prepared paper, 14.9 x 18.2. Boymans–van Beuningen Museum, Rotterdam. Photo: Fred Mijnheer.

25 *An Ox*, chalk and white heightening. (verso of illus. 52). Royal Library, Windsor Castle (inv. no 12796).

26 Engraving after a drawing by Botticelli, *Bacchic Procession* (detail from *Triumph of Bacchus and Ariadne*), *c.*1480–90, dimensions of detail 20.5 x 27.6. British Museum, London (A.III.III. P.V. 44, 104; A. Hind, cat. I, 26).

27 Perugino and Pintoricchio, *Moses's Journey into Egypt*, detail from *Events from the Life of Moses*, 1481–2, fresco. Sistine Chapel, Rome. Photo: Alinari.

28 *The Discovery of Honey*, *c.*1505–10, oil on panel, 79.2 x 128.5. Art Museum, Worcester, MA.

29 *The Misfortunes of Silenus*, *c.*1505–10, oil on panel, 76.2 x 126.3. Courtesy of the Fogg Art Museum, Harvard University, Cambridge, MA, Alpheus Hyatt Fund and Friends of Art, Archaeology and Music at Harvard Fund. Photo: Harvard University Art Museums, Cambridge.

30 Detail from *The Discovery of Honey*, illus. 28.
31 Detail from *The Discovery of Honey*, illus. 28.
32 *Stories of Prometheus*, *c.*1515–20, oil on panel, 66 x 118.7. Alte Pinakothek, Munich. Photo: Artothek.
33 *Stories of Prometheus*, *c.*1515–20, oil on panel, 64 x 116. Musée des Beaux-Arts, Strasbourg.
34 *Cleopatra* (the so-called '*Simonetta Vespucci*'), *c.*1485–90, tempera on wood, 57 x 42. Musée Condé, Chantilly. Photo: Photographie Giraudon.
35 *Head of a Youth/Young Woman in Profile to the Left*, pen and brown ink, brown wash and white heightening over preliminary indications in black chalk on yellow-brown tinted paper, 23.9 x 17.8. Cabinet des Dessins, Musée du Louvre, Paris (RF1870/1439). Photo: Service Photographique de la Réunion des Musées Nationaux.
36 Michelangelo, *Cleopatra*, *c.*1534, black chalk, 23.4 x 18.2. Casa Buonarroti, Florence. Photo: Alinari.
37 *Madonna and Child*, *c.*1485–90, oil on panel, 83 x 56. Royal Collections, Stockholm.
38 *Construction of a Building*, *c.*1515–20, oil on panel, 82.6 x 196.9. The John and Mable Ringling Museum of Art, Sarasota, FL.
39 Paolo Uccello, *The Hunt in the Forest*, 1460s, tempera with oil glazes on panel, 73 x 177. Ashmolean Museum, Oxford.
40 Paolo Uccello, *Rout of San Romano*, early 1450s, panel, 181.6 x 320. National Gallery, London.
41 Andrea Mantegna, *The Agony in the Garden*, (?) mid-1450s, oil on wood, 62.9 x 80. National Gallery, London.
42 Drawing on unprimed wood from reverse of *The Death of Procris*, illus. 6, perhaps for a decorative pilaster of a frame.
43 *The Liberation of Andromeda*, *c.*1515, oil on panel, 70 x 123. Uffizi, Florence. Photo: Foto Scala, Florence.
44 Detail from *The Liberation of Andromeda*, illus. 43.
45 Detail from *The Liberation of Andromeda*, illus. 43.
46 Detail from *The Liberation of Andromeda*, illus. 43.
47 *The Young St John the Baptist*, *c.*1485, tempera on panel, 28.6 x 23.5. Metropolitan Museum of Art, New York, bequest of Michael Dreicer.
48 Filippino Lippi, *Madonna and Child with SS Dominic and Jerome*, *c.*1485, wood, main panel approx. 203.2 x 186.1. National Gallery, London.
49 Hugo van der Goes, *Portinari Altarpiece*, *c.*1473–5, oil on panel, centre panel 252.7 x 304, wings 252.7 x 141. Uffizi, Florence. Photo: The Witt Library, Courtauld Institute of Art, University of London.
50 Domenico Ghirlandaio, *Adoration of the Magi*, 1488, 285 x 243. Galleria dello Spedale degli Innocenti, Florence. Photo: Alinari.
51 *The Immaculate Conception with SS Francis, Jerome, Bonaventure, Bernard, Augustine and Thomas Aquinas*, *c.*1520, oil on panel, 184 x 178. S. Francesco, Fiesole. Photo: Alinari.
52 *Seated Youth with Dog*, brush and brown ink and white heightening on blue tinted paper, 23.4 x 17.6. Royal Library, Windsor Castle.
53 *Portrait of a Woman as the Magdalen*, *c.*1500–10, oil on panel, 72 x 53. Galleria Nazionale d'Arte Antica, Rome. Photo: Foto Scala, Florence.
54 *Madonna and Child with SS Lazarus and Sebastian*, *c.*1480, tempera on panel, 165 x 123. SS Michele Arcangelo and Lorenzo Martire, Montevettolini (Pistoia). Photo: Foto Scala, Florence.
55 *Madonna and Child with SS Onofrius and Augustine*, *c.*1483–4, tempera on wood, 204.5 x 174.5. Private collection, Toronto. Photo: Diane Dwyer Studio, New York.
56 *Madonna and Child with SS Peter, John the Baptist, Nicholas of Bari and Dominic (*the *'Pala Pugliese')*, *c.*1485, tempera with oil glazes on wood, 166.4 x 113. St Louis Art Museum, MO.
57 *Madonna and Child with SS Catherine of Alexandria, Rose of Viterbo, Peter, and John the Evangelist* (the *'Innocenti Altarpiece'*), *c.*1495–1500, oil on panel, 203 x 197. Galleria dello Spedale degli Innocenti, Florence. Photo: Foto Scala, Florence.
58 *Adoration of the Shepherds*, pen and ink on white paper, 10 x 19.9. Gabinetto Disegni e Stampe, Uffizi, Florence (170 E). Photo: Foto Scala, Florence.
59 Detail from the *Adoration of the Shepherds*, illus. 58.
60 *Descent of the Holy Spirit* (design for an altarpiece), (?) before 1500, pen and brown ink over faint metalpoint indications on rose-salmon prepared paper, 14.9 x 18.2. Fondation Custodia (Collection Frits Lugt), Institut Néerlandais, Paris.
61 *Virgin with St Elizabeth* (study for the Washington *Visitation*, illus. 87), pen and brown ink over traces of black chalk on yellowed paper, 18.1 x 14.4. Gabinetto Disegni e Stampe, Uffizi, Florence. Photo: Alinari.
62 *Seated Figure at a Lectern and two Candelabra* (verso of illus. 61), pen and brown ink over traces of black chalk. Gabinetto Disegni e Stampe, Uffizi, Florence (286 E). Photo: The Witt Library, Courtauld Institute of Art, University of London.

63 *Immaculate Conception* (study for the Fiesole *Immaculate Conception*, illus. 51), red and black chalk, 23.8 x 27.8. Gabinetto Disegni e Stampe, Uffizi, Florence (552 E).

64 *Six Saints* (study for the Fiesole *Immaculate Conception*, illus. 51), red and black chalk on white paper, 14.4 x 27.8. Gabinetto Disegni e Stampe, Uffizi, Florence (555 E). Photo: Alinari.

65 *Incarnation with Six Saints* (study for the Uffizi *Incarnation*, illus. 88), *c.*1505, pen and ink, 20.1 x 24.1. Location unknown, formerly Bremen Kunsthalle. Photo: Bremen Kunsthalle.

66 Leonardo da Vinci, *Leda and the Swan*, *c.*1505–7, black chalk, pen and ink, 12.6 x 10.9. Boymans-van Beuningen Museum, Rotterdam.

67 *Madonna and Child with Angels*, *c.*1505–10, oil on panel, 116 x 85. Galleria di Palazzo Cini, Venice. Photo: Fotografia Giacomelli.

68 *The Holy Family with the young St John the Baptist*, *c.*1520, oil on panel, 118.5 x 87. Galleria di Palazzo Cini, Venice. Photo: Fotografia Giacomelli.

69 *Madonna and Child with Saints and Angels*, *c.*1495–1505, oil on panel, diameter 75. Private collection, New York.

70 *Virgin and Child with a Musician Angel* (study for the Venice *Madonna and Child with Angels*, illus. 67), pen and brown ink with wash and white heightening, 11.4 x 79. Gabinetto Disegni e Stampe, Uffizi, Florence (176 E). Photo: Foto Scala, Florence.

71 *Madonna and Child with SS Thomas and John the Baptist*, *c.*1510–20, oil on panel, 202 x 165. Chiesa del Crocifisso, Borgo San Lorenzo, Florence. Photo: Witt Library, Courtauld Institute of Art, University of London.

72 *Adoration of the Child*, *c.*1495–1500, oil on wood, diameter 160. Toledo Museum of Art, Toledo, OH, Purchased with funds from the Libbey Endowment, gift of Edward Drummond Libbey.

73 *Holy Family with the Young St John and Angels*, *c.*1495–1500, oil on panel, diameter 165. Gemäldegalerie Alte Meister, Dresden. Photo: Staatliche Kunstsammlungen, Dresden.

74 *Adoration of the Child with the young St John*, *c.*1500–5, oil on canvas, diameter 146. National Gallery of Art, Washington DC, The Samuel H. Kress Collection.

75 *Madonna and Child with Saints*, *c.*1515–20, oil and tempera on panel, diameter 137.8. Philbrook Museum of Art, Tulsa, gift of the Samuel H. Kress Foundation.

76 *Madonna and Child with the young St John the Baptist*, *c.*1495–1500, oil on panel, diameter 93. Musée des Beaux-Arts, Strasbourg.

77 Michelangelo, *The Holy Family* (the '*Doni Tondo*'), 1503–4, tempera on panel, 91 x 80. Uffizi, Florence. Photo: Alinari.

78 Raphael, *Madonna del Belvedere* (the '*Madonna of the Meadow*'), 1505 or 1506, poplar panel, 113 x 88. Kunsthistorisches Museum, Vienna.

79 Perugino, *Pietà*, 1495, oil on panel, 294 x 195. Palazzo Pitti, Florence. Photo: Alinari.

80 Antonio and Piero Pollaiuolo, *The Martyrdom of St Sebastian*, 1475, tempera on wood, 291.5 x 202.6. National Gallery, London.

81 Leonardo da Vinci, *Study of a Tuscan Landscape*, 1473, pen and ink, 19 x 28.5. Uffizi, Florence. Photo: Alinari.

82 Leonardo da Vinci, *Annunciation*, *c.*1472–3, oil on wood, 98 x 217. Uffizi, Florence. Photo: Alinari.

83 *Pietà with Saints*, *c.*1510, oil on panel, 190 x 112. Galleria Nazionale dell' Umbria, Perugia. Photo: Alinari.

84 Giovanni Bellini, *The Ecstasy of St Francis*, *c.*1480, tempera and oil on poplar panel, 124.4 x 141.9. The Frick Collection, New York. Photo: © The Frick Collection.

85 Giovanni Bellini, *Madonna and Child* (the '*Madonna of the Meadow*'), *c.*1505, canvas transferred from wood, 67.3 x 86.4. National Gallery, London.

86 Giovanni Bellini, *The Agony in the Garden*, *c.*1459, wood, 81.3 x 127. National Gallery, London.

87 *The Visitation with SS Nicholas of Bari and Anthony Abbot*, *c.*1490; oil on wood, 184 x 189. National Gallery of Art, Washington DC, Samuel H. Kress Collection.

88 *Incarnation with SS Catherine of Alexandria, Margaret, John the Evangelist, Peter, Philip Benizzi and Antoninus*, *c.*1505, oil on panel, 206 x 172. Uffizi, Florence. Photo: Foto Scala, Florence.

89 Detail from *Incarnation with Saints*, illus. 88.

90 Detail from *Incarnation with Saints*, illus. 88.

91 Leonardo da Vinci, *Madonna and Child with St Anne and a Lamb*, *c.*1508–10, oil on panel, 168 x 112. Musée du Louvre, Paris. Photo: Service Photographique de la Réunion des Musées Nationaux.

92 Leonardo da Vinci, *A River Running through a Rocky Ravine*, *c.*1483, pen and ink, 22 x 15.8. Royal Library, Windsor Castle.

93 Fra Bartolommeo, *God the Father with SS Mary Magdalen and Catherine of Siena*, 1508, oil on canvas, 361 x 236. Museo Nazionale di Villa Guinigi, Lucca. Photo: Alinari.

94 *The Volto Santo of Lucca*, *c.*1505–10, oil on panel, 160 x 120.5. Szépmüveszéti Múzeum, Budapest. Photo: Bridgeman Art Library, London.

95 *Madonna and Child with SS Dominic and Jerome*, *c.*1510–20, oil on panel, 208.9 x 205.7. Yale University Art Gallery, New Haven, Purchase from James Jackson Jarves.

96 *The Penitent St Jerome*, *c.*1495–1500, oil on panel, diameter 74. Museo Horne, Florence. Photo: Foto Scala, Florence.

97 *St Jerome in a Panoramic Landscape*, black chalk, 62 x 53. Gabinetto Disegni e Stampe, Uffizi, Florence (403 P). Photo: Foto Scala, Florence.

98 *St Jerome in a Rocky Landscape*, *c.*1495–1500, pen and ink, 23.6 x 20. Gabinetto Disegni e Stampe Uffizi, Florence (7 P). Photo: The Witt Library, Courtauld Institute of Art, University of London.

99 Andrea Mantegna, *St Sebastian*, *c.*1475, canvas, 257 x 142. Musée du Louvre, Paris. Photo: Service Photographique de la Réunion des Musées Nationaux.

Index

italics indicate pages on which illustrations may be found